Less Than One and Double

Recent Titles in STUDIES IN AFRICAN LITERATURE
▼▼▼▼▼▼▼▼▼▼▼▼▼▼▼▼▼▼▼▼▼▼▼▼▼▼

Bessie Head: Thunder Behind Her Ears
Gillian Stead Eilersen

New Writing from Southern Africa: Authors Who Have Become Prominent Since 1980
Emmanuel Ngara, editor

Ngugi wa Thiong'o: An Exploration of His Writings, Second Edition
David Cook and Michael Okenimkpe

Writers in Politics: A Re-Engagement with Issues of Literature and Society
Ngugi wa Thiong'o

The African Novel in English: An Introduction
M. Keith Booker

A Teacher's Guide to African Narratives
Sara Talis O'Brien

Women's Voices in a Man's World: Women and the Pastoral Tradition in Northern Somali Orature, c. 1899–1980
Lidwien Kapteijns with Maryan Omar Ali

Running towards Us: New Writing from South Africa
Isabel Balseiro, editor

Alex La Guma: Politics and Resistance
Nahem Yousaf

Recasting Postcolonialism: Women Writing Between Worlds
Anne Donadey

Colonial Histories, Post-Colonial Memories
Abdelmajid Hannoum

Aeroplane Mirrors: Personal and Political Reflexivity in Post-Colonial Women's Novels
Elizabeth Morgan

▼▼▼

Less Than One and Double

A Feminist Reading of African Women's Writing

Kenneth W. Harrow

HEINEMANN
Portsmouth, NH

Heinemann
A division of Reed Elsevier Inc.
361 Hanover Street
Portsmouth, NH 03801–3912
www.heinemann.com

© 2002 by Kenneth W. Harrow

All rights reserved. No part of this book may be reproduced in any form or by any electronic or mechanical means, including information storage and retrieval systems, without permission in writing from the publisher, except by a reviewer, who may quote brief passages in a review.

ISBN 0–325–07025–3 (Heinemann cloth)
ISBN 0–325–07024–5 (Heinemann paper)

Library of Congress Cataloging-in-Publication Data

Harrow, Kenneth W.
　Less than one and double : a feminist reading of African women's writing / by Kenneth W. Harrow.
　　p. cm.—(Studies in African literature, ISSN 1351–5713)
　Includes bibliographical references and index.
　　ISBN 0–325–07025–3 (hardcover : alk. paper)—ISBN 0–325–07024–5 (pbk : alk. paper)
　　1. African literature—Women authors—History and criticism.　2. African literature (French)—Women authors—History and criticism.　3. Women in Literature.　I. Title.　II. Series.
PL8010.H37 2002
809'.8927'096—dc21　　　　2001024298

British Library Cataloguing in Publication Data is available.

Paperback cover photo: From Jean-Paul Bourdier and Trinh T. Minh-ha, *Drawn from African Dwellings* (Bloomington: Indiana University Press, 1996). © 1996 by Jean-Paul Bourdier and Trinh T. Minh-ha. Reprinted by permission, courtesy of Moongift Films. Photo by Jean-Paul Bourdier.

Printed in the United States of America on acid-free paper.

06　05　04　03　02　SB　1　2　3　4　5　6　7　8　9

Copyright Acknowledgments

The author and publisher gratefully acknowledge permission to reprint the following material:

Excerpts from Judith Butler's *Gender Trouble* (New York: Routledge). Copyright 1990. Reproduced by permission of Taylor & Francis, Inc., http://www.routledge-ny.com.

Excerpts from *Powers of Horror* by Julia Kristeva, © 1982, Columbia University Press. Reprinted with the permission of the publisher.

Excerpts from *Lacan: The Absolute Master* by Mikkel Borch-Jacobsen, translated by Douglas Brick, with the permission of the publishers, Stanford University Press. Copyright 1991 by the Board of Trustees of the Leland Stanford Junior University.

Excerpts from Elizabeth Grosz's *Jacques Lacan: A Feminist Introduction* (New York: Routledge). Copyright 1990. Reproduced by permission of Taylor & Francis, Inc., http://www.routledge-ny.com.

Excerpts from *Feminine Sexuality* by Jacques Lacan, edited by Juliet Mitchell and J. Rose, translated by Jacqueline Rose. Copyright © 1982 by Jacqueline Rose. Copyright © 1966, 1968, 1975 by Editions du Seuil. Copyright © 1975 by Le Graphe. Used by permission of W. W. Norton & Company, Inc., and Macmillan Ltd.

Excerpts reprinted from Luce Irigaray, *This Sex Which is Not One*. Translated by Catherine Porter and Carolyn Burke. Translation copyright © 1985 Cornell University. Used by permission of the publisher, Cornell University Press.

Excerpts from Homi Bhabha's *The Location of Culture* (New York: Routledge). Copyright 1994. Reproduced by permission of Taylor & Francis, Inc., http://www.routledge-ny.com.

Excerpts from the novel *Nervous Conditions* by Tsitsi Dangarembga, copyright © 1988. Reprinted by permission of Seal Press.

Excerpts from Stephen Heath, "Difference," *Screen*, vol. 19, no. 3 (1978): pp. 51–112 reprinted by permission of *Screen*, Glasgow University.

Excerpts from *The Subject of Semiotics* by Kaja Silverman, copyright © 1983. Reprinted by permission of Oxford University Press.

Excerpts from *Tu t'appelleras Tanga* by Calixthe Beyala, copyright © 1988 Editions Albin Michel. Reprinted with permission.

Excerpts from *Une vie de crabe* by Tanella Boni, copyright 1990. Reprinted by permission of Les Nouvelles Editions Africaines Senegal.

Excerpts from *A vol d'oiseau* by Véronique Tadjo, copyright 1986. Reprinted by permission of L'Harmattan Edition.

Excerpts from *Burt* by Howard Buten, copyright 1981. Reprinted by permission of Howard Buten.

Excerpts from *The Five Books of Moses* by Everett Fox. Copyright © 1983, 1986, 1990, 1995 by Schocken Books. Reprinted by permission of Schocken Books, a division of Random House, Inc.

Excerpts from *The Slayers of Moses: The Emergence of Rabbinic Interpretation in Modern Literary Theory* by Susan A. Handelman. Reprinted by permission of the State University of New York Press © 1982, State University of New York. All rights reserved.

Excerpts reprinted by permission of The Feminist Press at The City University of New York from *No Sweetness Here and Other Stories* by Ama Ata Aidoo. Copyright © 1970 by Ama Ata Aidoo.

The problem of the articulation of cultural difference is not the problem of free-wheeling pragmatic pluralism or the "diversity" of the many; it is the problem of the not-one, the minus in the origin and repetition of cultural signs in a doubling that will not be sublated into a similitude.

[The space of cultural colonial discourse] is a "separate" space, a space of *separation*—less than one and double—which has been systematically denied by both colonialists and nationalists who have sought authority in the authenticity of "origins." It is precisely as a separation from origins and essences that this colonial space is constructed.

—Homi Bhabha, *The Location of Culture*

Contents

Preface		xi
Introduction: Insider Writers/Outsider Theory		xv
1	First Wave and Second Wave African Feminism: Butler and the Question of Gender	1
2	The Other (Side of the) Mirror	23
3	Jewish Abjection, African Abjection, and The Subject Presumed to Know: Kristeva and Beyala's *Tu t'appelleras Tanga*	43
4	Standing Like a Tower: Plagiarism, Castration, and the Phallus in *Le Petit Prince de Belleville*	97
5	Less Than One and Double: Irigaray/Bhabha, *Nervous Conditions/Assèze l'Africaine*	157
6	Division, Disunity, Disturbance, and Difference: Safi Faye's *Mossane* and the Challenge of Postmodern Feminism	247
7	City of Mud and Diamonds, City of Dis: Tanella Boni, Véronique Tadjo—A Feminism of the Cities	277

Conclusion: Rebuilding Dis: Words of a Second Wave	331
Bibliography	335
Index	343

Preface

What has been the problem of "applying" western feminism to African literature? Why is it that whenever a feminist critique of African literature has been written for the past twenty years, it has seemed necessary to the author to apologize for the use of western feminist theory, or to explain why western theory—Lacanian, Derridean—has not been applied? The usual reasons given for this reticence have been that western theory has been formed in a western cultural context, and is therefore appropriate only to western cultural texts, that western culture is essentially biased in its orientation toward the Third World, that it bears the marks of its colonial past even as it disavows that past. As this critique is being written by one such westerner, it might seem self-serving to deny these accusations, no matter how ill-founded they might appear or feel to me. However, beyond these questions of point of view—that is, who has the innate right or correct upbringing that enables that person to understand or speak about African texts—there is the more important question of what this resistance to western feminist theory signifies. What is gained and what is lost by the employment of western feminist theory; what is western feminist theory; what is the nature of the analysis or critique that employs it?

This study will attempt to address these questions by focusing on one branch of feminist thought, that which has been associated with the French feminists and those who have been influenced by them. This situates the theoretical apparatus within the sphere of psychoanalytical criticism, and leads to questions about *écriture féminine,* the subject and the problematics of the subject position, and most of all the nuances of language that entail close reading of texts. Those texts include some earlier writings by women authors, like Ama Ata Aidoo's story "Certain Winds from the South," Safi Faye's film *Mossane*, and more recent fiction by Tsitsi Dangarembga, Calixthe Beyala, Véronique Tadjo, and Tanella Boni, whom I am identifying as second wave feminist writers. How is it possible to read these authors in light of the work of Julia Kristeva, Luce Irigaray, Judith Butler, and, more broadly, the theoretical approaches influenced by Jacques Lacan? To answer this question, I have had to return to the thorny issues of the appropriateness of considering the Oedipus complex in an African context, or of the viability of such Lacanian notions as the phallus and castration for works involving women. This has been the challenge of a study whose goal was to read a body of exciting African writings through the optic of some of the best and most provocative feminist thinkers.

I am particularly grateful to a number of colleagues whose work has inspired me to venture along these lines, and these include first Odile Cazenave, whose own work, and astute critiques of my own, have made me feel the imperative to undertake this study. I have also been stimulated by the challenges of Keyan Tomaselli, and by reading the work of Susan Andrade and Irène D'Almeida, and discussing feminist issues with them. Clarisse Zimra has always provided the ideal of the inspired critic for me, and the brilliant work of Carole Boyce Davies has made it seem increasingly possible to bring to bear the powerful tools of feminist theory to the task of reading African literature. I am grateful to Obioma Nnaemeka for the support she has given me for this project, and am, like many, inspired by her inexhaustible efforts to combine scholarship with activism. Lastly, though her work is not discussed in this study, Assia Djebar's writings, films, and words have encouraged me to pursue the lines of thought that have guided much of this project.

Closer to home, it has been again my distinct fortune to have been able to compose this book while on sabbatical leave from Michigan State University, working under ideal circumstances in the home of Jean and Madeleine Sévry. And my wife, Liz Harrow, has given me all the support and feedback that I could have wished in making it possible for me to complete the work. My thanks to Olabode Ibironke for help in preparing this manuscript, to Barbara Goodhouse for her meticulous copyediting and to all the Heinemann editorial staff for their multitudinous efforts in helping to move this manuscript into publication. Most especially I thank Jim Lance for his generous support at every stage.

A word about the translations. In general, I have cited texts in their French original, whenever possible, with my own or published translations following. However, in the case of four texts I was limited to the use of three hundred words of the original French, what is defined legally as fair usage, and no more, due to the refusal of the publisher to grant permission. The publisher is Albin Michel, their author Calixthe Beyala, and the issue was my addressing the problem of her plagiarisms.

Introduction:
Insider Writers/Outsider Theory

The project of writing about African literature, especially by western critics, has always been plagued by the issue of outsiders propounding truths about the cultural products of other peoples. This problem, false though it may be in some regard, has been exacerbated in recent years by the development of complex critical theories whose distance from the literature has never seemed greater. Yet it is not an audacious or foolish act to bring the theories of postmodernism or western feminism to bear upon cultural works produced outside of the cultures in which the theories were elaborated. This is, in fact, the norm. Why then has the resistance to "theory" been so intense when it comes to African literature?

The history of Europe's relationship with Africa would be enough to answer the question, on a preliminary level: political and economic hegemony have done much to heighten apprehension about an extension of intellectual domination to the world of letters. Yet, such apprehensions have always seemed suspect to me. Could not the insights of Marxism or Freudian psychology be brought to different cultures, if one were aware of the adjustments required to account for historical or social difference? Could not the exciting and brilliant discussions that have animated feminist debates in recent decades be usefully extended to African women's writing? From the time of *Ngambika* (1986) to the present, this has been the challenge for those wishing to bring feminist criticism to African literature. This book represents an attempt to meet the challenge of employing that branch of feminist thought foregrounded by the French feminists of the 1960s and 1970s and continuing with those influenced by them into the

1990s, in the reading of recent works of African women writers and filmmakers.

I cannot claim that it is my experience in having lived in Africa or having read and taught African literature, as well as feminist theory, that particularly qualifies me for this task. It is rather that the nature of the task must be understood as multiple. While the Irène D'Almeidas, Obioma Nnaemekas, and Juliana Nfah-Abbenyis can bring their experience to bear on their analyses of African literature, others like Eloise Brière, Susan Andrade, and Odile Cazenave have acknowledged their foreignness, as they extended their feminist critiques to African women's writings. This is my goal as well, and as such I perceive my task as seeking to map a terrain best described in a passage from *Invisible Cities* by Italo Calvino, cited by Teresa De Lauretis in *Alice Doesn't*. It involves the city of Zobeide, to which the traveler arrives after six days and seven nights:

> Zobeide, the white city, well exposed to the moon, with streets wound about themselves as in a skein. They tell this tale of its foundation: men of various nations had an identical dream. They saw a woman running at night th[r]ough an unknown city; she was seen from behind, with long hair, and she was naked. They dreamed of pursuing her. As they twisted and turned, each of them lost her. After the dream they set out in search of that city; they never found it, but they found one another; they decided to build a city like the one in the dream. In laying out the streets, each followed the course of his pursuit; at the spot where they had lost the fugitive's trail, they arranged spaces and walls differently from the dream, so she would be unable to escape again.
>
> This was the city of Zobeide, where they settled, waiting for that scene to be repeated one night. None of them, asleep or awake, ever saw the woman again. The city's streets were streets where they went to work every day, with no link any more to the dreamed chase. Which, for that matter, had long been forgotten.
>
> New men arrived from other lands, having had a dream like theirs, and in the city of Zobeide, they recognized something of the streets of the dream, and they changed the position of arcades and stairways to resemble more closely the path of the pursued woman and so, at the spot where she had vanished, there would remain no avenue of escape.

Introduction   xvii

> Those who had arrived first could not understand what drew these people to Zobeide, this ugly city, this trap. (Calvino 52)

For De Lauretis, this city represents the world constructed on the basis of a phallocratic vision, the patriarchs' dream of woman as their possession, eternally pursued, eternally trapped. *Alice Doesn't* represents a reconfiguration of the vision, one which begins with the notion that it is not just men who see, construct, and pursue their desires in the world. Yet for one who has been turned from the West to the sights of Africa, it is astonishing how strong is the pull to read this parable of the city as representing the colonialist construction of "the dark continent." For the feminist theorists of the 1960s and 1970s that phrase was frequently borrowed from Freud to evoke their rebellion against psychoanalytical traditions steeped in male Viennese perspectives. But from an African perspective, the arrival of the outsider who seeks to construct a world based upon his own visions, and then to hold within it the original dwellers of that world, strongly suggests the familiar history of the western escapade known as colonialism. The woman forever pursued but never captured is nothing other than the "real" African, continually constructed by generation after generation of Europeans—always constituted by the inscriptions of the West onto what Christopher Miller has appropriately termed a "blank darkness."

"Dark continent" it has been dubbed. But to those who can stand apart from the mad pursuit of the colonialists, their vision has been more the reflections of what they have seen in a mirror in which they sought their own desires. Yet, though they laid out the streets, created traps even beyond their own imaginings, there were always original inhabitants to the land who were there, whose words, texts, signs, and discourses were present but not seen or heard.

Reading feminist theory has taught us to look for those discourses in the reflections at night, to see the other side of mirrors in which other desires are formulated and articulated. Yet it is not quite as simple as that. There is not just one perspective from which gender can be read or understood; not one African world, not one correct sight. De Lauretis points to this divided articulation in critiquing semiological analyses as being too limited. The notion of linguistic articulation, which we might compare with structural anthropology in its writings on Africa, "concerned as it was with minimal units and the homogeneity of the theoretical object, and 'vitiated [in Pasolini's phrase] by the linguistic mould,' was predicated on an imaginary, if not metaphysical, unity of cinema as a system, independent, that is, of a viewing situation" (44). It is precisely that "situatedness" that is our concern. De Lauretis describes it as consisting of the other components of the signifying process which semiological analysis tended to hide: "to hide the fact that cinematic signification and signification in general are not systemic but rather discursive processes, that they not only engage and overlay multiple codes, but also involve distinct communicative situations, particular conditions of reception, enunciation, and address, and thus, crucially, the notion of spectatorship—the positioning of spectators in and by the film, in and by cinema" (44).

The novel, like cinema, has its readers, its communicative situations, its discursive processes, all of which are marked by codes as well as situated contexts within which meaning is produced. For this study, it is the psychoanalytical codes that are brought to bear in particular to the task of discerning the obscure figure in the glass, while the historical and social contexts, though respected, are given less attention.

In Chapter 1, after an initial foray into African feminist criticism beginning with *Ngambika*, I explore the emergence of a first wave of women writers like Mariama Bâ and Flora Nwapa, and a second with Calixthe Beyala, Véronique Tadjo, and Yvonne Vera. It is not at all my intention to provide a survey or to respond to much of the excellent critical work that has been done, but rather to approach African women's writings, and the issues with which they are concerned, using that branch of feminist criticism that has been heavily influenced by psychoanalytical thought. Thus, the French feminists who were students or rebels against Lacan, the most well-known including Julia Kristeva and Luce Irigaray, have provided me with the means to begin a study of African women's writing. This is an exceedingly contested area because of the perception that this is a critical model that is inappropriate to African literature—a model developed in the West, marked by the phallocentrism of Lacan, not to mention Freud, and finally, refined into an abstruse form of postmodernism that is unnecessarily obscure.

None of these criticisms seems just to me. As I delved more deeply into, first, Lacanian analysis, and then the works of the French feminists, I discovered a number of things. The first is that the charges against Lacan, or even Freud, are often uninformed or ill formed. To be sure, many valid criticisms can be made of them—and indeed, I turn to feminist writers best known for radically criticizing their work. Yet at the same time, no psychoanalytic approach dispenses with their thought or categories, no matter how much their premises are contested. A close reading of Lacan reveals how reductive have been the ego psychologists' readings of Freud. A close reading of Lacan's critics reveals how reductive or obstinate are they who refuse to acknowledge Lacan's own ambiguities or neologisms, the best example being his reinvention of the concept of the phallus. A close reading of Kristeva and Irigaray reveals how nuanced they are in the development of a subversive set of strategies for feminist thought. When one ignores the nuances, Irigaray's morphological elaborations of the female body are mistaken for essentializing, the Name of the Father becomes simply the father, and the oedipus becomes a triangular relationship among persons, with no significant place left for the unconscious, not to mention language and desire, the two keystones to Lacanian and post-Lacanian thought.

The omission of the line of thought these feminist critics developed leaves us with a dependency upon anthropology, or those reductive offshoots of historicist approaches, the sociological or cultural, in which little work on the close reading of the text, its language, and its structural strategies is taken into consideration. This is not a call to return to the formalism of the past—far from it—or a dismissal of concerns over contextualization. One of the most misunderstood notions of the Lacanian symbolic is its relationship to the cultural context within which it is framed. When Lacan states that language and desire are already there in the Other, before the subject accesses them and makes them his or her own, what he means is that language and the shape of desire are enculturated, that they exist not as an abstract system, as in Ferdinand de Saussure's *langue*, nor simply as an individual instance of a general system, as with *parole*, but as a field that preexists the subject, that is accessed by the subject-in-process through the subject's relationship with the Other. That field is situated within a cultural and social matrix, is defined by that matrix.

Just because the symbolic is specific to a culture does not mean that the psychological forces that come into play in the development of the subject, the coming into language, the passage from birth into the life of a socialized being, are so radically different from culture to culture that the broad patterns that mark the one have no relationship to another. All cultures are marked by prohibitions, and most notably the prohibition of incest. Whether it is a strongly endogamous culture or one that is exogamous, there are always lines that divide people, always gender divisions that bear upon the way in which desire can or cannot be legitimized or realized. And most of all, there is always the pattern of entering into a symbolic order, with its language, its rules, its understandings of the world. We define those who cannot accept that order as psychotic—by "accept" I don't mean like or approve of, but understand and maneuver their way through. Most of all, it is the ability to differentiate that enables one to enter into the symbolic: to differentiate between the imaginary and the real being the first order of difference that is required. Finally, the risks of relegating to the symbolic the fixity of a universal pattern, a re-essentializing of the psychological on the level of the Other, are reversed in the challenges of Irigaray and her contemporary feminists, whose use of deconstruction as a "critical device," in Margaret Whitford's words, serves the "aim [of] the reorganization of the symbolic economy" (Burke, Shor, and Whitford 17).

The debate over the appropriateness of psychoanalytic criticism often turns on cultural specificity. We can say that a key concept that exemplifies this is the oedipus itself. For Lacan, the oedipus is crucial for normal development for without "passing through" the oedipus, the subject will not be able to enter into the symbolic, and will become psychotic. The role of the oedipus in Africa has been contested. For Marie-Cécile and Edmond Ortigues, psychoanalytic experience in Senegal demonstrated to them that the Oedipus complex pertains to all societies, although note must be made of the familial, social, and cultural context within which it is formed. Their study *Oedipe africain* was published in 1964, and their clinical practice in Dakar extended from 1962 to 1966. In all cases they noted the intervention of the father and the incest interdiction. The cultural context to which they tried to remain faithful involved a rethinking of the figure of the father in his relationship to those of the ancestors, and as a result the "nuanced" shape of the oedipus reflected this difference: "Dans le modèle européen du complexe d'Oedipe, le fils s'imagine tuant le père. Ici la pente typique serait plutôt: le fils se référant par l'intermédiaire du père à l'ancêtre déjà mort donc inattaquable et constituant ses 'frères' en rivaux" (79). [In the European model of the Oedipus complex, the son imagines that he will kill the father. Here the typical pattern is rather: through the intermediary of the father the son relates to the ancestor, who is already dead and therefore beyond any attacks, and constitutes his "brothers" as rivals.] They go on to describe the terms of the symbolic as reconstituting the conventional father-son rivalry into one in which the phallus is seen as collective, the ancestor unreachable, and the rivalry/identification pattern established between brothers instead of between son and father. The oedipal pattern holds within a different frame. Hortense Spillers comments on the conclusions reached by the Ortigueses: "From my perspective, then, *African Oedipus* is the term that mediates a new symbolic order. It allows us to see that 'father' designates a *function*

Introduction xxi

rather than, as Meillassoux points out, a 'genitor': the father is '*he who nourishes* and protects you, and who claims your produce and labor in return'" (Spillers 139). Allowing for differences, we can see how "father" here approaches the Lacanian Name of the Father when understood as a function and not simply a physical being.

It is this distinction that constitutes a response to Ibrahim Sow's (1977) objection that the oedipus is appropriate only for western cultures, and not African ones. Sow's hypothesis is that the oedipus, or more properly, Freud's Oedipus complex, is grounded in the concept of the concrete individual's "archeological" history—that is, a prehistoric psychological foundation, transmitted through the social replications of general family relations, universal prohibitions, and the unconscious memories of originary historical moments in which those patterns were installed. In short, Sow evokes the types of explanatory psycho-archeology Freud practices in *Totem and Taboo* (1913), in which he explains how in prehistoric times the sons of the original human pack rose up, killed the father, and instituted the rules by which patricide and incest would be forevermore prohibited. The inadequacies of such explanatory archeologies, for Sow, lie in the exclusion of the "horizontal," or what we might also call synchronic patterns elicited through culture and history (as opposed to the vertical prehistory of archeology). The result, for Sow, is a psychology removed from its social environment, and reduced to a monadic form of individualism:

> Mais le préjugé 'psychologiste' pur—individualiste—dans la conception du sujet, qui est probablement l'un des héritages culturels majeurs de l'Occident, inhibe une telle orientation de la recherche psychanalytique chez de nombreux auteurs. Freud, dans la plus pure tradition, a bien individualisé, au plan psychologique, le sujet, mais en une perspective limitée somme toute au simple psychisme individuel. (26–27) [But the pure "psychologicalist" prejudice—individualist—in its conception of the subject, which is probably one of the major cultural inheritances of the West, inhibits such an orientation of psychoanalytical research among many authors. At the psychological level, Freud, in the purest tradition, really individualized the subject, but with such a limited perspective as to constitute, in sum, a simple individual psychic life.]

It is hard to recognize the Freud of *Civilization and Its Discontents* (1930) in this description, but one can certainly understand this orientation toward Freudianism given the ego psychoanalytical schools that arose in the 1950s and that had such a wide impact. In Lacanian analysis it is quite difficult to accept this reduction of the subject to the archeological individual given the cultural, historical frame of the symbolic deployed by Lacan. The famous bars by which Lacan separates the signifier from the signified, the bar thats recurs in his strange algorithmic formulae, striking through La in L̶a̶ Femme, separating the Name of the Father from Desire of the Mother, are intended to resist any reduction to a "simple psychisme individuel."

Sow uncovers the classic archeological emplotment of western psychology in following the trail of the oedipus back to the patterns of the Fall, the Exile, the Banishment—the expulsion of the Adam and Eve from the Garden, the wanderings of Odysseus after Troy's fall—the familiar melange of Hebrew and Hellene in which the so-called Judeo-Christian tradition was said to reside. This is the primordial mythos of the West, for Sow, and he finds no western psychopathology that is not based on this foundation: "Toute psychologie et toute psychopathologie occidentales qui se voudraient compréhensives, quelles que soient leurs formulations, peuvent se saisir, en leur fonds commun, à partir de ce noeud primordial" (226). [Every western psychology and psychopathology that wishes to be considered comprehensive, whatever their formulations, could be grasped, in terms of their common foundation, starting with this primordial tie.] He concludes that it is illusory to detach the essential psychic human productions from their anthropological base. Which leads us to the oedipus.

Given the western base as Sow sees it, Sophocles's tragedy is translated via Freud into the ur-pattern of guilt and neurosis. If there is to be an African oedipus, it cannot be structured along the lineaments based on Sophocles's tragedy, if for no other reason than because "father" and "son" do not share the same relationship in the African context that they did in the ancient Greek, or more recent Viennese, society. Rather, we must seek the social and cultural motivations whose factors lead not to the death of the father, but to those of the fathers: "C'est ainsi que, dans les sociétés traditionelles, appartiennent au même champ sémantique: la prise violente du pouvoir total (social, culturel ou politique), le régicide politique décisif, qui est, en même temps, meutre des pères, et non du père" (227). [Thus it is the case that in traditional societies the violent seizure of total power (social, cultural or political) and decisive political regicide—which is, all the same, the murder of the fathers and not of the father—belong to the same semantic field.] The key lies in the site of the figure of the father—not in the individual, but in the "fathers": "la notion du père s'étend à tous les pères classificatoires, et toute atteinte portée contre le père s'étend, nécessairement, à tous ses pairs classificatoires" (227) [the notion of the father extends to all those classified as fathers, and every attack against the father is necessarily considered to be an attack on those classified as his peers]. Only in modern western societies can the notion of the father's function, according to Sow, be reduced to the individual.

While this interpretation both of the western and of African realities, with such broad generalizations applied to both, might be disputed on that ground alone, of greater importance is the fact that Lacan eschews any focus on the individual father per se, and signals the larger scope of the paternal function by employing the term Name of the Father. Sow wishes to construct a new sense of the subject's psychological ur-text grounded in African archeological patterns and social interrelations—all quite valid concerns. But the usefulness of Lacanian readings returns when we consider how effective the Lacanian approach is in its discussion of the subject's passage through a mirror stage, the state of misrecognition that accompanies the subject's separation from the mother, its identifications and rivalries that result in its entry into the symbolic as a gendered individual, and finally its acceptance of a sexual role hedged by social prohibitions and resolved through displacements. The problem returns, in brief, with the issues with which we began—the formation of the subject and its entry into a social universe that sets out its constraints and its permissible outlets for desire. Incest remains, and patricide remains, whatever the shape of the maternal or paternal function—and indeed those functions remain, however differentially they might be configured in different societies.

And, for that matter, so does the dominant heterosexual phallocratic structuring of society remain, whence the feminist discomfort with Lacanian privileging of the role of the phallus. In fact, what needs to be proved is not that social patterns in Africa differ from those in the West, or that psychic structures are framed by social patterns. The world of the traditional and the modern on which Sow's analysis depends, no matter how accurately conceived in general, disintegrates almost as quickly as one realizes that the very notions of traditional and modern are constructed around a modernist project of civilization in which African difference is always already assumed, and described as the inferior term. My turn toward western psychoanalytical or feminist thought is not based on the conviction that they are articulating universal patterns whose general applicability returns in the structural form of an oedipal relation or an incest prohibition. It is more in the confidence that the analytical tools of reading texts through such an optic can be successfully deployed in different cultures, that the difference is never so great as to justify a notion of Otherness, of radical, essentializing difference. Rather it is the case that the texts are culturally permeable, are permissive, and especially are all the more permissive to those readers whose acquaintance with their societies and cultural artifacts facilitates an embrace of the sort Abdelkebir Khatibi evokes in the notion of love in two languages—an understanding facilitated by openness to the differences, as well as by what Chris Miller insists upon as the insider's knowledge, the anthropologists' all too limited, but still necessary, understandings.

In the end, this entire line of reasoning strikes me as too self-satisfied. There is no way out of an impasse that seeks to deny a critical approach on the grounds of its cultural inappropriateness to the task, as every approach is marked by a set of theoretical constraints that mark both its value and its invalidity. I believe that the discussions that I attempt to set up between the feminist theorists and African women authors will have to justify themselves on their own terms, that is, on the terms of the readings. Those readings depend upon a series of principles embraced by Shoshana Felman in her presentation of Lacanian analysis, and which I utilize in the second chapter in my analysis of Ama Ata Aidoo's short story, "Certain Winds from the South."

In the chapters that follow, I attempt to present a series of readings inspired, in the end, by the revolutionary approaches taken by French feminists—the work of Julia Kristeva, Luce Irigaray, Hélène Cixous, Monique Wittig—and carried through in the brilliant commentaries of Shoshana Felman, Jane Gallop, Stephen Heath, and finally, inevitably, Judith Butler. The problems or revisions these feminists have posed with key Freudian/Lacanian concepts generally revolve around the notions of the phallus, castration, the oedipus, and especially the differences between female and male psychologies. In some cases, the complex role played by castration, especially for girls, has been rethought. Some, like Kristeva, Ellie Ragland-Sullivan, Julie Mitchell, and Gallop, have worked these concepts through with modifications or elaboration; others, like Cixous, Irigaray, Cathérine Clément, or Wittig, have been more critical, seeking to formulate new approaches that would undermine Lacan's phallocentrism. In this they are aligned more closely with Derrida. I have not sought to validate one position over another, but to use those aspects that seemed most pertinent to the readings. Thus in Chapter 3, which deals with Calixthe Beyala's *Tu t'appelleras Tanga* (1988), I explore Kristeva's crucial idea of the abject, all the while questioning her

Introduction xxv

attempt to anchor the concept in an archeological reading of the sort Sow has advocated, and which harks back to Freud's *Totem and Taboo*. It does not seem possible to ignore the Kristevan concepts of the semiotic and the abject in such works as Beyala's first two novels, where the imagery and characterization are so heavily marked by abjection, and where the mother-daughter relationship is crucial.

In Beyala's "Parisian" novels, beginning with *Le Petit Prince de Belleville* (1992), we seem to have encountered a new set of problems, a new author almost. In Chapter 4 I take up the problem of the subject forming an ego-position for itself, of establishing an independent image of itself, which cannot be considered apart from the tensions of castration and the son's relationship with the father. The convoluted issues of the Lacanian phallus and the passage through the mirror stage and the oedipus are considered, along with the ways in which the text evokes absences, "gouffres" or voids that mark the trajectory of desire. The massive plagiarisms that mark the text somehow sustain a reading that responds to palimpsests that lie beneath the surface of the narrative.

The echoes that mark *Petit Prince* and the doubles that characterize African women's literature suggest a connection to Chapter 5, which deals with Dangarembga's *Nervous Conditions* (1988). There I am interested in the ways that Butler presents the strategies for negotiating the passage to adulthood, especially for the woman, and especially for the one who must deal with loss, mourning, and the need to resolve one's relationship with a lost parent or sibling. Dangarembga captures so much of the essentials of this process in what used to be called the Bildungsroman with her pair of cousins, Nyasha and Tambu. Butler's exploration of Joan Rivière's theorizing about mourning and the incorporation of the other seems to have been perfectly tailored for Dangarembga's work. Ironically, the pattern of doubling appears again in "mirrored" form in Beyala's plagiarizing of Dangarembga's novel in *Assèze l'Africaine* (1994).

In Chapter 6 we pass to feminist film criticism, and especially Stephen Heath's groundbreaking article "Difference," in which the problems of using Lacanian and Irigarayan analyses for the study of women's roles, and the broader issue of resistance to phallocentrism, are raised. Difference, the feminine perspective, and the gendered gaze are presented in all their complexity in Safi Faye's feature-length film *Mossane* (1996). Questions of naturalizing or essentializing, in which she seeks to capture a Senegalese point of view, emerge in this film, along with the problems created by the perspective of the ethnographer, the profession Faye has followed in Paris for many years.

Lastly, the study concludes with two more recent "second wave" works by African women writers, Tanella Boni's *Une vie de crabe* and Véronique Tadjo's *A vol d'oiseau*. Here we can see how these texts have incorporated a set of relationships with the symbolic order in which many of the subversive strategies started in the earlier period, analyzed along psychoanalytical lines, now seem so much a part of the landscape. The borders that once divided—other/same, male/female, Europe/Africa, pure/impure, or, in Boni's image, mud and diamonds—begin to blur in these poeticized visions of a world in which dreams allegorize reality, and where new African feminine writing, singing, enchanting, permit a feminist reading from elsewhere to find its own voice.

Chapter 1

▼▼▼▼▼▼▼▼▼

First Wave and Second Wave African Feminism: Butler and the Question of Gender

Construction is not opposed to agency; it is the necessary scene of agency, the very terms in which agency is articulated and becomes culturally intelligible. The critical task for feminism is not to establish a point of view outside of constructed identities; that conceit is the construction of an epistemological model that would disavow its own cultural location and, hence, promote itself as a global subject, a position that deploys precisely the imperialist strategies that feminism ought to criticize. The critical task is, rather, to locate strategies of subversive repetition enabled by those constructions, to affirm the local possibilities of intervention through participating in precisely those practices of repetition that constitute identity and, therefore, present the immanent possibility of contesting them. (Butler 147)

Since its inception, African feminism has been concerned with social questions. In the colonial era, it was common for European colonialists to cast modernism as emancipatory: the civilizing mission would end slavery and bring "modern" thought and values to Africans, who were generally depicted as lacking those qualities. African women, like Muslim women in the "Orient," were depicted as being enslaved to their men[1]: the men presumably bought their wives, whose labor and property belonged first to their fathers when they were girls, and then to their husbands when they were married. Women were ostensibly kept in states of ignorance and oppression, so that the advent of European values, the argument went, would serve to free them by turning them into modern—that is Europeanized—emancipated women. For all the praise that has been heaped on

Mariama Bâ's *Une si longue lettre* (1979), little has been said to indicate how much she depicted her own education in the French school in this fashion (or that of her semi-autobiographical heroine Ramatoulaye). Flora Nwapa duplicates this positive vision of modernist western education in *Women Are Different* ([1986] 1995). Even though Bâ comes to question the forms of modernism adopted by her husband after independence, or even those adopted by her children in her mature years, it is not so as to question the fundamental project introduced all those years back by her French "maîtresse" under colonialism, but rather some of the abuses to which it led. Nwapa is even less critical than Bâ, going so far as to idealize her British schoolmistress.[2]

The fundamental project to which Bâ subscribed has been the dominant feminist position for most of the twentieth century in Africa, and it continues to remain paramount even as new outlooks are beginning to emerge. That initial, dominant strain we can call Africa's first wave feminism, in distinction from the emergent second wave feminism. These terms are certainly not intended to convey priorities in value, an evolution toward higher forms, a dialectal movement, or even any reference to Beauvoir's "second." Rather, it is an attempt to historicize a change that has been generated primarily through the writings of African women (though some note will be taken of the work of male authors) and through African cinema.

This is not the place for a lengthy disquisition on the use of the term "African": clearly general trends have their exceptions, occlusions, boundaries. I am talking about writers from "black Africa," not North Africa or, for the most part, South Africa; nor European writers of African adoption in any form. Nor, in the use of such terms as first and second wave feminism, am I seeking to establish some kind of prescriptive formula designed to elide the difference between the regions and people of Africa over time. On the other hand, it *is* possible to read African women's writings in terms of values generally accepted to be either feminist or of primary concern for women. Not all women authors will fall into this group: many of Aminata Sow Fall's works are a good example. And many African women writers eschew the label feminist, seeing in it the connotations of a western feminist agenda, of the sort indicated in the above references to colonialism and modernism, or look for the alternative term "womanism." Furthermore, in recent years African male authors have shown themselves to be preoccupied by questions concerning the role of African women, two most notable examples being Ngugi wa Thiong'o (in most of what he has written from *Petals of Blood* [1977] on) and Chinua Achebe, in *Anthills of the Savannah*. Sembène Ousmane has shown his interest in the condition of women for a longer time than most African authors. For these male authors, as for Flora Nwapa, Ama Ata Aidoo, Nafissatou Diallo, Mariama Bâ, Calixthe Beyala, Ken Bugul, Werewere Liking, Zaynab Alkali, Tsitsi Dangarembga, Bessie Head, Tess Onwueme, Zulu Sofola, Angèle Rawiri, and many others, the status and identity of African women have been of primary concern. These concerns have generated their own "first wave feminism" criticism, best exemplified in the volume of *engagé* criticism *Ngambika* (1986), edited by Carole Boyce Davies and Anne Adams Graves. The radical agenda conceived by the critics and editors of that volume sought to establish the legitimacy of the African woman as a revolutionary subject, one whose presence, contributions, and demands had been scanted. As committed criticism, the critics sought to redress the situation of revalorizing women's identities and commitments to struggle. In postcolonial language of the sort characteristic of *The Empire Writes Back* (1989), *Ngambika* would be seen as seeking to restore and validate women's agency, especially through the author's seizure of the word.

First wave feminism, then, was programmatic—a feminism whose politics were grounded in an Agenda the terms of which might vary, but whose concerns and presuppositions tended in the same direction. In general, oppressive conditions for women are built on a set of oppressors and a sociopolitical order that is served by that oppression. The earlier focus was on a colonial order whose European governor as commandant had power over the lives of the ruled. In Monique Ilboudi's *Le Mal de peau*, it is the colonial regional commandant who comes across an attractive African woman alone by a river and rapes her who symbolizes this unchecked power of the phallocracy. In Bâ's novels, or Myriam Warner-Vieyra's *Juletane* (1982), it is the African male—the father or husband—who comes to play the oppressor's role. The order is phallocratic, sexist, in novels from Senegal, Nigeria, Ghana, Cameroon, Kenya, Somalia, Botswana, and so on. And the depiction of the dominating patriarch can be located in the earliest writings of African women, in many of the earliest African films, as well as in such recent works as Souleymane Cissé's *Finye* (1982), or Beyala's *Les Honneurs perdus* (1996), where the protagonist's father is depicted as the conventional patriarch, in terms that accord perfectly with first wave feminism representations:

> "Did God permit women of today not to respect their husbands?"
> He started on styles of skirts, on girls who show their thighs and let the wind blow their hair, women who look men in the eye, refuse marriage proposals. (My translation; see p. 70)

In response, Beyala invites us to support the struggle of the patriarch's daughter Saïda to establish her independence, to become an independent woman, free to choose whomever she wants to love, free to live her life as she wishes. For Beyala, that autarchy is to be found in Belleville, the African/Arab quartier of Paris. There African social rules no longer govern, and women cannot be forced to marry, polygamy cannot be practiced, women cannot be compelled to stay at home and to cover themselves on going out. But as it is an African quartier, women can still live with other Africans, can still tell their children African tales, can still enjoy a social life marked by African culture.

Beyala's first wave feminism in *Les Honneurs perdus*, like that of Bâ, Emecheta, Aidoo, and most other African writers, is bound up in liberal humanist values that see the subject struggling to choose freely to live as she likes. The focus is placed on overcoming obstacles to that choice, obstacles that commonly derive from institutional patriarchy. What is assumed in first wave feminism is that there is a subject already there, prior to the choice, faced with the struggle, at times succeeding in her challenge and at times broken. The already present subject is the African woman. Both African and woman. Both identities given prior to the assumption of language, prior to the effects of acculturation or assimilation. In terms of insider/outsider or nature/culture binaries, "African" and "woman" are "inside" or natural, not constructed, not derived, but bodies whose contours are given, whose voices are there, ready to be spoken, ready to be heard.

Once that identity is given, it becomes possible to evoke the obstacles to her fulfillment, such as Saïda's father in *Les Honneurs perdus*, or innumerable other fathers and husbands, or patriarchs in general, whose authority is to be questioned. Bessie Head's Dikaledi can leave us wondering about the violence of that struggle to problematize the patriarchy, to castrate, rebel, scream, or die in anguish. But no matter how violent or emotional the struggle, the *terms of its engagement* are automatically, and thus passively and quietly accepted: the African woman is there, her story to be told, her voice to be heard.

It would seem that this is an eternal story, a never-ending struggle, and the critical apparatus brought to bear on it equally universal in its appeals to authenticity, independence, equality, justice, and decency—the humanist drama retold in African dress. Yet it is a humanism of which we should be suspicious, not because of its western origins or universalist appeals, all of which have a relatively easy, superficial quality to them, but because of its obscure side, its obscurantizing side—the same side that finds natural and normal a set of givens whose premises hold two qualities: (1) that they go without saying, and therefore are neither said nor defended, nor even noticed; and (2) that they function, like all identities, by exclusions whose costs and values are generally taken to be irrelevant, sideshows to the main action.

A second wave feminism would seek to call into question the givens. Not just for the sake of it, not to push iconoclasm to its limits, and especially not to adhere to a foreign code of nihilism. But because without such a querying, the unacknowledged, unnoticed, "natural" constraints of a repressive regime would be perpetrated, and the dance of revolt, reform, reinstitutionalization, and repression would continue indefinitely—just as patriarchy's work would continue to be accomplished in the same manner that western epistemology continued to be accepted in "postcolonial" times.

Here is where the work of Judith Butler, and especially her *Gender Trouble*, appears to be invaluable. For Butler, the charge of feminism is to question those basic assumptions that have gone unnoticed, beginning with the notion that there is something "there" when we use the terms "woman," "female," "sex," and "gender." And in our case, we would add, "African"—or its variants, such as "Nigerian," "Cameroonian," or "Peul," "Bamileke," "Wolof," and so on. In short, there is a range of terms and concepts that await being opened up, closed terms by which the formulation of the identity of "the African woman" is known and accepted—images of a being whose presence and identity are always already there. For Butler, "identity" and "subject" are the places to begin when asking, "Is there something there?" or "Is there something already there?"

Butler begins *Gender Trouble* as if it were the project of a collection like *Ngambika* that she wished to contest by stating that feminist goals presupposed, and constituted, "the subject for whom political representation is pursued" (1). She goes on to highlight not only the term "political," but especially "representation," as the key to the feminist goal of "foster[ing] the political visibility of women," a goal matched in the first sections of *Ngambika*. In fact, the majority of the chapters of *Ngambika* are devoted to the representation of women in male African writings: the first section of the collection is titled "Defining Women's Place: Female Portraiture in African Literature," and the second "Towards a Critical Self-Definition of the African Woman: Writers and the African Woman's Reality." Identity and representation figure as the basis for Boyce Davies's stress on the mimetic function of literature, one that "mirrors and/or recreates social, historical and economic realities."[3]

But in order for there to be representation, there must be a subject, and it is precisely the subject constituted by the exercise of power through the processes of the political and juridical system—ultimately as expressed in the symbolic order of the prevalent discursive system—that seeks its own emancipation from that same system. Under the guise of universal truths, natural structures, or even divine sanction, the constructedness of the subject—or even of the femaleness of the female subject—is obscured:

> In effect, the law produces and then conceals the notion of "a subject before the law" in order to invoke that discursive formation as a naturalized foundational premise that subsequently legitimates that law's own regulatory hegemony. It is not enough to inquire into how women might become more fully represented in language and politics. Feminist critique ought also to understand how the category of "women," the subject of feminism, is *produced and restrained* by the very structures of power through which emancipation is sought. (2; my emphasis)

If the "law" produces "a subject before the law" (Butler is using Derrida's term here), it can be seen by extension how various other subject positions are also produced within other institutional contexts—for example, the school, the bureaucracies of government, the sports world, the press, and so on—with varying differential consequences. One can occupy multiple subject positions from which an "I" can address others, and the specific context of time and place will dictate how those subject positions are produced, how they speak themselves. The categories of "African" and "woman" are no less variable, but also no less produced. It is hardly coincidental that the appeal to a feminist critique that calls for an understanding of how the category of "woman" is "produced and restrained by the structures of power" can be related to a similar appeal to an African critique of the category "African." In fact, the production of blackness, and especially of Africanness, in the structures of colonialism and of European thought, has been well studied by Christopher Miller (1985), V.Y. Mudimbe (1988), Anthony Appiah (1992), and Robert Young (1995). Perhaps it was the fulgurant excrescences of Negritude that pushed the critiques of race and of Africanity so far. But it is interesting to note that "the African woman" has proved to be much more resistant to the kinds of critique to which Negritude has had to submit, perhaps indicating the powerful force deployed by the heterosexual economy in naturalizing gender across various cultures.

Butler critiques Irigaray for generalizing, "globalizing" her analysis as though historical and cultural differences were not significant factors:

> [T]he power of her analysis is undercut precisely by its globalizing reach. Is it possible to identify a monolithic as well as a monologic masculinist economy that traverses the array of cultural and historical contexts in which sexual difference takes place? Is the failure to acknowledge the specific cultural operations of gender oppression itself a kind of epistemological imperialism, one which is not ameliorated by the simple elaboration of cultural differences as "examples" of the selfsame phallogocentrism? The effort to *include* "Other" cultures as variegated amplifications of a global phallogocentrism constitutes an appropriative act that risks a repetition of the self-aggrandizing gesture of phallogocentrism, colonizing under the sign of the same those differences that might otherwise call that totalizing concept into question. (13)

But is the problem here one of colonizing difference, or of a generalization of Irigaray's critique? If critique must be generalized to be persuasive, that is, traced through the specific historical and cultural contours of a given society, then no effective critique that extends across societies can be made. If one pushes the argument against generalizing to its limit, one will scarcely be able to construct a feminist critique of any sort, and if such critique is to be bounded by personal experience, so that only insiders can speak with authority, then we will be able to speak only about ourselves. Obviously agency will be destroyed under these circumstances—unless and until the term "ourselves" becomes sufficiently permeable to permit other voices, those excluded by the border police of inside/outside, to be heard.

It would be a mistake to see first and second wave feminisms, as I am calling these two stages of African feminist critique, as oppositional, tempting as it is to apply critique in such a way as to imply the inadequateness of a former system to its successor. Rather, first wave feminism also should be seen as productive, even of its own critique. The call for emancipation has turned back on the premises of first wave feminism, but not on its call for emancipation. In a sense, it has been something of the failures of first wave feminism, especially when confronted with the situation of the bulk of women living in African towns and cities under conditions of distress, that has driven the necessity for a second wave feminism to pursue the goals of emancipation. Those goals could not be met by any theorizing based on the "state of nature hypothesis," what Butler terms "that foundationalist fable constitutive of the juridical structures of classical liberation" (3).

It is the "state of nature hypothesis" that would present nature as a given, over against culture as a construct; sexuality as a given over against gender as a construct; and even the body as a given over against the mind as a construct. Similarly, if identity or even the existence of the subject is a construct, then some other "nature" will be located as having prior ontological status, be it instinct, drives, the libido, or even consciousness. Butler seeks to problematize Lacanian analysis for its assumptions about the human "substance" that is "there" before the infant begins to respond to the other, but to be fair to Lacan it must be noted that he tends to stress the fallaciousness of the belief in the existence of the ego, in the ego's own misrecognition of itself as a unified subject.[4]

More important, the state of nature hypothesis is built on what Butler terms a "metaphysics of substance," which can be deployed in a myriad of ways to establish the "nature" of being a female or a female subject. We might trace much of first wave feminism to the humanist notions of the subject for whom gender is an "attribute" of a person who forms the basic substance, and who is endowed with a "universal capacity for reason, moral deliberation, or language" (10). This is a Cartesian subject for whom appropriate actions serve the cause of social justice and individual freedom, and who never turns back reflexively to question the bases for the notion of subject itself, that is, for the terms of its own construction. *Ngambika* provides us with the appropriate symbol for this feminist critique with the image of the woman balancing a load of faggots on her head while carrying a child on her back. The inscription beneath her reads, "Help me balance this load" (epigraph to cover). (See Figure 1.1.) While the load might denote any number of burdens African women are made to bear, the burdens of gender of which the child on the back is the sign are not remarked upon. By burdens of gender I don't mean those inflicted on women, but rather the notion of gender itself as an attribute added to the person: the baby tells us this is a mother, that mothers must bear many loads, but not that the role of being a woman itself is extraneous to the person. The operative Foucaultian notion at stake here is that the order that serves to define and to delineate not only serves the interests of the structures of power that constitute the order, but hides the process of constituting the order which is seen as natural.

"Help me balance this load" thus can point forward to the load, appealing to the reader, interpellating him or her to join in the common effort, one to which all of us are called upon to respond. That is the burden of first wave feminism—one not so unnaturally borne at the time of Independence when new African states were being formed, when collective

Figure 1.1 Cover of *Ngambika: Studies of Women in African Literature*. Reprinted by Permission of Africa World Press and Red Sea Press.

efforts were the order of the day—and when revolutionary appeals were often cast in terms of dialectical material necessity. The "me" in the above phrase, "Help me"—the African woman, or even the "Africa" she might be called upon to represent—is not problematized as a construct, and any effort to do so might have been regarded as an impediment to her call to effective action—in contemporary terms, an impediment to the African woman's agency.

But it is fair to ask, who is the "me" in question, and what are the assumptions one is forced to make in accepting the "me" as natural, as a given. One such assumption is that we know who she is, but who are the "we"? Is it that "we" know who "we" are, that identity is given and known to the subject? Then how, one might ask, is it known, how communicated to others? More important, what are the boundaries, the borders of the "we," not to mention of the "I"? To ask this question is to broach the entire insider/outsider division that separates Africans from non-Africans, or Cameroonians from non-Cameroonians, or Bamileke from non-Bamileke. But Bamileke is a large category, and once again one could distinguish between those living in Bamenda from the community of Bamileke taking up residence in a non-Bamileke city like Douala.

The only answer to these questions of who is an African or a Bamileke and so on, would seem to be a "real" African or a "real" Bamileke, and the line that separates the real from the unreal is itself the most powerfully visible border of the sort Foucault was evoking, one that is policed in the interests of those defining the "real"; one that is so "natural" as to appear to be given, to be part and parcel of a metaphysics of substance, and that invariably must define the real in such a way as to exclude the Other from the category of the real.

It is perfectly appropriate to apply this same reasoning to the African woman, even though the genealogy for the construction of the real is different in her case from that of a multitude of other "reals." The problem can be turned by the commonsensical assertion that obviously there is such a thing as a Bamileke, a Cameroonian, an African, or a woman. We can dispense with such terms as "real," or any essentializing configurations, and still agree that we can use these terms of identity, even if we contest the exclusionary practices and thinking of identity politics. We can agree that the terms are relative, relational with respect to other peoples, to the "other" gender, and still see the substance of the identity as determined within a comprehensible system of relations. This leads us in the more radical existential direction taken by Beauvoir, whose formulation of the question is the leading quotation in Butler's *Gender Trouble*, "One is not born a woman, but rather becomes one" (Beauvoir 301).

Beauvoir takes the position that men so dominate our thinking about gender, so impose a masculinist point of view on our vision of what is natural and normal in society, that when one speaks of the universal, natural way of seeing or of being as gender neutral, it is actually the male markers of gender that are obscured, while the female presence is highlighted as conveying active and visible sexual markers. Men are "us" and women are "Other"; men are not visible, whereas women are there to be noticed as female. Men wear "ordinary" clothes and no makeup; women wear makeup and dress in "style" so as to be seen, and so on.[5] As women learn this behavior, learn to fit into this identity, they must "become" women—it is not something that is there, like an innate substance, a body, that is given.

In terms of first and second wave feminism, Beauvoir's approach would seem to bridge the space between the two. If one becomes a woman, assumes the role of a woman, it is obvious that that role will vary from society to society, regardless of the fact that it is a construction. If the burdens imposed on "woman" vary, the struggle to work together remains there for "authentic being" to assume. Neither the relativization of the burdens or of womanhood problematize the call for collective action; rather, they enhance our understanding of the presence of the burdens as burdens, and not as part of the landscape. But by putting the emphasis on "becoming a woman," one deemphasizes the particularity of the status and historicity of the African woman, and defuses the call of texts like *Ngambika* for the need for solidarity with men in the struggle of African people against western hegemony.

Obviously Beauvoir can be read forward or backward in the sentence "Help me to balance this load," because for her the issue of importance is less the problematizing of gender and subject as such than the relative discrepancies and oppression that attend the construction of gender difference. Irigaray pushes the envelope of the sentence by refusing to accept the basis for the discourse about gender. Where Beauvoir asserts that one "becomes a woman," Irigaray contends that the terms of the discourse about gender are framed within a phallocentric economy that adheres to notions, illusions actually, of a "masculinist substance" that provides the basis for "masculinist discourse." That discourse, grounded in binary logic, logocentric formulations, cannot adequately frame the terms into which the concept of woman would need to be cast in order to be adequate to the reality. Accused of essentialism, Irigaray is rather, I believe, iconoclastic in her own formulation of the possibilities of a discourse that would evade the structure of phallogocentrism. Central to this discourse is gender, the adequation of which can only be evoked by the term "not one."

"Not one" returns us back to the subject, the "me" in "help me," more than to the load, the object of the verb "to balance." But the "not one" marks her absence within the strictures of heterosexual and capitalist economies that define the oneness of woman according to a strictly regulated order, one whose particularities may vary, but whose form is generally defined by patriarchal structures.

The gamut of possible feminist readings of the *Ngambika* sentence matches the range of first and second wave feminisms in African feminist thought, and resembles Butler's summation of western feminist inquiry into gender, which is "underscored by the presence of positions which, on the one hand, presume that gender is a secondary characteristic of persons and those which, on the other hand, argue that the very notion of person, positioned in language as a 'subject,' is a masculinist construction and prerogative which effectively excludes the structural and semantic possibility of a feminine gender" (11).

"Help *me* to balance this load"—is the me "women" or "Africans," "African women," or people with burdens, people calling to us? It is not dissembling, a betrayal of that call, for us to ask questions about who that "me" is. By suggesting that it might be "African women," we raise the twin questions of identity and gender, and the issue of whether there is a relationship between the regulation of identity and of gender. "[H]ow do the regulatory practices that govern gender also govern culturally intelligible notions of identity?" (16–17). In posing these (Foucaultian) questions, Butler urges us along the path of querying *all* "substances," all given formulations that could be said to be bounded, and thus divided into an inside and an outside. The envelope of containment for gender or identity would seem to be clear. The regulatory practices that define women do so within the framework of the male/female binary that assigns limits and a format to govern our notion of each of these terms. "Bisexual" and "homosexual" begin to disturb the packaging, but only as disruptive, excluded terms in relation to an already structured mode of understanding and speaking about gender. Without eliminating gendered structuration altogether, as Wittig would seem to favor, some form of division among gendered categories, with their economies and exclusions, would seem to be inevitable. And the dismissal of gendered ordering would seem to be a virtual impossibility within present conditions.

But the reflections on the regulatory practices, with their costs and burdens, are not only possible but necessary. An understanding of the very fact that they function to naturalize their construction of gender is the prerequisite for any action to join in shifting the weight of the burden.

Butler's thoughts about gender would lead to a querying of all bounded entities, especially with respect to subject and gender, so that in the end it becomes clear that envelopes, skins that embrace and contain all ordered systems, be they sexual identity itself, anatomical systems, gender constructs, or the subject in all its various manifestations, are created by the repetitious performances that define their composition and behavior. They become "substances," "intelligible," to the extent to which they fall into the order that is governed by regulatory practices:

> "Intelligible" genders are those which in some sense institute and maintain relations of coherence and continuity among sex, gender, sexual practice, and desire. In other words, the specters of discontinuity and incoherence, themselves thinkable only in relation to existing norms of continuity and coherence, are constantly *prohibited* and *produced* by the very laws that seek to establish causal or expressive lines of connection among biological sex, culturally constituted genders, and the "expression" or "effect" of both in the manifestation of sexual desire through sexual practice. (17; my emphasis)

Thus "male" and "female" are constructed and regulated, and those in between or inconsistent with the heterosexual binary are created as Other, and simultaneously excluded. If first wave feminism seeks to help bear the burden, second wave feminism is much more determined to subvert the regulatory agencies that function to insure the continuation of "normal" and "natural" orders—in this case, that of the heterosexual economy of difference.

For Irigaray, that subversion comes through the site of femininity as "not one," as "a site of subversive multiplicity" ([1977] 1985: 19). For Foucault it was the figure of Herculine on whose body was written an ambiguous detailing of sexual identity—neither entirely male, nor entirely female. For Wittig, the lesbian subject is the only subversive possibility with which to oppose the patriarchal symbolic. None of these might provide an actual model for which second wave feminism in Africa will have much resonance, despite the echoes of such choices in Aidoo's fiction, and the stronger hints in Beyala's early fiction. But it will not be unreasonable to expect to find in the writings of Tonella Boni or Véronique Tadjo, among others of a younger generation of African women writers, some new sense of the necessity to explore the avenues of gender practice that the governing patriarchal regulatory agencies will experience as disconcerting, disturbing, subversive.

For first wave feminism, that subversion was expressed in revolutionary terms, with the demand to overthrow colonialist or capitalist structures, and to end exploitation and oppression engendered through western domination of African economies and states. If second wave feminism is undertaking a challenge to a metaphysics of substance that is guarded by border police, then we can envision its goals as being in harmony with the spirit of Foucault's image of the relatively unregulated order as encompassing "a world of pleasures in which grins hang about without the cat" ([1978] 1980: x).

For first wave feminists, the central problem posed by unsubstantial grins and their world of pleasures is one of agency. How is the pleasure afforded those free to express themselves outside the order of the law going to help the "African woman" bear her burden? She has a baby. How can she drop her role and abandon her responsibilities, even if that role and those responsibilities were imposed on her? And finally, how can she find the means to act, to assume her place, not to bend or break under the burden, on the basis of disembodied grins? Can the two images—the *Ngambika* woman and the grins hanging about—be sustained together, or are they fundamentally incompatible?

"Help me to balance this load." If we don't know, or recognize, how the "me," the subject who takes the form of the African woman, is produced—how there comes to be that woman carrying her child and bearing her burden—then we will be ill-suited to come to her aid. Concern over agency can't displace questions over identity—just the opposite: they pose them, and make them more acute. Agency presupposes an agent, an actor conscious of herself and her actions, and in first wave feminist terms it is a conscientizing actor, one aware of the sources of her oppression, and of the need to seek collective actions for collective solutions. At the limit, it is a Marxist notion of the individual who has risen above class interest, sees the workings of the dialectic, and understands the higher necessity to work for the long-term social good of a classless society. *That* woman and *that* burden have long been the subjects of Ngugi's and Sembène's fiction and cinema, along with that of a generation of anticolonial writers and Bolekaja critics.[6] The first wave feminism that marked that generation of the 1960s and 1970s, and that continues largely among male writers, sees women as oppressed by corrupt male figures of authority who continue to impose two forms of oppression: that of the village patriarchy, and that of the old colonial domination newly transformed into the abusive oligarchy of the independent African state. For these writers and thinkers, the African woman is formed by her traditions, empowered by her society and by the natural values inherited from the past, and ready to be helped to be free. There is no problem with her identity: "femme nue, femme noire" [naked woman, black woman] symbolizes Africa, proud and beautiful, ready to be liberated from the foot on her neck, and to assume her rightful place.

In such a vision, "patriarchy" is reduced to male abuse of power, so that all that is needed to correct the situation is to reform that abuse. In the end, humanist values, even socialist humanist ones, can take us no further, and as a result fail to address the fundamental nature of the workings of patriarchy as a regulatory agency that functions to create normalizing practices that perpetuate the unequal distribution of power—that keep the woman thinking it natural and inevitable to bear the baby on her back and the load on her head, and that the most she can hope for is to have others help lighten her load—shift it about, but not question the reflections cast back from the mirror that continues to maintain the same image. Who ever saw *grins* without a cat? And whose grins?

For Butler, paternal law doesn't function just to prohibit and deny women, as the Lacanian model of the Name of the Father would have it. It is also productive, "*generat[ing]* certain desires in the form of natural drives" (93). The female body, the one bearing the load, is both a figure of denial *and* a construction: she is "a construct produced by the very law [the female body] is supposed to undermine" (93). In this reading, that which represses the female principle, patriarchal law, is also responsible for its production. This would mean that the revolt against patriarchy is *already built into* the female as figure of exclusion, denial, or oppositionality. The parallel to Mudimbe's vision of the African's revolt against the European as doomed by the African's preexistent acceptance of the European terms of engagement, of the European episteme, is inevitable. As Butler puts it, "the repression of the feminine does not require that the agency of repression and the object of repression be ontologically distinct. *Indeed, repression may be understood to produce the object that it comes to deny*" (93, my emphasis). This being the case, the woman bearing the burden cannot be helped following the conventional Sembène model of women's liberation, and has not been substantially helped in most of Africa since independence, since the "female body that is freed from the shackles of the paternal law may well prove to be yet another incarnation of the law, posing as subversive but operating in the service of that law's self-amplification and proliferation" (93). As an example of such a figure, we can take the "Beyala" of the Grand Prix of the

Académie Française—in contrast to the Beyala of *C'est le soleil qui m'a brulé* (1987) and *Tu t'appelleras Tanga* (1988).

First wave feminism is based on an illusion: that of the humanist vision of a female body present prior to the effects of the law, to the symbolic order—the "true body before the law," whose emancipation, in fact, has not fundamentally altered the ratios of power in society, has not diminished the workings of patriarchal structure. And they will not be changed, according to Butler, by a revolution against paternal law because that which is revolting is itself an *inevitable* construct of paternal law whose existence is the condition for society itself. Radical as constructivism may appear, its ultimate argument is not to eliminate the mechanisms of construction—an impossibility—but rather to turn that law against itself by employing the force with which it has invested all that is excluded and denied by the law: "If subversion is possible, it will be a subversion from within the terms of the law, through the possibilities that emerge when the law turns against itself and spawns unexpected permutations of itself. The culturally constructed body will then be liberated, neither to its 'natural' past, nor to its original pleasures, but to an open future of cultural possibilities" (93).

The liberation of which Butler speaks has been the goal of feminist critique for Africa as for Europe, just as agency has been taken to be the requisite position for women to assume in order to achieve liberation. By posing the question about women's identity, one does not call into question agency because in order for there to be agency, *someone* must be there to assume it—and that someone, that substance as woman, as gendered and sexed being, subject, identity, or body, has been shown to be constructed, and thus, so the argument goes, unreal, artificial. The fear, then, is that in accepting the position of radical constructivism, the female agent will turn out to be determined by her culture, or by discourse, and thereby not be free to determine her own course of action. For Butler, this line of reasoning fails for two reasons. First, it relies on a "prediscursive 'I.' " There is no subject prior to discourse, much less to culture. Rather Butler postulates a multitude of subject positions each person occupies, converging in that location in which we locate our sense of ourselves. Second, Butler contests the notion that to be constituted by a discourse is to be determined. To be constituted by a discourse does not contradict the fact that it is we ourselves who use, speak, *perform* the discourse whose very performance constitutes us as particular subjects. When "I" speak, I am choosing to speak in a particular way. It is a way I have learned, that has been repeated before I was there, and that I have had to have heard in order to repeat myself, but as I use it, as I "say" it, as I enter into the role

Butler and the Question of Gender   *17*

of the one who speaks in such and such a way, I enact the role that constitutes my very position as subject. There is no "I" to stand apart from language and use it as a tool, to be taken up and put down without changing the hand of the user. "Language is not an *exterior medium or instrument* into which I pour a self and from which I glean a reflection of that self" (143–44).

The epistemological model of the self, which Butler rejects, sets an I in opposition to an Other as objects in a world to be perceived and understood. Agency, for such a model, is posited in first wave feminist terms as conscientization and action. But the subject and its agency established by such a model is grounded in a discursive tradition that *conceals* itself as it produces its own set of rules and models. The language of identity politics, with each "I" set over against its "Other," presupposes an unproblematic, undivided, natural substance for the "I" and "Other," subjects whose identities can function in blithe assurance of their knowledge—above all in this knowledge of themselves and of others: knowledge of the "real" me.

But to speak the "I" in discourse is to enact the split between the one who speaks and the one represented as oneself in speech; and the positing of the binary self/other carries the same weight of the discursive position as that in which the enactment of the male/female binary has been performed through the naturalizing regulatory agency of phallogocentrism. In opposition to the epistemological tradition, Butler seeks to locate the key problematic of identity within the scope of signifying practices, enabling her to recast the question of agency as one of the act of signifying. This permits her to avoid the "substantive 'I' " that functions "to conceal its own workings and to naturalize its effects" (144). Identity is not thereby lost, or uncovered, but seen to emerge through *practice*, as a "signifying practice," employed through the use of a rule-bound discourse, and not in total freedom from the past, culture, or language. The use of language in this case does not eliminate the necessity of learning previous usages and repeating them, nor from experiencing the effects of all such rule-bound practice, which is to conceal what it regulates and enforces. But awareness of the effects of such practice enables us to avoid falling into the deadly trap of the metaphysics of substance, with its reduction to the tediousness of identity politics and self-defeating notions about agency.

> Indeed, when the subject is said to be constituted, that means simply that the subject is a consequence of certain rule-governed discourses that govern the intelligible invocation of identity. The subject is not *determined* by the rules through which it is gener-

ated because signification is *not a founding act, but rather a regulated process of repetition* that both conceals itself and enforces its rules precisely through the production of substantializing effects. (145; Butler's emphasis)

As this practice comes about through repetition, reiteration, "'agency,' then, is to be located within the possibility of a variation on that repetition" (145). This is the key to Butler's distance from those who depended upon earlier understandings of agency and subversion. It is not the revolutionary overturning of an order she seeks, since it seems inevitable that we must operate within rule-bound systems of signification, that discourse and culture will continue to produce and conceal, and that these are the conditions under which we will be constituted as subjects. But the rules that produce rule-bound subjects also produce the very figures that "exceed," disturb, or oppose the normative subjects or values embedded within the discourse. If the discourse produces males and females, it can do so only by defining male/female according to bounded rules, and thus, by definition, opening up the possibility of there being those who do not fit within the binary male/female. The rules deny, but also produce, as Butler says, so that "alternative domains of cultural intelligibility" are enabled, allowing for "new possibilities for gender that contest the rigid codes of hierarchical binarisms" (145). The functioning of agency under these circumstances becomes truly subversive, because "it is only *within* the practices of repetitive signifying that a subversion of identity becomes possible" (145).

Here we can see the importance of Homi Bhabha's model for hybridity, as an "anti"-substantive approach to identity that escapes the binary logic of naturalized gender difference. We can see how the models of less than one and double, or Irigaray's multiple figuration of the female, function as resistant to the heterosexual *and* the patriarchal structurations. Most of all, we can see how the uncanny doublings we will identify in a range of African women's writings function as subversive or resistant to conventional hierarchical binarisms as they disrupt the models of mono-substantial identities upon which such hierarchies rest.

If repetitive signifying is what enables the subject to be generated, then it can be seen that subjects are not there prior to the practice of signifying, but emerge through that practice: subjects deemed to function according to the rules of the regulatory agency, as well as those deemed to be functioning outside those rules. In all cases, it is the *performance* of the signifying act that results in the constitution of the subject, which is what makes the act of mimicking so essential to the process.

Though *all* performances repeat earlier ones, as is obvious in the performance of an oral tale, it is especially parody that functions not only as a performance, but also as a self-conscious act by calling attention to its performativity. Parody renders visible what the rule-bound practices attempt to render natural, and thus invisible—that is, the act of performance itself. Butler points to the laughter unleashed by parody as an example of the subversive possibilities inherent within the signifying process:

> [T]here is a subversive laughter in the pastiche-effect of parodic practices in which the original, the authentic, and the real are themselves constituted as effects. The loss of gender norms would have the effect of proliferating gender configurations, destabilizing substantive identity, and depriving the naturalizing narratives of compulsory heterosexuality of their central protagonists: "man" and "woman." (146)

But if the parodist forgets her own position as equally constituted and naturalized by discourse, then the destabilization of the targeted parody would be overcome by the stabilized substance of the parodist's position, as is the case in Beyala's parody of the revolutionary speakers in the "villes mortes" campaign in Cameroon, presented in *Assèze l'Africaine*.

"Help me to balance this load" can now be read as a performance of one whose pain might be real, but whose meaning includes an awareness that who she is is not frozen in stone, but is engaged in the act of performing the role of the burdened African woman, the mother, the bearer of burdens, through the very repetition of the words she is speaking. She may continue to represent herself that way, feeling the weight to be overwhelming, the words to be inevitable consequences of her condition, the lament fixed by time and the previous behavior of her mothers and sisters. Or she may launch a new dance, speak the words with a new inflection, letting us know that although the burden is still there, there is now a new space opened up between herself and the image, a space in which there might now hang the faint suggestion of a grin, a surprising grin, faintly resembling a cat without a body.

Notes

1. This issue is explained clearly by Leila Ahmed in her disquisition about European colonialist thought and its exploitation of the modernist project of

emancipation of the Arab woman (see *Women and Gender in Islam*); Robert Young gives it a more general treatment in his *Colonial Desire*.

2. Nwapa goes so far as to have Miss Hill foresee the inadequacies of the incipient, newly independent Nigeria and criticize its immaturity, its inevitable inabilities to govern. Nwapa hammers this message home again and again. In her valedictory speech, Miss Hill tells her girls that she is apprehensive about Nigeria's impending independence because she fears the people are not ready for it, that they do not appreciate the meaning of independence, which is "awareness of Nigerians to their responsibilities in government" (48), and not just enjoyment of the perks of leadership. In Igbo, Miss Hill uses a proverb intended to chastise children for their impetuosity: "the person who ran, and the other who walked would eventually arrive at the same prearranged destination" (49). When Agnes moves into Enugu, working for the Ministry of Education, she sees the failures of independence in Miss Hill's terms: "To [those who took over from the British] independence meant living in the GRA—Government Reservation Area, taking over the positions of the British, driving cars like their colonial masters, but ignoring the grave responsibilities attached to the new positions. The British were not emulated by these new men" (63). Dora states the thesis most succinctly: "Dora did not see the reason for jubilation over the coup. Were those who were spared not guilty of bribes and corruption? Her teachers were right, independence came too soon. We had power thrust into our hands and we did not know what to do with it. We failed to use it judiciously" (72). Finally, Dora and Rose express their generation's abhorrence of the changes brought to Nigeria since independence: " 'The world is coming to an end, then.' 'No, not yet. It is our brand of civilisation. Our society is rotten' " (100). When Rose suggests the missionaries should have prepared them better for the harsh realities of the world, Dora corrects her: "No, we should leave the white missionaries out of it. Our own mothers did not prepare us for it either" (100). And Rose: "You see, Dora, we in Nigeria are in a kind of cultural melting pot. We have moved too fast since independence. Think of the colonial era. Things did not move too fast but we were sure where we were going. Since independence, we have had a civilian regime, a military regime, and civil war all between 1960 and 1974" (101).

There appears to be little or no distance between the author's apparent point of view and that of the former colonialist rulers. Is it then ironic that the principal women characters all thrive as businesswomen and as "modern" exemplars in the new urban environment, never looking back to the villages from which they had come? Simultaneously, the men appear as corrupt and as failures in one sense or another. This is a kind of feminist revenge writing, in which the old colonialist prejudices function as whips to punish the newly emergent African urban patriarchy and its social and political economies.

3. Cf. Boyce Davies's Introduction to *Ngambika*, in which she writes, "The social and historical realities of African women's lives must be considered in

any meaningful examination of women in African literature and of writings by African women writers" (6).

4. Butler elaborates on the issue of constructedness in *Bodies that Matter* (1993), where she disassociates herself from radical constructedness, reaching the conclusion not that everything is a construct, but that much that we take to be constructs, like gender, culture, and identity, and even much that we would be less likely to take as such, such as the body or sexuality, is the result of performativity and reiteration. She redefines construction so as to separate it from the question of the anteriority of the subject: "And here it would be no more right to claim that the term 'construction' belongs at the grammatical site of subject, for construction is neither a subject nor its act, but a process of reiteration by which both 'subjects' and 'acts' come to appear at all. There is no power that acts, but only a reiterated acting that is power in its persistence and instability" (9).

5. Cf. Butler's statement: "the female sex *is* marked, while the male sex is not" (10).

6. The "Bolekaja critics," as they have been dubbed: Chinweizu, Onwuchekwa Jemie, and Ihechukwu Madubuike. *Towards the Decolonization of African Literature* (1980).

Chapter 2

The Other (Side of the) Mirror

Western theory has been described as a kind of metonymic, superstructural extension of western culture in its domination of postcolonial societies.[1] The theory sits in a superior place, one inscribed for it by the western academy, and provides the means of accessing postcolonial texts. The apprehension widely felt by many who have written about African women's writing is that western theorists set about elaborating the correct schemata for analyzing texts, like colonial masters dictating canonical texts for the memorization of their colonial subjects. The "masters" provide the basis for the application of deconstructionism, Lacanian or Foucaultian analysis, which then informs the central works of Mudimbe, Gayatri Spivak, and Bhabha. Feminist writers continue the genealogy when such theorists as Alice Jardine and Butler reveal the influences of Cixous, Irigaray, or Kristeva, who were themselves greatly influenced by Lacan. Why bring in such a panoply of strong thinkers to a study of African literature when only one of those mentioned above is African, Mudimbe, the only one to have written substantially about African literature?

If I assume the risk of furthering this structural domination, it is because I feel that the argument against western theory is too narrowly posited, too limited in its understanding of the actual practice, too essentialist in its definitions of who is African or non-African, and most of all too much off the mark. The problem is not one of point of view—Afrocentric or Eurocentric being the conventional binary—but rather one of the issues that can be raised and analyzed. If it is true that Third World literature has often been read in a limited fashion, shoehorned inappropriately into a theoretical straitjacket, it is no less true that nuanced readings have been produced using theoretical tools from a broad range of thinkers that have strengthened the quality of the thought. A discussion may be productive even when reading across cultures. More important, even if all theory is constructed within a particular cultural context, it is not necessarily limited in its usefulness or interest by virtue of the cultural matrix or genealogical traces that it bears.

On a superficial level, African literature can be and has been misread by its readers. Those who know of Africa only as a textual construction provided by western media or popular iconography will be confined to a limited understanding, or misunderstanding, of most texts. Those who know well their own region or homeland in Africa, and who might wish to generalize from that to the rest of the continent, will also run the risk of constructing partial or weak models. Those who are convinced of the absolute truths of their theoretical guides might indeed seek to validate some theoretical model by finding verification in an African text, implicitly confirming the premise that western theory provides the thought and African texts the body. The notion of applying any theory to any text means essentially this: one stops listening to the text, and uses it to provide the proof for a previously elaborated argument. Rather than applying a theoretical argument, one can read a text bearing certain questions or issues in mind. It is not inappropriate for Trinh T. Minh-ha to suggest the model of a Buddhist who has managed to erase her ego as an ideal for the filmmaker who wishes to make films in Africa—especially a non-African filmmaker.

My goal is not to provide a model for the correct reading of African texts; it is not to prove that western theory is good for analyzing African texts, novels or films created by women. It is not to apply theory or to validate theory, but rather to find ways of reading that enable me to listen better to the critical discussions that have proven to be fruitful—fruitful to me in my appreciation of essential feminist issues. Those issues have been raised by important thinkers who have radically altered the ways we think about sex and gender, about society as a whole, especially as it bears the marks of patriarchy, about language as the carrier of gendered markers, and finally about the same old issues of domination that marked the concerns of African writers and Africanist theorists, like Frantz Fanon, for half a century and more. And by reading these theorists against and through African women's texts, their own assumptions and formulations will also be contested.

At the outset of this study, the challenge will be to take an approach that appears to bear no relation to African realities, one that is particularly distant from a straightforward realist vision of the world and of language, and to relate it to a text whose author has generally been viewed as providing a clearly articulated polemical argument through her construction of an accurate image of her society. In short, it will be a question of doing the impossible: reading Aidoo through Lacan. What an unintentional irony can be seen here: Aidoo, the self-proclaimed nonfeminist; Lacan, the anti-feminist neo-Freudian analyst, whose works have had a major impact on the development of contemporary feminist thought. The bridge between these two distant voices will be provided by Shoshana Felman (1987), whose reading of Lacan will enable me to interrogate my own initial readings of Aidoo's short fiction, and especially "Certain Winds from the South" (1970).

The initial question that interests me is framed by the issues of language. Specifically, what can be gleaned from the language of any text, and in this case a text composed almost entirely of dialogue, with much of the action implied by the speech—a text that performs language, that has been mistaken for an oral performance because of its emphasis on dialogue. Also, what are the limitations of the literal reading of "Certain Winds from the South" as a realist text; what are the limitations of reading as though an ego were addressing another ego? The ego-to-ego reading lies at the basis of approaches to Aidoo as an anticolonialist writer or a committed writer, or even as a feminist despite herself. The ego-to-ego reading has been most hostile to readings dependent on absences, the unsaid, to silence not as repressed speech but as unstated speech, to gaps and inconsistencies not as flaws in some schemata but as points of entry into other spaces.

For Lacan, speech always exceeds its intentions, or, more specifically, always exceeds the ego's intentions in the formulation of thought into speech. Ego-to-ego readings discard the excess, remove it as unimportant or irrelevant or not real. Ego-to-ego readings organize texts into coherent messages, thus fitting them neatly into the symbolic order. Such a reading of Aidoo would find her an anticolonialist. Such a reading would find feminist dicta in "Certain Winds from the South."

"Certain Winds from the South" is one of Aidoo's most successful works of early fiction. Published originally in *Black Orpheus*, along with "No Sweetness Here," and reprinted in the collection *No Sweetness Here* (1970), it belongs to a period when African fiction was thought to be under the unspoken obligation to assume its social responsibilities, that is, to lend support to the struggles of newly independent African societies to improve the lot of the people. The rhetoric was decidedly leftist, with the leftover project of engagée literature still dominant; the preferred modes of fiction were social realist. Attempts to move the center of realist fiction in a more abstract, parodic, modernist, "experimental" direction—as in the plays, novels, and poems of Wole Soyinka, the poetry of Christopher Okigbo, the fiction of Yambo Ouologuem, the cinema of Djibril Diop Mambéty—were attacked as elitist, westernized, and irrelevant to the lives and concerns of Africans. The authors were treated by the likes of Chinweizu as pandering to European audiences or as assimilated traitors.

For the Bolekaja critics, the first requirement to be satisfied by the realist fiction of the 1960s and early 1970s was that it be clearly comprehensible to its audience, and that its message serve a positive social function. The Rules for Reading were clearly preestablished for this fiction: it was to be read for its meaning, and its meaning was to be assimilable into a message—an ideological statement that would serve to conscientize its audience following an established ideological credo. The range of such fiction was considerable, and those displaying the least subtlety were to prove the most short-lived. But many of the dominant works, such as Chinua Achebe's *Things Fall Apart* (1958), Camara Laye's *L'Enfant noir* (1953), Cheikh Hamidou Kane's *L'Aventure ambiguë* (1961), and especially the fiction and films of Sembène Ousmane, respond to a number of these exigencies, though often not as simply and directly as the Rules of Reading would seem to require. Achebe's dictum that fiction be educational fits this credo; however, this is belied by the countervailing dictum he produced when he defined proverbs as "the palm oil with which words are eaten." Sembène's Marxist class conflicts, marked by colonial or neocolonial struggles, were cast in comedic terms in which the devices of humor, unessential or inconsequential to the message, functioned as supplements. In each case the movement of the language exceeded the obvious message, or more precisely, the obvious call for a message.

The Rules of Reading Aidoo's short fiction, as well as her early drama and prose, would seem to produce a consistent series of statements, to the effect that Africa in general, and Ghana in particular, has been victimized by the West; that the newly emergent black elite is continuing the patterns of exploitation of its white predecessors; that African males often continue the patterns by oppressing their wives, by forcing women into demeaning roles marked by sexual servitude to the exclusion of other productive social or economic roles; and by transferring traditional patterns of patriarchy onto the modern economy.

All of these messages can be seen to be present in "Certain Winds from the South." To begin, the story is structured by a diegetic frame story set in the present and a hypodiegetic narrative, or kernel story, set in the past. The frame story concerns the departure of Issa for the South, where he hopes to find work. His wife, Hawa, had recently given birth to their first child, Fuseni, and the action of the story is largely limited to Issa's informing his mother-in-law of his decision to leave shortly before he actually departs. M'ma Asana is left with the charge of informing her daughter about Issa's departure. She decides to comfort Hawa not by addressing safe words of commiseration to her, but by recounting her own story of abandonment by her husband, Hawa's father, a generation earlier. It was a story Hawa had never heard before. Like that of Issa, it involved a husband abandoning his bride, obeying a call for more prestige or wealth associated with the powers that ruled over the country from the South: in the case of Hawa's father, it was the British colonizers who called for soldiers to man their armies in World War II; in the case of Issa, it was economic hardship that drove him to migrate, since the North was dessicated and impoverished, and the South relatively prosperous.

One axis of the reading is provided by the tropes of wealth and poverty, and a second by those based on the structures of power. The frame story revolves mostly around the first axis, while the kernel story revolves around the second. Issa migrates south because the cola (kola) harvest is poor, the soil no longer fertile as it once had been. Even before Issa's emergence from the shadows into M'ma Asana's sight, she is remembering the more substantial harvests of the past, the more generous feasts of buckmeat and not merely duicker, in the celebrations of birth, as was fitting for the prestige attached to her family. In the present, one senses a shrunken and destitute family living under greatly reduced circumstances. Issa's decision to go south is not strenuously opposed by M'ma Asana, perhaps because she knows she cannot stop him, but more because she cannot deny the economic exigency that drives the decision. In her pride, she asserts that only the impoverished Gurunsi living to the North—the Voltans of colonial days—would have been willing to go south merely to cut grass or to exercise the most menial of functions in order to earn money. But the dry, bare days of her current life, like her aging and pain-wracked body, testify to a decline that she cannot negotiate, much less control. Issa departs, recapitulating a history of abandonment, driving the reader to see a pattern of significance in terms of gender that displaces the ostensible focus on the economy: women in the North wind up abandoned by their husbands who head south without them, with the one exception of Memunat, whose sexual liberties resulted in a fall in social status. She herself was forced to migrate to the city in the South where she became a prostitute.

In the kernel story, money is not the issue. M'ma Asana's husband comes from a well-to-do family, and he decides to join the army not because he is conscripted, but because, like Ken Saro-Wiwa's Sozaboy, he does not want to be "outdone" by the other boys who look so splendid in their uniforms.

The message in the kernel story becomes clear when the time comes for M'ma Asana's husband to leave for the battlefront, far from their homeland—far to the "South." When M'ma Asana's father-in-law protests that it is not their war and that his son cannot go, his words are obviously understood to be as powerless as those of M'ma Asana in stopping Issa. Everyone recognizes the prior authority of the British in determining who was to go and who was to stay. The kernel story concludes with a return to the economic trope as M'ma Asana refuses to go south in order to receive payment for her husband's death in the service—she wants him back alive, not money in compensation.

The story concludes with a return back to the frame where once again the economic trope prevails: despite their reduced circumstances, M'ma Asana decides to sell her kola nuts in order to buy a decent fish and prepare a proper feast for her daughter and grandson. Her gesture in the present repeats her earlier one in the past when she refused to give priority to economic necessity, to the call of wealth, to the duress of poverty: unlike the men who yield to glitter and thus choose to depart, she remains faithful to home and family, and teaches Hawa how to survive. Most important for the story's message, she offers her daughter a model not only by providing sustenance for the family, but by narrating her own story to Hawa. The larger message, then, supplanting that suggested by the two precedent tropes of economic duress and colonial authority, is that of feminine nurturing and strength, and especially that strength and nourishment to be found in the act of narration, in the mother's narration of her own story to her daughter. The abandonment by a father and husband is compensated by the performance of the mother's narration: the act of enunciation taking precedence over the condition of abandonment.

The story's "message" is thus multiple, and actually moves from one in which meaning takes precedence to one in which the performance, or the illocutionary function, supplants the immediate referential communication. The reader may choose to ignore this, to retain only the messages about economic injustice or oppression, about colonial domination, and finally about patriarchal failures and matriarchal successes. In that case the excess or supplement involving the act of enunciation, which actually defines how the story itself is performed as largely through the use of implied dialogue—an extraordinary performance in itself—would be ignored or downplayed. The symbolic function, so much in accord with patriarchal structures, would then prevail, and ironically would serve to undermine the very feminist impulse that drives the story's overriding message.

In laying out my interpretation of "Certain Winds," I never addressed you, the readers of this text, because my position and yours were implied, and hidden, in the hermeneutic practice to which we have become accustomed of extracting meanings and transmitting interpretations. The silence surrounding our communication somehow befits the pattern in which I speak and you hear, I deliver and you receive; my mind plays the game of exposing meaning, and you follow, see the meaning, get the point. In putting it this way—as Felman-Lacan would have it—I am constructing a binary pattern that echoes the popular view of the analyst-analysand relation. For Lacan, that popular view has nothing to do with the quite different and relatively more complex reality experienced in the analyst-analysand relationship. But leaving that complexity aside, there remains another issue of considerable importance, that of the role of the text in question. If the analyst is commonly thought to provide the interpretation for the analysand, exposing the meaning to the analysand and thus providing the basis of the cure, still it is the analysand who provides the text. To be sure, neither Freud nor Lacan operated on the basis of such a practice as popularly imagined in the previous sentence. But it is crucial to recognize that the popular notion of analysis, like the underlying assumptions of Rules of Reading criticism, leaves out of the process of interpretation any active role for the text itself. In the case of analysis, there is the equally passive role assigned the dream which is recounted by the analysand and contains a symbolic meaning discerned by the analyst and communicated to the analysand. The same wording could be used to describe Rules of Reading criticism.

The Felman-Lacan approach demands a number of major changes. For one, meaning is no longer important, or, to be more precise, the goal of the analysis after reading is not to decipher a text and lay its meaning bare for an audience, but rather to open a dialogue.[2] Next, the process of reading is not structured along a binary in which the teacher exposes and the student receives, but involves the text itself engaging a reading process involving both critics and readers.

Consider the opening lines of the story, appearing on the page a couple of inches below the title:

CERTAIN WINDS FROM THE SOUTH

> M'ma Asana eyed the wretched pile of cola-nuts, spat, and picked up the reed-bowl. Then she put down the bowl, picked up one of the nuts, bit at it, threw it back, spat again, and stood up. First a sharp little ache, just a sharp little one, shot up from somewhere under her left ear. Then her eyes became misty.
> "I must check on those logs," she thought, thinking this misting of her eyes was due to the chill in the air. She stooped over the nuts. (47)

The story seems to be pointing in many different possible directions. The wretchedness of the cola nuts, echoed in the reflection on the impoverished celebration of Fuseni's birth, serves as principal explanation for Issa's departure south when he tells her, shortly after this opening, "You yourself know that all the cola went bad, and even if they had not, with trade as it is, how much money do you think I would have got from them? And that is why I am going" (50). There are no further references to the cola until the very end when M'ma Asana says, "I am going to the market now. Get up early to wash Fuseni. I hope to get something for those miserable colas" (55). She concludes by stating that she will use the money to buy smoked fish and make a real feast, with "a real good sauce."

Aidoo would seem to be tying together the threads of the first axis of meaning, the economic, with the cola nuts, as they are laid out at the beginning and end of the frame story, and are given directly by Issa as the reason for his departure. However, we can see how this structuring of the frame, this instruction in valuation provided for us by the references to the "wretchedness" of the cola nuts, the "breaking" of trade, and the exchange of the nuts for the more valued fish and ingredients for tuo and sauce, is being positioned for us. Aidoo's narrator performs the same act—explaining the meaning, presenting us with questions and pointing toward answers—in her relationship to the story's principal character, M'ma Asana.

Thus M'ma Asana's "sharp little ache" is also presented in the opening paragraph, and our attention to M'ma's ache supplants our focus on the cola nuts. The ache seems to be linked to the misting over of her eyes, and although this trope is not carried through in the story, we are positioned above M'ma Asana in the second paragraph so as to see her as she is perceived not by herself, but by the story's narrator: she was "thinking this misting of her eyes was due to the chill in the air." Presumably the

The Other (Side of the) Mirror

narrator knows better, as the use of "thinking" implies that M'ma is mistaken. Otherwise, the narrator could simply have stated that the misting was due to the chill in the air. Ironically, the narrative soon moves from this run of direct discourse and narrated action into free indirect discourse, bringing together narrator and character, overcoming this initial distance.

If we take "thinking" as a distance marker between character and narrator, then we share in the empowered position and superior knowledge displayed by the narrator, and can judge the characters' reactions and thoughts as correct or incorrect, as self-deluded or insightful. But we never turn the gaze back on ourselves, never are invited to question our judgments or the narrator's position. The only direction the logic of the discourse invites us to follow is outward toward the implied social reality, not inward toward the enunciation itself or to the site of enunciation, as that would break the compact with realism into which we enter when we read this story on its own implied terms.

The site of enunciation, initially, is that of the panopticon, and ironically, the narration turns our gaze away from its point of origin, the narrator's seeing eye, to that of M'ma Asana's gaze as her first act recorded in the story is to see the pile of cola nuts. With her second act of spitting out the bitter cola in the second sentence, the reading of the first is readjusted to conform to the sense implied: the focus of the optical lens shifts. And this process can be seen to continue with every sentence until the last, when the picture is complete or in total focus.

If, however, we return to the cola nuts and to M'ma Asana's reactions in terms that go beyond those of simple monetary value, other possibilities are opened. The dominant role of cola nuts in the region is expressed not only in their position as a cash crop, but as a signifier of value per se. They are shared by distinguished guests to whom they are served as expressions of respect. Within the world of West African anglophonic fiction, one doesn't have to search far for images of this traditional sign of greeting and respect—a sign of respect conveyed especially to important male visitors. In this story, no male breaks a cola nut, serves it, and eats it. It is not a story of male friendship and relationships, but of male-female and female-female relationships. The cola nuts are sold in the end to serve the needs of a mother to lend support to her daughter. The wretchedness of the nuts, due to the wretchedness of the earth, the poverty of her land and the spirit of the men, reduces their value to a level commensurate with that of M'ma Asana's health, and to a stature commensurate with that of the small, single-mothered family—a far cry from the status of the family into which she married, "one of the richest" of the land.

Aidoo's use of the term "wretched" in the opening sentence carries several possible resonances that bear directly on the story as a whole. The most obvious is the correlation to the English translation of the title of Fanon's *Damnés de la terre* (1961), "Wretched of the Earth," a text that had achieved quasi-canonical status for Aidoo's generation of committed writers of the 1960s. Aidoo's rewriting of Fanon's grand revolutionary narrative is all too evident. Whereas Fanon leads us through stages of conscientization that are framed by the passage from servitude/colonization to freedom/independence, a movement of a people who came to know themselves in the act of rejecting the colonial ruler and his values, Aidoo leaves aside the narrative of the nation.

True, at one point M'ma Asana's father-in-law tells his son that he has no business going to war for the English: "You shall not go," said his father. "You shall not go, for it is not us fighting with the Grunshies or the Gonjas. . . . I know about the Anglis-people but not about any German-people, but anyway they are in their lands" (54). This conversation is placed within the context of the son's return home to explain that he has marching orders, orders that he must obey because "they were under the Anglis-people's rule" (54). The exchange opens the possibility for reading the story in terms of resistance, or as the adventure of the naive "sozaboy" turned bitter with experience of the real world. But such adventure tales, with their varied morals built around the acquisition of practical wisdom or greater experience, accompanied by a knowledge of self and one's relationship with the wider world—knowledge of self given in terms of class, race, or colonial status—have been the stuff of conventional tales of male initiation. Aidoo immediately deflates the situation with M'ma Asana's observation, "Of course his father was playing, and so was I" (54).

The kernel story does not move us into the world of the soldier's adventure. Within two lines of M'ma Asana's husband's departure, the news of his death is brought back, and we are led to direct our attention to M'ma Asana's womb, belly, and intestines, which are made to carry the weight of the news like the charge of the wretched cola nuts, now burning into her like a fire. Just as Hawa must bear the news of Issa's departure shortly after the birth of their child, so did M'ma Asana have to deal with the news of her husband's death three days after the birth of Hawa. The cycle of pregnancy, birth, and death on which M'ma Asana's reflections turn at the outset supersedes the linear track of history, world war, and revolution with which the wretched of the earth are caught up. Fanon's revolutionary dicta, after all, concern the men's march of history—one for which the women must defer their own *démarches* or *dévoilements*, their steps forward, their unveilings. For M'ma Asana, this site of History is what the South conveys. And the lure of money associated with all the other attributes of nation—jobs, government, power, foreign presences, and the Other—all the sources of "smartness" to which the men are attracted, generation after generation, has no power of attraction over her: "But I did not go. It was him I wanted, not his body turned to gold" (55).

The turn away from the South, from the Fanonian grand Narrative of History, from the male narrative of adventure, experience, and knowledge, can be seen in the attention to her small gestures, to M'ma's initial reactions that are recorded when she eyes the wretched pile of cola nuts.

M'ma Asana's gesture of picking up the bowl and putting it down again seems much more undirected than her eyeing the nuts and spitting. Within the context of a series of consequential acts and implied meanings, this gesture of picking up and putting down, the fact that it is a reed-bowl and not a calabash or other container, seems unimportant. Why is it mentioned? As in a dream, with its repetitions and obsessions, it could be linked to the indecisiveness of M'ma Asana in the face of a poor harvest, or it could be unlinked. Aidoo spins the chain of the narrative along a series of M'ma Asana's thoughts so that filling the bowl becomes suggestive of the sexual act joined to pregnancy. The roundness of the bowl—or its full contents—like that of a signifier filled with its proper meaning, a pregnant word full of sense, spills over into her thoughts of her own childbearing and that of her daughter. We are carried along as she leads us back to her home, unable to linger over the pile of cola nuts for more than a brief moment.

All of our speculation on the term "wretched" and the significance of the cola nuts is woven from these threads that are tied together by Aidoo to serve a Female narrative rather than a Grand Narrative, or a Male Narrative. Are we moving in a new direction in African literature, one that quietly departs from the foyers of authenticity and Afrocentrism, built on the foundations laid by Achebe, who had earlier constructed his own stories about men sharing cola nuts served by their wives and daughters? Or is it that all that Aidoo will have achieved, if we accept this task of constructing a new Female Narrative along the lines she lays out for us, is to have replaced one agenda with another? The core relationship of an author who speaks, a critic who interprets, and a reader who accepts the predigested meanings remains undisturbed. To disturb it, we can reject the filiations provided at each step, reject the English translation of *Damnés de la terre*, reject even Issa's rationale, as M'ma Asana herself does. "Issa has gone South now because he cannot afford even goat flesh for his wife in maternity. This has to be so, so that Fuseni can stay with his wife and eat cow-meal with her? Hmmm." (55)

A reading that rejects the South and the directions in which the winds blow might turn us more to the preoccupations with words that carry less precise directions, less clearly marked points of signification, while bearing the fuller weight of the signs, the signifiers, that mark off our dreams. The sexual organs are such signs. We have already seen how M'ma Asana characterized the news of her husband's death as a fire that "settled in the pit of my belly. And from time to time, some would shoot up, searing my womb, singeing my intestines and burning up and up until I screamed with madness when it got into my head" (54). As we see in the line that follows, the imagery of the fire's effect is soon joined to the physical reality, so that metaphor turns to metonymy, much in the same manner that free indirect discourse joins an external narration and an internal thought into one discourse. "Three days you were and suddenly like a rivulet that is hit by an early harmattan, my breasts went dry" (55).

The news, then, like the harmattan, passes into the physical plane created by the narrative: its heat and pain at this initial moment of reception, about which we learn toward the end of the story, is matched by M'ma Asana's recollection of it at the beginning of the story, shortly after she sees the cola nut pit, and then notices the traces of the old pits, now unused, that had once been full to bursting. The tie between past fecundity and present sterility is made, again, both metaphorically and metonymically: "at this time, in the old days, they would have been full to bursting and as one scratched out the remains of the out-going season, one felt a near-sexual thrill of pleasure looking at these pits, just as one imagines a man might feel who looks upon his wife in the ninth month of pregnancy" (47). From these reflections, M'ma Asana is led to reflect on the cycle of pregnancy, birth, and death, and thence to her husband's uncyclical moment of death:

> But there is only one death and one pain. . . .
> Show me a fresh corpse, my sister, so I can weep you old tears.
> The pit in her belly went cold, then her womb moved and she had to lean by the doorway. (47)

The word *pit* joins *womb, belly, and intestines* to the receptacles for cola nuts—the reed-bowl that M'ma puts down and picks up at the beginning, the current cola nut pits and the traces of the past ones. Thus, the "female" container of a child, and, by implication, that provided for a man's penis, functions as source and sign of fecundity. Aidoo's use of the female as receptacle, container—mother, sustainer—joined to the pits of the earth and the containers fabricated from its vegetation, contributes to a modernist totalizing vision of the feminine as source of tradition and of life. Aidoo constructs a unified vision of the African woman, one which she authenticates by signaling her status through M'ma's free indirect discourse as the insider. This signal is given in the line "one felt a near-sexual thrill of pleasure looking at these pits, just as one imagines a man might feel who looks upon his wife in the ninth month of pregnancy." Although this line can be read as direct narration, it blends into the following free indirect discourse so naturally as to suggest an unsutured discourse. Thus are naturally shared the narrator and character's gendered points of view, positioning themselves as women who can speak with certainty about the womb and its contents, but with less certainty about the male reactions to it. Later M'ma Asana's account to Hawa about how Hawa's father was attracted to the enticements offered by the South is given without uncertainty: "How could he sit by and have other boys out-do him in smartness? . . . Oh the stir on the land when they came in from the South" (53). The account leaves no room for doubt—none in M'ma Asana's eyes, in the narrator's, or in ours.

This we might call classical Aidoo: she projects a figure of power in whom a definite vision, secure positionality, and an assured account are summed up. The movement to read meaning in that summation might appear to be almost involuntary, like the force of the fire rising up and up the insides of M'ma. In more appropriate terms, we might liken it to the pit itself, the classically round shape of the container, the female as container.

How can we separate this image of woman as round container from self also as container? That self we might well equate with the subject whose self-understanding is shaped by the reflections of its own imaginary constructions of itself in the gaze of the other—in the reflections of the glass. Not Achebe's transparent glass that presumably reveals reality without filtering or discoloring, but the reflecting glass, the mirror whose imago Lacan takes to be essential for the mis-prision of the self, the construction of the ego. For Felman, the apprehension of this ego is the starting point for a psychoanalytical understanding of text. As of reader, analyst, and analysand.

For Lacan, the ego is not an autonomous synthesizing function of the subject, but only the delusion of such a function. The outcome of a series of narcissistic identifications, the ego is the mirror structure of an imaginary, self-idealizing *self-alienation of the subject*. It is a structure of denial; denial of castration (through a unified self-aggrandizement) and denial of subjectivity (through objectification of others and self-objectification) (Felman 11).

If M'ma Asana's supreme gift to her daughter is her narration, her story, which fills in the silence of twenty years, then it is the gift of the woman writer as teacher whose goal is to accede to the position long enjoyed solely by male writers in their monopolizing of the terrain of African literature. This is the burden of Irène D'Almeida's study of African women's literature, *Francophone African Women Writers* (1994), whose subtitle is "Destroying the Emptiness of Silence," and as such fits comfortably into the discourses of feminist writing about African women's literature for the past twenty years. As such, the models offered by African women's writing and their critics have generally been taken as positive, even when they have been of women who suffered mental breakdowns or physical abuse. The catharsis offered by such models, suggests Cazenave (1996), serves to highlight the discrepancies inherent in the normalizing discourse of mainstream patriarchal thought.

While this direction of analysis has several attractive features that ought not to be discarded in the service of a Felman-Lacanian reading, notably the emphasis upon restoring or reinforcing agency in the lives of African women, and upon exposing the naturalizing impulses of patriarchal structures, they do not go far enough in their analysis of the texts because of their insistence on a resolution that restores wholeness and harmony in a totalizing fashion.

It is denial that marks the story that M'ma Asana herself constructs, the kernel story that serves to fill the emptiness of the silence about Hawa's father, and that also serves to synthesize an autonomous figure in the person of M'ma Asana. Both M'ma Asana and her unnamed husband are rendered coherent and whole through the story; once we understand it, we understand them, and like M'ma Asana's own story, it functions to objectify M'ma Asana's husband. It also enables M'ma Asana to objectify herself. As the story is told to fill in the silence, to fill in the pits, restoring the fullness of pregnancy until they are "full to bursting" with meaning, with the substance of meaning, with pregnant meaning, it serves to bring into unity the dispersed elements of M'ma Asana's account, mirrored in her imaginary and unified into one symbolic whole: into "unified self-aggrandizement." Most problematically, this latter act—which lies at the core of the feminist claims of positive self-affirmation in African women's writing—bears the markings of the structure of denial—denial of castration. On this latter issue turns the whole difficult, central question of the usefulness of Lacanian analysis, especially when applied to a feminist approach.

Before undertaking a fuller consideration of the term castration, let us briefly note how it might be seen to apply in this story. Felman suggests that castration serves as Lacan's explication for the "self-alienation of the subject"—an attempt by the subject to deny that action or relation whose effect upon the subject is to drive it into division, dispersion, self-alienation. M'ma Asana's story is certainly intended as such a denial: it presents Hawa with an image of herself now as one whose life has also been slotted into a coherent story. And it is told so as to restore Hawa to a wholeness in the face of not only the absent father, but of her abandonment by her husband. It turns Hawa away from the spectacle of her own self-division, and toward the synthetic wholeness represented by M'ma Asana not only in her parallel actions in the past but in her significant reactions in the present. It gives wholeness to a temporality that had been fragmented by the disruptions of her past—war, loss of father, colonization; and of her present—poor harvest, and corrupt social and economic inequalities of contemporary, post-independent Ghana.

These disruptions had been presented to the reader from the outset through the images noted above, but also through the signs of such discrepancy and decay upon the body of M'ma Asana. But where the challenges of a decaying body are met and overcome by M'ma Asana's determination to pull her daughter through the current crisis, the same challenges face a less certain future for the men. The image of Issa's return with a pocketful of money to provide for the family is undermined by M'ma Asana's skeptical "Hmmm." Neither M'ma Asana nor her father-in-law can save M'ma Asana's husband. And although M'ma Asana can attest to the satisfactory outcome of her mid-wifery in the cutting of Fuseni's umbilical cord, she cannot give assurance about the outcome of Fuseni's circumcision. The image she employs in describing the latter is a classical trope of alienation:

> "When a grown-up person goes to live in other people's village . . . "
> "M'ma."
> "What is it?"
> "No. Please, it is nothing."

> "My son, I cannot understand you this evening. Yes, if you, a grown-up person goes to live in another village, will you say after the first few days that you are perfectly well?"
> "No."
> "Shall you not get yourself used to their food? Shall you not find first where you can get water for yourself and your sheep?"
> "Yes, M'ma."
> "Then how is it you ask me if Fuseni is very well? The navel is healing very fast. . . . And how would it not? Not a single navel of all that I have cut here got infected. Shall I now cut my grandson's and then sit and see it rot? But it is his male that I can't say. Mallam did it neat and proper and it must be alright. Your family is not noted for males that rot, is it now?" (49)

What strikes me about M'ma Asana's employment of the metaphor of the "grown-up who goes to live in another village" in reference to Fuseni's birth and circumcision is its oddness: it is generally women in a patrilocal society who are required to leave their homes, family, and village for another village when they marry. Although this pattern is not universal, it is the most common in West Africa and especially in the Sahel region that includes northern Ghana. M'ma Asana herself makes reference to her inclusion in her husband's family when recounting their past history. So, in a sense, the circumcision functions appropriately as a symbol and a metonymy for Fuseni's alienation/castration, his alienation of locus, his castration as enforcement of the symbolic order upon his body by the actions of the religious authority, the mallam. And it is made comprehensible—made whole—by the employment of the image of the woman who must also experience dépaysement, the feeling of loss and alienation in adulthood. The language M'ma Asana uses in addressing this issue of alienation is particularly striking: "males that rot" ostensibly refers to penises that become infected after circumcision. However, M'ma Asana's husband was also a male who rotted because he could not resist being "outdone in smartness" by the other boys. The contrast with M'ma Asana is thus made all the more powerful, as she refuses the money, the lure of the South, that was offered in payment to her as the widow of a soldier. Male dispersal would seem to continue through Issa's act of abandonment, and remains as a threat in the uncertainty about the outcome of the circumcision.

In the terms of the Marxist existentialist discourse of Aidoo's earlier fiction, M'ma Asana accounts for the threat of alienation, but not for the broader schemata of difference that subsumes castration and gender. The entry point of difference into the narrative's imaginary comes in the one inconclusive story contained within this kernel story, and that is the one involving Memunat.

> Who was this Memunat? No she is not your friend's mother. No, this Memunat in the end ran away South herself. We hear she became a bad woman in the city and made a lot of money. No we do not hear of her now—she is not dead either, for we hear such women usually go to their homes to die, and she has not come back here yet.
> But us, we were different. I had not been betrothed. (53)

Memunat sums up all of the main themes of the story, while turning them upside down at the same time. She "leaves home for another village," and unlike the penises that rot, succeeds in her endeavors to change her condition. She successfully emigrates and makes money. She successfully flees the dominant male authorities, her family patriarch, who has already engaged her upon the path of traditional marriage by accepting the brideprice cattle. She escapes from the narrow village confines with so much success that they no longer have word of her in the village, and she proves her staying power by not dying while away because she hasn't yet had to be brought back for her final days. In short, she appropriates the role of the penis that does not rot, and as such assumes the successful male role. According to the normalizing discourse of the village, she is a "bad woman"—the one who assumes the burden of the sign of difference so as to make normal the Same.

But by some slip in the symbolic logic of gendering and normalcy, M'ma Asana refers to herself and her husband as the ones who were "different"—different because she had not been betrothed. By implication, all the other girls had followed Memunat's ways, although she is the only one to have wound up "a bad woman in the city." M'ma Asana's difference, then, lies in her fidelity, her resistance to the boys with shiny shoes from the South. Like Sister Killjoy, like Anowe, like a host of Aidoo heroines, M'ma Asana is not seduced by the foreign glitter of the "Anglis," not concerned with their wars any more than with their money or their ways. But she cannot bring closure to the structures of her strong female identity as long as there is Memunat as the example of Mother Africa who has successfully defied the patriarchy and made a success of herself in the city. Memunat offers an alternative to the M'ma Asana model, and in her "badness" and independence assumes the real role of difference rather than M'ma Asana. After all, she was the only one really to "fall" and to have to go off to the city. It seems altogether appropriate that this seemingly minor, insignificant side story of Memunat, and the seemingly offhand comment concerning M'ma Asana and her husband's difference, should provide the basis for a supplementary structure that opens the way to the psychoanalytic reading. For Felman-Lacan points precisely to such a moment in the text, in our reading of the text, for the more telling unconscious signifier to appear.

If we admit into our analysis the reading of the text itself, presented as a discourse, a dream, that comes to know itself only in reflection, that is, only after the fact, after the act of narration, then we can separate the textual reading into an initial act of performance and a secondary cognitive act that gives rise to insight. Felman-Lacan proposed that the insight that accrues to the act of reading always comes in retrospect because insight is never transparent to itself: "Reading is an access route to a discovery. But the significance of the discovery appears only in retrospect, because insight is never purely cognitive; it is to some extent always performative (incorporated in an act, a doing) and to that extent always precisely is not transparent to itself. Insight is always partially unconscious." (15).

The "act" performed by M'ma Asana at this point is that of giving sustenance and strength to her daughter by telling her the truth about M'ma Asana's own abandonment, while it is also that of paying the price of that revelation by repeating to herself the hard truth about her failure to keep her husband with her. Finally, it is an act of informing her daughter who her father really was—an act that will complete the partial knowledge Hawa had up until that moment. The story of Memunat is performed as part of this multifaceted act, and is employed so as to set the stage for the dramatic moment of anagnorisis—the surprising revelation that will bring new knowledge, insight, and understanding. The moment of truth, in other words. But to get to that moment, M'ma Asana has to admit difference into a narrative of sameness. Memunat is clearly the sign of difference, but not the one M'ma Asana intended to evoke when she said, "But us, we were different. I had not been betrothed." Memunat inspires M'ma Asana to say "But," but the insight she brings to the Memunat story is framed by her own conception of herself and her husband as different.

The language she uses to evoke that difference is ambiguous—even opaque. For instance, when she marks her difference by saying "I had not been betrothed," that implies either that she hadn't yet been betrothed, much less married off by her father, that he had trusted her and therefore hadn't rushed to betroth her, or that she had chosen her spouse herself. Rather than resolve this ambiguity, she chooses this moment to reveal the identity of Hawa's father to her, leaving in abeyance the story of Memunat and the question of her betrothal. The flow of the text is clear in its direction: Hawa must learn who her father was so that now she can better appreciate who M'ma Asana is, and thus be enabled to follow in the footsteps of M'ma Asana ("Get up early to wash Fuseni" [55]), and not those of Memunat in chasing after Issa by going south.

"Going south" is the wrong way to go; Memunat "became a bad woman in the city." The story of Hawa's father, the kernel story, contains its own small cola, that being the story of Memunat—a story of badness and of difference attached to women who give in to desire, rather than circumcise their desires and remain home. Women who put kohl under their eyes, women who become rich, women who go south.

We can say, along with Felman-Lacan, that "the unconscious is a reading" (22), and that the reading of Memunat provides us with an opening onto the feminist readings I intend to pursue because it prevents the logic of a phallocratic order from closing down the process of reading by providing definitive meaning to the text. In this, I hope to be following Felman-Lacan-Freud in the goal of attending to the other side of the story, the Memunat side, which insists on going off in its own direction, on going south.

> This is in my view, the quintessential service that Lacan has rendered to our culture: to have derived from Freud a way of reading whose unprecedented thrust and achievement is to keep an entire system of signification open, rather than foreclose it, so that the small, unnoticeable messages can grow, by virtue of the fact that the big ones are kept still, open, and suspended. (Felman 16)

Notes

1. Most famously, Chandra Talpade Mohanty (1991) has written that "[f]eminist movements have been challenged on the grounds of cultural imperialism, and of shortsightedness in defining the meaning of gender in terms of middle-class, white experiences, and in terms of internal racism, classicism, and homophobia" (Mohanty, Russo, and Torres, 7). She has also written in "Under Western Eyes" (1991), the classic essay on the topic, that any construction of Third World feminisms must address "the internal critique of hegemonic 'Western' feminisms" (51), and that "one of the tasks of formulating and understanding the locus of 'third world feminisms' is delineating the way in which it resists and *works against* what I am referring to as "Western feminist discourse" (52). Similar claims have been adduced by African Ameri-

can and lesbian feminist critics, including Barbara Smith in "Toward a Black Feminist Criticism" ([1977] 1982), Barbara Christian (1986), and Alice Walker (1984).

2. I recognize that there are many different kinds of dialogues that can emerge. It seems fair to me that in her readings of African women's writings, Irène d'Almeida, as an African, will seek the intimacy of a discussion *entre soeurs*, whereas Odile Cazenave, as a Frenchwoman, will seek the more formal structure of a rational analysis. I, too, like Cazenave, will assume the more modest claims of one familiar with the house, as it were, but not born to its secrets and inner chambers.

Chapter 3
▼▼▼▼▼▼▼▼▼

Jewish Abjection, African Abjection, and The Subject Presumed to Know: Kristeva and Beyala's Tu t'appelleras Tanga

Why Céline?

For a Jew, it is difficult to read much of Kristeva's *Powers of Horror* ([1980] 1982), starting with her chapter on Judaism. After beginning with three chapters on the abject, the true subject of her study, she turns to Jewish monotheism in her fourth chapter as the source of a certain mode of thinking about the impure, about abomination as it appears in the form of food taboos, "corporeal alteration" and death, and about the feminine body and incest. All of this is generally subsumed under the economy of the binary pure/impure whose appearance she traces back to the Noah story.

The abominable is the quintessential form of the Biblical abject as developed in Jewish thought, and as codified in the Jewish Bible. It is linked to prior definitions of the abject, analyzed by Kristeva in the earlier chapters, where she builds upon notions involving individual psychology and "primitive" societies. The chapter on Jewish abjection is followed by a fifth chapter on Christianity in which the rigors of Jewish law that demand expulsion of the abject are contrasted with the mystical acceptance of sin/abjection as the condition for the remission of sin and the subsequent experience of the beautiful and of jouissance.

This leads to the final five chapters on Céline. There is a certain symmetry that follows these five chapters, as in the first five chapters. In chapter 6, Kristeva introduces Céline, just as she introduced the abject in chapter 1. In chapters seven and eight she develops the features of abjection in Céline's work—the images and themes that explain, in a sense, her choice of Céline for this study, just as she developed the psychology and sociology of the abject in chapters two and three. Finally, after having bracketed the discussion of Céline's anti-Semitism, she analyzes its appearance, mostly in his pamphlets, in chapter nine, entitled "Ours to Jew or Die," structurally placed in a position parallel to the fourth chapter, which deals with Judaism (each preceded by three chapters that lead to the discussion that brings in Judaism). Chapter ten, structurally placed in a position parallel to that on Christianity, deals with Céline's writing, and especially his style, which saves Céline, for Kristeva, by virtue of its beauty, its acceptance of the abject as a means of giving access to jouissance.

There is a final chapter, "Powers of Horror," an afterword as it were of four pages, that serves as an eponymous figure for the whole book, with respect to which Kristeva can situate herself. She avoids personal claims, but her valuations are writ large across the entire text.

Although the stereotype of the Jew, as say presented by Hemingway or Fitzgerald, is that of the *bavard*, the whiner who talks too much, too loudly, and especially too much about himself, the truth is that Jews, like the blacks of the Diaspora, typically make a clear distinction between speech intended for Jews alone, speech within the community, and that intended for non-Jews, the larger, amorphous, mostly Christian world assumed to be unsympathetic if not hostile to Jews. Jews, in short, have a "complex," like blacks, for whom a history of persecution and bigotry would be sufficient reason to explain it. Although the Jewish complex might be tied to two thousand years of life as a persecuted minority, it is more accurate to ascribe contemporary Jewish reactions to the Holocaust. The Holocaust makes the complex seem justified, just as the recent experiences of discrimination have had the most immediate impact on black thought, rather than the more remote, if more horrific experiences of slavery. The Jewish experience of the Holocaust means that the reading of the Bible that Kristeva presents to the reader cannot be the same as that of Jews themselves. Similarly, the chapters on Christianity and on Céline's redemption through the beauty and jouissance of his style cannot be separated in our readings from his anti-Semitism, especially when viewed across the dark years of World War II. Jews have in common with blacks the difficulty of disregarding their own historical experiences when engaging texts that come close to the bone.

The unspoken, assumed, maybe even repressed Jewish reaction to Christianity involves resentment and fear. This is because Christianity is the only religion that has taken the position that the adherents of another faith, its own parent-faith, are in the wrong because they did not go far enough, that they failed to recognize the existence of their own Messiah. "Paganists," Buddhists, Hindus, and Muslims could be excused their failures because Jesus wasn't a pagan, a Buddhist, and so on; the Jews not only failed to recognize him, they were blamed for his death. Jews are thus presented as traitors—to themselves, to Christ, and ultimately to humanity. Christians present this betrayal as though it were personally meant for them: Dreyfus betrayed France because he was a Jew; Jews "destroyed" Germany, and so on. Although Christians have managed to treat adherents of all other non–Judeo-Christian religions as ignorant and as damned, they reserved their pogroms and Inquisitions primarily for Jews. For the secular Jewish teleological reading of history, the Holocaust wasn't a surprise, but rather a logical culmination of centuries of persecution.

All this exposing of the Jewish abject, not as a question of pure/impure (in Kristeva's terms), but as an explanation for my discomfort in reading Kristeva's account of the successful workings of Christianity in contrast with the negative Jewish formulations of the abject, and in reading her account of the ultimately successful achievement of Céline rather than concluding with the horrors of his anti-Semitism. The Jewish abject—for us, not a question of pork, but of being roasted alive because of not being born Christian, or of being gassed because of being found circumcised. Not a question of purity, not even the oneness of God—the original sin of monotheism, reconfigured by Kristeva into various forms of monological thought—but persecution or even injustice. Jewish abjection as a music, a musical tradition so often in a minor key, tuned by history. She defines the Jewish abject by laws of kosher; but only some of us don't eat pork, whereas all of us have been marked by the experience of having been abjected from a Christian world for centuries, which explains the historical resonance with black culture, with Negro spirituals. The Jewish-black abject born of a mirrored relationship, one in which the self (as Jew, as black) is formed through the misrecognition of a reflected image of oneself—an image read in the imaginary of both cultures, especially in the United States, as having shared a similar history.

The Christian Other introduces the third term in the dyad, bringing the Law, the Name of the Father, the repression of an introjected Other, and its emergence through the play of the signified: the resurrection, supreme expression of the supreme abjection of the crucifixion. For Kristeva, who refuses sublimation, sin and jouissance form a unity.

The Kristevan/Lacanian universe is built on notions of a passage from an early stage in which the child is close to positive drives and forces that constitute his or her subjective self, to a later stage, that of the entry into the symbolic order where the price for sanity, for acceptance of the governing psychological authority and its symbolic sign realized in the Name of the Father, or Other, is repression. The normal person who succeeds in gaining access to the symbolic is able to recognize things as they are in the world, assign labels to them, and manipulate the syntax of language along with the demands of everyday living. Unlike the paranoid. And unlike the helpless child before its passage into the symbolic. Kristeva's originality lies in taking us back to an anterior stage, one that precedes the advent of the ego and of language. A stage in which the abject is of central importance, and the ego has yet to be built on secure foundations.

For Kristeva/Lacan, the ego is not a unified structure, and indeed cannot be identified with the subject, but is formed by the incorporation of an outside image, one that is mistaken for an inner essence, an inner being. Here, in the relationship between the self and the outside world, with the development of the ego and the recognition of existences outside of ourselves, the sense of the other, Lacanian thought identifies a beginning stage for the subject, with the initial focus on the mirror stage. Much postmodern feminist thought has been shaped by what follows: the widespread acceptance of the notion of the split ego, its birth in terms of the relation with the other, the importance of the image, and thus of the visual.

With the development of her notion of the semiotic, Kristeva distances herself from Lacan by turning her attention to a prior stage, one that precedes the mirror and its dyadic child-(m)other relation, and the imminent activation of the oedipus. Kristeva begins with a throbbing body and its uninhibited calls, its motions, rhythms, pleasures. This undifferentiated "semiotic" moves with the unstructured music of the soul, hence Kristeva's willingness to listen to the pre-language tonalities of Céline, as well as to focus on abjection and the borderline individual. In psychoanalytic terms, such an individual is situated on the margin between healthy/ill, normal/abnormal, psychotic/nonpsychotic. The terminology fails to convey the way in which the nonpsychotic person is viewed, because terms like healthy, normal, or well-adjusted are built around the assumptions of ego-psychology that Lacan/Kristeva reject. The borderline individual is one who has failed to navigate the oedipus successfully, failing thereby to introject the Other, to establish a repressive mechanism, and to acquire the means to develop a signifying system. Access to language, the formation of the unconscious, and ultimately a successfully developed mental life depend upon the individual entering into a three-way relationship, essentially the Oedipal triangle, following the fear of castration. The child-mother bond, the dyad typical of the mirror stage, is subject to the entry of the third term, the Other, that splits the dyad and the child's intimate play of projection, imaginary identification, and mirror imaging. The child becomes aware of the forceful restriction imposed on the dyad by the third term, and responds to the threat and force of its authority by identifying with the Other, and by introjection of the Other. The result of the introjection is entry into the symbolic, and with it access to a signifying system, to language, this the result of the introjection and repression of the Other which now functions through the phallus as a signifier.

The schematization of human development is built on this pattern of the dyadic structures of the mirror stage and its accompanying imaginary, passing into a triadic Oedipal and symbolic stage: a being is created who learns to use language after having come to an awareness of itself based on a visual, reflected image, or its equivalent, which it takes for itself. At each point the child, the individual in question, is subject to deluded or partial knowledge, and as such approximates the imperfection inherent in the subject's sense of self, an imperfection conveyed by such terms as misrecognition, multiplicity, fragmentation, heterogeneity, and borderline. The child of the mirror stage is seen as the first deluded being, the Cain who brought his ineffective sacrifice to his God, because in opening himself or herself up to the other there comes the sense of a difference between self and other, an end to the sightless unity of breast and mouth, of need and milk joined into a unity of satisfaction. Lacan focuses on the deluded sense of self the image/reflection returns to the child, its mistaken sense of itself as unified, as a complete and whole being united in body as in consciousness.

For Kristeva, there is a stage of human existence prior to this time, prior to the organization of the mental processes and drives into a mistaken sense of self/unity: this is a pre-narcissistic stage marked by fears of separation, a sense of oneself as a disorganized being, with forces, pressures, flows, and rhythms that stay with us, underlying all subsequent stages and development. There the force of creative energy that she identifies as the semiotic resides. It is gendered female rather than male, and provides us with our deepest, darkest fears, our sense of that which is thoroughly abject, repulsive, abominable—as well as joy, unnameable, extravagant, like jouissance. The fear of succumbing that can be seen in its traces left on a later stage of mastery and control—fear of being swallowed up, or being disgorged—also has its origins there. This is the celebrated stage where the drama of postmodernism is to be performed because its beauty, its effect, its style precede all the pretensions and bombast of a totalizing, humanistic, ideological, or rational discourse that would provide sense and wholeness to our lives, to the texts of our lives.

Kristeva runs the risk of celebrating the irrational in ways that might call to mind the early Nazi brownshirts or more recent skinhead movements. But for her, these partisans of violent destruction reacted to the sense of void not by embracing it so as to give expression to the strange force of the semiotic, but by enlisting the extravagance of their emotions in the service of some grand narrative of hatred. Abjection's police, rather than the partisans of jouissance. For Kristeva, there is no backing away from the full ugliness, repulsiveness of abjection. Céline's anti-Semitism is bracketed for five chapters, but when Kristeva finally discusses it, its repulsiveness is never denied or explained away, but rather taken as the central intellectual failing of Céline. And the fascination with "the powers of horror" never spills into admiration; Kristeva is not seduced by the psychotic, the borderline, the mystic, the paranoid, or the fascist. Nor does she construct a diatribe against those whose lives bring them into contact with the abject. Instead, the analyst is condemned to describe and to analyze the phenomena, and here the contradiction of the postmodern analyst catches up with her.

Kristeva, in the tracks of Lacan, follows Alexandre Kojève and the full generation of contemporary philosophers, analysts, and intellectuals shaped by post-structural developments who are not Aristotelian synthesizers or systemizers, but rather partisans, in a way, of rupture. "Partisans" not in the sense of adherents, but as of those who acknowledge the fundamental place of rupture in the individual's psychological economy. With the dissolution of the Cartesian self, the center of the subject is marked by a desert, a fearful emptiness or division. Not as in existential angst where the absence of an outside divine agency thrusts each individual back on herself. But in the sense of a fundamental rupture, leading to an empty or disjointed, decentered self over which all subsequent forms of organization into narcissistic self, into ego, into a being with a name, constitute a vain attempt to cover over this fundamental lack. And it is the return of this rupture, its sullied forms associated with expulsion, the repellent shit of the abject, that is driven by a force that emerges in proportion to the need to rationalize our existence. "The abjection of self would be the culminating form of that experience of the subject to which it is revealed that all its objects are based merely on the inaugural *loss* that laid the foundations of its own being" (5). Kristeva doesn't take us back to the origins of that loss. It is there, prior to our sense of ourselves as subjects separate from objects, prior to our recognition of self or other, but present in our fundamental existence.

And if there is loss, there must be a want that goes unfilled, unfulfilled. The centrality of loss and want to human existence can be measured only in terms of all the later, elaborate substitutions we erect in the vain attempt to satisfy the want, turned into need and eventually desire. "There is nothing like the abjection of self to show that all abjection is in fact recognition of the *want* on which any being, meaning, language, or desire is founded" (5). Kristeva describes this *want* as prior to being or to the constitution of objects, and as having as its only signified "the abjection of self" (5).

For Lacan, the role of the phallus is to signify desire, the object of desire, and as such it always conveys thereby its failure to provide the original object for which it is merely the sign. Similarly, the abject calls forth an infinite series of displacements whose original object is always lost. Lost, but so powerfully present within the individual's psychic economy that an entire, shared vocabulary and imaginary of the horrific can be constructed and disseminated. Among the various features of the abject whose appearance is recognizable—blood, excrement, decay, death—there also is to be found the feminine, what Kristeva calls "an 'other' without a name" (58), and whose repression can be tied to various sexual taboos, including especially that of incest. Kristeva traces this association of the female and the abject back to "primitive" societies—societies she initially designates as "so-called primitive," as if to question the usage of the term by Freud and later Claude Lévi-Strauss. Later she drops the qualifying quotation marks. Black/primitive abjection, as originary as the incest taboo, is analyzed as the preliminary stage to the advent of abjection, to the advent of Jewish abjection.

Freud's initial formulation of primitive society establishes a fundamental difference, based on the assumptions of the binary primitive/civilized employed in his day. In *Totem and Taboo*, written at the height of colonialism in 1913, Freud distinguishes between "primitives," who lacked access to abstract thought and who naively projected their fears and desires onto an external world, and civilized men, who had access to a self-reflective understanding of their own internal processes:

> It was not until a language of abstract thought had been developed, that is to say, not until the sensory residues of verbal presentations had been linked to the internal processes, that the latter themselves gradually became capable of being perceived. Before that, owing to the projection outwards of internal perceptions, primitive men arrived at a picture of the external world which we, with our intensified conscious perception, have now to translate back into psychology. (64)

Freud's interest in this stage of development lay in his attempt to reconstruct in the psychohistory of "mankind" the source of the social structures that came to mark all peoples. He found that source in the Oedipal model, with the traces of the primeval murder of the father by the sons, and the subsequent establishment of taboos against incest and murder. In passing, Freud noted that the process of projection that characterized "primitive" thought resembled that of creative writers whose fictional characters also served as the object for projection. Freud's ignorance of "primitive cultures" was evident in his unqualified acceptance of the most common error made by outsiders to "ethnic" cultures, the error of mistaking the mask for the spirit that "rides" it, or, to use a metaphor best adapted from much Yoruba iconography, mistaking the horse for the horseman. It was a mistake that served the colonial agenda well because it left intact a colonial structure that required "civilized man" to direct the development of "primitives"—those three-fifths men lacking the ability to think abstractly, to conceive of such categories as "civilized" or "primitive."

For Kristeva, the mask is a marker, like the poetic word, that signals the permeability of the boundaries that give definition to self, subject, object, and ultimately society. If Freud generally points us in the direction of the construction of the boundaries that define the individual and society, Kristeva points to their perviousness, in fact to the need that drives us to cross, to flow across boundaries—a need expressed in psychic disorders, but also and especially in the poetic word. The boundary that signals containment of the unimaginable, the rejected, the repressed, also signals the confinement of women: on the level of individual psychology, it is the incest taboo generated by fear of castration that explains the boundary; on the social level, according to Lévi-Strauss, it is the exchange of signs, like those of language, that explains and makes possible boundaries between cultures, groups, and castes within the group. Those initial signs were the women whose exchanges in marriage made possible the borders between "us" and "them," the limits within which the laws of exogamy and endogamy, of kinship, could function. As a consequence of transgressing the boundary, representations of the abject were formed, and they depended on repressions that required the feminine to be confined to fixed modes of behavior with set restrictions and rules. Menstrual blood and incest both shared the same taboo qualities, and depended on the feminine for their nature as taboos. If poetic language, like Céline's, represents the deviation from the straight line of reason, of the rules of language, then it would also exceed the strictures against murder and incest, effecting "a reconciliation with what murder as well as names were separated from" (61).

The act of joining with what we all "were separated from," along with our advent into the social economy and into language—even the inflection of poetic language—cannot be accomplished to any great degree without the risk of paranoia. To prevent this, we must succeed in gaining entry into the symbolic; this is what the identification with the Other accomplishes: not just access to language, through the effects of repression, but the ability to distinguish, to name, objects that are separate from ourselves. Without separation, there is only the child's blind cry of need and the breast-fed maternal milk. Separation, for the individual, is the condition for survival as a person with a name, and this is why the desire to be joined, to be rejoined with what we "were separated from," represents a threat. The threat of absorption, of an endless suckling, requires an equally powerful act of weaning, and a set of taboos, to accomplish the separation. The maternal-turned-prohibited, the devouring mother, is met in rituals of defilement; the powerful call of the initial dyad is warded off by fear, not of castration, but of total loss. Abjection—a warding off, an expulsion of the defiling, disgusting, repulsive, impure—in religious figuration always "converges on the maternal" (64). It is this aspect of religious ritual that Kristeva associates with what *she* calls primitive societies—the various forms of prohibition, of exclusions that can function because of the boundaries established between clean/dirty, normal/abnormal, human/divine. Kristeva's favored term is "propre"—clean and proper, in Roudiez's translation. "Clean" and "proper" might not quite accomplish what is desired by the exclusions set up in Soyinka's *Strong Breed* (1964), *The Road* (1965), or especially *Madmen and Specialists* (1971), in which "primitive," "tribal" exclusions cannot be distinguished from Christian symbology, Yoruba symbology, and especially the neo-genocidal symbology of a post-Biafran Nigeria. Black abjection is too mixed, too porous, for Mary Douglas's ethnographic examples, on which Kristeva relies for her understanding of "primitive" ritual, to work. The boundaries, margins, borders of Lévi-Strauss's models, of Mary Douglas's societies, represent those of a society impervious to the outside world: an anthropological vision of yesterday that never quite existed.

Not that systems of belief with notions of defilement weren't formed, and aren't still being formed. But the system of belief as signifier of a static social entity can signify little more than "the objective frailty of symbolic order" (70), and nothing about a presumed psychohistorical past. Yet that past is precisely what Freud attempted to reconstruct, working out of an ethnology as demoded as James Frazier's *Golden Bough*, and out of a Biblical reading, in *Moses and Monotheism* (1939), equally dependent on nineteenth-century scientific foundations/models. Kristeva's location of Judaism as the etiological source of western, Judeo-Christian abjectology, as we might term it, is by implication just as dependent on a model of development leading from primitive to civilized as is Freud's—a form of psycho-ontology that is recapitulated in phylogeny-history that leads us from the initial psychosocial formations of the abject, the primitive, the Hindu, and the Jewish, finally to the Christian developments with respect to the abject, preparing us for the final stage of Céline. These stages take us progressively from an initial unreflexive expulsion, the exclusion of the abject as the condition for accession into a normal social life, to the larger, programmatic prohibitions of Judaism, culminating in the resolution of Christianity, the positive solution to the human impulse to separate and exclude, achieved by the acceptance of sin as the condition of salvation.

Judaism, as St. Paul would have put it in his doctrine concerning the Law, constitutes the greatest obstacle to salvation, that is, to the successful management of sin, of the abject, because of its absolutism, the foundation of its acts of exclusion. Kristeva presents, with an unapologetic directness, the "taboos," the exclusions, the abjections or abjected, and the rejected in Judaism. She systematizes these elements by turning first to the binary pure/impure, tahor/tamei, as it appears in the story of Noah. Although she designates this choice as one possibility among many, almost as though any other would have done, it is significant that she chose the pair pure/impure, for two reasons. The first is that it is particularly appropriate to Leviticus, the book of the Bible she chooses to focus on, since it is in Leviticus that detailed instructions concerning what one can eat or not eat, concerning everyday life and not just the relationship with God, are provided. The instructions take the form of describing what is acceptable and what is unacceptable by defining the latter as impure or abject in one way or another (Lev. 11–20). As Kristeva wants to build a case that

Judaism passed from a religion of sacrifice to one of morality, of symbolic divisions between good and bad, with goodness as purity and badness as impurity, it is important that she focus on the binary that permitted her to encompass dietary, bodily, and feminine prohibitions.[1]

However, in doing so she represents Judaism in a way that warps its nature for most Jews, that is, as though the concern over purity, and the exclusion of impurity, were fundamental to the religion. The Jewish tradition, to the extent that one can speak of one, has been built around debate over interpretations of the Bible—Talmudic interpretations that include arguments among the rabbis, and even between the rabbis and God, especially over the ethics or hermeneutics to be derived from the scripture.[2] The Levitical code and symbolic order, its binary pure/impure, is closed and frozen; it leaves little room for a Talmudic discussion—one that Jews nonetheless insisted on holding despite the rulebound nature of the passages in question. And even without the disputations of the Talmud, it is now clear to Biblical scholars that the Bible is a compilation of several different voices of which those of the Levitical priestly authors stand most apart from the others. Kristeva has chosen one voice—the most rigid and legalistic—as if it spoke for the entire complex, polyphonic tradition.

Second, the choice of attributing central importance to the binary pure/impure deflects our attention from the far more important category of *kadosh*—holiness.[3] In fact, this is a term usually not presented within a binary: kadosh appears repeatedly by itself in the Bible, especially from the book of Exodus on, providing the Jewish reader with the basic call to his or her identity in terms of the relationship between God and humans. Kristeva quotes the key refrain, "You shall be holy, because I the Lord your God am holy" (104, quoting Lev. 19:2), but the effect of the line echoes the more common "I am the Lord your God." It is a call, one not unlike the call to the name by which Felman-Lacan accounts for the child's accession to the position of subject, and, eventually, into the symbolic order. As the call from the Other, it serves as the reminder of the presence of the Other in the Jews' status as subjects, and thus can be taken as the basis for the mechanisms of repression and speaking, naming, and separating, that give definition to the binaries pure/impure, holy/unholy.

Kristeva's argument is based on a model in which the end of sacrifice in Jewish religious practice, and the substitution (if not sublimation) of the symbolic order, what she terms the passage from a religion of sacrifice to one of morality (expressed in terms of pure/impure), results in the separation/distancing/repudiating of the abject. And for there to be a pattern to the abject, for it not to be an arbitrary collection, Kristeva must claim that this process of the intervention/interpellation of the Other, the unnamed God Adonai, functions so as to cut the dyadic tie of the child to the mother—in this case the Jew from the other. Jews are able to effect a rapport with God only by virtue of a separation from the impure, by maintaining a state of purity. The impure, which Kristeva finds in proscriptions concerning food and the body, has an underlying basis in the prohibitions concerning women—women who give birth, women who are menstruating. For Kristeva, these rules are extensions of the repression of the woman at several levels. The first, purely psychological, is the repression of the phallic mother—the mother as object of desire, and as desiring subject—a repression that only the fear of castration would be strong enough to achieve. The second, sociopsychological, recapitulates the struggle of the system of patrilineage, and presumably the accompanying patriarchy, to supplant that of matrilineage, if not matriarchy itself. The third, linked historically to the latter, would be the suppression of the cult of the Great Mother, and its replacement with the cult of God, Other, Father, Adonai, Elohim, depending on the author/redactor. It is this latter aspect, the weakest in Kristeva's argument, that she stresses throughout as being the basis for her interpretation of the Jewish abject. Thus, she states that the force that underlies Biblical thought concerning defilement is rooted "historically (in the history of religions) and subjectively (in the structuration of the subject's identity), in the cathexis of maternal function—mother, woman, reproduction. But the biblical test . . . performs the tremendous forcing that consists in subordinating maternal power (whether historical or phantasmatic, natural or reproductive) to symbolic order as pure logical order regulating social performance, as divine Law as attended to in the Temple" (91). The "forcing" in question is repression and exclusion, based on the association of impurity with maternal power. The "archeology of that impurity [reveals] fear in the face of a power (maternal? natural?—at any rate insubordinate and not liable of being subordinated to Law) that *might* become autonomous evil but *is not*, so long as the hold of subjective and social symbolic order endures" (91). Here, Kristeva might have cited the multiple injunctions against intermarriage with "others," the contamination that was repeatedly associated with various non-Israelite people, and which earned them their at times wholesale slaughter in the Biblical acccount.

However, to take the Biblical text partially, to serve her thesis, is to distort and totalize a text and set of beliefs and practices that were much more heterogeneous than that. Here lies Kristeva's primary thesis and principal problem: she insists on seeing Jewish difference as grounded in Oneness, monotheism, and an accompanying monologism. This might serve her purposes in explicating abjection, and in advocating the need to go beyond the strictures of too rigid a symbolic order, too absolute an intervention by the Other, too absolute the exclusionary practices of a fundamental(ist) priestly caste—all to be traced back to the binary pure/impure. The price she pays for so absolute a reading of the Jewish abject is Jewish dialogism and heterogeneity, central to the Rabbinical tradition and the Bible. Thus, one might cite, alongside the injunction against Jewish men marrying non-Jewish women, the marriage of Moses to a Midianite woman, and Moses's relationship with his father-in-law—a Midianite stranger who guided and directed Moses in the distribution of justice, the ultimate symbolic system of separation within the Israelite community. One could multiply these examples almost indefinitely, in citing just the major instances, as in the marriage of Joseph to an Egyptian woman, or in the Egyptian origin of Moses's name, his upbringing by the Pharaoh's daughter, or that most moving of loving couples, Naomi and her Moabite daughter-in-law, Ruth.

If the strictures against mixing at times overwhelm the reader with the rigor of their consequences—whole communities of non-Israelite men, along with their women, children, and even animals, are put to the sword—still, one finds equally present examples of kindness, understanding, and acceptance of the other—as in the rule that strangers must enjoy the same advantages of the law as the Israelites during the holy days, and especially the codification of generosity and compassion toward the poor, the outsider. The edges of one's fields must be left unharvested for gleaners. And one finds a series of rules listed in Exodus involving compassion, including the example cited by Kristeva—"Thou shalt not seethe a kid in his mother's milk." Whereas Kristeva interprets this as another example of separation, ultimately based on the rule of incest—that is, the kid and its mother must be separated—the context implies a rule grounded in compassion: even hunters cannot ignore the compassion one must have toward the mother's care of the young, thus maintaining the dyad and not separating the young and their mother. The rules requiring care for others as a central obligation are matched by concern over not violating the maternal bond: Kristeva cites the injunctions against taking a mother bird from a nest with eggs or sacrificing a cow with its young (Kristeva 105), but chooses to interpret these as examples of the incest taboo. For her, the milk in which the young kid is not to be seethed is deemed to "set up an abnormal bond between mother and child" (*sic!*, 105).

It seems to me a more natural reading to interpret the above rules as signs of the sanctity of the mother-child bond, rather than that of the incest taboo. Again within their context myriad examples permit readings to flow in opposite directions, testifying to the Biblical lack of unity. The abjection of the mother-child dyad might be read in the story of Ishmael, who is expelled along with his mother from Abraham's household at the behest of Sarah, with the seconding of God. However, the dyad also appears to be maintained at times: Abraham's grandson Jacob is directed by his mother, Rebecca, to deceive his father, Isaac, in order to obtain the paternal blessing. Likewise, Isaac's acquisition of Rebecca as a wife is joined thematically to Isaac's sadness over the loss of his mother, his need to bask in his mother's love.

Maternal love forms a broad current in the Bible, so much so that its force overwhelms the paternal function. The best example might be that of Moses, whose father is practically invisible and barely mentioned, but whose two mothers—one Egyptian, one Hebrew—play central roles in his life. Moses's insistence on knowing God's name yields him not only the multiplicity of Adonai, Elohim, Elohei, and so on, but the much more ambiguous and tantalizing Shaddai, which Fox glosses as possibly deriving from a Hebrew word for breasts (Fox 287, fn1). If Fox is correct, even the figure of God has not been totally divested of the maternal function.[4]

For Kristeva, the suppression of the maternal in that "colossus" of Hebrew monotheism attested to the Hebrew struggle against the matrilineal, matriarchal society associated with the worship of the Great Mother Goddess, that is, the Cretan, Mediterranean deity. Kristeva asks, somewhat rhetorically, would not the disposition attached to the laws concerning women and impurity "be an attempt to keep a being who speaks to his God separated from the fecund mother? In that case, it would be a matter of separating oneself from the phantasmatic power of the mother, that archaic Mother Goddess who actually haunted the imagination of a nation at war with the surrounding polytheism" (100). Kristeva goes on to establish the need to become separated from that mother in order for the child—in this instance, our figure for the Israelites as a whole, Moses—to be able to speak: "A phantasmatic mother who also constitutes, in the specific history of each person, the abyss that must be established as an autonomous (and not encroaching) *place* and *distinct* object, meaning a *signifiable* one, so that such a person might learn to speak" (100).

To complete the psychohistory, Kristeva puts forward—somewhat too facilely—the notion of a fundamental struggle between the cult of the Goddess Mother and the monotheistic, patriarchal Israelites.[5] The Israelites were certainly influenced by the surrounding peoples—most immediately Babylonians and Sumerians, the people of the Mesopotamian civilizations whose culture, language, and religions bear many obvious traits that strongly influenced Judaism,[6] but their religions were already complex syncretic practices hardly reducible to the single cult of the Great Mother. Furthermore, the focus on monotheism, a central aspect of Kristeva's argument in suggesting the Jewish establishment of a monological symbolic, strikes me as a construction of later interpreters who needed to assert a foundation of monotheism against such powerful polytheistic cults as those of the Greeks and the Romans—interpreters arising in the late Hellenistic and Roman periods, as Rudolph Bultmann has shown in his *Primitive Christianity*. The passages in Exodus, or even earlier, barely ever refer to polytheism as a threat, barely ever evoke a goddess figure as a competitor. Shaddai, the name of God employed in Exodus 6, suggests the possibility of the incorporation of a Mother Goddess into the cult of El. Kristeva evokes the figure of the Mother Goddess much as Freud evoked a pseudo-anthropology in his constructions of the Oedipus complex in *Totem and Taboo* (1913).

However, the ancient Hebrews were in close contact not only with the civilizations of Mesopotamia, but of Egypt as well. And it was the Egyptians who, above *all* other ancient peoples, allocated positions of authority and power to women in their society,[7] as to their gods. Here might that colossal revolution indeed have taken place—not in the erection of a doctrine of unicity, but in the displacement of the Egyptian maternal other by the Name of the Father, first in Egypt and then with the Israelites. With time, Adonai replaced Shaddai and became Adonai—one God—or what Lacan has termed The Subject Presumed to Know—a designation for the analyst who has put himself into the position of authoritative dispenser of truth vis-à-vis his patients: the analyst understood as the one who knows and understands the patient's problems, and the patient as one who must passively listen to the analyst's words to learn of her problem. This is the position developed through ego-psychology to which Lacan was most strongly opposed.

Kristeva's deployment of the notion of the taboo of the mother, grounded in the displacement of the cult of the Great Mother by the monotheistic Hebrew God, strikes me as being the intervention of The Subject Presumed to Know. It becomes a principle around which she organizes the entire Biblical structure of thought—a structure expressed in the binary logic of pure/impure, whose foundation lies in the suppression/repression of the maternal. Kristeva elevates this principle to the level of a mytheme, whose explanatory function can be seen as emerging in the following authoritative discourse: "Far from being *one* of the semantic values of that tremendous project of separation constituted by the biblical text, the taboo of the mother seems to be its organizing mytheme" (105–6). Kristeva goes on to deliver the authoritative source of this assertion by grounding it in psychology and anthropology: "Not only because psychoanalytical discourse on the one hand and structural anthropology on the other have discovered the fundamental role of incest taboo within any symbolic organization (individual and social); but also and especially because, as we have seen, the biblical text, as it proceeds, comes back, at the intensive moments of its demonstration and expansion, to that mytheme of the archaic relation to the mother"; and a few lines later, "the originating mytheme [is] present *everywhere*" (106; my emphasis).[8]

Much as Kristeva recognizes the psychological necessity to pass from the mirror stage to the symbolic, that is, to have the Other intervene through the fear of castration, much as she accepts Lacan's explanation that psychosis results from the failure to negotiate this passage, to introject the Name of the Father, her sympathies would clearly point to a nostalgia for those presymbolic accouterments of the psyche, those presymbolic stages in which the semiotic, maternal, feminine principles, as yet untamed by the oedipus, were dominant. And it is that sympathy that appears clearly in her description of the conquest of the stage of the Mother Goddess by the Hebrew Law of the Father. The "mytheme of the mother" becomes more than an organizing principle, it is a lost desideratum: "The priceless debt to great mother nature, from which the prohibition of Yahwistic speech separates us, is concealed in such pagan cults [as are condemned in the Bible]" (109). More concretely, Kristeva describes this passage from the cult of the Mother Goddess, from religions of sacrifice, to the Jewish religious condemnation of impurity, as being the foundational establishment of the monological symbolic: "A religion of abomination overlays a religion of the sacred. It marks the exit of religion and the unfolding of morals; or leading back the One that separates and unifies, not to the fascinated contemplation of the sacred, from which it separates, but to the very device that it ushers in: logic, abstraction, rules of systems and judgments. . . . Nothing is sacred outside of the One. At the limit, everything that remains, all remainders, are abominable" (111).

By focusing on the Levitical passages dealing with tahor/tamei, Kristeva marginalizes the far greater focus of the Bible on what is kadosh—holy, sacred. Rather than "overlay[ing] a religion of the sacred," the "religion of abomination" is at most present, side by side. Kristeva wants to restore unity to a text, and to a set of beliefs and practices, that partake much more fully of the differential oral and historical origins. Kristeva's "Nothing is sacred outside of the One" would require a reading of all the passages of the Bible through the squinty gaze of a legalistic priesthood, or, in this case, with a fixed postmodernist impulse to discover a single, overarching principle of repression of the feminine in the Hebrew symbolic. That discovery is true and false, depending on where The Subject Presumed to Know positions himself. Or in this case, herself.

Tanga the Abjected

Beyala dissolves the slash that separates the dyadic binaries black/white, Anna-Claude/Tanga, and posits an imaginary, narcissistic identification across the line separating black African/white Jew; she puts us in touch with the abject, in horror of the solid foundations of patriarchy. Maudlin, self-pitying, pitiful—*Tu t'appelleras Tanga* (1988) is so perfectly abject one wonders whether Beyala didn't steal her text from Kristeva's leftovers, Kristeva's own remainders. However, Tanga emerges out of a particular kind of detritus that forms part of the African urban landscape. Like Ouologuem, Beyala has stolen the images of decomposition and decay that Europe cast off, and the real question she poses for us is how the African woman's lament can be read when the terms of reading the abject have been so canonically set by Kristeva. Framed differently, the question is what happens when we read *Tu t'appelleras Tanga* by introducing a third term into the dyad. What happens when the French postmodern meets the African-Judaic abject?

If it is obvious that *Tu t'appelleras Tanga* is constructed around the logic of the abject, it may appear less obvious what the previous analysis of Kristeva's interpretation of Judaism has to do with the African text. Kristeva constructs a psychohistory with its roots in an assumed ur-history of a particular people, the Jews, and traces an evolution through their religious successors, moving down through the ages to the modernists and Céline. Her universalizing conclusion that "the originating mytheme is everywhere" can be read to mean that the incest taboo, the history of the displacement of the cult of the Mother Goddess, and the form of the abject that was initiated at that point, are also generalized.

After all, the expulsion of and disgust over bodily fluids and waste would seem to be universal. But abjection cannot take place without a prior reading of self and other, and the erection of lines, perimeters, and even barriers that can function *only* in the world, only in the concrete situation in which the individual finds him- or herself. The key to this process is not to be found in the ur-history of the psyche, and especially not in a historical ur-history to be traced back from the Christians to the Jews, but rather in the ur-foundation on which the symbolic structures of the present, as well as the imaginary, are constructed. And those foundations are as particular, as culturally relative, as is the symbolic itself.

It is this that permits us to speak of a Jewish abject, a "black" or "African" abject, meaning a process of abjection that responds to the valuations inherent in a current symbolic order. The temptation is to see human development as involving a psychological process whose origins can be traced back to earlier and earlier stages, to more and more deeply buried stages of ur-history. However, the human psyche is not a genetic pool of previously formed characteristics. Its entry into the world is one involving continual interactions of absorption and expulsion where every adjustment of the psyche is attuned to a cultural matrix inscribed within the symbolic codes. The symbolic does not come last in the developmental process, even if language is the end result of a series of stages of development. Like the imaginary, it is there at the beginning, always already there, giving cultural specificity to the forms of thought and action from which abjection eventually is born.

Kristeva's analysis poses the question of authority: how are we to accept the categories of western feminism, of the abject, without falling into the trap of sustaining the pattern of relationships built on privileging the (western) authority of The Subject Presumed to Know? However, if abjection can be read as Jewish or African abjection, or female African abjection, and not just abjection in general—that is, as grounded, like the symbolic, in a cultural matrix—then perhaps Kristeva, and the entire enterprise of western feminist theory, can be read through resistance and still successfully deployed as an analytical tool at the same time. This will be an organizing principle for this study.

However, the excursus into Kristeva's analysis of Judaism was a bit too extensive for it to be only that, and I prefer that it be regarded, in retrospect, as an example of Jewish paranoia, or at the least, Jewish abjection, just like that of Dostoyevski's Smirnikov, whose abjection was self-proclaimed in order to be denied. This abjection is of another principle, one of engaging the other while denying the engagement at the same time—a kind of sniveling that cannot be carried out alone. Or if alone, to a self that is simultaneously other.

This is the problem we have in bringing the subject of western feminism to the fore in our analysis of African women's writing—that of an approach that must bring out the abject by evoking a sniveling on both sides—the outsider's and the insider's. Abjection as sniveling functions in two ways: the sniveling is turned both inward and outward at the same time. The inwardness comes from the self-denigrating remarks, and the outwardness from their avowal as a form of expulsion—a simultaneous confession and denial. Sniveling also requires the outsider to perceive it as such, thus fulfilling the sniveler's need for self-punishment, while trapping the interlocutor into the position of judge, of one-who-knows, whose false sense of superiority is exposed, acknowledged, and mocked by the sniveler.

Tu t'appelleras Tanga begins with Jewish sniveling; through it, through the relationship Beyala builds between Anna-Claude and Tanga, we are able to build a bridge back to Kristeva and her chapter on the Jewish abject. Anna-Claude snivels, "Je vais mourir," evoking the fundamental link between the abject and the death drive, but she finishes the phrase with the word "femme," used in apposition: "Je vais mourir, femme" (5) [I am going to die, woman]. Her sniveling is thus addressed to an invisible addressee, "femme"—one woman, woman in general. She repeats the phrase, with variation, in the next sentence: "Les Blancs meurent aussi" [White people die too], again tacking on the apostrophe "tu sais" [you know], reinforcing the notion that there is an interlocutor, a racial other whose difference is evoked while simultaneously being denied by the qualifying "aussi." Affirmation and denial, the true marks of sniveling that build on Beyala's overdetermined oxymorons.

This opening confessional stance of a moribund first person chronicler recalls the beginning of Ferdinand Oyono's *Une vie de boy* (1956) in which Toundi also turns to a "semblable" [counterpart], a "Français" from Cameroon who, like him, had been expelled from the territory, and who is dying of the wound of his acculturation. Now, a generation later, living under the new dispensation of African independence, there is a kind of reverse optic: the voice that announces its mortality is that of a white woman; the interlocutor, another woman, African; both women are imprisoned in a fictive African country named Iningue—vaguely constructed so as to resemble Senegal, but more obviously based on the familiar Cameroonian setting of Douala to which Beyala generally returns in her fiction.

Anna-Claude is Jewish, a survivor of the Holocaust. Tanga is African, a victim of a murderous patriarchal order that seems to be demanding her sacrifice. Both women turn toward each other in a state of complete abjection, a mirror relationship of misprision in which the intervention of the Other would seem to lead not to the establishment of an independent subject position that enables the speaking subject, but to the annihilation of the possibility of speech. Abjection may seem to express itself through the signifying system of the symbolic, but it undermines that symbolic by the openness of its sniveling—speech that affirms and denies at the same time. Only occasionally does Beyala fall into the trap of preaching without sniveling. Far more often there is a kind of wallowing in misery that would seem to undo all reasonable boundaries.

Jewish abjection. Black abjection. The two meet at the beginning in a prison cell, and their encounter returns, insistently, like the repressed, to disturb the unicity of Tanga's account of her life. Like Toundi, Tanga can be apprehended only in her address to the other, the "tu" whose otherness as white Jew could not be greater, and whose sameness is the final solution of the confession, as the title *Tu t'appelleras Tanga* underlines. Simultaneously, Anna-Claude can only be apprehended in her address to Tanga. Just as Toundi was doubled on his deathbed by a stranger, so was Tanga.

Uncanniness, the mirror stage, and abjection in Anna-Claude and Tanga—Anna-Claude is forty and white, Tanga seventeen (sometimes sixteen) and black. How is it that their resemblance can be cast as uncanny? Both are strangers and doubles. As such they suggest two relationships of joint otherness and sameness—that of the self mirrored in the other, and that of the uncanny double. Both relations differ from abjection, although abjection is evoked with respect to both women in *Tu t'appelleras Tanga* from the outset.

In fact, the doubled relationships, like the novel's discourse itself, function on several levels that overlap and are intercalated within each other, without being subordinated to a single master narrative. We can best see this by analyzing the novel from two different angles: by examining its narrative structure, and by employing a psychoanalytical approach. The narrative begins with the encounter between Tanga and Anna-Claude in prison in Iningue. Anna-Claude addresses a somewhat distraught speech to Tanga, who doesn't respond. A third person account of Anna-Claude's earlier life in Paris follows. She decides to go to Africa in search of a phantasmic imaginary figure, "Ousmane," and eventually finds herself involved in demonstrations whose import she barely understands, leading to her arrest. In prison, she is placed in the same cell as Tanga, whom she meets thus for the first time. She prevails upon Tanga to speak to her, to recount her story. Tanga has been badly beaten, and at first refuses to reply. Eventually Tanga agrees to tell her story, and we leave the level of the frame, the extradiegetic level of Tanga and Anna-Claude's life in prison, for the diegetic level of Tanga's first person account.

There is no simple set of relationships that governs Tanga's autobiographical account; her association with Anna-Claude stands out as distinctly different from all of her other relationships. Yet, the qualities that define the mirror stage, the abject, and the uncanny, can all be seen in various degrees in these two narrative levels. We can approach the two levels with their two narratives as psychological discourses involving an "analyst" and an "analysand."

Anna-Claude prevails upon Tanga to tell her story, establishing the potential for an analyst-analysand relation. But Anna-Claude is already shown to be unstable, "unanalytical," marginal, from the outset. She is not presented as The Subject Presumed to Know, but the one about whom the other, the narrator, knows—the one who first employs the term paranoid:

> Elle lui [to Tanga] avait raconté sa vie jusqu'à la croisée des chemins, jusqu'à la folie, jusqu'à la mort qu'elle venait cueillir en Afrique. Elle lui avait dit la femme, Anna-Claude la paranoïque. Sur les murs de son appartement à Paris, elle dessinait des figures menaçantes pour exorciser le mal de vivre. (1988: 7) [She had told her her own life story, up to the moment when their paths had crossed, up to the time of her madness and the death she was coming to glean in Africa. She had told the woman of Anna-Claude the paranoiac. On the walls of her Paris apartment, she would draw menacing faces to exorcise the pain of living. (1996: 2)].[9]

"Le mal," the evil evoked by the narrator, can point in two directions: toward a poeticized/metaphorical sense of life constrained by malefic forces of oppression, or toward a psychological figure onto whom the feelings of guilt or fear are displaced. The narrator can lead us in the direction of an explanation—one which the narrator already knows—in which case the line between narrator and character is clearly established, and, more important, the distance from the character is clear. The opposite is the case here: the "mal" is left vaguely defined, and the narrator approaches the character with something that resembles free indirect discourse. These are the lines that follow directly those cited above: "Elle se levait à la nuit pleine, le corps nu, les yeux piqués de sommeil, allait du salon à la cuisine cherchant la figure du monstre qui hantait son repos. D'où le mal pouvait-il provenir?" (7) [She'd get up in the middle of the night, naked, her eyes stinging with sleep, go from the living room to the kitchen looking for the face of the monster that was haunting her rest. Where could the evil be coming from? (2)]. With this last sentence closest to free indirect discourse, the narration moves slightly back, leaving the narrative position in an indeterminate space: "Des bruits de la ville? D'elle? Des Autres? Ou tout simplement du calme exaspérant qui régnait depuis quarante ans, depuis la fin de son enfance depuis la fin de la guerre? Pas de réponse" (7) [From the city noises? From her? From others? Or quite simply from the exasperating calm that had been reigning for forty years, since the end of her childhood, since the end of the war. No answer. (2)]. To the narrative question, to Anna-Claude's question, no answer is expected. Anna-Claude's paranoia reduces her questions to symptoms, and her status to that of listener, one who waits for answers; it removes her, places her at a distance from, and beneath, that lofty space reserved for The Subject Presumed to Know.

Her relationship with Tanga, then, although structurally constructed so as to put her in the place of the listener, the analyst, is undermined from the outset by the narrator's description of her. And, in fact, as soon as Tanga begins to speak, Anna-Claude disappears. When Anna-Claude periodically returns, it is so as to return us to the present, outside of the action of Tanga's story, until the very end.

Furthermore, Anna-Claude's position is defined by *displacement*, not establishment. She is displaced, a borderline case, as Kristeva would call her: not so paranoid as not to be able to function in society; not always able to distinguish clearly between imaginary and real. The sign of the borderline is abjection—a state recognizable by the fascination with the abject, and by the need to establish one's own subject identity, an ego space not threatened by the tie to the other. Abjection is not derived from castration, that is, from the shattering intervention of the Other, but occurs prior to this, and involves an ego less well defined, a subject less clearly separated from the objects that surround it. Anna-Claude's abjection, vaguely linked to her Jewish identity, barely hinted at in this early reference to her fears of "le mal" emerging from the end of the war, becomes more definite when linked to her fantasies about Africa. Ab-jection, the expulsion of those excretions of the body's orifices, is also the expulsion of the feared other, often a mother—a devouring mother, whose threat consists in absorbing an uncertain self, an ego-not-yet-ego, a subject-not-set-off-from-other-objects.

In Anna-Claude's system of abjection, Europe is set against Africa. A professor of philosophy, she rejects the greatest figures of the western symbolic order, Kant and Hegel, in favor of the imaginary she ambiguously defines as "[le] mauvais-oeil, des fêticheurs, des marabouts" (7) [the evil eye, fetishers, marabouts (2)]. As abjection consists of an expulsion in response to the fear of absorption, it would seem natural that Anna-Claude's fantasies would be built around a logic of reversals: she courts what is feared, and in place of the menacing threat of spirits (evil eyes, fetishes) finds the image of love. Abjection—a fear that the other will absorb one, a fear of love and nurturing in which the boundaries between self and other fail to hold—a fear of the condition of borderline existence: "Folle, elle l'était vraiment. De cette folie qui questionnait sans jamais répondre, de celle qui créait le temps et l'arrêtait, de celle qui se réclamait de tous les lieux du monde où l'homme abolira les frontières. Les frontières demeuraient, la folie demeurait" (8) [She really was mad. The kind of madness which asked questions without ever replying, which created time and stopped it, claimed kinship with every place in the world where man abolished frontiers. The frontiers remained, her madness continued. (3)]. The frontiers are not completely effaced for her, or else she would be incapable of distinguishing between reality and fantasy. But on the borderline, she can construct the fantasy with enough elaborations to ward off her fears—fears of the "démons qui avaient persécuté son repos" (8) [demons who had hunted down her repose (3; my changes)]—and to fill in the blanks of her history. For in the end, it is not her Jewishness that manifests itself in her speech or acts, but her loneliness and vulnerability as a woman. And her dark continent is Africa, or more specifically, Ousmane.

If Ousmane is the embodiment of Anna-Claude's current fantasy, the object of an extravagant and unfulfilled desire, a figure who is a kind of substitute of the substitute object of desire normally constituted by a male love figure, he is not without precedent. His fantasmic predecessor, imagined by Anna-Claude to have been her husband in a prior life, was a man she had buried alive "pour outrage à la fidelité" (8) [for having desecrated faithfulness (3)]. To complete the fantasy, she provides her former self with twelve children, of whom two had died. The fantasy is marked by a reversal in power and fear: instead of demons pursuing her, and instead of pursuing an imaginary lover herself, she deploys her power over her husband, assuming for herself the role of the fearful mother (twelve children) whose threat consists in devouring, absorbing (burying alive). The outline of the fantasy erases another frontier, that between Anna-Claude and Tanga's mother ("la vieille la mère").

Like Anna-Claude's fantasy-husband, la vieille la mère's husband was "outrageous" in his abuse of fidelity. In fact, his relationship with his wife and his daughter, Tanga, was marked by the grossest kinds of infidelity imaginable. Furthermore, in la vieille la mère's fantasy about her prowess as a mother, she fantasizes that she gave birth to the same number of children as in Anna-Claude's fantasy—twelve. And the proportions of living to dead children are also the same, though reversed: ten to two. The only "explanation" for this resemblance between the story of Tanga's mother—which Anna-Claude has not yet heard—and Anna-Claude's fantasy is that it is a kind of absorption/introjection. Either Anna-Claude heard Tanga's story by this point, and the novel's chronology is unreliable, or Tanga has access to Anna-Claude's fantasy, although the narration does not have Tanga hearing it. It is possible to read Anna-Claude as a projection of Tanga, or vice versa, as the mutual fantasy they come to share is that the frontier between their identities can be erased by virtue of Anna-Claude hearing Tanga's story, or, concomitantly, by virtue of Tanga recounting her story to Anna-Claude.

The analytical situation is one that depends upon transference, or the analysand projecting a key identity onto the analyst, and on the analysand recounting her story to the analyst. The stability of Anna-Claude's identity, of the border between Anna-Claude and la vieille la mère, between the fantasy of Tanga's mother and of Anna-Claude-old-enough-to-be-her-mother, yields to the force of the discourse. Tanga's account becomes the whole story.

And yet it is also an eerie story. It requires the frame for its effect: Tanga's story must be heard as the story Tanga recounts to the infinitely vulnerable and abused, and somewhat absurd, figure of Anna-Claude. And if it both evokes and rejects the qualities of the analyst-analysand relationship, it also does the same with the relationship of uncanniness. Uncanniness is also a relationship of identity and nonidentity. It first makes its way into analytical literature in Freud's account of his encounter with his own image in a mirror, in his train compartment.[10] The "uncanny" sensation springs from the death wish, the sense of the threat of extinction springing from within and projected outward onto another. The other as self, again echoing the stage so close to the mirror stage—let's say its earliest phase—in which the relationship between self and other is uncertain, and where the break (Kristeva's "thetic" break) establishing the certainty of difference between self and other, subject and m(other) has not become a clear one.

Freud's account of this in "The Uncanny" is followed closely by Kristeva and Lacan, and has been the basis for an extensive literature on the double, with Conrad's "The Secret Sharer" having long served as a kind of ur-text.

Freud's own "ur-text" begins with his account of his uncanny reaction to his own mirror reflection in the train, but as was his wont, he traces that back to the earlier stage in which the child, as well as "primitive" humans, could not distinguish between ego and image, between ego and world: "The division between 'interior' and 'exterior' did not exist; the thought was equivalent to the act, the wish to its fulfillment. Everything was in everything, the 'ego' in the 'other' and the 'other' in the 'ego' " (Borch-Jacobsen 44)—a stage that Freud ascribes to "the old animistic conception of the universe" (Freud 1958: 240).

Like Kristeva, whose historicizing of the binary pure-impure depends upon a monological construction/reading of ancient Judaism, Freud seems to rely upon an equally limited, now long since discarded, concept of societies associated with traditional Africa, New Guinea, or with aboriginal peoples, whose mental processes and religious beliefs were taken to be radically other than those of "civilized" Europeans. For Derrida, that dependency on the supplementary societies of "primitive man" is explained by the underlying need of a logocentric economy to rely on the binary logic of the supplement. Lacan finally comes to reject this unfortunate feature of psychoanalytical history.[11]

However, if the mythopoetic reading of "primitive societies" is to be discounted, the same can not be the case with the individual's childhood stages that were the actual sources of Freud's, Kristeva's, and Lacan's analyses. There, the portrayal of the uncanny as the effect of the ego seeing itself *outside* of itself, is presented convincingly. Initially at the stage of primary narcissism, the child "doubles" itself in objects or beings it sees outside of itself, as a protection, according to Freud, against the destruction of the ego, a "preservation against extinction," a means of combatting castration" (Freud 1958: 235). The double, at some point, comes to be perceived as outside, while reflecting the ego at the same time, whence the feeling of the uncanny: "the ego *sees* itself outside itself, in an image all the more estranging because it is narcissistic, all the more alienating because it is perfectly similar. What had been one's own living identity (or identification) becomes, once represented, an expropriated, deadly resemblance—a frozen mirror, a cold statue" (Borch-Jacobsen 45).

Why does the original identity turn threatening? Freud explains: "But when this stage has been surmounted, the 'double' reverses its aspect. From having been an assurance of immortality, it becomes the uncanny harbinger of death" (235). Perhaps it is this shift of the double to weird and threatening that can be seen if we regard as the doubles Toundi (from *Une vie de boy*) and Tanga, rather than Toundi's Cameroonian counterpart, uncannily referred to as "le Français," and Anna-Claude, the neurotic outsider. Toundi and Tanga, the secret sharers, the ones whose accounts are given, also evoke the harbingers of their own deaths, and their fate of dying is given at the *outset* of each of their accounts.

More especially, we can note the indeterminacy in the separation between self and other in the case of Anna-Claude and la vieille la mère,[12] two women with "mirror" histories, two figures the reverse mirror image of each other. Anna-Claude is vulnerable and in need of Tanga, of Tanga's story, in order to be. La vieille la mère takes advantage of Tanga, "swallowing" Tanga's youth, destroying her childhood. The one image nonthreatening, sympathetic; the other antithetically antipathetic. The nourishing mother; the devouring mother. The relationship "unheimlich," uncanny, as in the spookiness of the evil eye, the fearful fetisher, the fearful spells of the marabout. The "true" mother falsely "eats" her daughter—eats her childhood, compels her to become a prostitute in order to procure money from her sexual activity, and when Tanga balks threatens to "eat" her soul. The relationship flips from "nourishing" to "being nourished" to finally "being eaten."

As Tanga tells Anna-Claude, "J'ai nourri son [her mother's] ventre. Mon rôle est terminé" (89) [I filled her (my mother's) belly. My role is finished. (63)]. And inevitably linked to this is Tanga's account of the maternal blackmail, all the more effective for being all the more maternal: "'Qu'est-ce que je vais devenir ma fille, qu'est-ce que je vais devenir?' 'Tant que mon cul marche, pas de problème.' 'Tu ne me laisseras pas seule, hein, ma fille?' 'Non, Mâ.' 'Jure.' 'Je te le jure'" (101) ["What's going to become of me, my girl, what's going to become of me?" "As long as I can move my ass, there's no problem." "You won't leave me to fend for myself, eh, my girl?" "No, Ma." "Swear it." "I swear" (71)]. More dramatically, "moi la femme-fillette soumise aux rites de l'enfant-parent de ses parents puisqu'il convient de commercer la chair pour les nourrir à cause du souffle de vie qu'ils m'ont donné" (30) [I the girlchild-woman, dutiful in the fulfillment of the rites of child-parent to her parents, since it's fitting that I sell my flesh to feed them always because of the breath of life they gave me. (18)]. "Souvent, j'ai pensé à cette rencontre qui m'avait enfantée, cette rencontre qui m'avait détruite en même temps qu'elle m'accouchait. Cette rencontre qui plus tard me dira: puisque tu es là, puisque tu es vivante, assieds-toi sur l'éboulis des siècles, nourris-nous de ton corps" (41) [I have often thought of that encounter which sired me, that meeting that destroyed me and at the same time gave birth to me. That encounter which was to say to me later: since you're here, since you're alive, have a seat on the debris of the ages; feed us with your body. (27)]. And finally, after Tanga's refusal, the curse: " 'Je te maudis,' me dit-elle d'une voix rauque. 'Tu va mourir dans les cacas et la pisse. Je te maudis . . . Et ces paroles que je prononce aujourd'hui se réaliseront, aussi vrai que pendant neuf lunes je t'ai portée dans mon ventre' " (60) ["I curse you," she says to me in a hoarse voice. "You'll die in shit and piss. I curse you . . . And these words I speak today will come true—as true as the fact that I carried you in my belly for nine moons" (40)]. "Sorcière, sale sorcière! Tu veux rentrer dans mon ventre par les pieds. Au secours! Elle veut me tuer. Mon Dieu . . . " (58) [Witch. You dirty witch! You want to get back into my belly feet first! Help! She wants to kill me. My God . . . (39)]. "Fous le camp! Salope! Tu veux ma mort. . . . Mais tu partiras avant moi. Nuit et jour, je vais prier le ciel. Il remplira ton sexe de pierres. Et les paroles que je prononce aujourd'hui se réaliseront, aussi vrai que pendant neuf lunes, je t'ai portée dans mon ventre" (57) [Get the hell out! Bitch! You want me dead. . . . But you'll go before I do. Day and night I'm going to be praying to heaven. It will fill your vagina with stones. And the words I speak today will come true, as true as the fact that I carried you in my belly for nine moons. (38)].

All three, Tanga, Anna-Claude, and la vieille la mère, are women whose lives reveal the fear or experience of abuse from men. Yet the mirror stage for them, with the girl-child's entrance into a subject-position, is built entirely around daughters and mothers. The uncanny fear of recognition of self in the other, along with the abject expulsion of the other in the self, is built around that mirror relation. And since the abject and the uncanny are expressed in a language, in a set of images and terms that are *culturally specific*, the abject of Tanga, her uncanniness, is both feminine and African. Without any strict anthropological identifications intended, we can call it polymorphously Cameroonian, one arising in the 1960s from the urban environment of New Bell, the quartier of Douala most familiar to Beyala.

Haunted by her mother's fate, her voracious exploitation, and her sniveling subordination to her husband, Tanga turns to the imaginary, to her own dreams, her artificially constructed reveries, as well as to a hyperbolically constructed discourse of the imaginary, to escape. But her escape route is also haunted by doubles, by doppelgängers who uncannily reflect her image. For Lacan, *the ego exists outside of ourselves*, outside of the subject, and is only mistakenly taken, in its reflection, for ourselves. In that misapprehension of the self, the ego, the perception of the image of ourselves standing upright before us is fundamental in our passage through the mirror stage. Tanga's story, the story of a moribund seventeen-year-old African girl-woman lying on her prison floor and recounting her story to her semi-deranged cellmate, is above all the story of that passage. We can recognize its elements: the play upon sight, the deployment of one's own word, Tanga's personal story, the absorption/introjection of the other, its mirror reflection/projection of the self, and the perception of one's self as *upright*. Underlying all these elements, finally, the "je," the tremendous importance attached to the sense evoked in the two first person indicators, "je" and "moi" (or "me"—in French the reflexive first person pronoun).

"Au diable Mâ! *Je* deviens une *tour*" (59; my emphasis) [Go to hell, Ma! I am becoming a tower. (40)]. The use of the first person brings us closer to the voice that thus addresses us so intimately. There is no more intimate voice, which is why it is used to give us access to feelings and thoughts; and its "truthfulness" is implied by what Philippe Lejeune calls a "contract" with the reader when the text is packaged as an autobiography. Even when it is not so packaged, it still bears the conventional signs, making it seem natural to evoke Beyala's Cameroonian origins when analyzing Tanga's polymorphously Cameroonian discourse.[13]

At the other end of the spectrum, "je" changes from a subject position into an object, as though one could refer to it as *the je*. When Rimbaud writes, "je est un autre" [I is an other], he moves us in this direction, which we could complete by writing, "je est autre" [I is other]. Tanga's formula is "Je suis autre" (17) [I am other], with the variants "je veux être autre" (20) [I wish to be other)], "je suis ailleurs" (34) [I am elsewhere], and "je veux exister autrement" (42) [I wish to exist in another way], and so on. *I* becomes frozen, becomes erected into a tower, an *I* we can see as though from the outside, in contrast with the *I* that confesses, the *me* in the depths of my soul revealing my soul's innermost hidden secrets. Abjection takes that inward feeling *me*, moves it outward onto that-out-there, and through displacements and projections turns the repressed or feared into that which is most distant, the horrific, threatening, disgusting, monstrous Thing-Out-There, the Thing from Outer Space. Tanga's space moves us continually between the two. Her favorite figure, the oxymoron, reveals the tension of attempting to maintain the two impossibly contradictory positions—a tension often resolved into the splitting into opposites: Tanga, Anna-Claude, both two and less than one at the same time, as Irigaray would have it.

At times the language strains at the margins of logic in evoking the movement of Tanga's thought. In walking away from Hassan, when she first meets him, Tanga narrates, "Je m'approche de lui en m'éloignant" (22) [I come near to him by keeping my distance. (13)], where the play of self and other is marked not only by the courting steps of distance and closeness, but where "lui" could also be read as Tanga's object of desire, or her desire itself. Her desire is as divided as her own perception of her identity, her ego-ideal, is doubled: her mother la vieille la mère, she la femme-fillette, a classic formulation of borderline identity. For the "femme," desire takes the ascendancy, leading her steps closer to Hassan and the sexual encounter he offers. For the fillette, it is more a dream of love, with a house, a field, birds and kids, which take on the clothes of desire. The more radical the split, the more unstable the dash between femme and fillette, the more the one turns her gaze on the other to find abjection. The mirror then does not return the imago of an ego-ideal, but of a broken dream that has built its shards on the discoordinated members of the fillette, long felt to be inadequate in the face of la femme standing before her. An inadequacy extending as far as her ability to speak, to share her thoughts with others: "Comment expliquer aux autres que je me hais? Certains matins . . . je prétexte une migraine. Je m'enferme dans la salle d'eau. J'attrape une miroir. Je regarde" [How do I explain to others that I hate myself? Some mornings . . . I pretend to have a migraine. I lock myself up in the shower room. I catch a glimpse in a mirror. I look]. The act of looking then splits in two, creating the reflexive form: "Je me regarde" [I look at myself (13)], and immediately the blurring of the subject, and its fragmentation: "Je me regarde jusqu'à me brouiller la vue. Le nez plat. La bouche lourde. Les seins maigres. Je m'asperge d'eau, de bassines d'eau pour retrouver les vertus de l'abysse natal. Rien ne change, rien ne doit bouger. Je suis née d'une déchéance" (22) [I look at myself until my vision is blurred. Flat nose. Heavy mouth. Pitiful breasts. I sprinkle myself with water, basins full of water to find again the virtues of the birth canal. Nothing changes, nothing must move. I was born from decay. (13)].

At this point in the novel, when we have barely met Tanga, and as she is recounting her initial meeting with Hassan, it is not too clear what her fall, her "déchéance," signifies. On the one hand, she is the femme-fillette, the child-whore driven into prostitution by her unfeeling mother. She thematizes the trope of lost youth in her narrative, bitterly indicting Africa as a land of poverty and exploitation, corrupt traditionalism, fallen cities and ridiculed peasants. Her fall is that of Africa's children, at least when viewed from an objective distance. Her dream of "real children" establishes the measure of the fall: "Des enfants, des vrais, pas cette enfance d'Iningué où l'enfant n'a pas d'existence, pas d'identité. . . . Des parents à entretenir et des coups pour obéir" [Children, real ones, not this childhood of Iningué where the child does not exist, has no identity. . . . Has parents to provide for and gets beaten so it will obey. (46)]. She goes on to create a pitiful portrait of the son of Tchoumbi, a child whose hands are torn with carrying luggage at the train station or the market: "Il avance lentement, tassé sous un sac de mil ou de maïs, ne répugnant pas à enfoncer ses pieds rongés par la vermine dans les ordures. Il mord sa lèvre inférieure. Ne vous étonnez pas. Ce n'est pas l'enfant qui souffre mais Iningué qui serre ses entrailles pour ne pas laisser échapper sa merde" (67) [He moves ahead slowly, huddled underneath a sack of millet or corn, quite disposed to dig his vermin-eaten feet into the garbage. He bites his lower lip. Don't be surprised. It's not the child suffering, but Iningué tightening its bowels so as not to let the shit escape. (46)]. Beyala continues this theme for the next two pages, concluding with the image of abject children—"tous ces enfants qui naissent adultes et qui ne sauront jamais mesurer la sévérité de leur destin, ces enfants veufs de leur enfance, eux à qui même le temps ne promet plus rien" (69) [all these children who are born adult and will never know how to measure the harshness of their destiny; these children who are widowers of their childhood, to whom even time no longer makes any promises. (47)].

The attempt to evoke these destinies with any sense of objective sociological distance is barely sustained, and never seriously developed at any length, because the limits, the walls of meaning that are erected by the external critic, like those of the self-contained tower, are too fragile to last: "Je deviens une tour. J'ai des frontières délimitées. Désormais, il faut une clef pour me pénétrer" (59) [I am becoming a tower. I have clearly demarcated borders. From now on, you'll need a key to penetrate me. (40)]. No sooner does Tanga emit these words than her mother curses her: "Et ces paroles que je prononce aujourd'hui . . . " and so on (60) [And these words I speak today (40)], bringing the tower down: "J'ai senti la malediction me tirailler les tripes" (6) [I felt the curse fire into my guts (40)].

If Tanga's déchéance as fillette constitutes one of the major tropes of the novel, then that fall is compounded—doubled—by her precocious womanhood. She works with her "cul," sells her sex, submits to her clients, and dreams of being a perfect little housewife. Her desire is lit when Hassan inscribes his extravagant sexual fantasies upon her body, denying the reality of her physical shape and features. Her own fantasy is shaped not only by the image of the happy housewife, but by that of the nurturing mother, again demanding the phallus, the object of desire in the form of the street-child Pieds-gâtés. Most of all, her fall as "femme" is multiplied first by a whole succession of motherly women, inhabitants of her quartier, who did not raise their children as much as groom them to provide income. Tanga's déchéance as femme was always already there, "son destin de femme [qui] surgit du néant allant vers le vide" (36) [her woman's destiny which has emerged from nothingness and is going towards the void (23)].

Although the above designation of the woman's space between nothingness and emptiness is used in reference to her mother, Tanga intends it to apply to all women, and especially to African women. This is why the abject is African: the destiny and the heritage are Tanga's, and though Tanga might have been a child of a fall, a falling away, it was a fall whose genealogy she was able to trace through her matrilineage. Except for a brief bit of incestuous dabbling, and occasional outings to his mistresses' bedrooms, Tanga's father plays almost no role in raising her. Rather, it is la vieille la mère, and her grandmother, who provide Tanga with a past.

Unlike Tanga, la vieille la mère was born "d'un miracle" (37) [miraculously]. Her mother, Tanga's grandmother, Kadjaba Dongo, "était une princesse Essoko" (37) [was an Essoko princess]. The princess's story reads like a folktale: she appears in the narration full-grown, attractive, and surrounded by suitors. Like the headstrong daughter, in the common West African cautionary tale related in *The Palm-Wine Drinkard* (1952), who refuses all the local suitors and runs off with a handsome stranger only to discover he is an evil spirit, the grandmother eventually accepts the one who lights the fires of her desire, and not the suitor chosen for her by her parents, as in the ending of the tale. As in the tale, the choice reveals itself to have been abject—a newly formulated image of the abject for an Africa itself, in the modernists' view, in a state of déchéance: "Elle [la princesse] se dressa pour découvrir le corps qui l'avait possédée, rencontra deux seins, un vagin" (38) [She (the princess) stood up to discover the body that had possessed her—and encountered two breasts, a vagina (24)]. The punishment for the violation of the borders of sexual desire is informed by the imagery of the abject: garbage and excrement. "Boue et immondices s'amoncelaient sur Kadjaba" (38) [Mud and dirt were piled on Kadjaba (25)]. Rather than being a mother, Kadjaba became an object of abjection. She gave up her child—Tanga's mother—and assumed the properties of negativity associated with abjection, that is, with the expulsion of the unwanted, rejected child:

> Cette naissance illégitime . . . l'envahit, la déposséda de tout ce qui n'était pas elle jusqu'à la poser en éternelle négation des autres.

> Elle ne se lava plus, ne porta que des pagnes coupés dans des sacs de farine et des chaussures militaires. Et pour rompre totalement, elle décréta qu'elle était sourde et aveugle. (39) [This illegitimate birth . . . invaded her, stripped her of everything that wasn't herself, to the point where she stood in everlasting negation of others. She no longer washed, wore nothing but wrappers cut from floursacks, and military boots. And in order to break with everyone completely, she declared herself to be deaf and blind. (25; my change)]

Kadjaba's child, la vieille la mère, carried on the heritage of her mother, that of embodying abjection and of seeking to expel what she felt to be the repulsive, the horrific within herself. Like her mother, her feeling of being wrenched off the foundations of her being was centered on her sexuality, which she thought to bring under her control by first stuffing and then emptying her vagina. At the age of thirteen, she found herself a palm tree:

> Elle s'accroupit, écarta ses jambes. Elle enfouit chaque noix dans son sexe. Elle sentait la brûlure, la griffure, elle continuait. Quand elle jugea sa coupe pleine, elle les arracha une à une, elle avait mal, le sang dégoulinait sur ses mains, sur ses doigts, les larmes coulaient, la morve aussi. Elle disait que la douleur était situation pour oublier le plaisir qui s'invente et se construit dans les alcôves. (40) [She crouched down, spread her legs. She pushed every one of the nuts inside her vagina. She felt the burning, the scratching, still she continued. When she decided her cup was full, she ripped them out one by one. She was in pain, blood was dripping down her hands, her fingers. Tears were flowing, her nose was running. She said that pain was the way to forget about the pleasure invented and constructed in bed. (26; my changes)]

What kind of experience is Beyala seeking to convey here in images so powerfully evocative, so glaringly bold for their expression of the landscape of African women? It is not pure abjection in the abstract that Beyala presents in this gruesome scene, but the abjection that gives rise to a daughter of nothingness headed toward emptiness within the walls of an African prison. Its meaning cannot be located in the hermeneutic transcription/translation of ethnographic or psychological fact, but in the excesses, the marginalia of meaning, so well expressed through the abject—the abject, beyond subject and object—beyond woman, beyond African, yet partaking of both. By introjecting the palm nuts, she takes control of the act of filling the vaginal space with African tokens of value. But the perversity of the act, its defiant quality of negation, is stressed in this "unnatural" self-immolation: on the one hand, it mocks the conventional "egg test" of virginity, and on the other hand functions as an act of self-deflowering.

It is in *C'est le soleil qui m'a brûlé* that Beyala narrates the egg test where the young Ateba is examined to determine whether she is still a virgin by an old woman who places an egg in her vagina. The repugnance of the old woman, and the humiliation of the test, are here reversed by Tanga's mother, who twice rejects patriarchal control over her genitals by assuming control over her own virginity and her own bodily spaces. But the price of that control is abjection, as though the anger expelled in the act could not be separated from its physical incarnations in both the human and the natural landscapes.

Tanga's birth, following rather rapidly after her mother's preternatural attempts to forestall male hegemonic control over her own sexual desires, and thus over the processes of insemination and birth, marks the failures of both her grandmother and mother to free themselves of that control. Tanga's subsequent affair with Hassan, her mothering of Pieds-gâtés, her stuffing of her own vagina with dirt, and by logical and symbolic extension, the abuse suffered by Anna-Claude and Camilla, attest to the continuation and universality of the trope of the abused woman, of the failures of women under all conditions and in all societies to acquire an independent and fully assumed agency. Yet this trope is not represented in simple miserabilist terms, as we have seen so often in the writings of African women, including especially many writings of those of the first generation, Emecheta, Nwapa, Bugul, Bâ.[14]

What marks Beyala's enormous distance from the authors of *The Joys of Motherhood* (1979) or *Le Chant écarlate* (1981) is the extravagance of her imaginary, her almost inevitable extension of the visual into the realm of "l'écriture féminine," where the wrenching of the real results not in a call to arms, the automatic lynchpin mechanism of the earlier versions of African feminist literature of protest, but in a far greater calling into question of the entire patriarchal structure, that is, of the symbolic order on which the patriarchal structures of thought and order rest. Beyala's evocation of the abject, then, is not an aberrant idiosyncrasy, but a more effective, wholesale challenge to the existing order, its norms, its naturalized values, its phallocentrism, than that of her predecessors who stressed the genuine, testimonial nature of their accounts.

Her generation, among whom could also be listed a Ben Okri and a Sony Labou Tansi, represents a second wave of feminist writing, consonant with the age of a new, harsh urban landscape. In the case of Cameroon, it was forged under the perennial rule of "Papa" Ahidjo, followed by his disciple Paul Biya, whose modes of governance have been overwhelmingly distant, implacable, and unresponsive to the needs of the governed, the people of Cameroon, with their *villes mortes*, and their increasing despair and repression.

Under such circumstances, the imaginary of the abject, seen here in the actions of mother and then daughter stopping up their vaginas, appears to resonate more with a fearful unreality than with the actuality of daily, brutal oppression as would be caught in the lens of mimetic fiction; only such an imaginary of the abject would be up to the task of taking on the powers of the order of horror. The literature of the African abject is not an import from an external theorist, nor is it an exotic item for export: it is the product of the QG, the quartier général, the generalized condition of contemporary life for most urban Africans.

The abject serves the African literature of our times because, as Mudimbe put it in *The Invention of Africa* (1988), the urban culture and landscape of contemporary Africa lie in between two worlds,[15] and thus correspond to the experience of the borderline patients who provided Kristeva with her models of the abject. Of course the borderline is not the only response to the meeting of two worlds: the creolization of Caribbean literature, the hybridity with which Bhabha associates the postcolonial, are not all marked by the negative signs of the abject. And it is not simply a function of the experience of the African woman living in today's urban conglomerates that explains the appearance of the abject in contemporary literature, as can be seen in the counter-examples of Aidoo (cf. *Changes* [1991]) or Sow Fall (cf. *Le Jujubier du patriarche* [1993]). Rather it seems to be the particular response of a younger generation, whose imaginary is much more permeable, their works informed with the wider and wilder semes of a hip-hop, westernized/international cultural setting, as can be seen in the early works of Beyala, Ben Okri, Véronique Tadjo, or Jean-Pierre Bekolo.

The abject is our point of entry into their works not only because of its excessiveness, its extremity, its violence; not only because it is a literature of the borderline, and by multiple extensions, of the unholy, the impure; but more fundamentally because of the instability of the subject position, especially in African feminist expression. Abjection centers around the fearful dimensions of the processes of introjection and projection. If Kristeva concerns herself with the introjection of the

Other, for the African abject the fearfulness of introjection, the acquisition and naturalization of the privileged norms of western culture, has been overlaid with competing, conflicting interests and with violent images of authority—metropolitan, national, and patriarchal all imposing their values.

La vieille la mère and Tanga inseminate themselves with palm nuts and African soil, elements of an ambiguous symbology. While both women act so as to assert an independent agency, neither succeeds either in achieving a fruitful result or in sustaining her independence. Their acts appear to be grounded in an imaginary that can be read either poetically as expressive of the extremity of their borderline psychotic state, or psychoanalytically as expressive of their sense of affinity with abjection.

What is there in the abject that serves their purposes so well, along with those of this literature and cinema? To begin, the fluidity of Beyala's expression, her almost immediate passage from a concrete scene into a poeticized or imaginary reverie in relation to the scene, marks the instability of the borders of the objects she employs in her discourse. The image of la vieille la mère filling her vagina with palm nuts is not surrounded with any of the precision of a ritual act with which we could associate a definite and authorized meaning. When Tanga concludes her description of the gruesome removal of the nuts, there is another shift onto a plane of reflection where once again the suggestive rather than the literal prevails. "Elle disait que la douleur était situation pour oublier le plaisir qui s'invente et se construit dans les alcôves" (40) [She said that pain was the way to forget about the pleasure invented and constructed in bed. (26; my changes)]. The use of "situation" instead of "condition" to describe "douleur" marks the first movement toward the vague and imprecise; the expression "dans les alcôves" marks a second, slightly jarring note since the figure of speech is based on an architectural model that harmonizes more with an urban house of ample dimensions than a village domicile. The attempt to escape love's pleasures by seeking a pain of her own making is all the more strange as she takes this action against her body precisely "pour qu'enfin les peines, les erreurs, les échecs n'encombrent pas son chemin" (40) [so that troubles, mistakes, failures wouldn't encumber her path in the end (26)], in the words that appear immediately before she stuffs her vagina.[16] Finally, immediately after this episode, Tanga recounts, "est venu mon père" (41) [my father came], an arrival that will result not only in the eventual birth of Tanga, but also in the completion of "les erreurs, les échecs" [the mistakes, the failures] that encumber la vieille la mère's path. The filiation that ties the two events is brutal in its immediacy: "Elle accoucha de moi. Mon père la trompa" (41) [She gave birth to me. My father cheated on her. (27)].

If this is irony, it is also a refusal to present the account with the logical clarity and rationality of a Cartesian ego. The ego against which the objects of the discourse are arrayed is besieged and defensive: "The abject has only one quality of the object—that of being opposed to *I*" (Kristeva 1). We can follow the direction of la vieille la mère's, Tanga's, Anna-Claude's, and Camilla's accounts, leading ineluctably toward the miserable death in the cell, along with the obscenity of the prison guards, the callousness of Hassan, of le vieux le père, and Monsieur John, pausing briefly at the occasional telegraphing of messages directly intended for the reader's edification, before we are caught up again in the extravagance of the narrative discourse. "If the object, however, through its opposition, settles me within the fragile texture of a desire for meaning, which, as a matter of fact, makes me ceaselessly and infinitely homologous to it, what is *abject*, on the contrary, the jettisoned object, is radically excluded and drawn toward the place where meaning collapses" (Kristeva 2).

What is drawn toward the place where meaning collapses is what there is in us that seeks the security of answers—answers that can only function as deferred positions of inquiry. Tanga's answer is to place the question of origins within a context in which the child is always already sold out in advance; where the child, the substitute for the painful palm nuts, the red earth, the "membre dressé tel un harpon" (38) [organ standing up straight as a spear (24; my change)] that Kadjaba mocks as an instrument of theft—"Mais, il va me voler ma fertilité" (38) [But that one is going to rob me of my fertility (24)]—is itself stolen, leaving a premature parent in its place:

> Souvent, j'ai pensé à cette rencontre [between Tanga's mother and father] qui m'avait enfantée, cette rencontre qui m'avait détruite en même temps qu'elle m'accouchait. Cette rencontre qui plus tard me dira: puisque tu es là, puisque tu es vivante, assieds-toi sur l'éboulis des siècles, nourris-nous de ton corps. Nous ne savons plus, tu sauras pour nous. (41) [I have often thought of that encounter which sired me, that meeting that destroyed me and at the same time gave birth to me. That encounter which was to say to me later: since you're here, since you're alive, have a seat on the debris of the ages; feed us with your body. We no longer know, you'll know for us. (27)]

"Détruite" at the moment of her conception, at the moment prior to her conception when just the possibility of her existence began to emerge, Tanga sees herself doomed by the piled up discharges of eternity, bearing the weight of a landslide on which she is seated: "assieds-toi sur l'éblouis des siècles, nourris-nous de ton corps" (41) [have a seat on the debris of the ages; feed us with your body. (27)]. Abjection seeks her out in the voice of the "rencontre" that created her; it speaks, incarnate, without a subject, and she, the "nourrisson," must become the "nourrice" of that which engendered her: "nourris-nous." The inversions of incest become the perversion of maternity; in place of an "I" with a voice, there is a body, a breast, a vagina to be filled, mouths to be filled, and the piled up weight of centuries bearing down on her. For Beyala, this "rencontre" has the attributes of the "African" heritage: the village past, the patriarchal present. For Kristeva, this encounter between the abject and its victim springs from the psychological burden implicit in each individual's early childhood—and is manifest in borderline subjects, pre-psychotic individuals, and poets. It brings "déchéance," "peines, erreurs, échecs," "douleur"— a history, an "éboulis" whose burden destroys (détruit) as it gives birth to (accouche) Tanga. "[I]t is a brutish suffering that 'I' puts up with, sublime and devastated, for 'I' deposits it to the father's account [verse au père—père-version]: I endure it, for I imagine that such is the desire of the other" (Kristeva 2).

"*Nourris-nous de ton corps.*" [Nourish us with your body]; "*tu sauras pour nous*" [you will know for us].

A massive and sudden emergence of uncanniness, which, familiar as it might have been in an opaque and forgotten life, now harries me as radically separate, loathsome. (Kristeva 2).

"*Je veux exister autrement.*" (Beyala 42) [I want to exist differently. (28)]

Not me. Not that. (Kristeva 2)

"*Je suis autre.*" (Beyala 17) [I am other.]

But not nothing either. A "something" that I do not recognize as a thing. A weight of meaninglessness, about which there is nothing insignificant, and which crushes me. (Kristeva 2)

"*L'éboulis des siècles.*" (Beyala 41) [The debris of the ages.]

On the edge of non-existence and hallucination, of a reality that, if I acknowledge it, annihilates me. There, abject and abjection are my safeguards. The primers of my culture. (Kristeva 2)

"*Tu t'appelleras Tanga.*" (Beyala 14) [Your name shall be Tanga.]

There we come to it. The primer to the culture where the threat of disintegration, of "non-existence and hallucination" can only be contained within the strong, iron bars of the cell, where abjection can be embraced so that if it annihilates, it will also give birth.

Tanga's birth, the birth of her "I," is marked by the violence of hallucination in which her projected, abjected fears return as phantoms that consume her. Appearing in multitudinous forms, until her death is finally achieved, they make their appearance in her infancy, shortly after her father began to wallow in the mire of his sexual infidelities. The forms of abjection Tanga experiences multiply and transmogrify:

> Certaines nuits où le sommeil râleur tient distance, je vois resurgir les fantômes qui m'entraînent dans leur paralysis. Je me débats. Je hurle. Ils me suivent, me persécutent, me heurtent. J'appelle mon père, j'appelle ma mère. Ils ne m'entendent pas. Je crie plus fort. Des monstres s'agglutinent autour de moi. Deux vautours à la place des yeux. Des cornes à la place des ongles. Ils me pénètrent, ils me lacèrent. Je vois mes tripes dans leurs mains. Ils rient des trous béants de leurs dents absentes. Ils attachent mes boyaux sur des amulettes et les suspendent au cou de mes parents. Je ferme les yeux, je veux qu'ils me laissent tranquille. . . . Je veux exister autrement. Je veux partir par les rues, me poster dans un coin, éventrer un homme. (42–43) [Some nights, when reluctant sleep keeps its distance, I see the phantoms emerge, dragging me into their paralysis. I fight back. I shout. They follow me, persecute me, collide with me. I call my father, I call my mother. They don't hear me. I scream louder. Monsters congregate around me. Two vultures where the eyes should be. Horns where the nails should be. They penetrate me, they lacerate me. I see my entrails in their hands. They laugh through the gaping holes of their missing teeth. They string my intestines on to amulets and hang them around the neck of my parents. I close my eyes; I want them to leave me alone. . . . I want to exist differently. I want to go through the streets, take up my position in a corner and disembowel a man. (27–28)]

The themes of Tanga's dream can be read repeatedly in the various forms of abjection recorded by Kristeva. For instance, when she talks about the abjection associated with food, or its connotations of uncleanliness or impropriety, she focuses on the "I" who not only refuses the abject object, the repellent food, but who refuses the desire of the "other," and thus is expelled by the very act of refusal: "But since the food is not an 'other' for 'me,' who am only in their desire, I expel *myself*, I spit *myself* out, I abject *myself* within the same motion through which 'I' claim to establish *myself*. . . ; it is thus that *they* see that 'I' am in the process of becoming an other at the expense of my own death. During that course in which 'I' become, I give birth to myself amid the violence of sobs, of vomit" (3).

Kristeva moves on to the most extreme form of abjection, that associated with death, the corpse—a form of waste that is echoed in the image of Tanga's innards reattached to her parents' neck, or to the bloodied nuts her mother extracts from her vagina. The imagery of the abject is drawn from blood, vomit, saliva, the slimy substances we produce at the margins of our bodies, because it is there, at the border between self and non-self, that the threat to the subject, the struggle to establish difference, the struggle not to be submerged, is experienced. "These body fluids, this defilement, this shit are what life withstands, hardly and with difficulty, on the part of death. There, I am at the border of my condition as a human being" (3). The struggle of life and death, death and birth, of the subject in the face of the monstrous with their toothless mouths that swallow "I" up, reconvert the inside "tripes" to outside amulets, ultimately is the struggle with the border itself. "Tu t'appelleras Tanga" [Your name shall be Tanga]—the inside turned out, white turned black—the other side of the bars occupied by repellent brutes, the other side of the mirror, the other side that makes this side possible, where I can huddle down as far from their shit and its odor as I can get. Tanga and Anna-Claude, safe on this side only as long as the bars can keep *them* out, as long as death stays in its place. "If dung signifies the other side of the border, the place where I am not and which permits me to be, the corpse, the most sickening of wastes, is a border that has encroached on everything. It is no longer 'I' who expel, 'I' is expelled" (4). Anna-Claude certainly goes crazy, is engulfed by Tanga's death as by the invading border that refuses to keep its distance. "In that compelling, raw, insolent thing in the morgue's full sunlight, in that thing that no longer matches and therefore no longer signifies anything, I behold the breaking down of a world that has erased its borders: fainting away" (4).

In his punishment of Anna-Claude, the prison guard deposits his "cigar," his excrement, in the cell containing the two women. They move away from it, seeking solace in each other. Tanga's death completes the erasure of the externalized border. "The corpse, seen without God and outside of science, is the utmost of abjection. It is death infecting life. Abject. It is something rejected from which one does not part, from which one does not protect oneself as from an object" (4).

> "Tu t'appelleras Tanga." (Beyala 14) [Your name shall be Tanga.]
> "Votre fille, c'est moi." (Beyala 189) [I am your daughter. (137)]

> Imaginary uncanniness and real threat, it beckons to us and ends up engulfing us. (Kristeva 4).

Kristeva concluded this threnody, unlike Beyala, not with the horrors of such an ineluctable fate inhabiting us all, destroying our last vestiges of difference, of sanity, but with the totalizing thought that the abject, which we all have dreamed, and which informed out histories in the unimaginable repeated acts of degradation and death in the slave trade, the Middle Passage, the Holocaust, can be reconciled with the familiar and even desirable modernist gestures of rebellion: the disruption/alienation of order: "It is thus not lack of cleanliness or health that causes abjection *but what disturbs identity, system, order*" (Kristeva 4; my emphasis).

If the slave trade had not been systematic and ordered, it could not have lasted four centuries nor entailed the deportation of 12–15 million Africans. If the gas chambers had not been administered with admirable order, they could not have killed 6 million in such short order. Is it a simple irony that the order Beyala would seek to disrupt is challenged by an imaginary that must draw upon the same devices of order that employ instruments of rape, torture, and death for its representations of the abject? "Devant l'horreur certaines gorges s'apprêtaient à vomir leur dégoût, mais le silence des canons s'engouffra en eux" (136) [Faced with the horror, some were getting ready to vomit their disgust, but the silence of the guns disappeared inside them. (98)]. In the final analysis, it is in language itself, in the discourse that slips away from the logic of syntax, that slides along the signifying chain, that the signs of abjection appear and do their work of abjection.

The passage from disruption of order in general to the specific form of the abject can be traced in the relationship between subject and object. When the demarcation between subject and object is clear, when the subject is fully constituted, and is able to assume the speaking position utilizing a first person locator, then the linkage between signifier and signified appears natural. But when the line between "I" and "it" is obscured, distracted, permeable—pervious—the convulsions of threat and desire shift ob-ject to ab-ject. The consequent permutations all seem to appear in *Tu t'appelleras Tanga*. When, as a child, Anna-Claude is tormented by other children, she takes refuge in reverie, just like Tanga, and the resultant fluidity of objects, now subject to projections without the walls of the real to defend them, leads to a hallucinatory experience, one where the desired and the feared or repulsive change place. Thus, the yellow star Anna-Claude and her family had to wear is changed, for her, into "l'étoile du coeur" (141) [the star of the heart].

Similarly, and more dramatically, Tanga's father—le vieux mon père—cathects desire onto the abject by finding sexual attraction in the elements of repulsion associated with the bodily orifices and their discharges:

> Il aimait cette odeur de poisson pourri, ces mamelles dégoulinantes, ces ventres qui épousaient des désirs sans prendre, ces ventres flaques d'eaux mortes. Il les aimait pour ce qu'elles renfermaient d'écoeurant, ces lieux publics, dépotoirs où se déversaient les déjections humaines. Il s'y vautrait et attendait, la langue pendante, haletant, il attendait le revomissement des ordures. (42) [He loved that smell of rotten fish, those oozing breasts, those bellies that were wedded to desires without taking anything, those sloppy wombs whose waters had died. He loved them for the sickening things they contained, those public places, the dumping ground into which human excrement was emptied. He wallowed in them and waited with his tongue hanging out, panting. He waited until the smut was spewed back out. (27)]

The borderline patient, for Kristeva, is defined within the oedipus: the incestuous desire for the mother, or of the mother, or a brutal separation from her, without the "paternal function" to establish the clarity of subject separate from object, the "unitary bent" between sign and signified, all create the conditions of possibility for abjection. Barely emerging from the confines of narcissism, still seeking to protect himself behind the walls that are "pervious," barely pervious, the borderline subject-position, neither subject nor object, allows its fluidity to infect the external world, the internal being, the inner workings of all existence: "[T]here was not yet an/other, an ob-ject: merely an ab-ject. What is to be done with this ab-ject? Allow it to drift towards the libido so as to constitute an object of desire? Or towards symbolicity, to change it into a sign of love, hatred, enthusiasm, or damnation?" (48–49).

It is in that indeterminate state that the choices in *Tu t'appelleras Tanga* are made. Tanga's father chooses to invest objects with desire as they constitute the elements of the body's inside that "show up in order to compensate for the collapse of the border between inside and outside. . . . Urine, blood, sperm, excrement then show up in order to reassure a subject that is lacking its 'own and clean self.' The abjection of those flows from within suddenly become the sole 'object' of sexual desire—a true 'abject' " (53). Tanga's father plays too small a role in *Tu t'appelleras Tanga* to provide us with any insight into the centrality of abjection for the women in the novel. However, his reduced role is matched by the impotence of his rhetoric, in which he attempts to assert a "traditional" paternal function, all the while abandoning his family, forcing them to make do on their own both emotionally and financially. Not unlike Toundi's father in *Une vie de boy* or Khar Madiagua Diob's father in *Vehi Ciosane* (1965), he represents the impuissant "African" fathers in much African literature, those whose displacement from positions of traditional authority is marked by their replacement by "pères blancs" of various kinds—there being both White Fathers as priests in *Une vie de boy* and *Le Vieux Nègre et la médaille* (1956), in the novels of Mongo Beti, as well as commandants, police chiefs, district officers, and so on.

With the end of colonial days, the powerless father remains, his current boss still an equally distant figure, but this time African, and no more marked by signs of fraternity or consanguinity than his white predecessors. And in all cases, whether colonial or postcolonial, it is the mother who fills in the gap created by the failure of the "paternal function," the absence of an effective Name of the Father to bring fear of castration. This is the situation that provides the opportunity for the eroticization of the abject, the situation Kristeva describes as resulting from the subject's compensation for the "collapse of the border between inside and outside": "a true 'abject' where man, frightened, crosses over the horrors of maternal bowels and, in an immersion that enables him to avoid coming face to face with an other, spares himself the risk of castration" (53). The fearful other within the maternal body becomes oneself, or at least a being possessed by oneself. "Abjection then takes the place of the other," and the abject is transformed into "the site of the Other" (54). This might explain the convergence of such elements as rape, excrement, verbal and physical abuse, lack of human feeling, and ugliness in the actions and language of the prison guards—the abject in the site of the Other. And it explains le vieux le père's "père-verse" attraction for the abject in women and bodily discharges—in the place of the "other." "Such a frontiersman is a metaphysician who carries the impossible to the point of scatology" (54).

Tanga's reactions are somewhat different. No less doubled/split in her identity than her parents, she, "la femme-fillette," is hedged by her "devouring mother" on one side, and on the other by the crude dismissals of her emotional needs and intellectual qualities by the men who see her only as a "pute," a youthful body useful only for sexual enjoyment. Tanga's dream of a middle-class life with Hassan shattered, she discharges her affections on the most disaffected—Mala, or Pieds-gâtés (Foot-wreck—literally, spoiled-feet), and Cul-de-jatte (Lame-leg—literally, Legless), the unnamed, legless chief of the street children. Both figures bear the attributes of abjection, with a range of repellent physical traits, and both awaken a maternal function in Tanga. As such, her eroticization of abjection enables her to provide for males whose coarse abuse of others translates into a simulacrum of authority. "When a woman ventures out in those regions it is usually to gratify, in very maternal fashion, the desire for the object that insures the life (that is, the sexual life) of the man whose symbolic authority she accepts" (54). If it can be noted that Tanga is not preoccupied with the abject in Mala or Cul-de-jatte, and that the qualities of abjection are here downplayed, this too conforms with Kristeva's analysis in which she posits the primacy of the relation with the mother over that with the male figure of abjection. "Very logically, this is an abjection from which she is frequently absent; she does not think about it, preoccupied as she is with settling accounts (obviously anal) with her own mother" (54).

Tanga's "settling of accounts" with her mother makes up a major theme in the novel, and indeed in Beyala's first three novels. In all three novels, though especially in *Tu t'appelleras Tanga*, the young female protagonist establishes emotional ties that disrupt, "disturb identity, system, order." That is the hallmark of Beyala's early work; it is what sets her apart from much of what had constituted African women's writing before her. Often it has been the unsaid, the silenced, or the revelation of abuse within the confines of what has been permitted for "female discourse" that has resulted in a literature of protest, and not a literature of the abject. Beyala's writing has opened the way to challenging the foundations of African patriarchy because she has been willing, unlike any other, to write out of the experience of abjection.[17] As such, she has broken new ground by redefining the possibilities for "l'écriture féminine africaine." Kristeva has noted this rare function, though she does not put her observation in terms of African women, for whom her restriction is all the stronger: "Rarely does a woman tie her desire and sexual life to that abjection, which, coming to her from the other, anchors her interiorly in the Other. When that happens, one notes that it is through the expedient of writing that she gets there." (54).

Tanga "gets there" repeatedly through a "[h]arebrained staging of an abortion, of a self-giving birth ever miscarried, endlessly to be renewed (54). One thinks of Tanga's adoption of Mala as a harebrained staging of both a birth and an abortion. But all of Tanga's acts of revolt, Hassan, Mala, Cul-de-jatte, are preliminary to the most harebrained staging of a self-giving birth—and that is her birth of herself through Anna-Claude. It is that birth that she ultimately succeeds in staging through recounting her story to Anna-Claude. The "expediency of writing," that is, of inscribing her life, and thus her identity, onto the other reinforces her anchoring in the Other, the substitute Other that the white in Africa has become.

Tanga's story, first and foremost, can be read as the story of her struggle to die and be born in and through her mother. That struggle returns in angry counterpoint to each "adventure" Tanga has, each attachment that takes her away from being the "femme-fillette" who must nourish her mother by ignoring her own desires. When Hassan presents himself, Tanga's rebellious "je ne suis pas une pute" is directed as much against her mother as it is toward Hassan. Tanga's struggle to name herself is against her mother's power to name her, to call her Tanga; Tanga's struggle to stand erect, the automatic position she seeks to assume when assuming her own subject position, is undermined by her mother's curses that level, flatten her, that place her under Monsieur John and all the other clients and lovers who situate her according to their own desires. Tanga's struggle with abjection is the struggle with her mother, for "[h]ow, if not by incorporating a devouring mother, for want of having been able to introject her and joy in what manifests her, for want of being able to signify her" (54), can Tanga become "femme" purely, "femme" anchored in an authorizing position she can make her own? Tanga's struggle goes beyond castration, the loss of a part, the mechanism that drives identification in the Other and the splitting from the mother: it is a total struggle: "It is not part of [her]self, vital though it may be, that [s]he is threatened with losing, but [her] whole life" (55; my intercalations). Tanga's struggle is the struggle of the borderlander: the struggle that encompasses the whole self.

But it is not completed through the story that is told on the level of the diegesis alone—because the African abject extends beyond the landscape of African city and village, which encompass the staging of the diegesis. Tanga's story is framed by the outer story of Anna-Claude and her prison experience with Tanga, and it contains the kernel, hypodiegetic story of

Camilla. The two white women extend the range of the abject onto another level where Tanga's own story can find completion. In a sense, it is this level of writing, of inscription, that sees the birth of Tanga's voice, story, and position as a subject. It is also at this level that her failed relationship with her own sister—who supplants her role as the "femme-fillette" who nourishes the mother—can be replaced by sisterhood, a sisterhood with the substitute figures of Camilla and Anna-Claude.

Tanga first presents Camilla by breaking out of the conventions that enclose the diegesis and addressing Anna-Claude directly, thus uniting extradiegetic and hypodiegetic narrative levels along with the two white women whose stories are central to those levels: "Et puis il y a la Camilla, *ta* soeur d'ici" (109; my emphasis) [And then there is Camilla, your sister, here (78)]. But Camilla is soon reintegrated into Tanga's story, providing all the openings for identification all the while establishing her difference: "Blanche perdue au milieu des désirs africains. Je ne peux pas ne pas te la raconter. Son nez est droit. Sa bouche si fine. Ses grandes jambes qui vont de table en table" (109) [A white woman lost in the middle of African desires. I can't not tell you about her. Her very straight nose. Her long legs that take her from table to table. (78)]. Most of all she is "femme," the ideal of maturity and especially independence, the two points of difference that mark her off from Tanga even more than the shape of her features or the color of her skin, because it is there that her problems of subject-autonomy are located.

Tanga's first, and last, responses to Camilla are in the form of denial. Her "I" sees in Camilla's otherness the same threat as that in her mother, in the abject—and thus, "Je ne veux pas reconnaître la Camilla. Je baisse les yeux. Je remue la tête. *Je* forme la négation" (111; my emphasis) [I don't want to recognize Camilla. I lower my eyes. I shake my head. I take on the form of denial.]. In response to Camilla's question whether Tanga belongs to the sisterhood of prostitutes—"le métier"—Tanga lies and says no—"Je ne suis pas une pute" (112) [I am not a whore]. Wanting to reach out to Camilla, but incapable of placing herself in front of what she feels she has to reject, she confabulates, readjusting the borders of the imaginary: "Je réajuste les bords. Je la persécute jusqu'aux W.C." (113) [I'm tidying up the edges. I pursue her straight into the toilet. (81)]. Tanga recounts, then, to Camilla as she would later do to Anna-Claude, and creates a life in the midst of the very elements evoked by her mother's curse, piss, and shit: "Un homme pisse en sifflant. . . . Et moi, je tirote les mots pour finir mon histoire" (113) [A man pisses as he whistles. . . . And me, I draw out my words in order to finish my story. (81)]. Pulled between the fabrications of her dream-account and the abjected elements with which she is surrounded, Tanga finds her "I" wavering, dissipating: "Les odeurs d'urine et de moisi s'infiltrent en moi. Ils me donnent la fièvre. *Je* n'ai pas de place. *Je* ne tiens pas en place" (113; my emphasis) [The smells of urine and mildew filter into me. They give me a fever. I have no space. I don't stay put. (81)].

But the account brings the two women together, despite the imagined dream, despite the men's urinals, and they reach out through their gaze to each other: "Nos regards, concentrés sur nos nombrils, s'embrassent sans se voir" (113) [Focusing on our navels, our eyes kiss without seeing each other. (81)]. They exchange positions, and Tanga, "la femme-fillette," becomes the interlocutor, the one whose assumption of the position of listener enables Camilla to recount her own litany of betrayal and despair. In approximate terms, they duplicate the relationship of analyst-analysand—at least as long as they are ensconced within the space of the W.C. that makes visible the abject.

Once out of the bathroom, back in the crowded space of the nightclub filled with men focused on sex, Tanga hesitates, wavers in the erect position she had assumed after hearing Camilla's story, and addresses frontally her own dreams of escape, now in the form of erecting her own "I": "Je veux m'ancrer au milieu de mes songes, m'élever au-dessus du destin. . . . Inventer" (122) [I want to anchor myself amidst my dreams, to raise myself above destiny. . . . To invent (87)]. Again the "femme-abject," she turns to the creation of her own text as the solution to her condition. And as she evokes this unique position of the abject-woman as writer, she does so again in terms that have a particular resonance in Africa, and especially in Cameroon/Nigeria/Benin, where the dead child is often seen to return in the newly born live one: "Mais n'est-ce pas le propre de l'enfant mort-né que de se raconter des histoires tout en fornicant?" (122) [But is that not the characteristic of the stillborn child, to be telling itself stories while fornicating? (87)]. Although Beyala shapes her question in the mud of the abject, and projects onto the adults the blame for the failures in Tanga's life, she frames Tanga's identity in terms of a marginality that we can only designate as that of the *abiku*—the "mort-né," resonant of an African imaginary that extends far beyond Kristeva's "harebrained staging of an abortion."

Tanga denies Camilla when she reemerges from the W.C., despite what their eyes convey to each other as their gazes cross. In answer to Hassan's question of whether she knows Camilla, she responds in the negative. She leaves with Hassan, embroiled in her lie. But though the dark side of rejection invades her, though hatred penetrates her, dispossessing her, she is able to position her self, her "I," in front of her hatred, examine it from the outside, prepare herself for the act of recounting and hearing her own story—passing from victim to a new embodiment of the mechanisms of death: she, the abiku child, becomes the poison that destroys the life of the child: "Je deviens le scorpion dément allié des ténèbres" [I am becoming the demented scorpion related to the darkness (89)], and as such can lay claim to the past lives—to the past: "Toujours la quête du mal. Elle me donne la mémoire" (125) [Always the quest of evil. She gives me my memory (89)].

Abiku-analyst—the position that Tanga can achieve is reached only through the telling of and listening to stories: to hers, to Mala's, to Cul-de-jatte's: she assumes the position not of The Subject Presumed to Know, but The Subject Who Listens. And it is in her abjection of her own self, one that she now recognizes, that she is enabled to take on this position. In her last adventure, in the lower level of the QG, she finds herself nameless—"J'ai perdu mon nom" (153) [I lost my name]—and surrounded by all the attributes of abjection: the kingdom of the legless man, the hideaway for homeless street children. It fills her with fear, as it is filled with repellent features: "Une odeur écrasante de poussière m'environne" (152) [An oppressive odor of dust surrounds me (109)]; "ombres déchues" (154) [fallen shadows]. Isolated, in the kingdom of the abject, she is like Alice in the woods with the deer—at the limit of identity, system, order: "the home of everything that does not respect borders, positions, rules. The in-between, the ambiguous, the composite. The traitor, the liar, the criminal with a good conscience" (Kristeva 4). Now the captive mistress of Cul-de-jatte, Tanga pushes the abject to its limits. We would expect this descent to the bottom to be the final preparation for her transubstantiation into the body of Anna-Claude.

At first Tanga mistakes Cul-de-jatte for an exploiter of children—a patriarchal Godfather of the underground: "Vous légiférez, vous détruisez. . . . T'es qu'un exploiteur" (156) [You legislate; you destroy. . . . You're nothing but a destroyer. (113)]. But Cul-de-jatte is not what he appears to be. He asks her to look: "Tu as perdu d'art de voir. Rien n'est plus rien. Il ne reste plus qu'à poser les yeux à l'horizon et attendre" (157) [You've lost the art of seeing. Nothing is anything any more. All that's left for you to do is fix your eyes on the horizon and wait. (113)]. Tanga looks, as if in a mirror, as if to recover that image of herself caught in the abject: "[N]ous restons l'un en face de l'autre, incapable de geste, semblables à ces ombres que sculpte le ventre de la lune, face à nous-mêmes, à nos statues rivées dans les contours angoissants du devenir" (157) [For a long while we remain facing each other, incapable of moving, resembling shadows sculpted by the moon's belly; face to face with ourselves, as if we were statues tethered to the agonising contours of the future. (113)]. Cul-de-jatte speaks. Recounts. Confesses his hopes and his despair. She listens, encourages, *maternal*, "mue par un désir de protection" (157) [moved by a desire to protect him (114)].

For Lacan, the symbolic emerges from the visual encounter effected in the mirror stage, and brought to its essential moment by the sight of the castrated figure of the mother, with the legislative intervention of the father. The image of the self is the ground for the ego. But the logic of the visual requires a phallocentric understanding of the symbolic, an understanding that requires the erect stance of the ego to be grounded in seeing as knowing. Tanga as listener brings us closer to the work of Irigaray, for whom the woman's access to the world is not limited to sight: "Vous existez puisque vous sentez" (157) [Since you have feelings you exist (114)]. Cul-de-jatte dismisses Tanga: "Tu ne sais pas ce que tu dis. . . . Parole de femme" (157) [You don't know what you're saying. . . . Woman's words. (114)]. But what Tanga-the-listener can now understand is informed by her experience of abjection—of the world in which they are completely caught and that she confronts. It is she who is able to render the evidence of that abjection into words: "N'empêche qu'entre ce qui est et ce qui n'est pas, il y a des plages de vide et de gouffre où peut habiter l'illusion de vivre" (158) [That doesn't mean that between what is and what is not there are no areas of void and abyss where the illusion of life can reside. (114)].

Although Cul-de-jatte tells Tanga that she doesn't understand anything, he still speaks. And as she encourages him—"Parle-moi de tes aventures" (158) [Tell me about your adventures. (114)]—he too begins to articulate the face of the abject—the allegory of the African abject as the underlying trope of Tanga's own narrative: "Dans ce pays n'importe quoi peut être n'importe quoi d'autre" (158) [In this country, anything at all can be just about anything else. (114)]. Cul-de-jatte's words, like Camilla's before, and Anna-Claude's before that, lead Tanga into the dyad begun with the mirror relationship at the start of the adventure to establish one's own ego. And it is an adventure that returns, again and again, like the abiku always before a fearful future. Soon Tanga will have Pieds-gâtés's death before her. And soon after that her own. At this decisive moment, she experiences the full repugnance for an abjection that threatens to swallow her up, as well as the seductiveness that accompanies the act of listening.

> Je ne veux pas de ces noces qui se célébreront dans l'abjection de la mutilation, au milieu de cette horde de désolés. Je ne veux pas épouser ce malheur. Pauvre et paumée, je le suis. Mais ces damnés, encore plus brutalement révélés à la malédiction, me rendent plus exiguë, plus inconfortable. Soudain j'ai peur de m'échapper de moi-même, de m'endormi dans l'étranger, moi dont le rêve est de partir, fuir la vieille la mère pour prendre la posture de l'envol. (158–59) [I don't want any part of this wedding to be celebrated in the abjection of mutilation, amidst this pack of desolate beings. I do not want to marry this misfortune. Poor and derelict I am. But these ones who are damned, even more brutally exposed to execration, make me more meagre, more uncomfortable. Suddenly I fear I'm escaping from myself, falling asleep on foreign soil, I, whose dream it is to leave, to flee from mother old one in order to put myself in the position for taking off. (114–15)]

Tanga cedes to Cul-de-jatte's seductive discourse, follows him into the full derangement of desire, enters the kingdom of the ego. "Je suis au royaume de moi, à l'assaut de moi" (160) [I am in the kingdom of myself. (116)].

Needless to say, the abiku child caught up in itself will sooner or later have to come to terms with its death. Tanga's story ends with the return to the cell, to Anna-Claude, whose intertwining into the story set in the present begins anew. Perversely, abjectly positioned before her, Tanga will wait for Anna-Claude, listen to her—open, ready to pass on the relay: "Elle sait que pour mourir, Tanga l'attendait, ouverte, offerte, pour lui donner à parler avant de passer les frontières et de s'étendre dans la nature morte" (176) [She knows that Tanga was waiting for her in order to die—open, offering herself, so she could give her words to speak before crossing the borders and lying down full length as a still-life. (127)]. And with Tanga's account passed on to her, Anna-Claude will assume the new identity of abiku-abject in the form constructed by Tanga both for herself and for Anne-Claude. "Elle sait que désormais aucun coup, aucune grâce, ne sauraient empêcher la femme-fillette de féconder la terre, de nourrir l'espace" (176) [She knows that from now on no blow, no grace will be able to prevent the girlchild-woman from fertilising the earth, from nurturing space. (127)].

"Il y a aussi ses morts" [Then there are her dead ones, too. (128)]. Kristeva's maternal abject, whose words become a source of nourishment. "Il y a aussi ses morts"—the final limits of the abiku, of abjection. "Ils anticiperont l'ombre de la peur qui l'avait cloisonnée dans le rêve. Ils annuleront portes et verrous. Elles céderont une à une, se fracasseront aux injunctions de la mort. Amour glaive de l'amour, Anna-Claude te brandira!" (176) [They will anticipate the shadow of fear that had partitioned her off in dreams. They'll invalidate every door and every bolt. They'll yield, one by one, shatter before the injunctions of death. Love the blade of love. Anna-Claude will brandish you. (128)].

Anna-Claude follows her interlocutor, now, and seeks to bring her own posture into line with Tanga's, erect before the spoken word. "Elle dressera sa silhouette dans le vide" (176) [She will hold her silhouette erect in the emptiness. (128)]. This is as far as she can go. For the narrator, she can't anticipate what the logic of the patriarch will do with the accounting that she will have to give of Tanga, of herself—what classification and analysis will bring to her story, to reduce it to an ordered and structured account—an account with a meaning. "Mais ça elle ne le sait pas. Pour le savoir, il lui aurait fallu connaître le gel de la conscience qui habite le monde. Il lui aurait fallu naître avec d'autres yeux" (177) [But she doesn't know that. In order to know that, she would have had to know the frozen state of consciousness which inhabits the world. She would have had to be born with other eyes. (128; my change)]. And who could ever say what accounting the abiku-girlchild could give of her experience of the abject?

In the end, Anna-Claude can best sum it up with the words, "Votre fille, c'est moi" (189) [I am your daughter. (137)]. But, of course, she is not understood, she is classified, filed away, and dismissed with the guard's words: "Laisse-la. . . . Elle est complètement maboule. On trouvera ailleurs" (190) [Leave her alone. She's completely off her rocker. We'll go look elsewhere. (137)].

Notes

1. The text in Leviticus dealing with priestly conduct and the prohibition against drinking wine evokes *both* sets of pairs, holy/unholy, pure/impure: Lev. 10:10: "so that there be separation between the holy and the profane, between the tamei and the pure." The juxtaposition of these two pairs is all the more complicated by the fact that the first terms of both pairs are *not* parallel, i.e., instead of pure:tamei::holy:profane, it is the converse: holy:profane::tamei:pure. The burden of the passage lies on the term "separation" or difference, and not the signifiers as isolated terms.

2. Susan Handelman (1982) sets off the Jewish tradition by suggesting its difference from that of Christianity: "Christianity claimed that it had the

final and validating interpretation of the now 'Old' Testament text. The word literally became incarnate. The Rabbinic tradition, by contrast, based itself on the principles of multiple meaning and endless interpretability, maintaining that interpretation and text were not only inseparable, but that interpretation—as opposed to incarnation—was the central divine act" (xiv). Handelman cites Lacan, who remarks that "psychoanalysis belonged to the exegetical tradition of midrash," which she glosses as "that genre of Rabbinic interpretation which is a searching out of the meaning of Biblical texts through methods close to free association" (xv).

3. Kristeva's choice of pure/impure rather than holy/unholy is significant for several reasons. First, she assumes an unproblematic translation of these terms, which then permits the clear notion of a set of binary opposites separated by a slash of oppositionality. The *Soncino Chumash* (Hebrew Bible, with translation provided by the Jewish Publication Society) gives tahor/tamei as clean/unclean. But Everett Fox (1995), one of the most meticulous of Biblical translators, gives "tamei/pure," glossing the untranslated tamei thus: "the term is not well served by negative translations such as 'impure' or 'unclean'; the Hebrew signifies that something is in a charged state and must not come in contact with the sanctuary" (525). "Pollution" and "contamination" are like terms that can only serve to complicate rather than to reduce the opposition to "tahor."

Fox considers the range of "pollutants" as arising from "territorial" problems, i.e., that which transgresses borders: "the border of what goes into the body, expressed through animals permitted and forbidden for food; the border between life and death, as expressed through sexual functions and discharges; and the border of outer surfaces, as expressed through skin disease, mildew on clothing, and mold on houses" (553). The pollutants are not concomitant with evil, but more with contagious, morally neutral elements, requiring ritual purification. "What was generally required was that the polluted person observe a period of separation from the sanctuary (or in more extreme cases, from the camp), to be reintegrated after either time alone or with the addition of laundering their clothes and/or washing themselves. In the latter cases, water was seen as acting as a purifying agent, not as a cleanser in the detergent sense (and so the word 'unclean,' so often used in translating Heb. *tamei*, is misleading)" (553). Like Kristeva, Fox depends here upon Mary Douglas (1966), who saw the system in Leviticus as "symbolizing the protection of boundaries in Israelite society" (Fox 555).

4. "And God spoke unto Moses, and said unto him, I am the Lord: And I appeared unto Abraham, unto Isaac, unto Jacob, as God Almighty [El Shaddai], but by my names Adonai [Yahweh—the tetragrammaton] was I not known to them" (Ex. 6:12). Although the name Adonai and Elohim run through the Bible, we also find El, and here especially, the

ambiguous Shaddai—a name given blithely in the King James English translation as Almighty, but actually less certain in meaning. As Shaddai is one of the least used names for God in the Bible, we might speculate that it represents a tradition that has been largely suppressed and supplanted by the Yahwehist and Elohist redactors. More generally, it points to the book of Exodus as being written over a palimpsest whose shadowy original emerges through such cracks as this rarely used name. Although not stated as absolutely by Fox, he notes that the ambivalent title Shaddai given God is tied to human fertility (Genesis 17:12), and further, "a possibly related Hebrew word means 'breasts' " (287 fn3).

5. Mary Douglas might have been Kristeva's source for this hypothesis as with her broader reading of Leviticus. Here Fox presents Douglas's thesis, which also supples the theoretical basis of his own: "I see Leviticus as the Book of Separations, the book in which are set forth distinctions between a whole range of aspects of ancient Israelite experience and practice: holy and profane; ritual purity and pollution; permitted and forbidden in sexuality and diet; Israelites and others; and priests, Levites, and common folk among the Israelites. This near-obsession with drawing lines (or, as Douglas has presented it, concentric circles) may in some sense reflect the position of Israel in the ancient Near East as a small beleaguered newcomer in a region of hoary empires, situated on land that was constantly invaded by both great powers and local foes. It may also be an echo of the larger Bronze Age and Iron Age process of change from the former, well-nigh universal worship of the Mother Goddess, to the later patriarchal societies with which the Western world still deals through its three monotheistic religions and their cultural outgrowths" (499).

6. See Jean Bottéro's *Naissance de Dieu: La Bible et l'historien* (1986), 36, 188, 196–201.

7. See chapter 3 in Leila Ahmed, *Women and Gender in Islam* (1992).

8. In seeking an organizing mytheme, Kristeva closely follows the work of Freud and Lacan. In *Moses and Monotheism* (1939), Freud writes, "I have never doubted that religious phenomena are to be understood only on the model of the neurotic symptoms of the individual, and are so familiar to us, as a return of long-forgotten important happenings *in the primeval history of the human family*, that they owe their obsessive character to that very origin and therefore derive their effect upon mankind from the historical truth they contain" (71; my emphasis). In his analysis of the mirror stage, Lacan indicates a similar belief in the psychic survival of human ur-history: "What I have called paranoia knowledge is shown . . . to correspond in its more or less archaic forms to certain critical moments that mark the history of man's mental genesis, each representing a stage in objectifying identification" (1977: 17).

9. Page references are to the 1996 translation of *Tu t'appelleras Tanga*. When no page reference appears, it is my translation, both here and elsewhere throughout the book.

10. "I was sitting alone in my *wagon-lit* compartment when a more than usually violent jolt of the train swung back the door of the adjoining washing-cabinet, and an elderly gentleman in a dressing-gown and a travelling cap came in. I assumed that in leaving the washing-cabinet, which lay between the two compartments, he had taken the wrong direction and come into my compartment by mistake. Jumping up with the intention of putting him right, I at once realized to my dismay that the intruder was nothing but my own reflection in the looking-glass on the open door. I can still recollect that I thoroughly disliked his appearance." Sigmund Freud, "The Uncanny," in Standard Edition of the Complete Psychological Works of Sigmund Freud (1958), 17:248.

11. Cf. Borch-Jacobsen's reference to *Ecrits* (1966) where Lacan "savagely ridicules" (57) Lucien Levy-Bruhl's concept of "primitive mentality" and "animism" as presented in *Totem and Taboo.*

12. Note the way in which Beyala has carried this doubling/indeterminacy to the naming of the characters: la vieille la mere; moi, la femme-fillette; la fille ma soeur, etc.

13. Thanks to Emmanuel Yewah in helping identify the sources of the following terms employed by Beyala in the novel: Kwem—Ewondo dish based on cassava leaves; jojoba—drink; megang—witchcraft among the Bamileke; Tchoumbi and Dakassi—Bamileke sounding names; Yaya—northern Cameroonian name; Ngala—name either from Douala or northwestern Cameroon; mala—a term resembling the Douala, as in na mala ("how are you"); Ga, Nga Taba, Essomba—southern Ewondo or Beti names (nga is also Bamoun for spider); Kadjaba—perhaps a southern name; Essoko—perhaps Douala.

14. See Obioma Nnaemeka's Introduction to her edited volume *The Politics of (M)Othering* (1997). Nnaemeka argues for the difference between male African authors, who mostly point out the negative consequences of the institution of mothering, and women authors, who also highlight the positive side of the experience of mothering. In general, Nnaemeka argues for a reading of women's literature that draws upon the positive features of resistance to patriarchy and oppression, along with the negative connotations of the latter. Further, she argues in favor of a more nuanced reading that would not reduce mothering, or the condition of women as represented in women's literature, to a simple status of subordination conveyed through a binary of oppression/liberation, but would see the gray areas that so often fall between the two: "the works themselves and the reality from which they evolve disrupt such binaries; . . . the central arguments of the works and their appeal (very instructive, I might add) rest on the authors' insistence on border crossings, gray areas and the ambiguous interstices of the binaries where woman is both benevolent *and* malevolent" (2).

15. Cf. Mudimbe's notion of this space as marginal: "Marginality designates the intermediate space between the so-called African tradition and the

projected modernity of colonialism. It is apparently an urbanized space in which, as S. Amin noted, 'vestiges of the past, especially the survival of structures that are still living realities (tribal ties, for example), often continue to hide the new structures (ties based on class, or on groups defined by their position in the capitalist system)' " (5).

16. In her study of the works of Beyala, *L'Oeuvre romanesque de Calixthe Beyala*, Rangira Béatrice Gallimore notes the various ways in which Beyala evokes ritualistic acts of violence and purification. For example, in *C'est le soleil qui m'a brûlée*, she writes, "La femme noircie et déséchée par le soleil se laisse pénétrer par les eaux de la pluie, celles qui, en même temps qu'elles nettoient, fécondent et fertilisent" (116) [The woman, darkened and dried out by the sun, let herself be penetrated by the rain waters, those which made her fecund and fertile while at the same time cleansing her.]. When Ateba kills a man with a knife, the blood spurts out from several wounds. "Le sang est ici le sang du sacrifice, qui nettoie et purifie" (117) [The blood here is the blood of sacrifice, which cleans and purifies.]. As for the state of madness that follows the murder, Gallimore follows Joseph Ndinda, who finds in the madness that which "a permis à la femme le retour à l'état mythique, celui de la pureté et de l'innocence" (118) [permitted woman to return to the mythic state, that of purity and innocence].

17. As these judgments might seem extreme, I should note that Ken Bugul's *Le Baobab fou*, Mariama Bâ's *Le Chant écarlate*, and, to stretch the definition of "African," Myriam Warner Vieyra's *Juletane* might be regarded as predecessors to Beyala's work, and that Werewere Liking has also moved in similar directions to Beyala. None of the above has grounded her work in abjection, as has Beyala; their work might be termed pre-abject.

Chapter 4
▼▼▼▼▼▼▼▼▼

Standing Like a Tower: Plagiarism, Castration, and the Phallus in Le Petit Prince de Belleville

The question of how to stand up isn't as obvious as it might seem. For Tanga, standing up like a tower might mean establishing her independence from her mother. For Toundi, it might also mean standing up to the Other, to the Commandant. However, Toundi's rebellion against the Commandant is often performed in secret, as with his spitting into the glass of water he is about to serve him. By the end of the novel, his rebellion has become generalized, and is perceived mostly in terms of his refusal to lower his eyes before the gazes of the Commandant and Madame. Indeed, Toundi's first step in freeing himself from his state of subordination comes through the visual perception of the Commandant's uncircumcised penis.

There were many steps that Toundi had to take after the initial liberatory sight—one that freed him from the restrictive, castrating fear of the Other. That psychological passage had its equivalent in his discovery of Madame's infidelity, a discovery that liberated him from the mesmerizing effect the sight of her had on him. Given Madame and the Commandant's superior position over Toundi, it seems obvious that Toundi's ascent into an erect posture constitutes the successful passage of the oedipus: the successful negotiation of the castrating fear of the Name of the Father, the successful break with the (m)other. In short, Toundi learns to pass beyond his status as a boy, even if he was the best, the highest placed of boys—"le chien du roi est le roi des chiens" (32) [the dog of the king is the king of dogs]—to become a man. He passed from being a colonized "boy" to a free man; from a "Français" to an African.

In his story of Toundi, Ferdinand Oyono has managed to encapsulate better than any other African novelist of anticolonialism this passage. And it is therefore not surprising that the key moment of representing Toundi's ascension comes through the image of his standing erect, like Tanga's tower. That moment comes in the prison where he has been beaten by the guards so badly that he is actually mortally injured. Not only does he refuse to cry out, he persists in standing and carrying his load of water on his head. In that moment, in those gestures before his fellow Africans, he demonstrates how to stand up to the white colonialists and to the worst of their threats.

He will eventually die after fleeing Cameroon, but in his death, as in his account left behind in his notebooks, he leaves a testimonial that will serve to encourage his compatriot "frère," and by indirection, all the other narratees of his account. The parallel to Tanga is a close one. In Tanga's death, she also leaves behind an example for others that will serve to restore her "semblable," her double, Anna-Claude. Her heritage also takes the form of an account. Like her black frère of the earlier generation, whose voice had been preempted by the superior civilized whites, Tanga's voice had been preempted by the ruling patriarchy: "Parole de femme" (157) [the word of a woman]—deemed worthless. And, as Irène D'Almeida points out, Tanga's story will "tuer le vide du silence," "assassiner le silence" (*Tanga* 13) [kill the emptiness of silence, murder silence]. As Toundi's is the story of the life of a "boy," Tanga's is that of "la fillette-femme." Toundi becomes a man, Tanga a femme.

Satisfying as this interpretation of the two texts is, it depends upon an allegorization of Toundi's and Tanga's accounts that necessarily subordinates them to a monological reading of revolt, that inscribes them into anticolonial and antipatriarchal agendas with a force that is directly proportional to the satisfaction we take in such understandings. Lacan affords us the opportunity for a dialogical engagement with the texts, especially with respect to the issue of their passage from child to adult, their act of standing erect.

The first thought one might have is that this act corresponds to the acquisition of agency that accompanies the formation of the subject— the subject position being necessary for speech and the entry into the symbolic. However, before that passage through the oedipus, before the thetic break is complete, the formation of the ego, as distinct from the subject, occurs. If the subject is a position from which intentions can be formed into speech, the ego is rather an image that is incorporated into oneself from the outside—as in the reflection of oneself in the gaze of the other, in the mirrored reflection of one's self. The re-

Plagiarism, Castration, and the Phallus 99

flection provides a sense of unity, an image of wholeness not experienced by the child in his or her multitudinous experiences of the world, or by the child's unassimilated and various perceptions and responses to external and internal stimuli.

The image of the self that forms the ego is acquired by the child that stands up to see itself. It is an image of the standing position, taken from the standing position: an erect position whose counterpart in the newly formed image of the self is the ego: "The ego erects itself (raises itself permanently and stably upright) only before 'itself,' by *anticipating* itself" (Borch-Jacobsen 48). Freudian psychology is built on the notion of substitution: in place of the object desired, in place of the person who is the object of desire, another word, another object, can be substituted. For Lacan, in place of the object of desire, another sign can be substituted. And because it is substituted, because the act of substitution implicitly defers direct access to the desired object, the satisfaction is always deferred, always incomplete. The ego becomes an object, and its desire for other subjects is always for "a false object, a decoy, a trap in which the ego pursues its own image" (Borch-Jacobsen 49).

That is the situation of the ego. Standing before an image of the self that seeks to reflect the wholeness and unicity of a perceived object, the self constructs for itself an ego. Always returned from the outside, where its original existence is to be found, rather than arising naturally from within. And it is that passage, that difficult passage marked by the misapprehension of self, that occurs without explanation. The transformation of the double from the narcissistic self to its uncanny other is conceived by Freud as a natural passage to a more advanced "stage"; as in the passage from child to adult, from "primitive" to "civilized." From less to more evolved. The ego thus formed, for Lacan, arises, rises into its standing position by seeing something that it takes for itself outside of itself. It is thus fundamentally self-deceived, and grounded in visual perception. "Indeed, only through vision can the ego raise itself before itself as a self-enclosed 'beautiful totality.' The erection of the ego is always the erection of a statue that I *see*, over there—triumphant, unshakable, fixed for eternity" (Borch-Jacobsen 49). It is this ego—"triumphant, unshakable, fixed for eternity"—that Toundi and Tanga are in the business of erecting for the sight of their doubles, and that is taken to be such in the readings I earlier identified as anticolonial and antipatriarchal.

However, Tanga and Toundi, or better still "Tanga" and "Toundi," do not become immortal. They die under miserable conditions. Their "victories" are the triumphs of their readers—implied victories that can be realized only in their successful transubstantiation into, incorporation into, the others—into the egos of the others. Their subject positions, their instances of enunciation, are assumed by their doubles, and the process of misrecognition, the repetition of the spectacle of unity, as in a film, is repeated in the spectators, or, in these cases, the readers of their accounts.

Because this external image of the self is visual, it is specular, and it serves as an instance for projection. This, we have seen, permits the construction of the abject when the subject does not feel itself to be securely differentiated from external objects. When the image is recognized, it provides the occasion for pleasure, for "jouissance," because that recognition is the recognition of self whose pleasure derives from the economy of the narcissistic self on which the child's identity is grounded. Thus, for Lacan, the subject perceives in the specular image "his inherent mental unity. What he recognizes is the ideal of the imago of the double. What he acclaims is the triumph of the salutary tendency" (Lacan 1984: 44).

What does the child see out there where it is seeing itself—what self does it see? We read the double's accounts of Toundi lying supine, dying; of Tanga curled up on the prison floor, dying. But their imagos are erect, erected like a tower, standing above the mud that clings to the soles of their sandals. "A chaque minute, à chaque seconde, à chaque heure qui se dévide et s'égoutte, je dois garder cela en tête: être présente, répondre présente, *droite* sous les soleils et les pluies, pour donner son souffle à l'histoire" (*Tanga* 26–27; my emphasis) [With every minute, every second, every unwinding hour that goes by, drop by drop, I must keep this in my head: to be here, answering yes to my presence, standing straight in the sun and in the rain, in order to give the story its breath (17)]; "je me hisserai sur un escabeau pour inscrire mon âme dans son désir" (32–33) [I'll hoist myself on top of a ladder to inscribe my soul into his desire (20)]; "je me posterai devant tout. Avant le monde, Moi, après le monde, Moi, toujours Moi" (56) [I'll put myself before everything. Before the world. Me; after the world; Me, always Me. (38)]; "Je veux m'ancrer au milieu de mes songes, *m'élèver* au-dessus du destin" (122) [I want to anchor myself amidst my dreams, to raise myself up above destiny (87)], and so on. This "je," this "I" posted before Tanga, represented before itself in the structure of "the objectifying Vor-stellung" (Borch-Jacobsen 59)—a representation that is a *standing before* oneself, is constituted as in the pose of the actor before the lens, that is, posed as a statue, a "stasis of being": "Now, this formal stagnation is akin to the most general structure of human knowledge: that which constitutes the ego and its objects with attributes of permanence, identity, and substantiality"

(Lacan, 1977: 17). What Lacan calls the world of knowledge, and what corresponds as well, specifically, to the sense, the meaning we ascribe to texts, the identities that we affix to characters in films and to their motivation, the sense of their lives and of the overall story, is all provided with "the *stability* of a substance and of what holds itself straight, raised, erected in the light, just as, imaginarily, the infant in the mirror did: 'The stability of the standing posture, the prestige of stature, the impressiveness of statues [are what] set the style for the identification in which the ego finds its starting point *and leave their* imprint in its forever' (Lacan 1953: 15)" (Borch-Jacobsen 60; my emphasis). (Lest it be argued that this model ignores the differences in social circumstances in societies, let it be recalled that that external image to be appropriated is always constructed within a social context, i.e., within a symbolic order—not in any universal, abstract sense.)

Our view of the ego, the I-tower standing before our regard, has focused on the person/figure/personage/character that we see, and that we see in ourselves. But the unicity of this vision is commensurate with, and for Lacan fundamental to, what sense we make of what we see. Knowledge assumes the same qualities as identity, and is as grounded in properties of imitation and identification, which is why Lacan regards knowledge as endowed with the properties of paranoia.[1] This quality of knowledge cannot be separated from the one who sees, who "understands" the elements of knowledge positioned before herself or himself, and for that reason knowledge is constituted into higher, statuesque forms—ideas. It is this last property of the speculating ego that gives us our understanding of Tanga or Toundi as imagos bound up in the dramas of decolonization or of "l'écriture féminine." "Indeed, for Lacan, the specular image, although admittedly an image of the ego, is simultaneously what *gives form to* the ego. The image is exterior . . . and 'superior' (the prestige of standing erect, of the human 'statue' to which the infant *raises* its eyes), and, moreover, formative: the ego (or the eye, if you will) forms itself in the image of the image, which by the same token reacquires the stature (and the 'standing') of a true Idea" (Borch-Jacobsen 62).

We would expect Beyala to have inscribed such a stature in the Idea which Tanga places before Anna-Claude, and to be sure, in their last words together, Anna-Claude evokes such an Idea to be placed in the spotlight: "[Anna-Claude] sait que l'angoisse est là mais qu'il faut travailler toujours et toujours à l'écloison de la lumière. Elle ferme les yeux puis dit à Tanga d'une voix mésurée: 'Continue ton histoire. *C'est elle qui me guidera*, c'est elle que tu dois me léguer' " (177–78; my emphasis) [Anna-Claude knows anguish is there but that she must ever and always work at making the light dawn. She closes her eyes then says to Tanga in a restrained voice: "Continue your story. It will guide me; it is what you must bequeath to me." (128–29)].

This stature of meaning freezes our action, our sense of originating action for ourselves and for others, once we perceive it there, before us, as the limit of knowledge. Borch-Jacobsen resists the statutory limit: "why, after all, should true life always be elsewhere, in front of me, in the double who augurs my death?" (Borch-Jacobsen 70–71). Tanga and Toundi stand insistently before us in their postures. But there is always an ironizing word that brings down the statue a notch, and even if invented in imitation and identification—the elements of paranoia, of monological unifications—it seeks to undermine at the same time as it reports what it sees. This turn of the subject is not the reflexivity of Absolute Knowledge that knows itself in the act of understanding, but that which revolts against the act of constituting itself as a unified subject. We begin again with the children, with Loukoum, le petit prince of Belleville, in an attempt to answer Borch-Jacobsen's question about whether there cannot be other options, other ways for the ego to be in the world—and most of all, whether the question of the ego cannot be posed not simply before just any mirror, just any double, just any object, but before a world of reflection and of objects constituted by an African imaginary.

Beyala and Plagiarism

In her *Lettre d'une africaine à ses soeurs occidentales* (1995), Beyala gives a definition of feminism that consists essentially in liberal humanist demands recognizable as those dating to the early years of "women's liberation"—that is, demands for equality in education and job opportunity, changes in social roles based on the treatment of women as objects of male desire; an end to male domination and female subordination (11). Aside from the occasional use of obscene terms, there is nothing shocking or subversive about Beyala's *Lettre*—except for the absence of subversive elements.

One could consider the approaches to feminism globally as entailing, on the one hand, humanist demands made within an existing liberal order in which the rules for justice and equity are inscribed, or, on the other hand, positions intended to subvert the existing order regarded as patriarchal or phallocentric. The former seeks to achieve its goals through reforming existing institutions; the latter through subversion or revolution. The former, reducible to programmatic demands, has long been the dominant trend in African feminism; in a sense, it is basically a modest approach in which, generally speaking, the principal demands for respect for women's rights (summed up in the radical rhetoric of the 1970s and 1980s in *Ngambika*²). The challenge to the conventions of normalcy in heterosexual gender roles, and to the dominance of the heterosexual economy, has rarely been mounted—and if so, only indirectly. Only recently can we say that radical feminist subversions, those strongly marked by the radical French feminist positions of the 1960s and 1970s, have had an impact on, or resonance with, African writers or filmmakers.

Beyala's "feminism" in *Lettre* is anything but subversive. But her plagiarism is—or could have been—just as Ouologuem had deemed his attack on French notions of propriety (propriété—property, cleanliness, propriety) to be. To return to Kristeva's definition of the abject as that which disrupts order, what *l'affaire Beyala* (the controversy over her plagiarisms) has shown is that while a writer's practice as a writer might be subversive, her sense of herself as a subject, that is, as an "author," might well be anything but.

In an article published in *Lire* (February 1997), Pierre Assouline provides a number of examples of passages in which Beyala plagiarized from various sources. He shows how four passages in *Le Petit Prince de Belleville* (1992) resemble those of Roman Gary's *La Vie devant soi* (1975); two in *Assèze l'Africaine* (1994) come from Paule Constant's *White Spirit* (1992); five more in *Le Petit Prince* were taken from Alice Walker's *The Color Purple* (1982), in its French translation; and two in *Les Honneurs perdus* (which earned Beyala Le Grand Prix du Roman from the Académie Française in 1996) were taken from Ben Okri's *The Famished Road* (1991; also translated into French in 1994). The passages in question were all obviously plagiarized, although some involved verbatim copying and others were more in the style of paraphrasing, or copying with rewording. When identical wordings were employed, the effect could be shocking.

Assouline also indicated that many more passages were taken from Howard Buten's *Quand j'avais cinq ans, je m'ai tué* (1981 French translation of the English *Burt*) and Charles Williams's *Fantasia chez les ploucs*. Buten's publisher, le Seuil, sued Beyala for plagiarism, and won the case on May 7, 1996. As Beyala republished *Assèze l'Africaine* in September and *Les Honneurs perdus* in October 1996, it appeared that she had not changed her practice despite the onset of the legal suit, and thus was dubbed a recidivist by Assouline.

The "affair" assumed dramatic proportions as Beyala responded vigorously in the press, in a number of ways denying any wrongdoing. In this, she was supported by *Jeune Afrique* (Mataillet, December 1996), and especially by Jacques Chevrier, who did not take the position that she had plagiarized, but that plagiarism was in fact intrinsic to the act of creating literature, if not to all writing, to all language usage.

My concerns with this issue are multiple. *Le Petit Prince de Belleville* is a novel in which the questions of abjection and doubling, seen in Beyala's earlier work, naturally lead us to the heart of feminist concerns over castration, the most contentious of issues for feminist critics employing a Lacanian analysis. The plagiarisms force us to ask at what level the subversions take place: within the text, between various texts, between the text and the reader, and finally within the larger social context. There can't be subversion without the threat of castration. Castration is the mechanism for establishing the symbolic order, both on the individual psychological level and on the level of the social order as a whole. Subversion is the refusal of that order. And plagiarism is an unacknowledged subversion of the legal and ethical order of the institutionalization of writing—of its inscription, performance, publication, and dissemination. Unwittingly, Beyala has placed these issues before us, and although one ought to be cautious about the employment of African folk figures as symbolic references, one can't help seeing in Beyala's posture the ever-recurring figure of the trickster in this affair.

In *Le Petit Prince de Belleville*, the rough edges of Tanga or Ateba in *C'est le soleil qui m'a brûlé* have been softened: figures like Pieds-gâtés, found in a box with maggots crawling over his legs, are gone. Belleville is far from New Bell, just as Spike Lee's Bed-Stuy or Harlem is often romanticized as in *Do the Right Thing* (1988) or *Crooklyn* (1994).[3] And it is especially far from the comfortable suburbs of Detroit where Howard Buten's *Burt* is set. Indeed, nothing could seem farther apart than Seven Mile Road and rue de Belleville or the park of Buttes-Chaumont, the "jardin" of Belleville. The irony is that the more violent and subversive novel is Buten's *Burt*, and that Beyala not only plagiarized *Burt* (or rather, its French translation *Quand j'avais cinq ans, je m'ai tué*) extensively, but that she systematically softens its hard edges—sweetens it, moderates its pain, and eliminates its violations.

Thus, Gil, the little boy protagonist of *Burt*, has uncontrollable fits and tantrums, has been committed to a children's psychiatric hospital or clinic, and has intercourse with his girlfriend at the age of eight, this being the culminating moment in the novel. Loukoum experiences none of these things. The episodes in *Quand j'avais cinq ans, je m'ai tué* are duplicated at many points in *Le Petit Prince de Belleville*, but without the extreme nature with which they are described in *Burt*. In place of intercourse, there is the suggestion of genital fondling; in place of the death of Jessica's father (Jessica is Gil's girlfriend), there is the divorce of Lolita's parents; in place of the children's psychiatric ward, there is the room over Monsieur Guillaume's cafe. In place of autism, the central trope of *Burt*, there is marginality. The threat represented by Le Pen is introduced at the beginning of *Le Petit Prince de Belleville* but is never translated into concrete acts; and Loukoum is never faced with the threat of being incarcerated in a psychiatric hospital.

But in all those instances, Beyala duplicates the action in *Burt*, most of the time down to the smallest detail. The scene in which Loukoum visits his friend Alexis and finds an autistic boy named Timothée is an example. Gil enters the "Salle de Repos" where he finds Carl, a "petit nègre de couleur" (*Quand* 56) [a little colored Negro]. Beyala turns this somewhat odd phrasing into her own, with her initial description of Loukoum's friend Alexis as a "petit Blanc de couleur" (36). In *Quand j'avais cinq ans, je m'ai tué*, Rudyard introduced Carl to Gil, and the following passages appear:

> Et puis il [Rudyard] a fait quelque chose de bizarre. Il a levé des mains devant les yeux et il a bougé ses doigts et puis il faisait Mmmm avec sa bouche comme s'il fredonnait mais c'était seulement un bruit pas de la musique.
> "Tu ne devrais pas t'asseoir par terre avec tes habits du dimanche," je lui ai dit. "Tu vas être puni."
> Il a levé le regard vers moi. Il avait les yeux verts avec des éclats marron dedans, comme Jessica.
> "Comme c'est vrai," il m'a dit. "Et pourtant, comme c'est loin."
> (. . .)
> Alors je l'ai suivi pasqu'il aurait pas dû écrire sur mon mur. Il est allé à la Salle de Jeux. La porte était ouverte. Je l'ai regardé par la petite fenêtre, il était là avec le petit nègre de couleur que j'avais déjà vu, celui qui est dingue. Le roux était à quatre pattes par terre avec lui et le petit garçon pleurait sans arrêt, pleurait, pleurait. Et puis le roux m'a vu. Il s'est levé et il m'a dit d'entrer. Je suis entré.
> "Je te présente Carl," il m'a dit. "Il mord."
> Il s'est levé et d'un seul coup il s'est mis à courir aussi vite qu'il pouvait tout autour de la Salle de Jeux et puis il s'est flanqué contre la porte, il a rebondi en arrière et il est reparti sans pleurer ni rien du tout. Et puis il s'est assis. Et puis il s'est levé. Et puis il a fait un cercle et il a marché sur quelques jouets et il s'est rassis. Je lui disais rien. Je crois qu'il savais même pas que j'étais là. Il a

ramassé un coussin et s'est mis à le bouffer. Ses yeux sont devenus tout drôles. Un qui regardait par ici l'autre par là. Il clignait des yeux et remuait très fort la tête. Il s'est mis à écraser les jouets dans le coffre à jouets.

"Tu devrais pas," je lui ai dit.

Mais tout ce qu'il a fait c'était de siffler. Et puis il s'est relevé et il est entré droit dans le mur et puis il s'est assis contre le mur et il a levé les mains devant les yeux et il s'est mis à gigoter les doigts. C'était la même chose comme faisait le roux dans la Salle de Repos.

Et puis Carl est tombé et il a roulé par terre et il s'est cogné très fort contre la jungle en plastique qui a failli lui dégringoler dessus mais finalement non, alors il s'est rassis avec le dos contre le mur et il s'est mis à se balancer et à cogner la tête contre le mur. Je voyais un petit endroit chauve derrière sa tête d'à force de la cogner. D'un seul coup il s'est assis tout droit et il a posé les mains sur ses genoux et il s'est tenu comme un petit garçon bien élevé. Je lui ai dit:

"T'es assis bien comme il faut, Carl, comme un bon petit citoyen." (*Quand j'avais cinq ans, je m'ai tué* 57).

[Then he did something funny. He put his fingers up to his eyes and wiggled them, and he like hummed, only it was noise, not music.

"You shouldn't sit on the floor in your good clothes," I said. "You'll get punished."

He looked up at me. His eyes were green with brown pieces, like Jessica's.

"So true," he said. "And yet so far."

(. . .)

So I followed him because he shouldn't have wrote on my wall. He went down to the Playroom. The door was open. I watched him through the little window, he was in there with the little colored negro boy I saw before, the one who is spaz. The red-haired man was crawling on the floor with him, and the little boy was crying and crying. Then the red-haired man saw me. He stood up and told me to come in. I went in.

"This is Carl," he said to me. "He bites." And he walked out of the room and closed the door. And I was alone with Carl. Who bites.

He got up and suddenly started running all over the Playroom as fast as he could and smashed into the door and bounced off and walked away without crying or anything. Then he sat down. Then he got up. Then he made a circle and walked on some toys and sat down again. I didn't say anything to him, I thought he didn't know I was there even. He picked up a bean bag and ate it. His eyes went funny. One over here and one over here. He blinked and jerked his head. He started to crush the toys in the toy box.

"You shouldn't," I said.

But all he did was whistle. Then he stood up and walked into the wall and then he sat down against the wall and put his hands up to his eyes and wiggled his fingers. It was the same thing that the red-haired man from the Quiet Room did.

Carl fell over and rolled on the floor and smashed into the jungle jim and it almost crashed on him but it didn't, so he sat with his back against the wall again and started rocking and pounding the back of his head against the wall. I could see there was a little bald spot on the back of his hair from pounding. Suddenly he sat up straight and put his hands in his lap and sat like a little gentleman.

I said, "You are sitting very nice, Carl, with good citizenship." (39–40)]

Shortly thereafter, an employee enters and Carl bites him on the hand. The action that follows is roughly duplicated, step by step, in *Le Petit Prince de Belleville*. Here is how Beyala turns the scene:

Il y a là un gamin à quatre pattes. Il pleure tout le temps. Il porte ses habits du dimanche avec une cravate et une chemise blanche.

"Je te présente Timothée," fait Alex.

Et moi je regarde. J'ose pas bouger.

"Approche," me dit Alex, il va pas te manger.

Je fais quelques pas. Alex sort et il me dit: "Fais attention. Il mord."

Il a refermé la porte. Et je me retrouve seul avec Timothée qui mord. Il saute, il hurle, puis il s'arrête et me regarde avec un oeil qui regarde par ici, l'autre par là. C'est drôle, ses yeux. Je suis tout retourné, alors je souris à l'anglaise, l'air de rien.

Soudain il se lève, il se met à courir comme un Indien. Il s'arrête. Il se flanque derrière une porte. Il repart sans rien dire. Il se remet à quatre pattes. Il se relève. Il va à la penderie. Il sort des vêtements et les jette par terre. Il regarde autour de lui. Ses yeux tournebiscotent. Puis il écrase les vêtements avec ses pieds.

"Tu devrais pas," je lui dis.

Il répond pas.

"Tu dois pas salir le linge," je dis encore. Si t'arrêtes pas, Monsieur Guillaume va t'en foutre une."

Il fait *Brrrr*! C'est du bruit comme l'orage. Il recule. Il se cogne contre la barrière du lit. Il se lève. Il se rassoit avec le dos contre la porte et il cogne sa tête contre le mur. Je vois un petit cercle chauve derrière son crâne. Tout à coup, il s'arrête. Il va s'asseoir derrière la porte. Il croise les bras. Il se tient comme un honnête citoyen. (38–39)[4]

[There is a kid on all fours. He is crying all the time. He is wearing Sunday clothes with a tie and white shirt.

"This is Timothy," Alex goes. Me, I look, I don't dare budge.

"Come closer," Alex says to me. He won't eat you.

I take a few steps. Alex goes out and tells me, "Watch out. He bites."

He closes the door again. And I find myself alone with Timothy who bites. He jumps, he screams, then he stops and looks at me with one eye that goes one way and the other that goes another. It's funny, his eyes. I'm all confused, so I smile acting real cool.

Suddenly he gets up, begins to run like an Indian. He stops. He flings himself behind a door. He starts up again without saying anything. He starts again on all fours. He gets up. He goes to the closet. He takes out clothes and throws them on the floor. He looks around himself. His eyes are spinning. Then he crushes the clothes with his feet.

"You shouldn't," I tell him.

He doesn't answer.

"You shouldn't get the laundry dirty," I say again. "If ya don't stop, Mr. William's gonna smack you one."

He goes, "Brrrr!" It sounds like a storm. He backs up. He knocks against the bedrail. He gets up. He sits down with his back against the door and knocks his head against the wall. I see a small bald spot on the back of his head. All of a sudden, he stops. He goes and sits down in back of the door. He crosses his arms. He makes himself into the perfect gentleman. (My translation; see 38–39)]

Beyala abbreviates Buten's text somewhat, but retains almost all of the action, the language, and the "tics"—the sounds and wording that give the original (translation) its flavor. The scene is an oddity in a sense, since Timothée does not reappear in her version, and would seem to be there mostly to evoke sympathy for children whose vulnerability extends to the point of suffering drastically, especially in light of the failure of those in charge of them—in this case the adult male, Monsieur Guillaume, another inadequate father figure. In *Burt*, Carl's autism is presented as indicative of the extreme margins of the human existence where the norms of authority fail, where the Name of the Father has not yet entered to establish its presence. It is at the core of *Burt*, a novel about the resistance to the Name of the Father, to the Law of the Father, in the manner of Ken Kesey's *One Flew over the Cuckoo's Nest*, or even Salinger's *Catcher in the Rye*.

Beyala's employment of this scene is much less obvious: it has no sequel, and stands apart from the action. In reading *Le Petit Prince de Belleville* by itself, the scene seems loosely woven into the narrative, in contrast with *Burt*, where it is integral to the novel's main theme. When one reads both novels side by side, the effect is dramatically different from almost any other reading experience. The interaction between the two is shocking when one finds many examples of systematic plagiarism, especially in those portions of the text involving Loukoum and any other children. Eventually, a kind of textual dependency is created, in which the reader comes to expect to find the action and the language duplicated, abbreviated, and refashioned. It is as though a strange new sort of crime, an open theft, is being carried out before our eyes. The narration of the theft is carried along by itself: the one text speaks, the other mimics. And as the former builds toward a climax that is effective and moving, one anticipates a similar pattern and denouement.

This doesn't quite happen, for a number of reasons. One, to be cynical, is that Beyala plagiarized several sources. Thus, for example, we have in the stories of the adults echoes of other narratives that have nothing to do with the *Burt* sequences, ones in which Loukoum is witness and not actor. This is most evident in the drama involving M'am and Soumana, and their relationship with his father. Soumana is a figure of misery, and is easily recognized as the clone of Celie from *The Color Purple*. Gary's *La Vie devant soi* also furnished Beyala with character-relations and material with which she constructed the narrative involving the adult characters. In addition, much of the evocatory power of *Le Petit Prince de Belleville* lies in its narrative counterpoint where each chapter, more or less, begins with a passage presented by Abdou, generally addressing an anonymous interlocutor, ostensibly a white Frenchman. In those passages, there is no dialogue or action: Abdou's interior thoughts and feelings are articulated often in highly poeticized and moving fashion. The sequence of his monologues creates a text unto itself, one that interacts dialectically with the main diegesis narrated by Loukoum.

In short, although *Le Petit Prince de Belleville* is a work of considerable theft, it is in the end a novel that stands by itself, that coheres, if imperfectly at times, that is effective, in fact. It is Beyala's work. The reader who has not read her source texts would not find a text that revealed in any obvious way that portions were not original. And the reader who will have read only the English versions of *Burt* or *The Color Purple* will be far less shocked than those whose acquaintances with those novels was through their French translations, because Beyala often copied the French wording and the verbal mannerisms employed in the translations.

The effect upon the reader who has read the translated versions, however, is striking, and can best be compared to Freud's reaction to seeing his reflection in that train compartment mirror in not quite recognizing himself: the feeling of the uncanny. At times the uncanniness comes across in a phrase or an action that seems vaguely familiar, but can't be placed. At times it is wrenching and painful. The overall effect, in the end, is to have seen something that should have been hidden—to have witnessed a violation, a crime.[5]

But this is a crime of letters. The courts evaluated the case and fined Beyala 100,000 francs. She decided not to appeal the decision, and the original version in French was still being sold in bookstores in France in 1998, but was halted by 2000. The financial and legal penalty may appear significant to some, but in truth represents a paltry sum considering the great success Beyala's writings have achieved—signaled by the high sales of her books and the major awards they have garnered.[6] Her success is also evidenced in terms of the media, as she has become a major figure on the French literary landscape, appearing often on TV and radio.

Her "affair" was widely reported in *Le Monde, Libération, Figaro, Jeune Afrique, Le Nouvel Observateur*, and elsewhere in the press.[7] The charges and countercharges reverberated throughout the media during 1996 and 1997, carrying into 1998. Her striking appearance was as much subject for comment as her writings: Beyala took the place of le petit prince, and made herself, and not her writings, the issue. And she did this *not* as Jean Genet or Bretyen Breytenbach or Hunter Thompson had done, proclaiming themselves to be outlaws, thieves of the established bourgeois order, but rather as a maligned and victimized African woman—a poor, simple countrygirl ("cambroussard" being her favored term), a victim of racists, sexists, and left-wing journalists. In short, Beyala turned from subversive to media star whose challenges to the dominant order were represented as being entirely a form of intratextuality, and therefore both legitimate and nonthreatening. Whereas her defenders would occasionally cite postmodernist rationales for plagiarism, she denied any wrongdoing and counterattacked her critics.

The reactions from those whom she plagiarized ranged from silence (Romain Gary being dead), to somewhat bemused indulgence (Constant), to anguish and anger (Okri). Paule Constant found it "surréaliste" that an African would steal from her, a European, to evoke her native Africa: "C'était presqu'un hommage, je l'ai d'abord pris ainsi" (Assouline, *Lire* 9) [It was almost like paying homage, and at first I took it that way.]. Then Constant imagined the "impuissance" and "frustration" that Beyala must have been experiencing in order to resort to such maneuvers. Constant brings in the personal relationship, and thus the inevitable sense of propriety, for a text in which each choice of a word was made, each allusion, each adjective chosen in relation to the imagined text. At seeing her work so closely read and followed, her imaginary Africans turned into "archétypes africains," Constant says she was "étonnement amusée," but an underlying enervation emerges in her admission that her reaction is marked by "points d'ironie," especially in her revulsion at the rationalizations Beyala employed for the plagiarism: "je m'insurge avec force contre l'idée complaisemment exploitée que 'tout le monde' plagierait 'tout le monde' " (Assouline, *Lire* 9) [I strongly revolt against the smugly exploited notion that "everyone" plagiarizes "everyone."].[8]

Ben Okri's reactions were much more emotional and angry. If Constant displayed amused curiosity and irony, Okri found himself thoroughly annoyed: "Ecrire est affair d'amour, et cette femme a tout sali et m'a fait passer des nuits blanches" (de Gaudemar, *Libération*, May 29, 1997: 7) [Writing is an act of love, and this woman has dirtied everything and given me sleepless nights.]. He goes on to describe his feelings, his pain: it was as though a car had been continually running over his legs. He then responds to her self-justifications: "Mais il ne s'agit pas simplement de moi. L'idée répandue par elle et selon laquelle la littérature africaine est naturellement plagiaire est non seulement fausse mais dangereuse, malfaisante, car elle laisse croire que tous les écrivains africains sont de constants emprunteurs. C'est insultant pour eux et pour la littérature" (de Gaudemar, *Libération*, May 29, 1997: 7) [But it's not simply a question of me. The idea she spread and according to which African literature naturally plagiarizes is not only false but dangerous, harmful, because it allows people to believe that all African writers continually borrow. It's insulting to them and to literature.].

Two notable interventions in support of Beyala appeared in the *Jeune Afrique* issue devoted to "le cas Beyala." Marcel Péju finds plagiarisms occurring naturally, as in Racine's adaptation of Euripides. He dismisses the issue involving Ben Okri's *Famished Road* on the ground that regional customs between Nigeria and its neighboring Cameroon are similar, thus explaining the appearance in both texts of passages in which a woman grabs a man by his testicles. Political practices in both countries being similar, descriptions of bribery in the two texts would also naturally resemble each other. However, examination of some of the plagiarized passages reproduced in *Lire* shows that Beyala did not inadvertently copy Okri, but consciously took his wording in the French translation and incorporated it into her own text. Péju goes on to naturalize the act of plagiarism, arguing on the one hand that common experiences inevitably give rise to similar texts, that is, that it is unintentional, and on the other hand, that Beyala only borrowed seven passages from *Quand j'avais cinq ans, je m'ai tué*, and that she had "sagement" reduced them to two. By my own count, Beyala took passages from *fifty* pages of Buten's novel, and although some of the passages were brief, some continued for pages at a time. It is hard to see how anyone could have looked into the case, and then concluded that Beyala's only fault was to have responded too precipitately in accusing her opponents of racism and misogyny, or of being politicized in their charges—"left-wing journalists."

Jacques Chevrier quotes Barthes to the effect that "a text is composed of multiple citations arising differentially from multiple sources." But Barthes claims such quotations function as "dialogue, en parodie, en contestation" (quoted in Mataillet, *Jeune Afrique*) [dialogue, as parody, as struggle]. To a certain extent, it is impossible to have a dialogue when one of the partners is hidden; impossible to parody a text whose identity is not only hidden, but presented as one's own, as being part of one's own text instead of being set off by parody.

Chevrier turns to a Bahktinian image of language, and claims: "Dans ces conditions, tout livre renvoie nécessairement à d'autres livres et, telle une rivière, toute création littéraire possède obligatoirement une double orientation, d'un part vers l'amont d'où elle puise ses sources, d'autre part en aval dans l'accomplissement de son dire" (quoted in Mataillet, *Jeune Afrique* 76) [In these conditions, every book refers necessarily to other books and, like a stream, every literary creation necessarily has a double perspective, on the one hand looking toward the sources, and on the other hand downstream in the fulfillment of its expression.]. Chevrier goes on to claim that African literature is especially given to the "heterogeneity" indicated by Barthes's observations, and that "francophonie" is marked by the space of multiple identities. Chevrier notes the previous attacks on African authors like Ouologuem, Camara Laye, and others, and concludes that the attacks on Beyala belong to the past when the author and his work were considered sacred; that now, the author and her work must be demystified, following Philippe Soller's argument that the text belongs to everyone, to no one, but can only be "l'indice d'une productivité qui comporte aussi son effacement, son annulation" (77) [the index of a productivity that also includes its erasure, its annulment].

These arguments are all true, and false. They ignore the element of theft, that is, of the deliberate hiding of the quotation marks. That doesn't change the fact of intertextuality, but creates another usage besides those indicated by Barthes, and that is recourse to practices outside the law, outlaw quoting. Everything Chevrier and Péju say functions to deny this practice, to understate Beyala's actions, as though she did not plagiarize or the plagiarism were not significant, or that everyone plagiarizes—that plagiarism is not really wrong. The subversive defense, then, is defused, is tossed out, in a typical pseudo-intellectual fashion that functions so as to turn the subversive act into a subversion on one plane—that of letters—while converting it into a nonsubversive act on another, that of social life.

Unfortunately, this is the defense Beyala herself took, in a sense mimicking the very defusion of *Burt's* subversive qualities into innocuous words and acts. Two more quotes from the *Jeune Afrique* issue speak directly to this issue, an issue that we need to view in terms of the Beyala public personality, the figure of Beyala—the virtual, media presence we can acknowledge by restoring the hidden quotation marks and by referring to her as "Beyala." For Aminata Sow Fall, "Beyala" is the victim of the troubling climate in contemporary French society; as she pointedly puts it, "Quand Yambo Ouologuem a été accusé de plagiat, personne n'a fait un tel battage" [When Yambo Ouologuem was accused of plagiarism, no one made such a fuss over it]. Discreet in her discourse, Sow Fall states, "Pour ce qui est du comportement de Calixthe Beyala, chacun choisit sa manière d'être. Mais, à livrer le moindre de ses faits et gestes aux médias, on prend des risques" (quoted in Mataillet, *Jeune Afrique* 71) [As far as Calixthe Beyala's behavior is concerned, everyone chooses their own way of behaving. But, to expose her smallest acts and gestures to the media is to take risks.].

Most pertinently, Caya Makhélé also addresses the issue of mediazation:

> Elle a bâti sa réputation sur la provocation, avec un discours radical porté par une écriture travaillée, poétique et efficace. Elle est la réussite littéraire africaine la plus médiatisée de ces derniers 10 années. On l'invite à parler aussi bien de politique que de cuisine

et de dessous féminine. *Elle conforte une certaine idée de l'Afrique tout en déplaçant cette même idée vers une révolte qui peut paraître convenue. Son univers donc agence pour paraître choquer et conforter à la fois.* (Quoted in Mataillet, *Jeune Afrique* 72, my emphasis) [She built her reputation on being provocative, using a radical discourse conveyed in an intricate, poetic, efficient style of writing. Hers is the best publicized African literary success in the last ten years. She reinforces a certain idea about Africa while shifting that same idea in the direction of rebellion that can also appear reassuring. Her universe thus functions by seeming to shock and reassure at the same time.]

It seems to me that Makhélé is quite accurate in this characterization of "Beyala," that is, as one whose success, won through an oeuvre whose first novels broke new and important ground for African literature, and especially for African literature authored by women, has created a public persona whose words shock only to comfort, whose home truths are safe half-truths, functioning like public pronouncements—or pronunciamentos, as Sony Labou Tansi would have put it.

Half-truths about Africa provide the spice of what Ambroise Kom objects to in "pineapple literature" ("L'univers zombifié de Calixthe Beyala," *Notre Librairie*). Although I believe Kom is actually prudish in his displeasure with Beyala's strong language and open portrayal of sexual, or even vaguely lesbian acts, it has always been true that Beyala sought to instruct the reader, from time to time, from the position of The Subject Presumed to Know. Media success, fame, and the considerable financial success that accompany them can perhaps account for the fact that in her public defense of the charges laid against her, especially in *Lire*, Beyala assumed the posture of The Subject Presumed To Know, or, to be more specific, The African Women Presumed To Know, dispensing home truths to a sympathetic French audience, especially the *Figaro* readership, who would be certain to be impressed by her achievement in winning the Grand Prix du Roman of the Académie Française.

In her defense in the conservative *Figaro* (January 25–26, 1997: 23), Beyala begins with an image that is spiced with African flavor and intended to downplay the significance of the charges against her. She writes, "By looking for fleas on a shaven head, one winds up finding a speck of dust and taking it for a fig" (my translation). She immediately passes from the issue, so lightly dismissed, to her person, and in the course of the four columns of print constructs an image of herself that is intended to complement the striking portrait of her smiling face in the center of the article. The large headline reads, "MOI, CALIXTHE BEYALA, LA PLAGIAIRE!"

[Me, Calixthe Beyala, the Plagiarist!]. The large font "MOI," with her name heading the page, announces a major presence, whose *appearance* is written large, whose *shock* is displayed by the outraged tone and the exclamation point, "LA PLAGIAIRE!," and whose subsequent *comforting* response is built upon her construction of the kind of African that the French public will feel comfortable with—not a Genet or Ouologuem, bad boys of 1968, but the poor countrygirl (cambroussarde)/ghetto-girl-made-good, whose sanctification by the Academy is rewarded by her gratitude to the French!

The portrait she creates emerges in the following passages, a portrait that combines elements of defiance, outrage, irony, and smug self-satisfaction. Rather than reconstructing the totality of her argument, I am presenting here the elements of her discourse that constitute the self-portrait, as well as those that provide her justifications for her writing practices:

> Today I ask myself, can you be born in a slum and be completely recognized as a writer in Paris? Let's be accurate: I am neither Racine nor Molière. But myself . . . simply myself. With my female weakness, my African laughter, my anguish as a writer, my joys as a mother, my little nothings . . . .

> La cambroussarde que je suis, la pied-nu d'Africaine que je représente . . . [The countrygirl that I am; the barefoot African that I represent . . .]

> Que Monsieur Assouline veuille donc avoir l'amabilité d'éclairer la lanterne de cette pauvre Négresse venue de nulle part, déplacée, charriée, sur ce qu'est la plagiat.

> Je ne cherche pas à défendre ma peau. [Let Monsieur Assouline have the kindness to enlighten the dim wits of this poor Negress, come from nowhere, displaced, swept around, on the question of what constitutes plagiarism.
>   I'm not looking to defend my own skin.]

> Je peux vous jurer sur la tête de ma mère . . . . [I can swear to you on the head of my mother . . . .]

> J'attendais des excuses en règle de ce monsieur, je l'avoue avec perplexité (comme il se doit, même chez les sauvages . . .). [I was waiting for excuses, that were in order, I must confess with some perplexity (as is in order, even among savages . . .).]

> Un soir, alors que je regardais le ciel, y cherchant en vain des étoiles, des mots de ma grand-mère me traversèrent: "L'excuse, ma fille, est le dessert des grands hommes."
> Je fit mon deuil de ces excuses méritées, sans haine ni passion. Je ne pensais qu'à une chose: jouir paisiblement, avec mes amis, de ce prix, tout en dansant le makossa sur le rythme de Joseko Bi-bop, un chanteur africain qui nous a rendu hommage en nous dédiant un disque. [Note: It is difficult to tell whether the "nous" employed here is the royal we, indicating that Beyala has passed from the use of an ironic mask to that of the sovereign.] [One night, as I was looking at the sky, looking in vain for the stars, my grandmother's words came to me: "Excuses, my daughter, are the dessert of great men."
> I mourned the passing of these well-deserved excuses, without hate or passion. I thought of only one thing: to enjoy in peace, with my friends, this prize, while dancing the makossa to the beat of Joseko Bi-bop, an African singer who rendered homage to us in dedicating one of his records.]

> Naive je le suis et je le confesse. [Naive I am, and I confess it.]

> *Les Honneurs perdus*, que l'Académie française a eu l'amabilité de récompenser de son prestigieux prix et qui fait la fierté de tout un peuple, de tout un continent [*sic*!] [*Les Honneurs perdus*, which the Academy Française had the goodness to bestow as its most prestigious prize, and which is the source of pride of an entire people, an entire continent.]

> D'ailleurs, je ne suis qu'une pauvre femme. [However, I am only a poor woman.]

Beyala next adopts the form of a mock-testimonial:

> Je soussignée, Calixthe Beyala, reconnais avoir plagié tous les écrivains de France et de Navarre . . .
> Je reconnais plagier dès que j'écris Je, car J'appartiens forcément à un autre. [I, Calixthe Beyala, the undersigned, do admit to having plagiarized all the writers of France and Navarre . . .
> I admit to plagiarizing from the moment that I write. Because I belongs, by necessity, to an other.]
> I admit to being at once teller of tales and a reader.
> I admit my ignorance as to the meaning of the word plagiarism . . .

I appeal to his great generosity so that he might pardon me, once and for all, for being just an African, an African oh so ignorant of so many things about the Parisian world of letters, a Negress who is where she is not supposed to be.

When he pardons me for having won the Grand Prize of the Novel from the Academy Française, which brought so much joy to Africa: it's well known, we don't deserve such happiness.

Thank you again to France, which welcomed me, gave me my daily bread and a roof over the heads of my children.

Thank you again to the members of the Academy Française.

Thank you, simply, to my readers who continue to support me, despite the cabals against me. (My translation; see p. 23)

Thus Beyala puts herself into the position of speaking for all of Africa—an Africa of the bidonvilles, ignorant, country, barefooted, an Africa that is grateful to France for having provided her, and people like her, with the opportunity to raise herself to such eminent heights as those of the recipient of the Grand Prix mentioned three times in her piece, as well as the Prix Tropique (mentioned once). Thus the attacks on her were essentially attacks on all Africa, including especially those Africans whose success was the goal of France's grand edifice, la Francophonie. Her irony works not so much to distance her from these stereotypes of the African "Negress"—after all, her grandmother's traditional lore is incorporated into her defense—as to turn the mirror of prejudice against her accusers, especially Assouline,[9] whose vision of her as the scheming African turns into a reflection of a supposed racist vision of all Africa.

It is fascinating how the heart of Beyala's defense—her counterattack, actually—is the ironized and glorified self-portrait, centered on the Je which is not-Je at the same time. The irony not only erases the country bumpkin subject, it proposes the sophisticated subject of the ironist whose presence and authority are guaranteed by the two awards she repeatedly mentions in her defense, and by the full weight of the French establishment ensconced in the archaic Académie Française. Yet even there, in the construction of this "Beyala," the original figure—the palimpsest of herself—appears in the formulation she gives of herself as a writer, that is, the author as other: "Je reconnais plagier dès que j'écris Je, car Je appartiens forcément à un autre" (Beyala 1997: 23) [I admit to plagiarizing from the moment that I write. Because I belong, by necessity, to an other].

But Beyala will not adhere, in this position in the spotlight, to the earlier dicta of the abject. Certainty and denial replace otherness and indefiniteness: the border is securely locked in place as she evokes a range of familiar arguments in justification of her practice. To wit:

- African orality is transmitted from mouth to mouth, enriched each time it is taken up by the griot; thus it is the property of no one person;
- Literature is in perpetual movement, never closed, but like a stream. Here, in this passage written one month after Chevrier penned his defense of Beyala in *Jeune Afrique*, Beyala picks up the same language and imagery employed by both Péju and Chevrier. Thus, she writes, "I am neither Racine nor Molière," following Péju's reference to Racine as one who incorporates the earlier work of Euripides. And she duplicates Chevrier's figure of the "rivière" both upstream and downstream. She writes, "A text . . . [is] like a stream, it does not achieve its participation, its inscription in the Universal-Whole except by enriching itself through to its sources upstream, and by its encounters with other texts downstream" (Beyala 1997: 23; my translation, see p.23). (Her imagery here, if not a plagiarism of her own defenders, is nonetheless an unacknowledged borrowing.)

Instead of resting on this position, Beyala returns to denial, asserting that her usage of passages resembling those in Okri's text was a natural coincidence, a position she claims is validated by Juillard's and Okri's rejection of Assouline's proposals. In fact, Okri inveighed at length against Beyala in an article in *The Guardian* titled "Famished Road Feeds French Book Fever" (November 26, 1996), in which he stated, "I want people to read me, but I don't want people to steal from my work."

Beyala's response is ultimately that she did not plagiarize, but rather read and spontaneously evoked the material she had absorbed: "when I set myself at the task of writing, certain sentences engraved in my memory can spontaneously spring out of my pen" (my translation; see p. 23). She denies that a few phrases—or even ten or twenty ("let's be African," she writes, "and exaggerate") could constitute a book, and that the ensemble, created by the writer within the context of her book, refashioned the old into something different and new.

These arguments appear to be more self-serving than rigorous when measured against the array of parallel passages Assouline assembled, and the court suit which she lost. And they downplay the extent to which she went in borrowing long and multiple passages. When one looks closely at the systematic pillage of passages taken from almost fifty pages of *Quand j'avais cinq ans, je m'ai tué*, her arguments appear ludicrous.

In fact, the arguments justifying the use of previously published material seem insignificant in comparison with the strident tone and broad irony with which she positions herself as "une Négresse qui est là où elle ne doit pas être" [a Negress who is there where she is not supposed to be], a "pauvre Négresse venue de nulle part" [poor Negress come from nowhere]. On the one hand, as previously noted, the irony functions to turn the accusation of racism and sexism against her accusers, especially Assouline. But the "Je" who is writing that she is only a "pauvre Négresse venue de nulle part" remains both invisible and powerful simultaneously. Invisible, because in mocking the image putatively assigned her by her detractors, she doesn't offer any other speaking voice in its place other than that of the winner of the Grand Prix. Beyala presents herself as "moi . . . simplement." But that "moi" is framed by a headline, a large photographic portrait, and the aura of the Grand Prix winner. She is "simple" only in denial. And in that posture of denial, of parry, counterattack, and thrust, she seeks to hurl back that same castrating force of reprobation that was present in the initial charges laid against her.

Thus, in a phrase ironically parodying the passage plagiarized from *The Famished Road*, she writes, "[Assouline] est si pressé qu'il tient d'une main le cul de son pantalon, de l'autre . . . Quoi? Son scoop" (1997: 23) [{Assouline} is in such a hurry he holds the seat of his pants with one hand, and with the other . . . What? His scoop]. In the Okri passage in question, a woman grabs a man by his pants and then seizes his testicles. Beyala's version, in *Les Honneurs perdus*, follows closely Okri's wording. She writes, "Sa femme ne l'écouta pas. Elle l'attrapa par le pantalon et le traîne. Il tenta de se libérer de cette poigne de fer, qui, en plus du pantalon, agrippa ses testicules" (27) [His wife didn't listen to him. She grabbed him by his pants and dragged him. He tried to free himself from this iron grip, which, in addition to his pants, had hold of his testicules]. Okri's French translation reads, "La femme cessa de l'écouter. Quand nous passâmes devant la foule, nous vîmes qu'elle avait entrepris de le traîner en le tirant par son pantalon. Il essayait de se libérer de sa poigne de fer, qui, sous le pantalon, avait même aggripé ses parties génitales" (56) [The woman stopped listening to him. When we passed in front of the crowd, we saw that she had set about dragging him, pulling him by his pants. He tried to free himself from her iron grip, which, under the pants, had even grabbed onto his genital parts]. Beyala becomes the one who "ceased to listen" to Assouline, and in her mockery of him, grabs him by the seat of his pants with one hand, and with the other dispenses with his scoop.

Beyala attributes the violence of her imaginary to the Road—that is, to the street scene in New Bell and Belleville. In response to a question about this feature in her work, in the December 18–31, 1996 *Jeune Afrique* interview, she writes:

> Je n'ai pas un discours violent. J'ai un discours inattendu. Je suis née à contre-courant. J'ai fait l'école de la rue, dans les bidonvilles de Douala. J'ai vécue à Belleville, à Paris. Cela me sert de colonne vertébrale. Tout ce que j'écris part de mes expériences personnelles. . . . Et ma langue, c'est celle de Douala. Je ne parle pas un français de Paris. . . . Je viens de la rue et je n'ai pas quitté la rue." (76)[10] [I don't use violent speech. I employ an unaccustomed speech. I was born going against the tide. My schooling was in the streets, in the slums of Douala. I lived in Belleville, in Paris. That served to give me a spinal cord. Everything I write comes out of my personal experiences. . . . And my speech is that of Douala. I don't speak Parisian French. . . . I come from the street and I have not left the street.]

The imaginary with which the family structure is constructed in Beyala's first three novels always involves a father who is weak, absent, killed off, and so on, while the mother remains to raise the children—usually girls. This figure of the absent father is joined to that of an abusive father (Tanga is raped by her father when she is a girl), and more generally to the abusive male figures who inform much of Beyala's first three novels. The plagiarized passage taken from Okri's work figures in this fictional imaginary, in which the central and minor characters are often portrayed as helpless, as being in the grip of a malevolent force that sweeps them along the dusty roads of their lives, battering them, if not literally castrating them.

The figure of the abused woman seeking revenge is a less common one, although she appears in Bessie Head's fiction, especially in the story "The Collector of Treasures," where one finds the most violent depiction of revenge as castration. Dikeledi, the abused wife seeking to preserve her independence, and rejecting the return of her abusive husband, refuses to "listen" to him when he informs her of his plans. She waits till he sleeps, and then enters the hut: "She re-entered the hut and closed the door. Then she bent down and reached for the knife under the bed which she had merely concealed with a cloth. With the precision and skill of her hard-working hands, she grasped hold of his genitals and cut them off with one stroke. In doing so, she slit the main artery which ran on the inside of the groin. A massive spurt of blood arched its way across the bed" (103).[11]

Beyala uses the image of castration in her defense of her right to speak. This claim is so powerful that it supplied D'Almeida with the title of her study of African women's literature—"Destroying the Emptiness of Silence," taken from *Tu t'appelleras Tanga*—and it is a refrain that runs through much of the feminist criticism of African women's literature. We can view the imagery of silencing, and the sequelae in the above passages dealing with symbolic or actual castrastions, as a central trope in African feminist literature and criticism. To understand that trope, we must give some consideration to the central issue of castration for a psychoanalytic reading, which will then provide us with an approach to *Le Petit Prince de Belleville*.

Castration and the Phallus: Freud/Lacan

Lacan's position on castration is derived from Freud, and it is central to the main tenets of his thought.[12] Elizabeth Grosz gives a succinct summary of Lacan's position when indicating how a group of feminists, whom she calls "the dutiful daughters"—including Julia Kristeva, Juliet Mitchell, Jacqueline Rose, Monique Plaza, Cathérine Clément, and E. Ragland-Sullivan—share Lacan's basic assumptions:

> Each claims that the Father's Law or the oedipal interdict is one of the necessary conditions for the existence of the social, in whatever form it may take. Each affirms that the child must be definitively separated from its immediate, maternal dependencies, which threaten it with suffocation or annihilation and the loss of an independant position or place in the social. And each affirms that, because of his purely cultural or signifying role in paternity, the father (or the Father's name) is ideally placed to perform this operation. (184)

The "separation" of the child from its "maternal dependency," what I have earlier referred to as the splitting of the child-(m)other dyad in the mirror phase, or what Kristeva calls the "thetic break," is brought about by the fear of castration, the "castration complex." Grosz's summary is categoric on this point: "Only with castration and the oedipus complex is the subject's definitive separation from the immediacy of its lived experience secured: it is now able to designate and replace its experiences with representations. If the mirror stage initiates the field of signifiers, marked by pure difference, the castration complex generates signs, which organize and render these signifiers meaningful" (45). And Kristeva confirms this interpretation with her claim that "[c]astration puts the finishing touches on the process of separation that posits the subject as signifiable, which is to say, separate, always confronted by an other: *images* in the mirror (signified) and semiotic process (signifier)" (1984: 47).

In negative terms, without the threat and fear of castration, the child does not separate itself from its maternal dependency, will not successfully complete the process of substituting sign for object, of distinguishing self from other, of bringing signifier and signified into those sets of relations, exchanges, and substitutions by which the semiotic, the symbolic, the signifying system itself, functions. In its most radical form, the failure to effect the break through castration will leave the child without the ability to distinguish its imaginary from the real, creating the conditions for psychosis. Put more mildly, the ineffective intervention of the threat of castration—due to the weakened presence of the Law of the Father, would negatively impact the child's introjection of the Name of the Father, the basic condition needed for the signifying process to be established. And as a result, the symbolic order, and its accompanying social order, will have less of a hold on the child's mental operations. In short, the "social construction of subjectivity" (142), along with a "stable identity" and a "determinate sexuality" (142), depends upon the successful imposition of the castration complex. On the register of language, accepting the authority of the Name of the Father and his phallic status "is the precondition of the child's having a place in the socio-symbolic order, a name, and a speaking position" (142).

The emphasis on castration and its meaning for Freud, Lacan, and Kristeva does not appear to be exactly the same: Freud links it directly to the Oedipus complex and its resolution, emphasizing its strength in creating the mechanism of repression, and its ultimate role in enabling the child to formulate a proper superego. For Freud the balance between superego, ego, and id needs to be in an appropriate equilibrium, or else neurosis or hysteria will develop. And as he saw his age as one in which the powerful figure of the father lent strength to the mechanisms of repression, he was particularly concerned about overly strict mechanisms of repression that would give rise to neurosis. For Lacan, and especially Kristeva, the modern period posed the opposite threats: the fragmentation of the family, the absence of the father, the increased rates of divorce—"the deficiencies in the paternal function"—all signify "a crisis in the symbolic."[13] Lacan's radical opposition to the notion of an innate or innately formed ego, to the need to strengthen the ego in defense against the superego, his "anti-mimetic Oedipus" in which the analysand is enjoined *not* to identify with The Subject Presumed to Know, but with his or her desire, all attest to the *fragmentation* of the unities and identities Freud had in mind when he conceived of the positive workings of castration. More important, Lacan shifts the emphasis of the oedipus, and of castration, from the immediacy of the actual family relations experienced by the analysand to that of "language"—that is, to the acquisition of a speaking position, to the positioning of the subject within language, within the symbolic order, and thus to the use of a signifying position.

Lacan views the use of language and the important relations into which the child enters as varying according to the dominance of the imaginary or the symbolic. In general, the child's development and use of a signifying system is built upon an increasing ability to defer and to substitute. Displacement and transference are built around these abilities, as is the use of language. It would be wrong to speak of castration as entailing, for Lacan, the literal meaning of a physical action upon an actual physical body. The significance of the action in the imaginary already implies a threat that is translated into the terms of representation, that is, of language, of the signifier. And the relations impacted by the threat of castration involve a relationship with a being whose identity and position for the child are imbued with processes of projection and mirroring, and especially of desire, that also involve substitutions and deferrings.

"Desire" for Lacan is no longer to be understood as an immediate physical sensation, but as a sensation bound up in a relationship with the nurturing presence of a being finally understood to be separate, to be other: commonly a mother, though obviously better understood as the maternal other, whence (m)other. Similarly, the threat of castration does not come from the father, but from the one whose function of imposing a law of denial on the satisfaction of desire is transferred into the symbolic order as the signifier of that function, whence the Name of the Father.

Castration, for Lacan, depends upon the complex and contested notion of the phallus. For Lacan, the phallus is transformed from its status as an object to a signifier—it must be denied/deferred/transformed into a substitute object in which desire is bound up in a signifier of that desire, and ultimately, as it is introjected/internalized, transformed into the signifier that enables the process of signification to occur, the signifier that signifies the fact that signification is occurring—the signifier of signifiers. The process of introjection and transformation, of "annulment" and "raising up" the phallus to the function of signifier (Borch-Jacobsen 219) is what is meant by castration for Lacan, for only castration/annulment would be powerful enough to cause the child to internalize and repress the phallus. The imaginary phallus, an object bound up in the crosscurrents of desire as discerned in the other, must be substituted for, and the substitute phallus is that symbolic signifier.[14]

Thus, the phallus must be seen not as a penis, not as object but as signifier in a transformative process acting on human desire, a substitute for an originary object of desire perceived in the other, now transformed into a signifier. Lacan states this directly in "In the Meaning of the Phallus": "the phallus is not a fantasy, if what is understood by that is an imaginary effect. Nor is it as such an object (part, internal, good, bad, etc. . . .). It is even less the organ, penis or clitoris, which [it] symbolises. . . . [T]he phallus is a signifier" (quoted in Mitchell and Rose, 79). "[T]he phallus is not a question of a form, or of an image, or of a phantasy, but rather of a signifier, the signifier of desire" (Lacan [1968] 1975: 187). Signifier of desire, signifier of signifiers—the phallus functions to enable the displacements through which repressed desire is manifested into language. Furthermore, the child, now become subject, must deal with the issue of castration not in terms of the loss of the penis, as in the Freudian Oedipus, but in terms of the effects upon his or her sense of who he or she is at the moment the child comes to the realization that it is impossible *to be* the mother's object of desire: "The solution to the problem of castration does not arise from the dilemma to have or not to have it; the subject must first recognize that he *is* not it" (Lacan, quoted in Borch-Jacobsen 219).

Although the phallus does not refer to the penis for Lacan, it almost seems that Lacan holds to the Freudian terminology of "phallus" and "castration" out of a kind of stubbornness, as though insisting not only that his followers adhere to his thought, but that this be done in the face of a linguistic contrariness. The first "meaning" of phallus is the desire of the mother (Borch-Jacobsen 220). But desire, as seen above, is already more than drive, need, or demand, all Lacanian terms entailing differing degrees of immediate expression of biological need versus substitutions within a symbolic order. Desire requires the desiring subject to be able to defer the immediacy of a need, to be able to address another to meet that need (i.e., to be able to demand), and to be able not only to defer satisfaction literally, but to be able to defer satisfaction through displacements. If the phallus is the desire of the mother, this is first of all because the mother can already transform the immediacy of a drive or need into the substitutive action of desire, because she can perceive the object to be separate from herself as subject, because she is the focus for the satisfaction of the child's needs as well as being bound in a relationship with the father. The child seeks to be desired by the mother. What the mother desires, then, is what the child seeks to *be*, whence the notion that the child seeks to be the "phallus," precisely the thing "castration" prevents him or her from being.

But we have already seen that the phallus qua object of mother's desire, that is, qua mother's desire, is transformed into a signifier. Why *phallus* as the key term to fill this function? Here Lacan departs quite a bit from Freud. Freud needed an originary myth to justify his reading of castration, and he found this in the primal horde of male agemates who kill the dominant ruling adult male and replace him collectively, installing the prohibition against murder and incest. This reading is found to be compatible with the comparable interpretation of the Oedipus myth, a story of sons, fathers, mothers, sexual drives, and punishment. Lacan's phallus is too bound up in the relationship between subject and language, into substitutions if not sublimation, for that primal myth to suffice. Nonetheless, Lacan, like Freud and Kristeva, who also needed to perform readings on originary "historical" sequences, could not leave phallus as simply desire of the mother, or desire of the other, or object of that desire (all equivalents, and *adequate descriptors*). In an attempt to historicize the term phallus, Lacan turns to the Greek mysteries in which the phallus functioned as the insignia of the family name,[15] and as the symbol of desire. More important, as the incorporation of the phallus is the condition for the subject to pass through the mirror stage and become a full subject, by *seeing* itself in the imago, the ideal self reflected back by the gaze of the other, that is, to "see" itself as a whole, full-standing being—an *ego*—the phallus came to be seen as the signifier that denoted the ego. The ego, mistaken for a whole and unitary being and (mis)perceived as such, is taken as that which is equivalent to the posture of erection. Thus, to be the object seen as desirable in the mother's eyes, to be seen as whole, full standing, and eventually as the object of an absolute act of prohibition or denial, is to be the phallus. And as the object of the mother's desire is precisely what she cannot have—since the nature of desire is to seek to acquire what one doesn't have in order to be different from what one is—the child must learn to find another mode of being other than that provided by its mirrored relationship with that mother.

That other mode of being consists not in being the object of the mother's desire, the phallus, but in a doubled position of identification in relation to the father, that is, to the one whose Law imposed the split with the mother. The doubled position consists in the revolt against the Father's Law, the rejection of the bar to the status first established by the formative ego in the mirror stage; and in the identification with the Father as the figure of authority, Law, whose relationship to be the object of desire of the other consists not in *being* it but in *having* it. Thus, the effect of castration first is to effect the child's split from the image of itself as being the object of the mother's desire, and next to resolve the relationship with the father, which involves the question of having the phallus. "The solution to the problem of castration does not arise from the dilemma to have or not to have [the phallus]; the subject must first recognize that he *is* not it" (Borch-Jacobsen 219).

Once the child has come to this realization, he or she will cease to identify with the imaginary phallus, the object of the mother's desire, just as the mother too, integrated into the symbolic with its Law, must transfer/displace/sublimate the object of her desire into the signifier of that desire. The mother must substitute the symbolic phallus for the imaginary, a process of displacement that the child must also accomplish.

At this point, according to Lacan, the child enters into the classical Freudian rivalry with the father, and interprets castration as a "real privation: the father is the one who *has* the phallus, since he violently deprives the mother (and hence also the child) of it" (Borch-Jacobsen 221). As Borch-Jacobsen explains it, at this point the child is not seeking to have the mother, as in the classical Freudian Oedipus, but to *be* the maternal phallus, "in his capacity as ego." But "being" the maternal phallus, the mother's object of desire, is no longer simply possible with the presence of the father, who himself apparently, and increasingly evidently in the growing child's eyes, enjoys the "possession" of the mother's desire.

For Lacan, the rivalry the boy experiences at this point will naturally exceed that of the girl, as she can more easily resolve the situation by acceding to the pattern that will restore the object of desire to her either in the form of becoming the desired object (the one to receive it, passively, from he who has it), or to acquire it through her own body. Her access to "symbolic castration" is facilitated by the societal roles she can expect to be able to play as a woman. The boy, in rivalry with the father, must also identify with him in order to "have" the phallus.

The third phase for the boy will bring a resolution to this situation. He realizes that the father enjoys possession of the phallus by virtue of his social authority, but he lacks the position of authority from which the effect of Law can be articulated, and so the boy must come to accept the father's possession of the symbolic phallus. The imaginary phallus, so much more closely bound to objects identified with the site of desire, must be rejected, and in its place substituted the symbolic phallus, "the signifier of [the mother's] desire, the substitute for the x that she desires (in which she desires herself) 'beyond him' " (220). This symbolic phallus will not be something the boy will be, but, as with the father with whom he comes to identify, something he will come to possess and to give. The *object* is gone, and the signifier takes its place: the Other, as the father's place is deemed to be, replaces the phallus: the Name of the Father is assumed. But as one cannot identify with a signifier, since a signifier is precisely *not* an object for which it is the stand-in, his relationship to the mother's desire is not to become its object, but to stand in the place of that which signifies the mother's desire, and that is the place occupied by the Name of the Father.

What is it that enables the boy, or we should say here the child, since the process is similar in the case of both genders, to effect this break from the rivalry for the maternal phallus? Phrased differently, what compulsion would be strong enough to break the powerful dyadic bond between mother and child? For Freud it is castration, understood as fear of loss. It seems to me that all children experience this in relation to the mother as part of the process of weaning, first on a physical level, and eventually on the levels of the imaginary and the symbolic. But as Freud insists on directing this threat of loss to the genitals, he gives primacy to a mythos based on size, the absence or presence of the penis, on the viewing of adults' genitals, and the expected set of reactions involving inadequacy, fear, and envy. In other words, Freud polarizes the reactions in terms of radical gender difference, and in so doing imposes a priority on the physical over the symbolic. Lacan stubbornly holds on to this pattern, *despite* his insistence that phallus doesn't equal penis (but rather is the mother's object of desire), and that the fear of castration and the phases of the oedipus are *all* grounded in a relationship between the subject and the other that involve maneuvering desire through the shoals of prohibition and permission.

The most astonishing reading the Lacanian approach gives rise to involves the key question of how the child ends the rivalry with the father and comes to occupy a position that will not bring a total end to the "agency of the phallus as the object *desired* by the mother" (Lacan, quoted in Borch-Jacobsen 223). The classical Freudian Oedipus has the resolution lie in the child's decision to identify with the father who possesses the symbolic phallus. The boy-child, afraid of losing *his own penis*, his own basis for enjoying the mother's desire, accepts the role of substitutions by identifying with the father, so as eventually, as one in that position, to win the rights to the desire of the other. But though Lacan does not leave the resolution to the child alone, and moves in a direction less grounded in male anatomy, the resolution calls for a split and an identification that is gender specific. As in a weaning, it is the *mother*, he claims, who must effect the child's separation, must give the child the understanding that in place of being the object of the mother's desire, her "phallic double," the boy must acquire possession of the symbolic phallus by giving up the rivalry with the father and become reconciled to an identification with the father. The boy is presented with this solution as the natural outcome, while the girl will have a different path to follow. For Lacan, she does not have to make the identification with the father since, lacking a real penis, "her access to symbolic castration, which enjoins her not to be the imaginary phallus, [is made] almost natural" (Borch-Jacobsen 222). Here the Freudian, Lacanian, and Kristevan classic position is least acceptable, as they argue that the girl, experiencing the split, the effects of castration, less acutely than the boy will thereby enter less completely into the symbolic. Borch-Jacobsen calls Lacan to task on this point: "[T]he fact of not having a real penis makes her access to symbolic castration, which enjoins her not to be the imaginary phallus, almost natural. (This solution may actually be found to be a little too 'simple,' even from Lacan's point of view, for isn't this a surreptitious resurgence of the reference to the *reality* of the difference between the sexes, to the reality of the 'hole' that the girl hastens to fill through an imaginary identification with the phallus?)" (222).

For boy and girl, the key role of generating the split is performed by the mother. The mother must come to this position, and to convey it to the child, and this Borch-Jacobsen terms the castration of the mother! "The pivotal moment of the Oedipus is not, as in Freud, the threat of castration by the rival father; it is the castration of the mother insofar as she recognized it symbolically: 'I do not have (the right to have) the phallus, and therefore you cannot be it, unless you yourself become a father, by receiving/giving in your turn the symbolic phallus that you are not" (Borch-Jacobsen 223). Why "the symbolic phallus that you are not"? Because the signifier consists precisely in not being, but representing, as in a substitution.

If the girl does not "become a father," she is no less obliged to give up the imaginary maternal phallus, to accept symbolic castration. The path seems more tortured for her; the use of "phallus" for "object of desire" all the more difficult to sustain. But the pattern in all cases leads to splitting and identifications that are marked by the processes of displacement and substitution.

But this is what desire itself entails: the acceptance of the notion of the substitution of the originally desired object by another, one that stands in place of the original. Desire is grounded in the notion that one seeks to become what one is not, to fill the lack-in-being experienced as having-a-desire, as wanting something outside of oneself needed to change the present state one finds oneself in. This is the position to which the child accedes in completing the passage through the Lacanian oedipus—for the boy, rivalry with the father is conflated with arriving at an identification with the father, or more precisely, with the one who possesses the phallus; for the girl, to identify with the mother whom she comes to recognize not as the one who has, but who is, the phallus. The relationship to the phallus shifts from that of one seeking possession of an object, to *one of being* a possession, to being, to identifying; thus, according to Borch-Jacobsen, we can consider the phallus at this point as being "the signifier of the subject, insofar as the subject identifies himself in it ('represents his identity' in it) under erasure, in the mode of a forbidden, barred, repressed identification: the subject is the phallus insofar as he is not it, insofar as he 'metaphorizes' himself in it and defers his own identity in it" (Borch-Jacobsen 224).

The language of castration and the concept of the phallus as penis disappear in the ontological notion of being under erasure, bringing us closer to Jean-Paul Sartre's notion of being as a condition torn between the competing exigencies of the for-itself and the in-itself. Lacan's formulation reshapes entirely the way we respond to the Freudian Oedipus because the approach taken to signifying systems as grounded in substitution and difference, and not in transcendental being, not in unitary identity, carries through to both the philosophical and the psychological understandings of being. Borch-Jacobsen brings this together under the heading of Kojève's influence upon Lacan:

> [M]an is what he is (a desiring subject, and ek-static transcendence) only by not being what he is (a transcendent object, a given identity). If the phallus, in Lacan, is posed as the universal "object" of desire, this is because it eminently embodies the identical-and-objective-being of the imaginary ego—that is, what the human subject, if he wishes to live up to his vocation, must perpetually negate, overcome, transcend, and desire. In it, the subject desires himself as the object he is not, as the non-object he *has to be*. (Borch-Jacobsen 225)

Thus formulated in terms of a subject that must accede to a position entailing negation, overcoming, transcendence, and desire, it would seem to be altogether possible to conceive of this process without accepting

Lacan's insistence on the language of the classical Freudian Oedipus, the language of phallus as penis and castration as physical threat, but rather to employ phallus as "desire of the other" and castration as "threat of loss." This is not to deny the role of gender in this problematic, but rather to take it out of the specific cultural and historical matrix upon which a late nineteenth century Viennese, or indeed a modern European society, is inscribed, and to leave room for the relatively different modalities of various African or African-European societies to be brought into play.

This insistence on the retreat from the language of the classical Oedipus should not be seen as an attempt to soften Freud/Lacan's position or to make Lacan more palatable to his feminist critics.[16] Rather, it would seem to be compatible with the basic assumptions upon which Lacan's revision of Freud is based. To begin, the Lacanian transference of emphasis from the real to the symbolic passes through language, through his rereading of Saussurian linguistics for which difference provides the basis for the signifying chain. But the play of difference—of what something is and is not perceived to be—is grounded in culture. Where one culture sees differences, say in the gradations of race in the historical Caribbean societies, and thus assigns a multitude of names for people who range from "black" to "white," the contemporary American society sees only one difference, black and white. "Black" in England is "white" in the United States, in the case of people from the Indian subcontinent, and so on. As language is not universal, but culturally relative, so are subject positions constituted by language—a concept fundamental to Lacan: "[Language] signifies, not because it expresses thoughts or pictures reality, but because it constitutes subjects as historically and geographically, culturally specific beings" (Grosz 99).

Thus we are not surprised that the phallus functions as a symbol across different cultures and in different time periods in a radically variable manner, as we have seen in the Greek representations that so influenced Lacan in his choice of phallus as symbol for the object of desire. Clearly the "family insignia" in ancient Greece signified differently from those of medieval Europe or Japan. Its functioning in the positioning of gender, or as a "location within a hierarchized social geography" (Grosz 121), can only cut across cultures if it is transformed/substituted as signifier. It can become signifier of signifiers, freed from the signified, freed from the penis, only if the cultural specificity, along with the physical reality of the object, is annulled and replaced by the signifier.

Phrased differently, if the fetishist transfers the object of the original desire onto a shoe, it will not matter what form or material constitutes the shoe—all that will matter, in the economy of the libido, will be its function as object of desire. This is the basis of Grosz's critique of Lacan: "The Law of the Father cannot be the universal condition of culture: it remains the form of specific cultures. Without this historical qualification, Lacan's work has the same air of inevitability as biologistic accounts" (145).[17] Arrogant though Lacan may have been, in the final analysis his work was dedicated to subverting the authoritative position of The Subject Presumed to Know, the analyst with whose position the analysand was supposed to identify. Not identity, stated Lacan, but desire was to be the goal of the analysand—the embrace of a desire that would not enable the subject to be constituted as an identity, an ego, but precisely the opposite—a nonbeing.[18]

Kristeva and Irigaray: To Disrupt the Symbolic or Not

Julia Kristeva and Luce Irigaray, whom Grosz dubs respectively dutiful daughter and rebellious daughter, both also focus their attention on the mechanism of castration. For both, the role of the mother is of considerable importance, although their approaches to the maternal role differ. For Kristeva, the maternal can be accorded a space she designates as the *chora*, a pre-imaginary space in which the pre-oedipal drives and their articulations can circulate. Those drives are named the semiotic by Kristeva, and they constitute a substratum of human psychical processes continuing to exist throughout life. It is this presymbolic set of drives and articulations that Kristeva designates as feminine, and the space within which the drives circulate as the *maternal* chora. It is also to the mother that the demands originating in these drives are made, and it is she who becomes the object of the desires thus generated. She becomes thus the phallus: "As the addressee of every demand, the mother occupies the place of alterity. Her replete body, the receptor and guarantor of demands, takes the place of all narcissistic, hency imaginary, effects and gratifications; she is, in other words, the phallus" (Kristeva 1984: 47).

Now it is precisely castration that separates the child from "too close an identification with the image of the (phallic) mother" (Grosz 156), thus enabling the child to enter into the symbolic. Kristeva follows Lacan closely in this interpretation of castration, but unlike Lacan she places an emphasis on the positive, creative qualities of the maternal semiotic, which often breaks through the constricting, unifying, totalizing pressures of the symbolic. The effects of the semiotic are sometimes dubbed "irruptions," irruptions in the symbolic, disruptions in the social, rational order we have come to associate with the avant-garde, in harmony with the entire spirit of modernism—from T.S. Eliot's anesthetized patient to Samuel Beckett's absurdist clowns. Grosz indicates Kristeva's formulation for the spirit of disruption as appearing in the guise of "madness, holiness, and poetry," all effects of "transgressive breaches of symbolic coherence" (153).

We have seen to what degree Beyala relied upon the sense of transgression in *Tu t'appelleras Tanga*, and indeed in the composition of her first three novels. However, the effects of the transgressive, like modernism itself, cannot remain permanently disruptive. Eventually, as the example of T.S. Eliot demonstrates, the shock value is translated into its opposite, the normative standard by which *all* value is measured, as it becomes the new symbolic order. We can note this in Grosz's description of Kristeva *and* Irigaray's positions, positions we now associate with the new dominant, postmodernism: "Both Kristeva and Irigaray affirm a polyvocality and multiplicity lying dormant within prevailing representational systems—an uncontrolled, excessive textual force or energy" (173). Kristeva would have seen how these terms, originally invested with transgressive force, would have been recuperated and eventually turned into substitutes for disruptive political practice: "In reconverting the semiotic back into a new symbolic, its energy is dissipated in the conservation and stabilization of the symbolic" (Grosz 165).

At its extreme, when transgression becomes style alone, strengthening the line between the imaginary and the symbolic, or, in Kristeva's terms, the semiotic and the symbolic, the result can be a rigidified and reinforced symbolic order that denies all plurivocality within the political realm. This is clearly the case with "Beyala," whose anchoring of her defense in the institution of the Académie Française establishes a clear *political* demarcation between those African institutions she critiques and the French establishment whose neocolonialist policies in Africa, and especially in Cameroon and Senegal, her fictional settings in Africa, have been dominant. Thus, for Kristeva, if the avant-garde is threatened on the one side with total effacement of the lines/posts around the symbolic, that is, with psychosis, it is threatened on the other with authoritarian politics, the opposite extreme, fascism "in which the disruptive semiotic processes are rechanneled into both a (narcissistic) love relation with the charismatic leader, and to a rigidified body organization hierarchized in even tighter form through this identification" (Grosz 165).

It is not quite the case that Beyala has passed to this opposite extreme, although the term "narcissistic love relation" tied to a "rigidified body organization" might not seem too inappropriate. Ironically, it is precisely the disruptive features of *Burt* that are toned down in *Le Petit Prince de Belleville*, disruption against an order primarily identified with the psychiatric institutions that emprisoned, misunderstood, mistreated, and imposed themselves upon Gil. In *Le Petit Prince de Belleville*, we don't have such institutions in the front rank, although they do play a number of secondary roles.

If we were to chart Beyala's changes from *C'est le soleil qui m'a brûlée*, *Tu t'appelleras Tanga*, and *Seul le diable le savait* to *Le Petit Prince de Belleville*, using Kristeva's formulations, we would look to the daughter's revolt in each of the first three novels in terms of an attack upon the symbolic as constructed in terms of the subject and the text. For Kristeva, the symbolic affords a "stability which insures a cohesive, unified speaking subject and a coherent, meaningful text" (Grosz 152). The symbolic could be seen in the order the mother attempted to impose on her daughter by invoking the force of the community's approval or disapproval of the actions, almost always entailing the mothers' attempts to control and regulate their daughters' sexual behavior. The daughters' revolt would be seen in terms of the semiotic and its chaotic irruptions into her life, her dreams and thoughts, her text, one of "madness, holiness, and poetry."

For Irigaray, however, the focus would be less on the symbolic as a regulatory agency imposing unity and coherence than on its gendered nature imposing an oppressive order on women. The dominant symbolic order for Irigaray is patriarchal, and although Kristeva and especially Lacan would not disagree with that, neither of them could foresee a revolt that dispensed with that patriarchy without destroying the mental stability of the subject and inducing psychosis. Where Kristeva calls for an avantgarde, Irigaray calls for a new woman, a new textuality to be inscribed in society as in writing, a new "écriture féminine" that would reject the repressions entailed in the functioning of "maternity under patriarchy"—an unacceptable condition that "curtails the mother's possibilities of expression, [and] 'exiles' the daughter from her origins and her potential development as a woman" (Grosz 182). Thus, "plurality" and "alterity" become gendered attributes to be claimed in opposition to patriarchy's "monosexual model" (Grosz 173).

The pattern of mother-daughter relations, which Freudian, Lacanian, and Kristevan analyses describe in terms of a dyadic closeness requiring castration, imposes a set of restrictions on the possibilities of the mother-daughter relationship, identified by Irigaray as what "patriarchy requires of women" (Grosz 182). For Irigaray, "psychoanalysis does not allow a space for restructuring or reconceptualizing female relations, or reinventing a body-to-body and woman-to-woman relation with the mother" (Grosz 182). To the argument that even here, Irigaray is too confining in ignoring class or race as equally important regions of the dominant symbolic, Irigaray would respond that race and class, no less than gender, are structured by the dominant symbolic order, and that each bears the marks of a patriarchy that serves the interest of the same dominant male establishment. In advancing this argument, Irigaray approaches Kristeva's position with respect to the symbolic, even if their relation to Lacan is at variance:

> For Kristeva, power relations are explained in terms of degrees of adherence to symbolic norms. The symbolic is the "system" against which semiotic subversions are directed. As the unities comprising the state and its various instrumentalities, signifying practices and their norms, and subjectivity integrated under the illusory mastery of the ego, the conception of power she utilizes is a globalized, integrated totality. *The oppression of women and the structure of patriarchy is* [sic] *merely one long form of oppressions* [sic]—*class, race, religious—all of which are equally effects of the symbolic structure.* (Grosz 168; my emphasis)

And for Kristeva, the disruptive effects of the avant-garde have effects upon the entire symbolic order, regardless of the identity of the author or his or her intentions.

Le Petit Prince de Belleville: The Son's Revolt

Le Petit Prince de Belleville is marked by a number of nodes of disruption, but interestingly enough *none* of them involves a daughter in revolt against her mother. The earlier pattern of the devouring mother and rebellious daughter is gone, and in its place are a series of voids, "gouffres" that function like desire—testimonies of beings always in quest of what Lacan would term the phallus, always to suffer disappointment, the aftertaste of castration.

In Beyala's previous three novels, the subversion was not playful: it wore the brutalized face of abjection, where abuse and repulsion marked many of the characters and the landscape. The novels were set in Africa—the first two in a popular poor quartier, ostensibly New Bell in Douala, and the third in a village—but they were not written so as to immerse the reader in an African ambiance: there is no great feeling of getting to know the "real Africa" in all its sights and smells in any of the novels, any more than one could find this in Ben Okri's fiction. The action takes us to the characters' feelings, reactions, and close relations, and not to the social institutions, barely evoking the actualities of an urban or rural environment.

Le Petit Prince de Belleville represents a major change. Like Ben Okri and Buchi Emecheta, Beyala had come to Europe at an early age—seventeen in her case. By the time *Le Petit Prince de Belleville* appeared, she had been out of Africa for fourteen years (1978–92), and was ready to set her work among the African exile community of Belleville, the popular quartier of Paris. For the first time, the novel's protagonist is not a young woman—not an autobiographical subject in any sense—but a ten-year-old boy, Loukoum, a kind of sweet but street-smart kid whose function in the novel is a split one. On the one hand, he is the narrator of an autodiegetic text, and more specifically provides us with the narrative eye that sees the action while only marginally or not at all involved. He conveys to us the child's views of the adults' actions, thus giving the novel something of its shock value when sex or painful emotional issues between adults are raised. On the other hand, he also has his own story, his own interactions with other children, with little or no interaction with adults.

The miserabilism of the first three novels, and especially the bitter notes of protest against male abuse, are largely attenuated, although still present, especially in the case of Loukoum's two "mothers," M'am and Soumana. In its place, there is a much lighter tone, matching the ironic, demystifying gaze of the naive—a familiar technique in which the outsider's view of social norms affords a social critique. *Le Petit Prince de Belleville* also presents us with a wider range of white characters in a variety of roles and relationships, from white prostitutes to Loukoum's best friend, his girlfriend Lolita, the social worker/feminist Madame Saddock, and his teacher Madame Garnier. Belleville is depicted as having a mixed and hybrid culture, just as its inhabitants are often shown to be long-standing residents or citizens of France, or even second generation French. The African homeland is often evoked, especially in the monologues of Abdou, Loukoum's father—but mostly as a nostalgic memory. The world of Loukoum is circumscribed by his family's apartment, his school, the local café, and Monsieur Guillaume. Most significantly, he expresses himself in the idiom of the kids of his quartier, Belleville, the poor African and Arabic neighborhood in Paris's Nineteenth Arrondissement.

Beyala splits the narrative of *Le Petit Prince de Belleville* into two parts, the father's and the son's. The portions of the text written by Abdou, the father, head the chapters, and are italicized and presented as interior monologues. Loukoum, the eponymous hero, functions frequently as a witness to the novel's action, and is thus as "exterior" to the narrative as his father in his monologues is "interior," except for those sequences where Loukoum as the principal actor, gives us a conventional first person narrative.

The style of the two narratives is radically different as well. Whereas Loukoum's narrative understandably resembles Gil's in *Burt*, Abdou's entries are all highly poeticized, abstract, and often polemical. He places himself at the center of his polemics, and at his own center lies the "gouffre," the rupture that encompasses his *mal de pays*, his longing for his homeland, his wives, and Loukoum, his son. He is the patriarch. But he is also the exile, the immigrant, the poor African street sweeper on the bottom of the French hierarchy. He is thus seated between two worlds, one that he reconstructs in his memory and imagination, and that he tries to use to fill the second in which he lives, a patriarch in decline ruling over a lost realm.

To hear Abdou's story as he recounts it in his series of monologues, he is the victim: his son is taken out of his care and placed in school where French education supplants his Malian, Qur'anic schooling and upbringing; his wives change from docile housewives to independent and assertive women; the prestige attached to his culture, religion, race, and language is lost, and in its place is its opposite, the generalized scorn held by the French. He suffers from "the poison of exile," and to hear him articulate his uneasiness in his opening monologues with such eloquence and poetry is to experience great sympathy for him: "Thus, bit by bit, others come to disturb us. To lend out my son to authorities other than my own—to men and women whom I do not know but who, they say, are qualified to teach. And so the child escapes my control" (my translation; see Beyala 1992: 5).[19] Then Abdou turns his regard on himself. The image he constructs is pensive, meditative, sensitive, and anguished. And most of all, it is turned inward, as in a mirror gaze that returns us to the specular image of a lost soul:

> I no longer recognize visible mirrors.
> Each new day nourishes my haggard eyes.
> Other words are formed against my own.
> The jargon of generations of those who possess knowledge, science.
> And my soul? Oh well, my soul clings to impossible voyages.
> At odds with myself because of exile's poison.

I belong so little to this world that I prefer to surrender. (My translation; see p. 5)

Abdou signs this missive "Abdou Traoré, père vénéré" of Loukoum, as though he were an elder weighed down by the knowledge of tradition, the burden of his years, and his proximity to death. Practically an ancestor—the "père vénéré."

However, as we get to know Abdou better, we see another portrait: not that of an old, but a middle-aged man. Not a grandfather, but a father whose oldest son is apparently the ten-year-old Loukoum. Not so distant from French language and customs that he cannot express his complaint with eloquence; that he cannot take advantage of the social security system by claiming false "allocations familiales" for children born to him out of wedlock; that he is not attracted to women who dress in an erotic, European fashion; that he cannot drink alcoholic beverages in cafés. In short, when Abdou turns gay blade, he is completely different from the one whose portrait he paints for himself and for us in his monologues. He is literally "méconnaissable."

This different Abdou appears in an almost miraculous transformation when Mlle. Esther displays her wares. "It's my Papa. Dressed to kill. Pink jacket. White shirt. Big beige hat. And beige raincoat casually draped over his shoulder" (my translation; see p.63). Mlle. Esther and Loukoum are both astonished at the sight of him: "She can't get over it, that's obvious, and me neither. My papa looks like a young man. Sure he looks a lot older than lots of guys I know, but not like someone with two wives, four kids and a job with the Paris sanitation department. And I look at him, eyes wide with astonishment" (my translation; see pp. 63–64). As Abdou turns on the charm—"So there is my papa sweet-talkin' Miz Esther" (my translation; see p. 64)—Loukoum experiences all the frustration and rage of the full oedipus rivalry, along with the contrary obligation to accept and identify with his father: "When I hear Miz Esther laugh like that, I want to strangle him and to shove my hand into my papa's face. And I can't because it's my father" (my translation; see p. 64). This is the classical double bind that the oedipus causes: "the boy must simultaneously identify with the father (so as to have the phallus and to become masculine) and not identify with him (so as not to be his rival, so as not to be the phallus of the mother)" (Borch-Jacobsen 222).

Except for this moment, however, Abdou and Loukoum's relationship is not marked by rivalry, but by loss, and in particular the kind of loss brought on by dislocation and reinstallation, the condition of the immigrant. Abdou's lament can be viewed as that of the African forced to submit to European values, but, left unexpressed, is the larger grief of the patriarch who has been supplanted by the foreign Other, like Oyono's "boy" who may be no more than the "*chef* des boys" while also being the "boy des *chefs*." The wording of Abdou's complaint evokes a reading in which we can see the forceful apparatus of desire at work—desire in the Lacanian sense of a need constantly in search of substitute objects that, as substitutes, can never bring satisfaction, repletion, or wholeness.

> Get crackin'! Find a way! Steal! Pillage! The essential thing? Don't get nabbed. I know these words. They keep me company and keep me at a safe distance from the abyss. They give my weariness free rein and fill me with dreams. They come and go in my head like a ball in my hands. (My translation; see Beyala 1992: 19)

Abdou describes himself roaming the streets at night, insomniac, finding nothing to fill the void: "Nothing here, nobody here, only a void in the interior night where the friend is resting and who, then, will keep watch? Me. My ghosts. My land" (my translation; see p. 19). And he evokes the emptiness of Africa, "là-bas," over there, where the call of Europe in response to the expression of desire echoes back the interior void—desire's call: "Pourtant, là-bas, sur cette terre qui ne nous appartient plus, le tam-tam murmurait" (Beyala 1992: 20).

> And yet, over there in that land that's no longer ours, the drum used to murmur. Mouths would quietly voice the hope: Money, money! It is there, in that limpid country across the seas, amidst the cars, the streetlights, and the cracked walls. . . . Mouths would say: There's money, millions to be gathered, everywhere, with your hands, with your head, with your heart, with your bottom. . . . You'd have to find a way. Get crackin'! (My translation; see p. 20)

However, it is not the fleeting fortune, the millions with wings, that Abdou gathers. His "phallus," his object of desire, slips increasingly into the familiar image of the glorified woman: "But then there is woman. There she is, immense, unattainable, present and so distant. She comes in, an ocean and flames, places her lips on my soul that has passed out" (my translation; see p. 56). Abdou's reveries of the idealized woman continue, suggesting the mirrored reflection of his own *imago* of wholeness, erection, perfection: "Let me take care of it," his dream woman cries, "Let me

Plagiarism, Castration, and the Phallus 139

strengthen that tower you wanted to build and which is being crucified by your exile" (my translation; see p. 56).

Lacan's reading of this romantic love imaginary as evidence of the man's narcissism would seem to be perfectly appropriate here. "[R]omantic love relations involve . . . 'putting her on a pedestal' (the projection of the man's narcissistic self-conception) and/or a reduction to the position of a sexual object (receptacle of active masculine desire)" (Grosz 134).

Abdou would seem to have it both ways, for no sooner does he dream of this ideal woman as the "océan et flamme" than she is repositioned back into the same old familiar place: "I cling to her breast, her belly, the warm tuft of her sex, as I would a new land, a new dawn" (my translation; see Beyala 1992: 57). This dream woman, the woman in the dream who becomes Lolita, Mlle. Esther, and even for Loukoum his own mother Aminata (indeed, as she is no less idealized, in her own way, than Jessica in *Burt*), so close to the *object* of desire, or to its earlier incarnations, the *objet a* that is nothing but the plaything of sexual demand and its imaginary constructions, is now easily recognized as woman-as-image, woman, that is, without her own status as subject: "What is more clearly affirmed is not her subjectivity but her ability to be reduced to desired object, which she shares with all women in patriarchy. She is a sexual receptacle, property, object, lacking, wanting, what men have" (Grosz 134). And she is no less real for being Abdou's dream woman, no less a dream when she takes the form of Mlle. Esther, Aminata, or their earlier incarnations in Soukouma or M'am. In fact, it is precisely her continually shifting form that confirms her role as phallus, as object of desire, when seen, fantasized, courted, or loved by Abdou. Or by Loukoum, because it is this patrimony, above all, rather than the Qur'an, the "tradition" or the knowledge of the elders, that Abdou imparts to his son.

Abdou's loss of Loukoum to the French, through Loukoum's gradual adaptation to the French language and customs of schoolchildren, is inseparable from the loss involved in all the changes Abdou has to accept, his displacement as patriarch. The loss of frontiers we earlier associated with abjection here returns, like repressed desire, in the substitution of new frontiers in place of the old—the Qur'an, Allah's word, the father's place in the home, in his chair:

> "I have a son who will not continue my line
>   He has moved his borders. He has set up his world inside your world, friend, there where I cannot penetrate, for his nation, *your*

nation, friend, was made to protect itself jealously. No entrance, I can't get through any more.

Today, without any real kinship, without love and full of remorse, my world is exploding in a shower of fire inside my skull. (My translation; see p. 223)

When we turn to Abdou's "patrimony," to his heir Loukoum, we see the same pattern duplicated, not only with Loukoum's romanticizing of Lolita, and the loss she represents for him, but in the same recursive turn from image or object back to self-erected ego, the same twists and turns of desire's path, designed to fill the lack, to "remplir l'absence." Thus, toward the end, when Loukoum, like Gil, turns his "little boy" eyes to the larger world around him, he sees the same cracks, fault-lines, and gaps through which Kristeva would expect the discordant irruptions of the semiotic to become manifest. Here, in Loukoum's questioning and groping, it is mostly the more visible shape of the narcissistic subject, and even more the palimpsest of Gil, that emerges in his discourse:

> Me, I really wonder why the need for love. Why there is suffering. Why there are blacks. Why men, why women? Where do these differences come from. Where do the dead go. I realize that in spite of school, I don't know anything at all. At all. . . .
>
> I think of Lolita. I am sad. I am unhappy. Especially when I see a girl walking along and I think it's her. . . . At times, I don't want to think any more. I want her to leave me alone. To let me breathe. I am worn out. . . . I write all the time. But I am happy with my fate. If Lolita writes me, I'll be in heaven. If she doesn't write, I'll make do with my fate, between my parents, the blacks of Belleville and school. Keep your mind busy while you wait, I tell myself. That's what I have to learn about life: to fill the gap [*remplir l'absence*]. (My translation; see p. 246)

The Oedipus is structured around the necessity of the thetic break, the fear of castration that is brought to bear upon the child-mother dyad through the agency of the Other. In *Le Petit Prince de Belleville*, the paternal function that underlies the Other is continually disrupted. In Abdou's own monologues, he evokes the pain of being supplanted by the French Other, by his loss of status and feeling of emptiness. And in each relationship, a series of substitutions for the mother-child-father triad is effected whereby each of the figures in the African family reaches out to a European other across the lines of the Oedipus triangle. Loukoum has his Lolita, but also his best friend Alexis—the petit "blanc de couleur" who reaches across the white-black bar (a cross-copy of the French translation of "colored" in *Burt* given as "petit nègre de couleur" in *Quand j'avais cinq ans, je m'ai tué* (56) ["little colored Negro boy" in *Burt*]); and he has a white mentor/ego ideal, Pierre Peletier, who tutors him in French.[20] In order to understand these relationships with others, we must turn to the paternal model who constructs his own cross-cultural, unique alter ego, "l'ami."

"L'ami," Abdou's French Other, is, like Loukoum's imaginary horse "Blanco" (the copy of Gil's "Blacky"), an imaginary friend: he is ostensibly a white Frenchman who is an invisible alterego, and also a silent interlocutor whose wife enjoys the very freedom Abdou fears his own wives will seek to acquire. "L'ami" is Abdou's uncanny double—and his uncanniness is conveyed in the invisible image of Abdou that it casts back: "You, friend, you pass by and you do not see me. It's true that I don't exist. I am something that is transparent, a sheet of paper carried off by the wind" (my translation; see p. 114). Like the neologism "blanc de couleur" that Beyala employs in reaction to the "nègre de couleur" in *Quand j'avais cinq ans, je m'ai tué*, the uncanny double functions as a racial oxymoron, the white reflection of the invisible blackman, the blankness reflected back on the immigrant for whom the anguish of his own otherness opens up the gap of nothingness: "A car almost knocked me over. The driver grumbled. He raised a threatening arm. He wants to destroy this leaf that I've become and that's getting away from him" (my translation; see p. 114).

The contingency of Abdou's disarray cannot be limited to his personal psychological past alone, because the allegorical nature of his relationship with this generic Frenchman rests upon the historical foundation of France's colonization of Africa, and, to be specific, of Mali, Abdou's homeland. The misrecognition occasioned by the vision of the mirror image is heightened by the colonizers' inscription of their own imago on Africa's "blank darkness." This, too, forms part of the foundation of Abdou's anguish, as he articulates it in his address to the white other: "I really want to tell you about my country other than what you've read in books. I know that you won't believe me. All the same I'm suffering and I no longer know what to do with my anguish" (my translation; see p. 114).

The function of "l'ami," first of all, is to listen. He is the addressee of Abdou's discourses, Abdou's monologues, addressed as if to a silent Other. Thus l'ami permits us to imagine a reception and a response to Abdou's words—a dialogue. We can think of him in two ways: as a listener whose presence forms part of a dialogue, and as an analyst silently listening to the analysand. In the latter case, we could understand the bond linking him to Abdou as involving a transference, evidence of which would be seen in Abdou's projection onto l'ami. This appears in a remarkable image Abdou constructs in an effort to bridge the gulf between them: "I won't remove from your skull ten thousand years of prejudices. The pain of life separates me from you. But if you spent a single night on the path of insomnia, where your fatigue is transformed into a long dark day, then my life would come across to you" (my translation; see p. 98).

Here the need to have the Other understand, to have him changed into a comprehensive figure whose otherness is transformed into openness, into receptivity, is figured in terms of the transformation of opposites: night to day, sleep into insomnia, distance into proximity, and eventually, and most importantly, other into self. This is close to the identification to which the son must surrender in his rivalry with the father. But it is also a call to the father to change, to the Other to yield, to be able to receive the gift of the child, his life—"then my life will come across to you." For this to happen, the father as Other must be seen to relent in the absoluteness of his prohibitions, of his own ties to the maternal other. And in the course of the novel, Abdou shows himself as incapable of doing this. The signs of his resistance appear directly in his relation to the two maternal figures who still maintain a strong sexually active personality with respect to Loukoum, Mlle. Esther and Loukoum's own mother, Aminata. Both women, as we see in the scene in the park, focus their sexual attentions primarily on Abdou.

The maternal function, however, is divided and doubled: in addition to the sexually active and attractive Aminata and Mlle. Esther, there are the two maternal figures in Loukoum's life, M'am and Soumana, whose roles are more maternal than sexual, especially in their relation to the father. Soumana never comes to accept this, even up to the time she dies, whereas M'am has had to live with it for a long time. They have become mostly mothers, whose function is primarily to care for and feed their husband and children, to keep the home as a sanctuary for the family, to preserve the economy of the paternal authority within the family and society.

This is so strong a function that we are not surprised that M'am can continue in this role even after Loukoum learns that she is not his mother; nor are we surprised to learn that the husband accepts his wife as sexual partner for only a limited number of years, before consigning her to the role of mother, and not lover. In order for this rejection of the wife to occur, we would expect to find some other sign of the castration in their relation, some sign of the female as "vagina dentura." This we can see from the beginning with the appearance of the French schoolteacher, Mme. Garnier, whose authority over Loukoum is asserted against M'am. We can see it in Loukoum's distinction between his identity within French institutions, including school (la gynécologie), and at home (la civilisation): "J'm'appelle Mamadou Traoré pour la gynécologie, Loukoum pour la civilisation" (Beyala 1992: 6) [For the birth certificate, my name is Mamadou Traoré; in civilization it's Loukoum]; between his age for the French ("For official records, I'm seven") and for the Africans ("and ten seasons old for Africa") (my translation; see Beyala 6). Most of all, he is placed under the tutelage of the woman schoolteacher, called "maîtresse" in French, who establishes a new authority over him, one which functions to separate him from his role as African child and to substitute a new set of normative values for his French identity: "Mamadou, you should have told me you didn't know how to read. Didn't your parents ever tell you a little boy shouldn't lie?" His response, "To begin with, I'm not a little boy. And next, I do know how to read, Miss" (my translation; see pp. 7–8), cannot hold for long. He learns that reading Arabic is not reading, that his mother insists on putting him under the authority of the school, and that the rhythm of his life was henceforth to be marked by the hours and vacations set by school.

Thus it is not surprising to note that no sooner does Abdou appeal to l'ami to open himself up to Abdou's life than the female other to M'am and Soumana, that is, the female as authority, and thus as danger to male authority—ultimately as devouring mother—will appear. The first line of Loukoum's narrative that follows Abdou's "then my life will come across to you" is "Miss Garnier gave us the course in nat science" (my translation; see p. 98). We recall Abdou's line, in his opening monologue, "The magic of contradictory thought escapes me" (my translation; see p. 5), followed by the demonstration of "raisons contraires" (contradictory thought or reasoning) of sorts, in the teacher's disquisition on the division of animal species into opposing families—vertebrates, invertebrates; warm-blooded, cold-blooded; useful and harmful. And when the lesson concludes with the description of the hierarchy of species, with man at the top, we see Loukoum not bewildered by the pattern, but rather pleased: "As a theory it pleases me." He immediately associates the notions of division and hierarchy with his family: "I really wonder where you can categorize my family" (my translation; see p. 98).

In the end, Mlle. Garnier does not assume the role of a threatening figure. Beyala borrows heavily from *Quand j'avais cinq ans, je m'ai tué* in the construction of her character, so that in the scene that follows the natural science lesson, the visit to the zoo, she appears as rather kindly and considerate toward Loukoum, and exercises a reasonable authority over the children whose original wildness in *Quand j'avais cinq ans, je m'ai tué* is much attenuated in *Petit Prince*.

Just as the mother figures are doubled, so too are their white counterparts, and we are not surprised to find the logical extension of Mlle. Garnier carried to its ultimate limit in the person of a second young white woman, one who enters directly into the lives of Loukoum's family. It is M'am who first brings this white double into their home in the midst of the crisis Soumana is experiencing as a result of Abdou's new affair with Mlle. Esther. Soumana's state of mind can be seen in her negligence of her children, leaving M'am in the position of having to care for them. As Madame Saddock enters their apartment, her first words, reported by Loukoum, convey her role: " 'It's unacceptable,' she goes. 'Intolerable. You've got to fight! Don't count on me to do it for you.' " She is described as white, wearing a camel hair coat, and with a head full of blond hair, "which makes her look quite striking" (my translation; see p. 84). Her language—"Intolérable!" [Unacceptable]—conveys the image of the aggressive western feminist, of the type Kristeva found to be misguided and narrow-minded. Here she is all the more seen as such because her rejection of the woman-as-mother/woman-as-submissive-wife is couched in racial and cultural terms. She is "une Blanche," the white woman whose passion takes the form of the need to free the black woman from the confines of her traditional role. She is also the agent of a modernity whose project of the "modern" woman requires as its counterpoint the "traditional woman," the symbol of Africanness as tradition. Thus the accouterments of female modernity: white skin, camel hair coat, blond hair, "*remarquable.*"

Her fight cannot be carried out through M'am and Soumana, ostensibly because only the African woman can free herself. But the more fundamental reason is that she is already implicit in their function as all-giving mother, and that they already represent the threat to the independent identity of the male-child Loukoum, who does his best to stand in the place of his father in rejecting Madame Saddock. As M'am's love and Soukouma's plight make it all but impossible for Loukoum to split from them, the weaning requires a substitute, M'am and Soumana's double, Madame Saddock, who must herself help him to find another place (recall that Loukoum is given the place *next* to Mlle. Garnier on the bus—she is his "p'tit copain," another difficult position from which to make the break).

This she accomplishes with her second visit to their home—again in the absence of Abdou. Once again her entrance is prepared by Abdou's monologue. This time he is expatiating on how women compensate for his sense of exile, how they comfort and remake his soul: "They. Women. They know how to invent me. . . . I travel over their bodies that open up to my caresses and I fall asleep in the open arms of heaven. Exile moves further off." Beyala's irony against the romanticizing, philandering Abdou is at its height as she follows this discourse with Loukoum's opening line, "Madame Saddock, you only need to look at her to tell, is a first-class ballbreaker" (my translation; see p. 115). He then launches into an attack on her interference in their lives as an example of the cultural insensitivity of women whose aggression against men is a form of castration—"une casse-couilles" (ballbreaker). "What's she gotta go prophesying all that women's revolution for, which it's done a lotta good here in France, but it's a natural catastrophe for the immigrants. Say what you want, French women have suffered sexual racism. They have their reasons! But Soumana and M'am have never had to complain about sexual harassment. There's no tragedy or dead body here. So I don't quite see what Madame Saddock expects from all this" (my translation; see p. 115).

Abdou prepares the ground for Loukoum to reject Madame Saddock, not as a colonizer insensitive to African traditions, but as a woman who is sexually unsatisfied, and free—that is, as one not integrated into the patriarchy. He tells Loukoum he's Abdou's heir, that everything Abdou has will one day be his. "So listen carefully. That kind of woman is like a weed, the kind that spreads her legs for anyone. Gotta never listen to them. Never!" Such women, he blithely states, are frustrated: "Nobody, no man wants to have anything to do with them. That's why they're making all these revolutions" (my translation; see p. 88).

The echoes of Walker's *The Color Purple* are strongly felt in Beyala's construction of Soumana as victim, like Celie, as in the scene between Abdou and Soumana following Madame Saddock's first visit:

> And he turns to Soumana.
> "Give me a glass of water," he goes, real fucking calm.
> She raises her eyes and looks at him.
> At first, her face doesn't move. Her wide, flat nose stays the same. Her thick lips, too, like prunes. Only her large eyes are glittering. Like they'd love to kill a snake." (My translation; see p. 87)

As "l'héritier" of Abdou, Loukoum does not commiserate with Soumana, despite Abdou's mistreatment of her. Her complaints about Abdou to Madame Saddock fall on deaf ears, as he ironizes: "Listening to her, you'd say she's the world's worst treated woman and deserves the Nobel Prize as the most humiliated woman in the world" (my translation; see pp. 116–17). Nonetheless, Loukoum does have sympathy for Soumana, and although he rejects Madame Saddock, his rejection is played out more in cultural terms than along the phallocentric lines laid out by his father. The text vacillates. Sympathy is checked by irony, just as identification is checked by castration. The function of castration, shifted onto Madame Saddock, is overlaid with Celie's revolt in *The Color Purple*, with Gil's marginal rebelliousness and dysfunctionality in *Burt*, and with Beyala's desire to bring together a critique of western feminism as well as African patriarchy. Loukoum wants to be the heir: he rejects the notion that African women were abused. But he is also sensitive and quick, and the failures of Abdou appear before his eyes without excuse. Thus, while he demurs, "Me, I wouldn't want to be Soumana's heir, I swear to you! An eighty-five kilo black woman, where every kilo's uglier than the next, that's weird," he also takes note of the mothers' submission and the abusive use of force against his sister: "The women have prepared couscous. It's very nutritious. Except that Fatima won't stop crying. My dad gave her a hit" (my translation; see p. 88).

Uncomfortable with the need to reject his mothers, his defense of his father requiring his own acquiescence in the misery experienced by his sister and mothers, Loukoum can easily displace his revolt onto the uncanny figure of Madame Saddock: half woman/half man, sympathetic to the plight of the African women whose very culture she rejects, she appears as the ghost of the devouring witch whose words alone in *Seul le diable le savait* were able to destroy others. " 'The pig!' says Madame Saddock. 'What a bunch of shit!' " (my translation; see p. 118).

The irony could not be richer here. Loukoum revolts against the figure who is a mother-double, and Beyala turns, at this critical juncture, to her double-text, *Burt*, for the terms of the revolt. For it is Gil, the one who cannot stand to hear obscene words, who forms the model for Loukoum's subsequent reactions: " 'You shouldn't say "shit,"' I goes to her. 'It's a dirty word.' " Beyala turns back on her own dicta in *Tu t'appelleras Tanga*, to "tuer le vide du silence," as she brings Madame Saddock into the *upright* position of the woman who will not yield the agency of speech: "But she got up saying, 'Shit! Shit! Shit!' " She underscores this with the cultural claim based on Western ideals: "I'll say dirty words if I want to, Loukoum. We live in a Republic" (my translation; see p. 118).

It is finally at this point that Loukoum breaks with his own role as passive recorder of events, and assuming fully the stance of Gil's revolt against social phallocentrism, turns to his own act of murder, killing the threat to his identity by severing the strangling umbilical cord of his mother: "I was in a really bad mood. I didn't know what to do. So I leaned over like I was a cowboy, pointed at her with the finger you're not supposed to point with, went *bang-bang*! and I killed her" (my translation; see p. 118).

The break must come from the mother if the weaning is to be complete; the child cannot do it on his own. Madame Saddock's response brings this about. "Now there's someone I wouldn't want my daughter to marry" (my translation; see p. 118), she says, with the phrase carrying the unstated implications of racism that line the discourse of the far right in French no less than in American society. Thus the castration of the mother, as Lacan would have it, can be seen in this figure of Madame Saddock, who carries out the function of the devouring mother, the one who must be rejected, and whose solicitude must be seen as the flip side of emasculation. She is the western-feminist-presumed-to-know against whom Beyala poses the uncertain dikes and fences erected by the romanticizing, despairing Abdou.

While Loukoum follows the traces of Gil in his western-style revolt against patriarchal institutionalism, Abdou carries through to the end his lament of the exiled patriarch who has lost his wives and his son.[21] The disjunction between their two narratives grows deeper with each succeeding episode, as Abdou expresses loss and emptiness, and Loukoum greater independence and even fulfillment in his love for Lolita, with no accompanying sense of a revolt against his father. And then, appearing through the crack in the text, following Loukoum's reception of a letter from Lolita—just as in the scene in which Gil had received his letter from Jessica—there emerges, like the semiotic maternal pulsation, the return of the repressed. The despairing mother, the failed revolt, the broken figure of Soumana, whom Loukoum would never have wanted to become, erupts at the end, with a presence that provokes once again the sense of uncanniness before a force that will not respect the boundaries of things, that will invade and take hold of us, despite all attempts to ignore it: "For a minute, I thought about Soumana; nobody talks about her and yet she's here in every object, in every breath of air that goes through the house" (my translation; see p. 250). And like the ghost (*nègre* in French) of Alice Walker, Beyala concludes, "Oh! Dieu, il s'en passe des choses chez les nègres" (250) [Oh! God, there's some weird stuff goin' on with the blacks] (my translation).

Notes

1. That gaze of the "static Being" before whom we stand when first coming to an understanding of ourselves as selves functions both as a model/basis for the ego and its understanding of the nature of knowledge, and as external locus for consciousness in whose gaze we stand. Its stability and theoretical nature coalesce in the image of the statue that holds us in its gaze: "The 'ego-world' is a statue: as hard as stone, as cold as ice, it is *standing in front of* the ego that is petrified there—that is, in the ego world, it both gazes at and petrifies itself" (Borch-Jacobsen 60). This Medusa property recalls Bhabha's evocation of the evil eye in Meiling Jin's poem: "Only my eyes will remain to watch and to haunt, / and to turn your dreams / to chaos" (Bhabha 46; see 52ff. for "evil eye").

2. Carole Boyce Davies lists seven traits to what she terms "a genuine African feminism," beginning with a recognition of "a common struggle with African men for the removal of the yokes of foreign domination and European/American exploitation" (8). The remaining may be summarized as follows:

—the recognition of inequities within traditional societies, reinforced by colonialism, resulting in a specific African feminism, despite affinities with international feminism

—acknowledgment of significant social and political positions enjoyed by women in precolonial times

—advocacy of those institutions which are of value to women, and rejection of those that work to their detriment; rejection of a simple importation of western women's agendas

—respect for African women's self-reliance and cooperative work ethic

—recognition that following struggles for national liberation women must enter into new stages of struggle against the men who had fought for national liberation

—examination of African women's avenues of choice both in traditional and contemporary societies. (8–10)

3. The romanticizing in *Crooklyn* is grounded in the nostalgic recollections of childhood, and does not jar with the viewer's sense of reality. *Do the Right Thing* seems to me to strike a note much closer to *Le Petit Prince de Belleville* with its familiar and "loveable" neighborhood types, its local hangouts—a pizzeria in the former, a café in the latter—and its atmosphere, which is generally nonthreatening, despite the evocation of social problems and poverty. Crime does not figure in either the film or the novel in any significant way. And there is a governing moralism that is generally evoked in response to the threats of racism from the dominant culture.

4. All this is largely absent in the English translation of *Le Petit Prince de Belleville,* in which many of the most egregiously plagiarized passages were deleted and the text rewritten. Ironically, the translation lacks much of the spice of the original, despite the fine work of the translator, Marjolijn de Jager. This is understandable when one sees Beyala picking up Jean-Pierre Carasso's rendering of Buten's English "colored" as "nègre de couleur" and transforming it into "blanc de couleur"—an untranslatable wording, translated back by Marjolijn de Jager simply as "coloured"!

5. This reading of Beyala's plagiarism should be set in contrast with Christopher Miller's analysis of Ouologuem's plagiarisms, which Miller correctly characterized as creative transformations of Graham Greene's *It's a Battlefield* into a new text, one that is entirely Ouologuem's own. Ouologuem's initial defense of his practice was to claim that the publishers had omitted the quotation marks which he had placed around the material taken from other texts. The presence of the quotation marks, however, would have rendered *Devoir de violence* incomprehensible. Subsequently, Ouologuem published *Lettre à la France nègre,* in which he took a stronger anti-conventional position. There he defends the "nègre," or ghost-writer, who is urged to plagiarize, in ironic counterpoint to the whites' production of texts with integrity, "wholeness." By having the "nègre" plagiarize, Ouologuem would have him "thus become the controller of the interpenetration of textual bodies in a system that had become doubly perverse"—perverse in the false wholeness of the "white" famous writers, and in the castrated status of the "nègres" who produce texts for them (Miller 1985: 227). This is a continuation of Ouologuem's project in *Le Devoir de violence,* which Miller describes as subverting (225) the binary (original/copy, authentic/inauthentic, etc.) terms on which conventional textual authority is based. Ouologuem works out this logic in *Lettre à la France nègre* in such a way as to "spoil the distinction between original and copy," i.e., to subvert the bases of bourgeois society such as Ouologuem knew it in the late 1960s—to "upset the principle of sole authorship and property as well as the founding basis of authenticity" (225). The challenge Ouologuem mounts to the conventional literary social world of his day is all the more striking in its contrast to Beyala's continual reference to the Académie Française award as the basis for her defense.

6. *Les Honneurs perdus*—1996, Grand Prix du Roman, Académie Française. *Assèze l'Africaine*—1996, Prix Tropique.

7. I am grateful to Madeleine Borgomano for sharing much of her research on this "affair" with me. See her paper, " 'L'Affaire' Calixthe Beyala ou les frontières des champs littéraires," presented at the APELA (Association pour l'Etude des Littératures Africaines) colloquium at Brussels in September 1997.

8. Compare this with Gallimore's far more indulgent reading, not only of the issue, but of Constant's reaction. In reference to Beyala's claim that

once a sentence leaves its original context, it automatically takes on a new sense, Gallimore states, "Paule Constant semble confirmer cette dernière déclaration de Calixthe Beyala. Ce n'est que quand on l'a prévenue du plagiat que 'ça lui a sauté au visage' " (208) [Paule Constant seems to confirm this latter declaration of Calixthe Beyala. It was only when she had been alerted to the plagiarism that "it leaped into view"]. She attributes this failure to recognize it because the passages "avaient revêtu un autre sens" and "portaient en eux un autre dynamisme" [were dressed in a new meaning and carried within them another dynamic]. Gallimore glosses over Constant's more cynical reactions. Finally Gallimore concludes in academic fashion, dodging the ethics of the issue: "Comme le but de notre étude n'est pas d'analyser la problématique de l'originalité et de l'authenticité de la poétique de Beyala, nous ne nous sentons pas tenue de prendre partie de cette controverse. . . . En fin de compte, il nous semble que l'idée d'intertexualité peut alimenter le processus créatif pour produire une oeuvre originale comme c'est le cas en musique où on peut retrouver un air de Mozart retravaillé dans Beethoven" (210–11) [As the goal of our study is not to analyze the problematic of Beyala's originality and the authenticity of her creative practice, we do not feel obliged to take sides in this controversy. . . . In the final analysis, it seems to us that the idea of intertexuality can feed the creative process to produce an original work, as in the case of music where one finds a Mozartean tune reworked in Beethoven.].

9. Beyala lampoons Assouline in her 1998 novel, *La Petite Fille du réverbère*.

10. I am not disputing these claims for Beyala's first three novels, but still can't help remark that the language changes in *Le Petit Prince de Belleville*—and the "street" locution "que je dis" (meaning "I say," or better "I go") used in place of a narrative "je dis" (as in "je dis, 'Où va-tu?' ") is to be found in *Quand j'avais cinq ans, je m'ai tué*. It is presented as a marker of Loukoum's street speech in *Le Petit Prince de Belleville*, but does not appear in any of Beyala's other novels, despite their settings in the streets of both New Bell and Belleville.

11. Let me note that in her defense against the charge of plagiarizing the Okri passage, Beyala claims that she was merely describing a common practice, "que c'est là une practique courante chez les femmes africaines, d'ailleurs illustrée par les contes et les chansons, une sorte de coutume regionale" (Mataillet 74) [that it is a common practice among African women, furthermore illustrated through tales and songs, a sort of regional custom].

This line of defense ignores the structural similarity in the two passages, and the even more striking similarity in the two wordings. Interestingly, the key word Beyala changes is Okri's "parties génitales," rendering it "testicules," and, as Borgomano notes in her discussion of the passage, "Beyala" employs an even more direct discourse when she states, "Je décris une femme qui empoigne un homme par les couilles" (Mataillet 73) [I am describing a woman who grabs a man by the balls]. "Couilles" means "balls" in English, and Borgomano qualifies Beyala's language here as "crû": "Calixthe Beyala déclare, plus crûment encore" (Borgomano 7) [Calixthe Beyala declares, still more crudely]. Crudely—directly. The image of street talk here corresponds to Beyala's construction of "Beyala," at the same time that it talks back to the man who refuses to listen.

12. In her introduction to *Feminine Sexuality: Jacques Lacan and the Ecole Freudienne*, Juliet Mitchell gives a full account of the importance of the castration complex, not only for Freud and Lacan, but for the entire profession of psychoanalysis:

> The question as to what created this difference between the sexes was a central debate among psychoanalysts in the '20s and '30s. Lacan returned to this debate as a focal point for what he considered had gone wrong with psychoanalytic theory subsequently. Again Lacan underscored and reformulated the position that Freud took up in this debate. Freud always insisted that it was the presence or absence of the phallus and *nothing else* that marked the distinction between the sexes. Others disagreed. Retrospectively the key concept of the debate becomes transparently clear: it is the castration complex. . . . Lacan returns to the key concept of the debate, to the castration complex and, within its terms, the meaning of the phallus. He takes them as the bedrock of subjectivity itself and of the place of sexuality within it. . . . In Lacan's reading of Freud, the threat of castration is not something that has been done to an already existent girl subject or that could be done to an already existent boy subject; it is, as it was for Freud, what 'makes' the girl a girl and a boy a boy, in a division that is both essential and precarious.
>
> The question of the castration complex split psychoanalysts. By the time of the great debate in the mid-twenties, the issue was posed as the nature of female sexuality but underlying that are the preceding disagreements on castration anxiety. In fact all subsequent work on female sexuality and on the construction of sexual difference stems from the various places accorded to the concept of the castration complex. It stands as the often silent centre of all the theories that flourished in the decades before the war: the effects of its acceptance or rejection are still being felt. (6–8)

13. Cf. Borch-Jacobsen: "On the contrary [to the Freudian conditions of the Oedipus], the crisis of the symbolic is spread all over: the 'deficiencies' of the paternal function, the 'foreclosure' of the Name of the Father, the perpetual calling into question of the 'Law' and the symbolic 'pact,' the confusion of lineages and the generalized competition of the generations, the battle of the sexes, the loss of familial landmarks. In other words, the crisis of

symbolic identification is everywhere" (226). Borch-Jacobsen goes on to point out that Lacan's call for a "symbolic Law" is a kind of "analytic myth," that the Lacanian Oedipus is "not the Oedipus as it is, it is the Oedipus as it *must* be" (226).

14. It is on this point that Derrida, in *Spurs/Eperons* (1979) and "The Purveyor of Truth" (1975), formulates his criticism of Lacan. If Lacan claims to have displaced Cartesian certainties of being with the model of the unconscious presented in the form of language, those logocentric certainties return with the deployment of the phallus as the "transcendental signifier."

15. "[T]he phallus is not a question of a form or of an image, or of a phantasy, but rather a signifier, the signifier of desire. In Greek antiquity, the phallus is *not represented by an organ but as an insignia*" (Lacan [1968] 1975: 187).

16. Note that during the entire history of the development of the theory of the castration complex, there were numerous debates over the nature of castration, whether gender was an innate, historical given, a cultural construct, a question of imprinting and behavior, of object attraction. For Karl Abraham, castration fear was fear of lack of potency (Mitchell, Introduction to Mitchell and Rose [1983], 15); for Ernest Jones it was fear of extinction of sexual desire. Mitchell's able summary of Lacan's position once again demonstrates how the main tenets can be articulated without having to refer literally to the physical body: "the analysand's unconscious reveals a fragmented subject of shifting and uncertain sexual identity. To be human is to be subjected to a law which decenters and divides: sexuality is created in a division, the subject is split; but an ideological world conceals this from the conscious subject who is supposed to feel whole and certain of a sexual identity" (Mitchell and Rose 26).

For Freud, as Mitchell notes, the "prohibition only comes to be meaningful to the child *because* there are people—females—who have been castrated in the particular sense that they are without the phallus" (16; my emphasis). "If, as in Abraham's work, the actual body is seen as a motive for the construction of the subject in its male or female sexuality, then an historical or symbolic dimension to this constitution is precluded. Freud's intention was to establish that very dimension as the *sine qua non* of the construction of the human subject. It is on this dimension that Lacan bases his entire account of sexual difference" (17). If "historical and symbolical dimensions" are factors on which gender identity is based, they are nonetheless constructions, relative to different cultures and historical periods. Most of all, as constructions, they cannot be reduced to a single, central mythos as the Oedipus has become.

Starck found castration anxiety "in the loss of the nipple from the baby's mouth" (Mitchell and Rose 18), thus paralleling my argument in favor of weaning as the model for loss and separation. Franz Alexander and Otto Rank trace castration back to the birth trauma. Mitchell cites Freud to make clear that the fundamental loss, as far as he is concerned, is the loss of a penis (cf. 18). "To Freud the castration complex divided the sexes and thus made the human being, human" (*sic*, 18).

Lacan's dependence on Freudian thought is at once clear and confusing. For Lacan, "The castration complex is *the* instance of the humanisation of the child in its sexual difference. . . . If the specific mark of the phallus, the repression of which is the institution of the law, is repudiated then there can only be psychosis. To Lacan all other hypotheses make nonsense of psychoanalysis" (Mitchell and Rose 19). As I stated above, however, the terms "phallus" and "castration" seem quite different when used by Freud and Lacan. For Freud, phallus is inseparable from penis. For Lacan, it is object of desire, and on the imaginary level, *objet a*—with a base grounded in a constructed mythos.

To the argument that losses or threats not involving the penis are also operant, Freud/Lacan respond that only fear of loss of the phallus can account for the distinction between the two sexes (Mitchell and Rose 19).

17. Stephen Heath argues along similar lines when he states that the "logic of the penis/phallus" that is, the use of "phallus" to denote signifier, along with the choice of the term phallus based on its function in infantile sexuality, and its functioning as a visual object in classical symbology, is grounded in the very patriarchal society that gave rise to the forms of subjectivity defined in terms of the phallus: "What is at stake and shut off in the logic of the penis/phallus is the history of the subject in so far as that history might include effects of social organization, and, for example, of patriarchal order" (50). Heath goes on to argue that the foundation for the logic of the phallus/penis and its role in the construction of subjectivity lies precisely in a construct—a representation founded on a fundamental mythos: "That such a logic may really describe the production of subjectivity in a relation of sexual difference in a patriarchal society is not necessarily in question; that production, however, cannot be inverted—except to reproduce and confirm its established terms—into the fixed point of an origin, the translation of a vision. The vision, any vision, is constructed, not given; appealing to its certainty, psychoanalysis can only repeat the ideological impasse of the natural, the mythical representation of things" (50).

18. Cf. Borch-Jacobsen: "The Lacanian Oedipus is not the Oedipus as it is; it is the Oedipus as it *must* be. It is the anti-mimetic Oedipus, the identificatory anti-model to which the analyst, through his silence, enjoins the analysand to conform: 'Identify with my desire'; '(Do not) be like me'; 'Imitate the inimitable.'" Borch-Jacobsen goes on to state that Lacan's model was not, as it was with Freud, *Oedipus Rex*, in which the rivalizing Oedipus also "submits to the interdiction" (Lacan, quoted in Borch-Jacobsen 226), but the Oedipus of *Oedipus at Colonus*, who "voluntarily tears out his eyes and

rails, unreconciled, against the curse of existence" (226). Lacan finds in this older Oedipus a being oriented toward death, the condition of nonbeing, "the preference on which a human life must end . . . the triumph of being-toward-death" (227).

For Borch-Jacobsen, Lacan has made analysis "the rite of symbolic castration: the harsh initiation of the 'harsh desire of . . . desiring,' the tragic schooling of the tearing away of self and total disidentification, the infinitely painful access to that 'place from which a voice is heard clamoring "the universe is a defect in the purity of Non-Being"'" (Lacan, quoted in Borch-Jacobsen 227).

19. All citations from *Le Petit Prince de Belleville* (1992) from this point on will be my translations from the French text, unless marked "(Beyala 1995)," in which case they refer to the English translation by Marolijn de Jager, published by Heinemann as *Loukoum*.

20. As for the white Other whose authority supplants the paternal function of his own father, Loukoum is witness to a series of such figures erupting into his life, until in the end not only has he himself changed so as to be unrecognizable to his father, but Abdou himself has become totally "other." After his imprisonment, Abdou loses all his authority as African Other. He is no longer the breadwinner—it is his young son Loukoum who has assumed that role, with the active participation of M'am. The sacred authority of the father's chair, normally reserved just for him, is violated and lost, even if he recovers the right to sit there on his return. Most of all, his authority, his hold over M'am is lost forever, and with it goes his "Name," his "Law," the high position signaled in his habit of chewing on his cola nut: "Then, he pursed his lips and spat colanut juice straight as an arrow which cleared the windowsill and landed in the courtyard: *splat*!" (my translation; see Beyala 1992: 21-2). Now the much changed Abdou is deflated, penitent, and even suppliant: "Tell me woman, how could stand me for so many years?" (my trans.; see 248).

21. Cf., for example, the following passages:

> That my son is my blood. I have seen his life, this life which I have passed on to him, I know that he is the most precious of my earthly possessions, the only one I possess in my own right. My son. My continuity. I had to make him become an imitation of me. For better or for worse, his character had to flow out of mine. . . .
> Is it too much to ask that a son be the image of the father?
> . . . But you know, friend, little by little my son was no longer listening to me. Or when he lent me an ear it was with a pout, the pout of a television announcer. . . .
> Today I see my son.
> He has discovered the vocabulary of Paris. Words scratched in by wind and weather.

He has acquired other ways of saying hello.
He knows rituals that throw me.
He feels repugnance at eating with his hands.
He imposes other conformities.
He imports tastes, preoccupations.
He passes from one universe to the other without worrying about it. He judges ours, feels contempt. My stories amuse him. . . .

Friend, my son no longer listens to me. I feel emptied of myself, robbed and ransacked of my last dream, to the last of what is beautiful. (Beyala 1995: 144)

Chapter 5

Less Than One and Double: Irigaray/Bhabha, Nervous Conditions/Assèze l'Africaine

The language of colonialism was marked from the beginning by doubling. A politics of "acculturation" was replaced by one of "assimilation," in which the first goal of doubling the metropolitan "culture"—that is, its economy of identity bound up in the notion of civilization—mapped onto the "blank darkness" of the African, was succeeded by the project of transforming the African into a Europeanized double, an "assimilé," an "évolué," a civilized man. If women were generally left out of this formula, it was because the neutral status ascribed to the notion of civilization in the early and even mid-twentieth century was deeply masculinist, so that the goal of a French or British education was to create a man of letters, a subaltern administrator, a cleric, a teacher, or a veterinarian—all posts occupied by men, except for teachers in some cases.

There the exception led naturally to the doubled doubling for women. As Flora Nwapa shows in *Women Are Different*, and Mariama Bâ in *Une si longue lettre*, in the years before and after World War II, schooling for women, directed and taught by women, often missionaries, was provided so as to create a class of wives appropriately formed for the rising cadres of educated African men. The women were doubly doubles because their models, the women who taught them, were themselves still subordinated to a male order, and were themselves struggling to double the men who monopolized the vote, the economy, and most professions.

The notion of doubling, as we have seen with Lacan, is bound up with the formation of the subject, and the subject's apprehension of himself or herself, in the misrecognitions of the mirror stage, misrecognitions to which conventional thought has attached the concept of identity, and Freud the concept of ego. Lacan, then, could dismiss the notion of a double self in that the self to be doubled is actually an imagined or constructed entity, one mistaken for a given identity or projected onto another and taken to be oneself. Alternatively, the subject's identity could be seen to be formed in the act of enunciation, a formula central to feminist thought and to Bhabha's thought, inasmuch as it is through the framing and enunciating of a discourse that we have to assume a position in which to use the first person singular pronoun. But even there, we find doubling. The source of the discourse lies in the appropriation of the Other whose displacement, as phallic-signifier, is made possible only through the split effects of castration. The "I" enunciated in the discourse is immediately separated into the "I" of the enunciation (the act of enunciating) and the "I" of that which is enunciated (the "I" who functions as a character in the text); that is, the "I" constructing the discourse, and the "I" constructed in the discourse. Tzvetan Todorov takes this split one step further in contending that there is still the "I" needed to construct the "I" of the enunciation, as though it were the case that every time we were to think of ourselves, the self ("I") about whom we are thinking must be held, seen, at a distance apart from the one doing the thinking. The mirror, then, would be insufficient to describe the doubling effect since what we see is only the constructed image of ourselves, and never the one who is seeing. In other words, we can see "ourselves," but not see ourselves seeing ourselves—never see our seeing.

These inversions seem increasingly empty until one returns to the question of what is implied by the double. The self and its double, as we have seen in the model of colonialism, are bound up in notions of authenticity. Very rapidly in the course of colonialism, ideologies of acculturation and assimilation were confronted with epistemes of authenticity: the "authentic" African was being corrupted by assimilation; the "évolué" was a false being, half-savage, half-civilized, fallen from a natural state of purity, and thus prone to indecision, ambiguity, corruption, and dishonesty. Such half-beings are evoked in Conrad, but more especially in Joyce Cary, whose Mr. Johnson serves as a particularly distasteful example of the colonial fantasy.

The double, so configured, relies upon essentialist or originary formulations, by which any transformation of an original would constitute a falsification—repetition being based upon binary notions of original/copy, true/false, or copyrighted/plagiarized. The logic of the supplement put an end to the long-standing predominance of the priority placed on originary, authentic, or essential being, presence, or property. For Derrida, presence was marked by its supplement, requiring the very thing that lay outside its delimited sphere of being or presence for its own completion. And if the supplement was not always a double, there was a way in which the recognition of its indelible link to the originary presence was troubling—uncanny—as in the recognition of a self external to what one had settled comfortably into believing was only oneself.

If the misrecognition of the mirror stage is not uncanny, it is only because we have domesticated, made our own, our reflected image. Freud's first reaction in the train, then, was the natural, first impulse, only later mastered by the processes of appropriation that accompany recognition. One doesn't recognize oneself: one constructs a familiar, a doubled spirit to carry oneself, one's self brought into the unitary essence of "oneself." And that process is not accomplished by oneself, in the solitary space of a bathroom with a mirror, behind locked doors, locked in with one's self, but from the beginning of one's entry into relations with others. "What a cute baby." "Isn't he cute." And "he," "cute," and presence are born, recognized, appropriated.

The process is obviously not immediate. It requires repetition, distance, and the play of approaching, distancing or going away—"fort, da."[1] But when the words begin to make sense, when they enable one to see, to see oneself, others, to sense distance, and to speak from a site where one is in possession, then the doubled-back image, a "she," "cute," "sensitive," "enervated"—all these properties turn into predicates—become tied to one's language and a continually reinforced set of terms/images that are ultimately formed into sentences beginning with "I am. . . ."

Our first seeings are not double. We see and feel ourselves as one. But the minute we commit that feeling to speech, we reconstruct an image and reflect it back on ourselves both by our words and by the reactions to ourselves that we set up. That double meets the original double constructed through the processes of the mirror stage, and sets the stage for the reaction of recognition or of the uncanny. It is there, at that moment of sensing the exteriorization of our image, that the multiple models of "double or nothing," of self or other, or the in-between experiences half-sensed by less than one or doubled occur.

African women's literature is frequently marked by such "secret sharers," invisible interlocutors whose image sends back either a sense of recognition, a reflection of self, if not a veritable shock of recognition, or a more distant other on whose features one can recognize the projected forms of a narcissistic or desired projection. Thus, Ramatoulaye's portrait of herself requires the invisible and silent interlocutor, Aissatou, whose mere presence as reader of Rama's letters is needed for Rama to construct herself in a self-portrait built of words. In Aidoo's *Changes*, Esi's form can take shape only when set against Opokuya, who first comes on the scene as an altered double to her friend: "Compared to Esi, Opokuya was definitely fat" (14). Without the double, the original can only be an invisible being, a specter like Tutuola's "complete gentleman" who has to give back his body parts because, as a ghost being, there is literally nothing there.

But the first name one would expect to be given to Esi's double, Ramatoulaye's double, or their innumerable counterparts in various texts by Emecheta, Aidoo, Nwapa, Bâ, would be "sister"—"Ah my sister" (*Changes* 23); and an inevitable response *requesting and acknowledging presence*, the adult version of "fort-da," call-response, would automatically ensue: "Hi, how are you. I am well, and you? How are you? Can't complain. How are the children? They are fine. And those in boarding, have you seen them lately, and how are they? And our little daughter, how is she? Oh, she is fine. You have been hiding! No, it's you who've been hiding" (33).

For the generation after Bâ, the exuberance of recognition is often muted by a more restrained sense of self, a less tightly woven image of self bound in the other. From "sister" we pass to cousin, and the bond to the double in *Nervous Conditions* and *Assèze l'Africaine* becomes marked by greater ambiguity and struggle. Clearly, as the uncertainty implicated in the processes that lead to doubling, beginning with the mirror stage, is multiplied, as the young women are increasingly estranged from their mothers, not by the effects of a castrating Other, but by the superimposition of a second set of colonial and postcolonial cultural imperatives, both doubling and replacing the first Name of the Father, so, too, are the relations with the double sister/cousin complicated and compromised. The double is at once more distant (cousin); more vulnerable (bulimic, suicidal); and as she is increasingly different (better educated, gifted, or wealthier), she also becomes more of a projected/displaced version of the original disrupted, misrecognized self.[2]

If it is self and sister that form the first image, the first projection of the imaginary, this arises only in denial of an earlier, more overwhelming figure of the doubled self, and that is the mother herself. Here, we can postulate that the fundamental processes of identification and castration operate on so powerful a level that the doubled figure always will be returned as a displaced other, one in whom the feelings of recognition and appropriation will be grounded in sensations of pleasure and pain. Resemblances in appearance, behavior, or modes of speech can be seen as such displacements mistaken for the reflected, doubled image: production turns reproduction into imitation, mimesis, and opens up the fundamental strategy available for all doubles: the mime and the masquerade. These are the two, divergent strategies open to women, according to Luce Irigaray, for whom the problematics of doubling come down to resisting or playing the game of the patriarchal order. Put in this way, miming and masquerading become questions of double or nothing, because the former entails a mimesis consciously undertaken so as to establish a distance from the expected figure of the woman, and thus simultaneously to make present the place of the one putting on the mime, the one who *is not*. The masquerade entails no such putting forward of the figure behind the mime, but rather its disguising, its disappearance behind the mask. In African terms, the spirit that rides the masquerade takes over the masquerade, transforming it entirely into the other.

This is where Bhabha's mimic stands apart from Irigaray's specifically feminine strategy, because for Bhabha the mime is already marked by the doubling/split inherent in the act of enunciation, and not in gendered role playing. Further, the conditions of colonialism make it virtually impossible for the colonized to achieve the perfect doubling of the colonizer whose "civilizing mission," on the one hand, demands that he seek to "civilize the natives," but whose fundamental beliefs in racial superiority build in limits to the possibility of transforming the native. The result is mimic men who are "less than double": "[I]n the slippage between identity and difference the 'normalizing' authority of the colonial discourse is thrown into question" (McClintock 63).

For Anne McClintock, Bhabha's analysis is flawed because of his disregard for the gender oppression of the hybrid colonized. Similarly, she sees Irigaray as failing to take into account the oppression engendered under imperialism, leaving both Bhabha and Irigaray as having proposed *partial* strategies. According to McClintock, Irigaray devises an "essentially female strategy," and thus "paradoxically reinscribes precisely those gender binaries that she so brilliantly challenges" (62). More generally, McClintock's critique of Irigaray and Bhabha centers on agency. As the displacement of colonial authority, according to Bhabha, arises out of the ruptures within its own discourse, McClintock sees no place in Bhabha's work accorded "the military strategies of the colonies" or "shifting social contradictions" (63). McClintock queries whether it is sufficient to locate agency in the "internal fissures of discourse," and sees Bhabha as projecting historical agency onto "formal abstractions that are anthropomorphized and given a life of their own," so that "abstractions become historical actors; discourse desires . . . etc." As a result, "social relations between humans appear to metamorphize [*sic*] into structural relations between forms—through a formalist fetishism that effectively elides the messier questions of historical change and social activism" (63–64).

The answers McClintock is seeking are built into the questions she poses, with "agency" the key word. In calling for agency as the measure of critique, McClintock places it on a metatheoretical level at which its significance is taken for granted. Bhabha's turning of the narrow absolutism of original presence, or historical determinism, back into open, indeterminate concepts or strategies does not reduce agency or formalize his terms of analysis. McClintock wants to see "historical change" and "social activism" driven by actors whose self-conscious assumptions of their condition and the means of changing it can be determined by a straightforward reading, as though historical agency were structured as unproblematically as mimetic realism. There is no mediation, in this critique, between word and act, between historical condition and the writing or reading of it. Bhabha's introduction of ambivalence into the colonial discourse does not remove agency from those who resisted colonialism; it rather deconstructs the phallocentric basis for colonial discourse, enabling strategic positions assumed during the colonial period to be read along a number of different tracks.

One track might be seen to emerge in the variable response to evangelical Christianity, as is stressed by Achebe in his historical fiction, and as Bhabha foregrounds in his chapter in *The Location of Culture* on mimicry, ambivalence, and colonial authority, "Signs Taken for Wonders: Questions of Ambivalence and Authority Under a Tree Outside Delhi, May 1917." In both Achebe and Bhabha, it is initially those naive questions posed by the "natives" to the missionaries and their Book that locate the site of resistance. As the force, the fist behind the missionaries makes itself felt in the police actions of the District Administrators, or in the expansion of the colonial state, the modes of resistance are split, and multiply. Bhabha, of course, takes this resistance to the English book, to its inherent assumptions about full presence divided by the unstated assumptions about authority, to its conclusion by identifying new forms of native cultural hybridity that extend the initial naive questioning to the undermining ruses of mimicry and mockery:

> Culture, as a colonial space of intervention and agonism, as the trace of the displacement of symbol to sign, can be transformed

> by the unpredictable and partial desire of hybridity. Deprived of their full presence, the knowledges of cultural authority may be articulated with forms of "native" knowledges or faced with those discriminated subjects that they must rule but can no longer represent. This may lead, as in the case of the natives outside Delhi, to questions of authority that the authorities—the Bible included—cannot answer. Such a process is not the deconstruction of a cultural system from the margins of its own aporia nor, as in Derrida's "Double session," the mime that haunts mimesis. The display of hybridity—its particular "replication"—terrorizes authority with the *ruse* of recognition, its mimicry, its mockery. (115)

Another track might emerge in the attempt of women to "recover the place of [their] exploitation by discourse" by "play[ing] with mimesis," as with Irigaray. McClintock reads these tracks as simply unidirectional: "If Irigaray challenges Lacan's masculinism and argues for mimicry as a specifically female strategy (an essentialist gesture that elides race and class), Bhabha, in turn, bypasses Irigaray and refers only to race, eliding in the process gender and class" (64).

McClintock's critique is wrongheaded here, as she deliberately ignores Irigaray's evocation of Freud's reference to women as the "dark continent," and likewise ignores Bhabha's multiple deliberately constructed *parallels* to feminist strategies in his text. For McClintock, the strategies of mimicry suggested by Irigaray and Bhabha are written into closed, genderized frameworks, so that mimicry's usage by women, according to Irigaray, leaves out gay strategies, and Bhabha's reinscription of mimicry as a male strategy, failing to acknowledge its gendered specificity, erases female agency. "By eliding gender differences, however, Bhabha implicitly ratifies gender power, so that masculinity becomes the invisible norm of postcolonial discourse. By eliding racial differences, Irigaray, in turn, ratifies the invisibility of imperial power" (64–65).

McClintock's critique sets forth requirements: the requirements for agency entailing the specific, explicit reference to struggle along lines of class, race and gender—the "articulated categories" she sets forth at the beginning of her study (4). But these terms become formulaic fetishes themselves, no matter how much one believes in the necessity for committed struggle, so that critique is reduced to an act of measurement according to standards generally taken for granted, and reading is limited to the literalism required by mimetic discourse. It is not too much of a stretch to see Irigaray's mimicry reacting across the genderized language of her text to apply to colonial subjects equally oppressed by phallocratic orders, including the discursive; and it requires no real stretch to see Bhabha's reinterpretation of métissage as taking on forms of mimicry that undermine the colonial discourse of assimilation, also corresponding to the amibivalent discourses of class or gender logocentrisms.

Such a stretch will be undertaken not so as to defend Irigaray or Bhabha, but rather so as to return to the act of reading their strategies through the lens of doubling, or rather doubling by approximation, as contrived in the fiction of African women writers. With that reading, we will return to Dangarembga's *Nervous Conditions* and Beyala's haunting of that text.

Irigaray

Irigaray provides the perfect model for the double by mounting the challenge to Lacan's mirrored constructions in her *Speculum of the Other Woman* ([1985] 1992) and *This Sex Which Is Not One*. The speculum curves the mirror back on itself, refusing to return the images straightforwardly: turning in on itself like a vagina whose two lips close, touch, and form a self-caress that cannot be reduced to any unitary formulation—*not one*. The looking glass that refuses to return the image just to one side of the room, of the society; just one bathroom for men, another for women; one phallus to be, another to have; this is Alice's looking glass, and in it Irigaray sees Alice and Ann crossing into each other's story, through the borders of a space that refuses to be read as effecting separation, refusing fort-da: "Who spoke? In whose name? Filling in for her, it's not certain that she's not trying to replace her. *To be even more (than) 'she.'* Hence the postscript that she adds to what was said to have taken place: 'He even wants to have a baby with me.' Then they fall silent, differently confused" ([1977] 1985: 20–21).

Alice's supplementary addition doesn't add clarity or unity to the text; it doesn't help distinguish Ann from Alice. It sets up the situation in which the drive to impose the coordinates of the symbolic order—be they familiar divisions of class, race, or gender—is aroused. Who better to enact this desire than a surveyor? "That's the moment when the surveyor, of course, is going to intervene" (21). The use of the present tense moves our attention to the narrator whose presence is not hidden and whose descriptions fail to clarify, unify the text: "*But how can he tell them apart?* Who is she? And she? Since they are not the sum of two units, where can one pass between them?" (21). In *passing*, the white mask deceives the reader into thinking the mimic is what she is not, white. White becomes a site of constructed identity—like an ego read from the imago. And when the man would likewise pass into that space divided by two lips that are not the sum of two units, what unitary readings will be then imposed on that moment of jouissance, and what excess will be then attributed to the mysteries of the dark continent?

"We are luminous. Neither one nor two. I've never known how to count. Up to you. In their calculations, we make two. Really, two? Doesn't that make you laugh? An odd sort of two. And yet not one. Especially not one. Let's leave *one* to them: their oneness, with its prerogatives, its domination, its solipsism: like the sun's. And the strange way they divide up their couples, with the other as the image of the one. Only an image" (207).

Irigaray, and in fact that generation of feminists linked to Lacan and the rebellion his work engendered, center their attack on phallogocentrism in this play of numbers that refuses the unitary method of counting, attributable across the centuries not to an originary mode of Hellenic thought, but to the reiterative processes of patriarchy reinscribing its logic onto those whom it rules. Just as patriarchy has returned, with its differences altered but its structures intact, so has the post-Lacanian feminist resistance returned to the issue of the unified subject, the humanist construction, as the key to its subversion of phallocracy. "I love you" (208), the division between subject, object, and the articulation of desire bound repeatedly into a difference that underwrites patriarchy. But then rewritten: "our two lips cannot separate to let just *one* word pass. A single word that would say 'you,' or 'me' " (208). For McClintock, the double lips, like "l'écriture féminine," constitute a female strategy. But they are no more essentialized as a physical structure than is the phallus as a penis: phallocracy and patriarchy are systems grounded in the mimetic substitution of resemblance, the process of metaphorization that naturalizes and thus dissembles behind the reflection of the real. The splitting of language, the call to speak, the calls across the systematizing of phallocracy, extend beyond the reductive economy of sexual difference and cry out for an equally subversive reading:

> Closed and open, neither ever excluding the other, they say they both love each other. Together. To produce a single precise word, they would have to stay apart. Definitely parted. Kept at a distance, separated by *one* word. . . . The unity, the truth, the propriety of words comes from their lack of lips, their forgetting of lips. . . . Men and women have children to embody their closeness, their distance. But we?

> I love you, childhood. I love you who are neither mother (forgive me, mother, I prefer a woman) nor sister. Neither daughter nor son. . . . I love you, your body, here and now. I/you touch you/me, that's quite enough for us to feel alive. (Irigaray [1977] 1985: 208–9)

Irigaray's two lips cannot be *only* vaginal, without separating, dividing, and reinscribing the *one word*. If it is woman whose sex is not one, it is also that which exceeds woman, as in the French "la personne," whose gender is feminine whether referring to a male or female. And it is that "elle" that resists the digital structuration of one and two, that embodies the mystery in resistance: "Whence the mystery that woman represents *in a culture* [my emphasis] claiming to count everything, to number everything by units, to inventory everything as individualities. *She is neither one nor two* [emphasis in original]. Rigorously speaking, she cannot be identified as either one person, or as two" (26).

This is the same rigor that denies life and death the privilege of exclusive boundaries, as in "les morts ne sont pas morts," or in the figure of the *abiku*, whose Yoruba specificity has been lost in the appropriation of the figure across the continent and the Diaspora. The readings of abiku or Birago Diop's deathless figures of death are continually reinscribed in the phallocentric rendering of African religions into safe compartments, like fetishized formulae for African essence. The freedom of Irigaray's "woman" doesn't lie in any essential, physical trait, but in the liberty with which her text permits us to *read* her. Thus, just like Trinh T. Minh-ha, who insists in *Reassemblage* (1982) and in *Woman, Native, and Other* (1989) on standing *next to* her cinematic subjects, and not in their place, not to speak *for* them, so, too, are we placed in a position that enables us to hear and read *otherwise*—to assume the only agency that escapes from the reinscriptions of phallocracy: "One would have to listen with another ear, as if hearing *an 'other meaning' always in the process of weaving itself, of embracing itself with words, but also getting rid of words in order not to become fixed, congealed in them*. For if 'she' says something, it is not, it is already no longer, identical with what she means" (Irigaray [1977] 1985: 29).

It is this "she" who discovers the technique of mimicry. And she discovers it through touch that subverts sight: the speculum turns and curves the image back and within where intimacy, not distance, where touch, not sight, nor the scopic gaze, prevails: "Within themselves means *within the intimacy of that silent, multiple, diffuse touch*" (29). This touch is the point at which a new language can find its point of departure. Its undermining of the unified (subject) image is reflected back in multiplicity, in the shards of the mirror:

> Must this multiplicity of female desire and female language be understood as shards, scattered remnants of a violated sexuality? A sexuality denied? The rejection, the exclusion of a female imaginary certainly puts woman in the position of experiencing herself only fragmentarily, in the little-structured margins of a dominant ideology, as waste, or excess, what is left of a mirror invested by the (masculine) "subject" to reflect himself, to copy himself. Moreover, the role of "femininity" is prescribed by this masculine specula(riza)tion and corresponds scarcely at all to woman's desire, which may be recovered only in secret, in hiding, with anxiety and guilt. (30).

Thus the denial of distance and sight, of seeing as knowing, and the privileging of feeling, touch, and nearness: "Nearness so pronounced that it makes all discrimination of identity, and thus all forms of property, impossible. Woman derives pleasure from what is *so near that she cannot have it, nor have herself.* She herself enters into a ceaseless exchange of herself with the other without any possibility of identifying either" (31).

Irigaray's last lines here come so close to the figure(s) of Tanga/Anna-Claude that it would seem Beyala was responding directly to their call. The blurring of the lines of identity of self/other responds, as well, to Kristeva's understanding of the abject, not to mention Freud's uncanny. When the Same loses its hard edge of difference from the Other, the basis of the phallocracy is undermined—this being the central thesis of radical feminism: "Now, this domination of the philosophic logos stems in large part from its power to *reduce all others to the economy of the Same*" (Irigaray [1977] 1985: 74).

None of this order of resistance laid out by Irigaray has been dissipated by her critics, but rather has become itself a form of accepted truth, thus making it more vulnerable to deployment as a frozen, rigidified category of thought. Her brief appeal to a strategy of mimicry, questioned and ultimately dismissed by McClintock, holds the seeds for a fresh approach to the African feminist text, and to the doubles that inform it. Here Irigaray is closest to Bhabha in her assertion that it is the "discursive mechanism" that must be subverted. If McClintock sees this as a formalist approach, in which agency is inscribed in the abstraction of discourse, one only has to remember the well-known lines of Cheikh

Hamidou Kane's *Aventure ambiguë* (1961), in which Kane asserts that following the cannons of military conquest, it was much more the canons of the French language, of French education, of the *alphabet* that demolished the walls of Fulbe (or Senegalese, or indeed African) culture and identity. Not the book as fetish; but the discourse of whose authority the book was only the sign.

What if one only feigned reading? Feigning, like assimilating, cannot be done without a successful degree of appropriation—of taking the other and making it one's own, on one's own terms. From within, feigning may entail a mockery, a mockery of mimesis that is only possible if the mimic herself is not taken in. But the risk of being taken in, submerged within the role, ridden as the spirit rides the masquerader, is real:

> [T]he masquerade has to be understood as what women do in order to recuperate some element of desire, to participate in man's desire, but at the price of renouncing their own. In the masquerade, they submit to the dominant economy of desire in an attempt to remain "on the market" in spite of everything. . . .
> What do I mean by masquerade? In particular, what Freud calls "femininity." (Irigaray [1977] 1985: 133-34)

In contrast to masquerade, Irigaray calls for the subversiveness of mimicry: "One must assume the feminine role deliberately. Which means already to convert a form of subordination into an affirmation, and thus to begin to thwart it" ([1977] 1985: 76).

The greatest masters of this strategy can be seen already in Oyono's brilliant mimics—in *Une vie de boy* and *Le Vieux Nègre et la médaille*, which are all about the act of subverting through mimicking. And Beyala has picked up extraordinarily on this playful quality of Cameroonian humor, as has Jean-Pierre Bekolo in *Quartier Mozart*, especially in the characters of Atango, Samedi, Chien Méchant, and Chef du Quartier. The transcription from playing at one role of subordination to another is almost automatic, as can be seen in the various types of women and black characters that inform the theatre of Genet. Or, in radically different circumstances, in Jean Rouch's *Les Maîtres fous* (1954) where the Haoukas' trancing is what enables them to enter into the spirit of mimicry of the colonial rulers.

But Irigaray would take us one step further: it is not roles or subject positions by themselves that must be mimicked, but the discursive basis for the subject:

> To play with mimesis is thus, for a woman, to try to recover the place of her exploitation by discourse, without allowing herself to be simply reduced to it. It means to resubmit herself—inasmuch as she is on the side of the "perceptible," of "matter"—to "ideas," in particular to ideas about herself, that are elaborated in/by a masculine logic, but so as to make "visible," by an effect of playful repetition, what was supposed to remain invisible: the cover-up of a possible operation of the feminine in language. ([1977] 1985: 76)

One can read this appeal as to an essentialized feminine language. But one can also read it, across the optic of an African perspective, as an appeal to the subversive, other space of the African who has had to modify and suppress his/her speech in order to assume that invisible position of the "boy" standing next to the door, awaiting the Commandant's orders. (Given the circumstances of these two examples, it is easy to see how the construction of blackness, like femininity, is grounded in oppositionality.)

The words that come next in the master's script, to fetch the glass of water, to serve it, to play the docile, expected role, are turned back on the commandant by his docile servant's act of spitting, unobserved, into the glass. *His* pleasure lies elsewhere. And it is there, in another space, in an otherwise turn, that Irigaray looks for the mimic to complete her act—the " 'elsewhere' of female pleasure." To arrive there involves the act, like Alice's, of crossing back through the mirror, because "[t]hat 'elsewhere' of feminine pleasure can be found only at the price of *crossing back through the mirror that subtends all speculation*," a mirror, in other words, that provides the subject with "the necessities of the self-representation of phallic desire in discourse" ([1977] 1985: 77). The disruptive excesses which Irigaray calls for all relate to this fundamental reconfiguration of the basis for *discourse* upon which the ground of subject identity is based. Lacan is rewritten—but only after his mirror stage is appropriated by Irigaray.

Which takes us to the mirror and its doubles—the figures that emerge from "the processes of specula(riza)tion that subtend our social and cultural organization" ([1977] 1985: 154), and not just our individual ego formation. Irigaray's revolution through the mirror, her fragmentation of its surface, is aimed at the effects of a flat surface whose reflection presents an image as natural as the economy of desire it subtends—"the *flat mirror*, that is . . . what privileges the relation of man to his fellow man. A flat mirror has always already subtended and traversed speculation" (154)—a speculation reflected in mimetic narrative and its cinematic double, the conventional cinema and its look.

The subject that gazes at the cinematic mirror will always be looking without ever finding what the phallic signifier has been substituted for. But for the "dark continent," there is more than the lack of a substituted object of desire that is experienced. Irigaray's heartfelt "what subject has ever found in it, finally, its due," has multitudinous resonances that reemerge in the bittersweet laughter of Oyono's "pequenots," or of Bekolo's "gars chauds"—those especially sensitive to the excluded space and sensations of the " 'other' . . . reduced by it to the hard-to-represent function of the negative" (154). As the double that remains ensconced within the hard surface of the mirror, "she" reemerges in Irigaray's double gaze across its surface, through its opacity, past its reflections: "To interpret the mirror's intervention, to discover what it may have kept suspended in an unreflected blaze of its brilliance, what it may have congealed in its decisive cut, what it may have frozen of the 'other's' flowing, and vice versa of course: this is what is at stake" (154).

The new relation that emerges in Irigaray's prose assumes the form of liberation as it subtends a new cultural organization emerging from subjects whose forms begin to take shape only in the reflection of the curved surface—"a curved mirror . . . one that is *folded back on itself*, with its impossible reappropriation 'on the inside' of the mind, of thought, of subjectivity. Whence the *intervention of the speculum and of the concave mirror*, which disturbs the staging of representation according to too-exclusively masculine parameters" (155). Then Irigaray can envision the relation of woman "to 'herself' *and to her like*" (155; my emphasis).

Before turning to those relations in this ideal form, African literature has embraced the flat surface that reflects and projects the doubled image of women "as objects or the possibility of transactions among men" (155). The generalized ambivalences to which this possibility has given rise—women carrying weapons or messages for men in Algeria's or Zimbabwe's revolutions, women transferring the wealth of one family to another as part of the process of exchange, women who serve to rationalize colonial ideologies by justifying the "civilized mission" of emancipating native women—may be seen as endless. Before considering Dangarembga's and Beyala's own narratives of miming and doubling, we will look to the flip side of Irigaray's speculum, Bhabha's "less than one and double" mimic men, the others whom we can take as "her like" in Irigaray's terms.

Bhabha

To understand Bhabha's concept of the mimic men, it will be necessary to trace his notions of dislocation, his dislocations of the notions of presence in conventional definitions of identity. Though he is best known for his privileging of the term "hybrid," it must be understood that his usage of the term is not centered at all on biological mixing, or even cultural borrowing. It is not "métissage," which focuses our attention on the person, or the object that is the product of combining different objects, beings, or cultures. Rather, it is the effect felt at the site of enunciation under particular historical circumstances—circumstances of transplantation, dislocation, often under the stress of compulsion, and more particularly under the conditions of colonialism. The text that continually hovers over *The Location of Culture* is Fanon's *Black Skin, White Masks*, not that of the ideologue of revolution with his three-stage formulae of decolonization, but the psychiatrist, the analyst of disruption, rupture, *dépaysement*.

The site of sitelessness, properly "dépaysement," is the best point of departure because it evokes the conditions of migrancy and transplantation that provide the basis not only for Bhabha's ruminations, but also for a large part of what is commonly taken to be African literature, that is, written African literature, and especially Europhonic African literature. On the one hand, an important segment of Africa's population has long had the experience of migration. One only has to think of Aidoo's "Certain Winds from the South" to recall the patterns of economic and even military migrations, especially those that characterize regions marked by considerable differentials in wealth. Much of the story of post-Independence Africa is the story of people from one region seeking work in another—witness not only South Africa and its neighbors, but Gabon, Nigeria, the West African coast versus the interior, Kenya and its neighbors, and so on. In addition, the vast rural migration to urban centers, and finally the horrific flood of transplanted refugees for generations, the dislocations occasioned by war, famine, desertification, or economic strife based on ethnicity, have meant that Africans have had to move, to learn new languages in order just to survive, and have seen their families split by the departures of wage-earners or fighters for long periods.

All this is the massive ground onto which one other kind of migration should be added: that of the intelligentsia, including all too frequently those who write literature. There the migrations are linked primarily to educational and economic constraints, although a considerable dosage of political coercion has figured in this as well. Thus, it is actually rare to find an African author who has not studied or worked abroad. Uncommon might be the permanent nomad like Nuruddin Farah, but common is the Soyinka who received his university degree in England, only to return and depart from Nigeria repeatedly; and not uncommon the Emecheta, Okri, Osundare, Dangarembga, or Beyala who have taken up residence abroad, or whose "African" experience, recorded in the novels, is grounded in the memory of childhood years. Even the older generation of Oyono or Tchicaya U'Tamsi attended lycées in France, and if they returned to Africa, like Oyono, it was to go back abroad for many years as ambassador. Reading the autobiography of Birago Diop provides one with the sense of the extraordinary amount of travel, of peripatetic living, that marked his life until his retirement from the colonial service; and the same could be said of Léopold Sédar Senghor, until he took up responsibilities as president of Senegal, or of Hampaté Bâ's Wangrin, the interpreter for various administrators.

Whereas the older generation of writers, starting with those associated with Negritude and continuing through the 1960s, wrote as if often responding to European interlocutors, countering European prejudices by affirming their own beliefs, in recent decades African writers have turned their attention increasingly to internal conditions in their own societies and to a critique of post-Independent regimes. Anticolonial or even anti-imperialist writing is largely superannuated, while self-critique is prevalent. Even the most ardent critics of neocolonialism, like Sembène, have come to focus less on the interferences from the "Metropole" than the local attitudes of dependency and intercommunal strife, as in his film *Guelwaar* (1991).

Sembène, ensconced in his "Keur Ceddo" for years at Yoff, might well be seen to contrast with Dangarembga or Beyala, who live respectively in Berlin and Paris, and who are approximately half Sembène's age. But even in *Guelwaar*, one has to take note of the same phenomenon of displacement: of Guelwaar's three children, one has left Thiès for Dakar where she earns money as a prostitute for herself and her family back home; another lives in Paris, has acquired French citizenship, and on his return to his father's funeral is not only seen to be out of place, but speaks French rather than Wolof and displays contempt for the local society. Only the third and last son, who is handicapped and therefore presumably discouraged from traveling, has remained at home. And, of course, the film turns on the issue of foreign aid, so that even those who have not left cannot be said to be unmarked by the disruptions arising from the interaction of their society with the world economy.

The disruptions may not all take the form of *dépaysement*. Unfortunately, it is often the call for the opposite—the fundamentalist nativism or "authenticity" that sees itself as the site of the true and original culture or people—that gives rise to the most murderous forms of rejection of the other (Rwanda, Burundi, and Congo offering recent examples). It is this danger that Bhabha senses in his appeal to Fanon, who was "far too aware of the dangers of the fixity and fetishism of identities within the calcification of colonial cultures to recommend that 'roots' be struck in the celebratory romance of the past or by homogenizing the history of the present" (9). Rather, Bhabha focuses on the experience of relocation, relocation of the "home and the world," taking up the title of Satyajit Ray's film version of Rabindranath Tagore's novel, and describes it using the Freudian term "unheimlich," unhomely, the effect of the uncanny misrecognition felt before the image of the double. The "unhomely" for Bhabha is the central experience of our time, especially for the literature of the colonized: it is a "paradigmatic colonial and post-colonial condition, it has a resonance that can be heard distinctly, if erratically, in fictions that negotiate the powers of cultural difference in a range of transhistorical sites" (9). The reason why so much African literature, and especially African cinema, has turned on "women's issues"—forced marriages, polygamy, the right of women to work, or simply to assert the values of their lives independent of their husbands' or fathers' control—can be seen in the particular effect of the unhomely as the disturbance caused by the change in attitudes toward "the home and the world," the private and the public spheres. Specifically, what was once private, and whose recognition as private required its protection from the public gaze, has become, like the unveiled woman, a shocking sight, the site of shock. The "disavowal" of this publicity of the prohibited has been at the core of the reaction against "feminism" or "westernization," or "western feminism"—a disavowal that turns on the subject's sense of himself or herself in the "new" or "modern" spaces of Africa. Civil society, inasmuch as its dominant layers can be said to generate a subject position, feels *itself* threatened: in the Sudan women are barred from taking public transport with men, much less dancing with them; the imposition of Sharia in northern Nigeria is now taking the same form. There is "uncertainty at the heart of the generalizing subject of civil society, compromising the 'individual' that is the support for its universalist aspiration" (10). That universalist aspiration is often accompanied by the most violent of edicts: in Kinshasa after Laurent Kabila assumed power, women were forbidden to wear short skirts or provocative clothing, as had also been the case in Algeria in the late 1960s (by the 1990s the veil had been reimposed).

This has been the struggle of the feminists: not just to remove the official boot, but to realign and make visible the hidden configurations of the home, and even more, to make visible "the forgetting of the 'unhomely' moment in civil society," thereby "specify[ing] the patriarchal, gendered nature of civil society and disturb[ing] the symmetry of private and public which is now shadowed, or uncannily doubled, by the difference of genders which does not neatly map on to the private and public, but becomes disturbingly supplementary to them" (10). As a result, it is now in the redrawn domestic space that are felt "the normalizing, pastoralizing, and individuating techniques of modern power and police: the personal-*is*-the-political; the world-*in*-the-home" (Bhabha 10–11). It is no coincidence that Dangarembga focuses on Tambu and Nyasha's struggles under the domestic regime of the paterfamilias Babamukuru, and that it was precisely from this dimension of *Nervous Conditions* that Beyala mostly "borrowed" wholesale for *Assèze l'Africaine*.

The direct response to the overtly oppressive configuration of patriarchy has often been an equally overt demand for rights, equality of opportunity, support for "family codes"—the liberal humanist formulae through which western feminism as a social movement has made its claims, as if based on a universal code. Less direct has been the appeal to an authenticity and an originary text, as can be seen through cracks of Cissé's *Yeelen*, Gaston Kaboré's *Wend Kuuni*, or more especially in Dani Kouyaté's *Keïta* with its reenactment and canonization of *Sundiata*. Bhabha makes reference to Marshall Sahlin's concept of western bourgeois culture as one that generates knowledge through an integrated, open, expanding code, in contrast to the concept of culture as a static "homogenizing, unifying force, authenticated by the originary Past, kept alive in the national tradition of the People" (Bhabha 37). Both poles can be seen in the feminist debate in Africa—a sort of duel between *Finzan*, with its modernist agenda, and *Keïta*, with its validation of tradition.

The problem with both positions, aside from the social program for which they are mobilized (and which is not automatically placed in one direction or another—cf. Negritude), is that they are both narratives that ignore the process by which they are narrated—they ignore the split between what Bhabha calls the subject of the proposition (*énoncé*) and the subject of the act of enunciation (36), as if the enunciation originated its own act of enunciating and narrated itself. The space Bhabha claims to be opened by the general conditions of language in the production of meaning, the enunciation of a proposition or narrative, is what he calls Third Space, denoting thereby that condition of language that "lies between" and that cannot accommodate self-awareness or the "prise de position" of the subject. This is the enunciative split, a linguistic parallel to the split in the subject occasioned by the introjection of the Other in the processes of the oedipus. The "disruptive temporality of enunciation" introduces ambivalence into each narrative that erects value, asserts meaning: "The production of meaning requires that these two places be mobilized in the passage through a Third Space, which represents both the general conditions of language and the specific implication of the utterance in a performative and institutional strategy of which it cannot 'in itself' be conscious. What this unconscious relation introduces is an ambivalence in the act of interpretation" (35). The solidity on which a national or cultural identity is founded, as in a *Sundiata*, evaporates as one considers that none of the multitudinous *Sundiata*s can ever exist without first being performed, and secondly without its performance being taken to express a set of values, "Malinke" values, whose origins, as in those of the Bible or the Qur'an, are considered transcendental. Hence the "mirror of representation in which cultural knowledge is customarily revealed" (37) is destroyed, just as the mirrored double, taken in the imago as the subject, loses its unity and becomes "less than one and double."

> The intervention of the Third Space of enunciation, which makes the structure of meaning and reference an ambivalent process, destroys this mirror of representation in which cultural knowledge is customarily revealed as an integrated, open, expanding code. Such an intervention quite properly challenges our sense of the historical identity of culture as a homogenizing, unifying force, authenticated by the originary Past, kept alive in the national tradition of the People. (37)

Bhabha's commitment against the notions of originary culture—easily extended to gender—focuses on this ground of the ambivalence that lies at the heart of the enunciative act, and that demolishes the assumption that "meaning and symbols of culture have . . . primordial unity or fixity; that even the same signs can be appropriated, translated, rehistoricized and read anew" (37).

Aside from past ideological constructions of Negritude or authenticité that sought to do precisely that, one can read the contemporary efforts to reconstruct griots, tricksters like Ananse, abiku, deities like Ya, Mammy Watta, Eshu, or Shango, and a multitude of other signs of Africanity, as continuations of the same earlier processes that reify while they erect signs of Africa. The African woman is no less subject to these inevitable processes—she too emerges, as if by herself, like the Mammy Watta from the depths, effortlessly and transcendentally.

In response to this inevitable process, Bhabha makes his claim for the necessity to acknowledge hybridity in culture, this the consequence of recognizing the split in enunciation and its effects upon the production of cultural meaning. "Hybridity" takes us beyond culture as well, although it is best evoked for Bhabha in the context of colonialism—and by extension, patriarchy. This is because in colonialism, as in patriarchy, the erection of the unitary subject is dependent upon economies of difference that totalize the Other—"a tradition of representation that conceives of identity as the satisfaction of a totalizing, plenitudinous object of vision" (46). Bhabha characterizes the relationship between the colonial "I" and the colonized Other as one involving sight, and once again draws upon the mixed visions involving gender and race to accentuate the process of splitting that occurs in the familiar scenario of the male gaze, this time as felt by the migrant woman, Adil Jussawalla: "as even now you look / but never see me" (47). The subject—here the poet—speaks, "and is seen, from where it is *not*; and the migrant woman can subvert the perverse satisfaction of the racist, masculinist gaze that disavowed her presence, by presenting it with an anxious absence, a counter-gaze that turns the discriminatory look, which denies her cultural and sexual difference, back on itself" (47). Bhabha then plays on the "transitiveness" of the act of seeing through an examination of the "phrase of identity," which can only be spoken by putting the "eye/I in the impossible position of enunciation. *To see* a missing person, or *to look* at Invisibleness, is to emphasize the subject's *transitive* demand for a *direct* object of self-reflection, a point of presence that would maintain its privileged enunciatory position *qua subject*" (47). There is a price to be paid for this privileged position, as can be seen in the demand that is frequently translated into situations involving an abusive male ordering around his wives and daughters, without concern for or awareness of their feelings or desires, or even more, against their deepest held desires—whence the extreme literary portraits of women broken in conditions of depression, anxiety, insanity, and self-destruction.

Bhabha doesn't stop there: the second reading follows on his alternate stress placed on the object of the predicate, that is, the invisible (wo)man: "To see a *missing person* is to *transgress* that demand; the 'I' in the position of mastery is, at *that same time*, the place of its absence, its *re*-presentation" (47). When this Eye/I is the instrument of scopic desire, and gazes on the Other as woman and as exotic, her "anxious absence" turns that gaze back onto itself, turning demand into alienation. What the camera work and text of Trinh T. Minh-ha so brilliantly *makes visible* in her repeated re-presentations of breasts, among other body parts, in *Reassemblage*, is that very absence of the eroticized Other, its negations of presence, and especially the returned, absent gaze.

"To see a missing person" is to see a double, to see "en double." If colonialism has been the site for such doubling, it is because, as Bhabha puts it, it is the place of an identification caught between demand and desire. The one built on the rhetoric of the colonial mission, the demand of the colonialist that the colonized change skin, become civilized, eat with a fork, renounce the ancestors. The other built on a desire of the colonized for positions of prestige, met by the refusal of the colonizers. One thinks of the substantially elevated figure Birago Diop cut in colonial times when he was an administrator of veterinary medicine over the vast territory of the French Sudan; at one point he came to blows with a white man over the privilege of seating in a movie theatre. For Bhabha, the place the évolué is invited to occupy, that of the "black skin, white mask," entails a "doubling, dissembling image of being in at least two places at once . . . mak[ing] it impossible for the devalued, insatiable évolué (an abandonment neurotic, Fanon claims) to accept the colonizer's invitation to identify: 'You're a doctor, a writer, a student, you're *different*, you're one of us' " (44).

In Africa, and under patriarchy, the educated or wealthy woman now represents difference; her position poses the problem of finding an appropriate title by which she can be addressed: "Madame le Ministre," "Madame le Professeur." In African urban societies, it doesn't take a minister to raise the issue of the gendered challenge to male authority where house servants still function as "boys" who must obey the orders of a "madame." Aidoo has captured this succinctly in the lines from her story "For Whom Things Did Not Change": "When a black man is with his wife who cooks and chores for him, he is a man. When he is with white folk for whom he cooks and chores, he is a woman. Dear Lord, what then is a black man who cooks and chores for black men?" (1970: 17).

For us, the question left unposed by Aidoo is, what is the black man *for whom* the black man cooks and chores, and by extension what is the black woman in the "master's" position? The answer is the Other, in a colonialized or patriarchal structure, and consequently the site of a splitting, a setting off of otherness as "the tethered shadow of deferral and displacement" (Bhabha 45). The servant, like the colonized, the woman who cooks and chores, does so in response to a demand for identity imposed on him or her for an Other: "The demand of identification—that is, to be *for* an Other—entails the representation of the subject in the differentiating order of otherness. Identification . . . is always the return of an image of identity that bears the mark of splitting in the Other place from which it comes" (45).

The identity that will emerge from the "Other place" and is doubly split, exactly as in the two readings of "To see a *missing person*." Aidoo gives it a postcolonial setting, and Oyono a colonial setting, but both demonstrate completely how the awkward grin and dance show can be transposed from gendered to racial masks as long as there is the question of identity posed under the gaze of the Other.

It is in *response* to this splitting of identity that the fiction and cinema of authenticity—for example, *Things Fall Apart* or *Wend Kuuni*—have been constructed. I will not take up here the task of trying to show why this approach has been so strong, so dominant in African literature and cinema, except to remark that it is not coincidental that a patriarchal order, reasserting itself against the patriarchy of the colonial order, should have given birth first to the panegyrics of essentialism in Negritude, and later to a literature of *témoignage*. For Bhabha, what is of importance in considering the mode of mimetic realism is how it has structured a discourse of identity grounded in a "perspective of depth"—a *"perspective of depth* through which the authenticity of identity comes to be reflected in the glassy metaphorics of the mirror and its mimetic or realist narratives" (48). Calling upon Barthes's evocation of "l'effet du réel," Bhabha speaks of the "arresting [of] the linguistic sign in its *symbolic* function" (48), which has as a consequence the freezing of the signifier into the sense imposed by the signified. This does not come without consequence: *resemblance* is privileged, and as a result of the focus on the signified, a "vertical dimension" is created within the sign, a dimension Bhabha calls the "dimension of depth." It is there, in the *sense* of a profound depth, that the language of Identity is formed—that language, that is, of an identity with depth, meaning, profundity, importance, presence, weight, and so on. This ontology correlates with the "unified" or unitary self inherited from the Enlightenment tradition, the introspective self explored by the Romantics, the self exposed in anguish, truth, and fidelity in the autobiographical explorations of those granted *sight*, or better, *insight* into the human heart.

If African realism doesn't always seek to follow this path of exploration for the individual, it frequently does for the culture, the people as site for a collective identity, equally tied to a signified whose meaning has been authenticated through the discourses of anthropologists and their native informants. Where this has stopped has been at the threshold of the laughing mask, the fictions of parody and comic dismissal, as seen in Ouologuem,

Oyono, Djibril Diop Mambety, Bekolo, Henri Lopes, Sony Labou Tansi, Ahmadou Kourouma, and often Beyala (beginning with *Loukoum*) and Aidoo.

Where works like those of Nuruddin Farah, as well as Dangarembga's *Nervous Conditions* or Beyala's *Assèze l'Africaine*, take us is not to the place of authenticity—although at times their reconstructions of "the village" bring us close to such sites—but to a more conflictual terrain where the ostensible singularity of the mirrored image cannot hold, and the split into the double occurs. For Bhabha, this is exemplary of the "representative postmodern experience," and indeed reading Dangarembga and Beyala inevitably leads to the experience of aporia that is radically different from, radically opposed to the angst of existential despair that was so bound up in the dialectical conflict related to sublimation and authentic being. It is not an image in depth, then, but one that fits Bhabha's evocative phrase "the tethered shadow of deferral and displacement," and that results in a "disseminating self-image," one that exceeds, overlaps and superimposes itself over the "analogical consciousness of resemblance." This the strategy of *doubling* (Bhabha 49).

This point of excess, occurring at the moment of the discursive response to the demand from the Other, provides the possibility for resistance—indeed for Bhabha is marked by the sign of resistance:

> Each time the encounter with identity occurs at the point at which something exceeds the frame of the image, it eludes the eye, evacuates the self as site of identity and autonomy and—most important—leaves a resistant trace, a stain of the subject, a sign of resistance. We are no longer confronted with an ontological problem of being but with the discursive strategy of the moment of interrogation, a moment in which the demand for identification becomes, primarily, a response to other questions of signification and desire, culture and politics. (49–50)

The questions of signification and desire that have driven the demand for identification in Africa have centered around the politics of the home, where the identities of wife, mother, "modern," "traditional," and even free and slave, have been played out, fought over, and ultimately determined. The results have not always been settled with signs of integrity and unity—although the artifacts of popular culture have always been located in such comforting sites: it is there, most of all, that the safe binary opposition of traditional/modern, as an explanatory solution to the ambivalence of splitting, has been sought. And much of pop culture has turned on that binary (invariably identifying "African" with the former, and western with the latter). But the process of articulating such safe solutions has required the conventional symbolic strategy of turning the reader, or the viewer's gaze, away from the site of enunciation into the fullness of the image, of the imaginary; in other words, privileging the signified.

The figure of the double, as Bhabha puts it, "cannot be contained within the analogical sign of resemblance. . . . For post-structuralist discourse, the priority (and play) of the signifier reveals the space of doubling (not depth) that is the very articulatory principle of discourse" (50). And if this principle marks language, it also marks the colonized relationship, the patriarchal relationship to the Other—a relationship doubled in desire and demand, leaving the subject divided, torn between "partial positions": "The desire for the Other is doubled by the desire in language, which splits the difference between Self and Other so that both positions are partial; neither is sufficient unto itself" (50).

Bhabha continually plays on the splitting in language and in the subject, borrowing heavily from Lacan. Meaning, and being, inseparable in the image as in the Other, undergo processes of substitution, a characteristic that is absolutely fundamental to Bhabha's understanding of colonial structures and their narratives. Thus, the assertion that "the access to the image of identity is only ever possible in the *negation* of any sense of originality or plenitude" (51) is true because the image can only ever be constructed *or* appropriated—written or read—through processes of displacement: the image is a "metaphoric substitution, an illusion of presence," and because it is a substitution, it functions simultaneously as a metonym, "a sign of its absence and loss" (51).

The same holds true for the place of the Other: "The Other must be seen as the necessary negation of a primordial identity—cultural or psychic—that introduces the system of differentiation which enables the cultural to be signified as a linguistic, symbolic, historical reality" (52). The representation of the Other "is always ambivalent, disclosing a lack." If that lack is not immediately apparent, if the colonial Other always presents itself as embodying a primordial identity, it is because the process of substitution and exchange by which the phallic signifier functions to establish the authority of its Name—Father, Fatherland, or its colonial metonym Motherland, Metropole—inscribes a "normative, normalizing place for the subject." But, as in castration, that Name cannot be introjected through identification without rupture: it is "the place of prohibition and repression," and even more in the colonial context, the site of "a conflict of authority" (52).

Nothing would seem to make this splitting in the process of identification plainer, more visible, than the évolué's mixed response to the modernist appeal. Ramatoulaye's eager welcoming of the French school, her schoolmistress, and everything it implies for her freedom, her enthusiasm for "progress," and especially her sense of agency in the rebuilding of a new country, must be seen in the perspective of her representation of herself as a faithful Muslim, faithful to her traditions and to the values of her upbringing. Seen from the other side of the colonial border, one has only to consider Conrad's depiction of the "cannibal" pilot or Cary's Mr. Johnson to read not hybridity or mixture but the ambivalence and instability inherent in the discourse of the civilizing mission. "Identification," as Bhabha puts it, "as it is spoken in the *desire of the Other*, is always a question of interpretation," and in the unconscious processes of the acts of interpretation lie inevitable displacements and substitutions. The Other remains present, split in its writing and its reading—in "the process of the subject's signification in language" and in "society's objectification in Law" (52). It is fundamentally split, and it is this split that lies at the heart of the colonial relationship, the colonial enterprise, and the colonized's re-reading and re-writing of herself.

If the question "what is the African woman" has been answered *for* the African woman since the 1930s—"femme nue, femme noire," African dancer, spirit of the land and the blood, embodiment of warmth, inspiration that moves the poet's pen, and so on—in more recent times, her seizing of the word and image has often enough still resulted in the presentation of her voice and image as embodying a set of distilled characteristics, such as patience, malleability, endurance, independence, and strength, that continue to freeze the processes of identification and impose a set of signifieds intended to restore depth—a depth resulting from "the *analogical* relation between superficial form and massive Abgrund" (53). The depth of the metaphorical narrative.

When Tanga looks with cross-eyed impatience at the prison guards of her cell, and when Anna-Claude feigns the need to piss in the prison grounds when being taken to her interview with the commandant of the prison, we are in the presence of a different kind of look: that of eyes that reiterate the refusal of the narrative of patriarchal power. Eyes that look squint-eyed, the "evil eye" of Jussawalla's poem that remains "to watch and to haunt" (53), because the eyes that look back and refuse cannot see what the Other has attempted to present as all that is there. These eyes Bhabha calls partial eyes because of their "destruction of the *depth* associated with the sign of symbolic consciousness," and, it must be added, because of their reluctance to reconstruct new signs of a symbolic consciousness based on the same preconceptions of depth. If African women's writing is divided between these two tendencies—as can be seen in Anne-Laure Folly's prescriptive film *Femmes aux yeux ouverts* (1993) versus Flora M'mbugu-Schelling's phenomenological *These Hands* (1992)[3]—nonetheless, we can find in much African literature and film, and especially recent efforts of African women's writing and film, the vision of "partial eyes" that "bear witness to a women's writing of the postcolonial condition." And here Bhabha is most explicit in explaining how this strategy, one that harmonizes with the common feature of doubling, serves as a means of resistance to patriarchy: "Their circulation and repetition frustrates both the voyeuristic desire for the fixity of sexual difference and the fetishistic desire for racist stereotypes." Bhabha continues, using the evil eye as the site for feminist resistance: "The gaze of the evil eye alienates *both* the narratorial I of the slave and the surveillant eye of the master. It unsettles any simplistic polarities or binaries in identifying the exercise of power—Self/Other—and erases the analogical dimension in the articulation of sexual difference" (53).

Bhabha identifies the "force" of the evil eye as arising not in what it restores in purity or authenticity, but in the disruptions that highlight or make visible the sense of a space, his third space, between two authorized or opposing narratives of authenticity: Master/Slave, or Modern/Traditional. Identity is no longer grounded, but elided, and this elision is made possible by the one who both is and is not what she seems to be, or seems to see: the evil eye is a haunted absence of being, and its strategy is thus one of "duplicity or doubling." The effect of doubling is ambivalence, undecidability, the negation of presence, the "uncanny sameness-in-difference." But that is exactly the strategy of the mime, who is both same and different simultaneously, not through an act of metaphoric substitution, but through "the act of *becoming* through a certain metonymic logic disclosed in the 'evil eye' or the 'missing person' " (53–54).

This logic is built on the double play of sight: while the one appears to be seeing, simultaneously she who seems to be there is absent, invisible; the look on the apparently visible face masks that more deadly gaze of the invisible eye. Medusa as mom, Fatma, bonne-à-tout-faire, the Commandant's maid-cum-bedwarmer, the maiden of virginal beauty whose breasts so excited the viewers in the prenuptial celebrations descried in *Things Fall Apart* or at the dances in *Song of Lawino*—the evil eye has one (un)identifying characteristic, its invisibility, that is, its mask. And it is in this play that Bhabha makes most explicit how the *doubling, miming strategy* employed by the evil eye defines the act of feminist subversion: "There is a specifically feminist re-presentation of political subversion in this strategy of the evil eye. The disavowal of the position of the migrant woman—her social and political *invisibility*—is used by her in her secret art of revenge, *mimicry*" (56).

There is a double action involved in the mimicry which Bhabha presents under two forms: the fading away of the "I" as it appears in the "field" of the Other, a sense of transparency that takes over in the act of enunciation, so that what appears clear seems to emerge as though by itself; and the emergence of the subject through that same act of enunciation, the claiming of self and space for the subject, for the woman, whose refusal is not one of ending silence, but of ending the role of one who is *spoken for*. Mimicry subverts the passive acquiescence of being spoken for by signing, and making visible, the substitutive gesture—like the logic of the supplement that Derrida describes as "compensatory and vicarious . . . an adjunct, a subaltern instance which *takes-the-place* . . . [but] produces no relief, its place . . . assigned in the structures by the mark of an emptiness" (1976: 145).

The resolution of this reading into a subversive political act, one that permits us to read the strategy of doubling and mimicry as variants of the evil eye and invisibility, stems from Bhabha's sense that the ambiguity introduced between colonized and colonizer, or their equivalents in the sphere of gender oppression, is fundamental not only to the reality of their relationship but to the resistance to it as well, and this becomes apparent only in the act of enunciation.

That relationship is described as one in which the "shadow of the other falls upon the self." From the play of that shadow on the variable surfaces of self and other emerges a cultural difference "as an enunciative category": "It is the 'between' that is articulated in the camouflaged subversion of the 'evil eye' and the transgressive mimicry of the 'missing person.' " The strategy permits "the violation of a signifying *limit of space*" (60), without which the very means to think a subversive strategy would not be possible. Neither a purely formal approach, as McClintock would have it, nor a mere reconfiguring of patriarchy as of colonialism, it is rather the indispensable condition upon which subversion becomes possible.

Bhabha achieves eloquence in invoking the strategy of subversion that thus emerges, a strategy based not on the liberal-humanist appeal to "the fullness of Man" but the "manipulation of his representation." Through mimicry and doubling, it becomes possible to exercise power "at the very limits of identity and authority, in the mocking spirit of mask and image;

it is the lesson taught by the veiled Algerian woman in the course of the revolution as she crossed the Manichaean lines to claim her liberty" (62–63)—an action that transgressed multiple boundaries. The transgression disrupts patriarchal authority, as much as colonial authority, revealing behind the play of mimicry, the play-acting of doubleness and ambivalence, the threat of an effective strategy: "The *menace* of mimicry is its *double* vision which in disclosing the ambivalence of colonial discourse also disrupts its authority" (88).

Tsitsi Dangarembga

The Name of the Authority in *Nervous Conditions* is Babamukuru, and it is in the doubling of the daughters that we will be looking for the mimic's reflected signs of challenge to the split features of authority in the novel.

Nervous Conditions is a novel of masquerades and mimics, and it is not always clear which is which. It is a novel of doubling through opposition rather than resemblance. It is a novel that addresses itself directly to feminist concerns more than practically any other novel of its times, and yet not only does its author take her distance from feminism, especially western feminism, she has not written her novel along the lines of the grand experiment of *l'écriture féminine*. In fact, *Nervous Conditions* is closer to the classical realist narrative, with its voyage of self-discovery and development, as Bildungsroman. Through the notes of resonance it has struck, it, like Mariama Bâ's *Une si longue lettre*, has reached a semi-canonical status as emblematic African woman's novel.

The first masquerade, the marketing. "The exchanges upon which patriarchal societies are based take place exclusively among men," according to Irigaray (echoing Lévi-Strauss). As a result, "Women, signs, commodities, and currency always pass from one man to another" ([1977] 1985: 192). *Nervous Conditions* is presented as the sign of the African woman's novel. The two presses that have published it, the Women's Press in Great Britain (1988) and Seal Press in the United States (1989), are "women's literature" presses; the cover of the 1989 Seal Press edition bears a painting of a young African woman dressed and adorned as a villager, in a village setting; the cover also carries an approving quotation from Alice Walker. The title and the novel's epigraph are from Fanon's *Wretched of the Earth*, and although the quotation is from Sartre's preface ("The condition of the native is one of nervousness"), the reference is canonical Third World. The back cover carries a portrait of Tsitsi Dangarembga with a flamboyant hairstyle, with further quotations making explicit the novel's contents involving the "bitter reality of women's lives in modern Africa," and their "determination to be both free Africans and free women in a patriarchal society." Lastly, the note "About the author" on the back page informs the reader that "Tsitsi Dangerambga was born and raised in Zimbabwe," and that she "studied medicine and psychology before turning to writing full-time."

The second masquerade, the genre. *Nervous Conditions* is a novel. The cover bears in large letters under the title the words "A NOVEL," in a font twice the size that used for the author's name. The fictional aspect is reinforced by the quotation on the cover, beginning with the words "That rare novel," and the back cover stipulates, next to the price, "Fiction." When one turns to the opening words of the novel, one reads, "I was not sorry when my brother died" (1). And as one continues, one discovers that the first person voice that addresses the reader, and that continues throughout the novel, belongs to Tambudzai—Tambu—the novel's young heroine who is clearly the subject of all this "Bildung" and emancipation and "coming of age" signaled on the back cover. The reader's natural inference would be to assume, or at least wonder about, a tie between the author and the narrator-protagonist. That is not the consequence of naivete or duplicity, but the simple consequence of a long-standing tradition of first person accounts that address the reader—as in autobiography in which, as Philippe Lejeune has put it, there is an "implied contract" between reader and author. In autobiography that implied contract entails the understanding that the author's words speak the truth about the author, the one whose identity is given on the cover. Here, there is a kind of implied contract, despite the signals that this is a work of fiction, that the experiences presented in the book bear a valid correspondence to the reality they describe, and that that correspondence is guaranteed by the author, who is, like her protagonist, a young African woman, "born and raised in Zimbabwe," and who obviously succeeded in her studies, as did Tambu, to make something of herself (a student of those difficult subjects, medicine and psychiatry).

Whose masquerades? As our reading of the novel continues, we discover that there is a second young woman who plays a major role in the novel, Tambu's cousin Nyasha, who was born in Zimbabwe, or rather Southern Rhodesia to be more precise, but who passed a significant portion of her childhood abroad, that is, in England, and whose difference from the other children, as a result of this period of growth abroad, created problems in her relationship with her family and in her adaptation to Zimbabwean society. But as the novel is not narrated in her voice, but rather in that of her cousin Tambu, the reader does not naturally identify her with the implied experience of the author. Rather, that identification, or better, that masquerade, is reserved for Tambu, whose "coming of age" is signaled on the back cover (next to Dangarembga's picture).

All of this is a bit tongue-in-cheek—like masquerade, because the "implied" aspects of the contracts, the understandings, are all conventional, depending not only on marketing and presentation, but the habits of reading bred by acquaintance with long-standing genres of fiction whose effect, whose punch, whose "reality," or better, "reality effect," is created by such devices as first person narrative and intimate, personal details, along with descriptive passages that expose the reader to the "realities," if not the exotic, unknown features of a foreign culture. For the family member the "reality effect" is not felt through the introduction to new worlds, but in the recognition of familiar details. The masquerade with which the author embellishes, or disguises, the narrative voice would be experienced differently by different readers.

In the case of *Nervous Conditions*, one could well image a Zimbabwean, or Shona, reader reading this novel with that sense of familiarity, whereas the foreign, and especially non-African reader, would not—and would not see masquerade, but rather portrait—a "moving story" being more appropriate to the latter than to the former. Yet for one with a passing knowledge of Zimbabwean history, and of Africa itself, there are some troubling features that disturb the sense of identification and acceptance of the characters and mise-en-scène. The first, and most obvious, is the lack of reference to the fighting that was raging in the country, and especially in the region around Umtali, where the action of the novel was set, at the time of the events in the novel, the 1960s. That fighting entailed Zimbabwe's protracted struggle for independence, usually referred to as the second Chimurenga, and it has frequently been the subject of contemporary Zimbabwean literature.[4]

It is difficult to interpret an absence. It could form part of the novel's strategies, as Charles Sugnet has claimed.[5] It could signal a failure on the part of the author to be faithful to the reality she is ostensibly constructing for the reader; it could be irrelevant, somehow, to the novel's subject, although it is hard to overlook a war! It could, however, not be noticed by readers unfamiliar with the details of Zimbabwe's history—in fact, one would think, the bulk of the readers of the Women's Press or Seal Press.

How does an absence affect a masquerade? Obviously, it can only be noticed by those with some prior notions of the feature being represented by the mask. This takes us to the second point of disjunction: the narrator's reactions to her home. Here it is important to distinguish between the narrator and the character of Tambu, because although the novel is narrated in Tambu's voice, from her first person point of view, she is narrating from some point in time, presumably not too long, after the events that occurred, so that we have a split between Tambu-as-narrator and Tambu-as-character.[6] But regardless of whether we take Tambu's reactions to be those of the young girl in her family's homestead or those of the older, better educated young woman, it is difficult to accept her descriptions of her home as dirty and squalid, such reactions seeming to fit much more an outsider accustomed to different conditions and norms of cleanliness than those with a village upbringing. Yet the youthful Tambu repeatedly calls attention to the dirt and squalor of her surroundings, as though these features called attention to themselves. The tuckshops at the local market are described early in the novel as "pale dirty tuckshops, dark and dingy inside"—an outsider's reaction—although she identifies them as "magrosa," a word whose meaning is provided for the non-Shona speakers: "which we call magrosa" (2). Similarly, when Nhamo returns home from the mission school, it is to his "squalid homeland" (6). It is possible to interpret this as implicitly focalized through Nhamo's eyes, but Tambu returns to such terms as "squalor" and "dirt" frequently enough for the reader to associate them with her point of view. Thus, she writes, "Before he went to the mission, we had been able to agree that although our squalor was brutal, it was uncompromisingly ours" (7).

Tambu's preoccupation with cleanliness is made explicit when she learns she will be going to live with her uncle at the mission. Her books will be clean, her clothes will be clean, and "I would be able to keep myself clean too" (60–61). This is in contrast to her homestead, where dirt reigns: "I knew, *had known all my life*, that living was dirty and I had been disappointed by the fact" (70; my emphasis). In the mission, she is "[f]reed from the constraints of the necessary and the squalid" (93), and when she returns home for Christmas, her first words of reproach to her mother are "why didn't you clean the toilet any more?" (123).[7]

That Tambu is shown to have undergone change, as Sugnet claims, is indisputable, is central to the novel. But that she felt her home to be squalid and dirty before she has been exposed to other values and has begun to change is very difficult to believe, as our standards of dirtiness and cleanliness are among the first things we absorb as normal and natural. But such standards pass from "natural" to "unnatural" when we begin to assume another role, a masquerade with its disjuncture between inside and outside. These first two masquerades hover around the implicit presence of the author lingering in the narrator's voice. That presence, made so evident in the details of the cover, the "About the author" note, Dangarembga's portrait, and the novel's first person narration, along with the "insider" perspective and use of Shona terms, does not accord well with Tambu's reactions to dirt, and to some extent, with her precocious thoughts and "westernized" reactions to the sexist behavior of her brother and father. This reader's response, however, shifted dramatically on learning that much of what is drawn from the facts of Dangarembga's life fits the character of Nyasha much better than Tambu.[8]

Dangarembga, like Beyala, is constrained to describe village life as an outsider—and that fact explains the sense of the above discrepancies. From a close acquaintance of Dangarembga, Thompson Tsodzo, I learned that Dangarembga went to Britain when she was still in elementary school. According to Tsodzo, "She must have been around ten years old or so. Her parents did their Master's degree there, returning around 1968 with their three children, Tsitsi, Gwinyai and Rudo."[9] He continues, "Tsitsi was at a Convent school doing Form 4 ('O' levels) . . . ; she was already a rebellious child (smoking and drinking, etc.), and her very conservative parents did not want her to come near young men." To this portrait, Tsodzo adds that by the time her family had returned from England, they no longer maintained their ties with their rural family, which lived about ten miles from the mission, but that "Tsitsi visited the village against her parents' will. She has always been a person of the people. I would say that this was the time when she learnt about life in the villages, where she did not live herself but was very interested to know about." What the evidence from Tsodzo's letter makes plain is that it is Nyasha and not Tambu for whom Dangarembga's life served as a model, thus explaining the sense of disjunction relative to some of the narrator's reactions. It also suggests that many of the older Tambu's experiences were drawn from Dangarembga's own experiences, suggesting that Dangarembga "split" herself into Nyasha and Tambu, to some extent, so that "the two characters depict the two stages of her personal development" (Tsodzo).

Lastly, on this biographical note, Tsodzo comments on her family, again making it clear that it was principally Nyasha's, and not Tambu's, family that was modeled after Dangarembga's. Thus, Dangarembga's father, like Babamukuru, "came from a poor family. . . . [He] worked as a herd boy (looking after cattle) at the same mission where he later became principal and was said to be a very polite young man. Things changed when he returned from Britain with a Master's degree in Education." As his wife's family was wealthy and eminent, he now associated with them instead of his poor relatives, becoming "a very austere person." His wife "became the opposite . . . very polite, submissive to her husband and greatly liked. . . ." The children were "pampered" and "not allowed to speak in Shona or play with low class children." Tsodzo interprets Dangarembga's own rebellious attitude as being directed against her father's snobbery, her mother's submissiveness, and the deference of the rest of the family to her now powerful father.

My interest in this account of Dangarembga's life is not based on the notion that there is some kind of truth to be uncovered in reading through the novel to the author's life, though I fear such an impression might naturally have been created by giving these precisions. They tell us nothing about the narrative, about the processes by which fiction is read, and very little about their creation, much less about the "truth." They do, however, suggest that this particular novel might profitably be considered in terms of the strategies of masquerade, and further, as a close reading reveals, of both mimicry and the problematics of assimilation as well. We might wish to claim that *all* fiction bears these traits—masquerade, mimicry, and their accompanying qualities of hybridity and doubling. But they emerge from a subtextual level when account is taken of the first two masquerades here evoked, the marketing and the reality effect produced by the narrative voice when viewed in terms of the insider/outsider opposition. They point, in fact, to the heart of this novel.

At first glance, it seems crystal clear that Irigaray's distinction of masquerade/mimic applies to *Nervous Conditions*. At any given moment, we may find any one of the adult women putting on the mask of the docile, feminine woman in order to seduce the men into doing the women's bidding. A prime example would be Lucia's request to Babamukuru for a job. Lucia is depicted as the most independent and powerful of the women in the novel, and her actions greatly disappoint Nyasha and Tambu. As they take their complaints to Lucia, she responds, "But you, Nyasha, are you mad! Babamukuru wanted to be asked, so I asked. And now we both have what we wanted, isn't it?" (160). What this, and many other episodes, will make plain is not whether masquerading or mimicry was employed, but the difficulty in distinguishing between the two.

For Irigaray, the masquerade is a feminine strategy outlined by submission "to the dominant economy of desire in an attempt to remain 'on the market'" ([1977] 1985: 133). It is, conversely, Freud's notion of "femininity" arising from woman's desire to satisfy man's desire for her to be his complement (220)—in Lacanian terms to be the phallus for the man. It is "alienated or false," according to *This Sex Which Is Not One*, because it entails the submission of women to the economy of male desire, rather than an affirmation of their own.

Lucia sells herself to Babamukuru as a woman, to Nyasha and Tambu's disgust, in order to get a job: "he wanted to be asked." She plays to *his* desire. But she wanted the job, wanted to ask for the job, wanted to want his want, just as her physical need had earlier led her to return to Takesure's bed despite her obvious scorn for him. "And now we both have what we wanted." Nyasha's refusal of the game of the mask is obviously "madness" to Lucia, because to refuse to see where power lies and thereby to play along with it so as to get what one wants is to cut off one's nose to spite one's face—madness. Precisely of the sort that defines Nyasha's subsequent bulimia, her "nervous condition." The difficulty lies in knowing when the masquerade is self-consciously adopted by the woman as a means of manipulating men, or when it is unconsciously assumed, and thus is "false" to the woman's desire; when the role playing is indistinguishable from the woman's own sense of herself; when the mask cannot be seen as separate from what lies underneath it; when the mask doesn't come off, and when the makeup doesn't come off. In Irigaray's terms, this would be when the woman couldn't distinguish between masquerade and mime. But it is instructive to look a bit more clearly at these terms in their French originals, with their etymological origins, to see where the nuance of difference lies.

The term "masque," indicating the painted form of the face worn as a disguise, has as its origin "mascha," a Latin term for witch, coming to mean a false face that makes people afraid (Littré 465).[10] The term "masque" comes to mean an ugly or malicious girl or woman, or witch, in various regions of France and Germany. An allied meaning is a "femme de mauvaise vie" (464), a "loose" woman. It is also a theatrical term, and corresponds not only to the mask worn by the players, as had been the case in ancient theatre, but to the play as well. Starting in the sixteenth century, women as well as men began to wear masks, as the older military usages gave way to Renaissance role playing. Its connotations of falseness and role playing never entirely shed its original association with wily women.

This seems to have been carried forward with the term "maquillage" as well. Maquillage means "makeup" in English. Its original French definition is as a theatrical term designating face-paint, the means employed by an actor to play an older or younger person, "le plus souvent jeune" (435). Again the term, in its earlier usage, implied deception, all the more as it is defined as a "terme de coulisse," coulisse connoting not only the backstage of a theatre, but the hidden backstages of life in general. Makeup is thus not so much an enhancer of natural beauty or decoration, as a falsifier, a means of deception, especially as it is associated with women: "beaucoup de femmes du monde se maquillent" (435).

The last term, "mime," also has its ancient Greek and Roman origins in the theatre, and refers to actors playing in comic, light, and popular plays, indicating the one who imitates. All the classical definitions associate the term with comic vulgarity, and one of them with women! The associated qualities of buffoonery and freedom suggest lightness, the absence of seriousness, and can easily be linked to Bekolo's "chaud gars" of the quartier. Irigaray's usage of the term, then, as a woman who imitates, who plays at a role, in freedom, and for her own freedom, would seem to be appropriate as a reappropriation of the male role and its corresponding liberties.

Irigaray locates the strategy of the mime on the level of discourse where women's "play with mimesis" allows her to "convert a form of subordination into an affirmation" ([1977] 1985: 76). Whereas the masquerade involves a disguise that hides (female desire), mime is so openly displayed that it exposes, "by an effect of playful repetition, what was supposed to remain invisible: the cover-up of a possible operation of the feminine in language" (76). It means "to unveil," as this is effected through discourse, because through mime woman is try[ing] to recover the place of her exploitation by discourse, without allowing herself to be simply reduced to it" (76), while in masquerade, "the woman loses herself by playing on her femininity" (84).

The problem lies in knowing when the mime turns into masquerade, when the playful repetition fails and becomes loss, when there is a recouping and when an act of being recouped; when playing at subordination fails to achieve the conversion to affirmation, or when it only partly does so, while rubbing the paint of the mask off on the face beneath. The investigation into masquerading in *Nervous Conditions* reveals an almost endless array of configurations of such subtlety and range as to lead one to question whether any strategy of miming, as can be claimed in the above case of Lucia, can ever be completely free from the losses engendered in masquerading.

Dangarembga's introduction of this element into her novel is very subtle. Toward the beginning, we see Tambu feigning innocence and naivete, as would be expected of a young girl in her first discussion with her father, Jeremiah. He is speaking to his son, Nhoma, blustering and blathering about how wonderful it was that Nhoma was so intelligent, unlike Jeremiah, who would otherwise have been able to provide his family with all the conveniences that Babamukuru had given them. As Jeremiah is notoriously lazy, he wants to make out that it was the natural gift of intelligence that Nhamo, like Babamukuru, has that accounts for his success, just as it explains his own failure. But as Tambu is actually the quick-witted one, she naively asks if "Mukoma," that is, Babamukuru, was "sharp at his lessons." Without reflection, her father naturally replied, "Not exactly that. . . . Not exactly sharp" (5). Then he realizes the trap he has fallen into, and goes on to explain Babamukuru's success as luck, he having had the chance to go to the missionaries at an early age (rather than as a result of hard work, which would leave Jeremiah without excuses for his own failure).

Without seeking gain for herself in this interchange, Tambu plays at the role that allows her entry into the male discursive space. Whether she has "recovered the place of her exploitation by discourse" through her mime cannot be determined by the context as there are no recorded consequences to her intervention suggesting that her father or brother perceive any such "recovery," or even that she sees it in gender terms, or in any terms other than clever manipulation of her father through language. But it sets the stage for her relation with him, and simultaneously stages the strategy of miming for the reader to credit the narrator's judgment that this is a trap into which her father has fallen.

The sequel to Tambu's first recourse to feigning can be seen in the scene that occurs shortly thereafter when Tambu pleads for a chance to sell mealies in town so as to raise money for her school fees. Her father is opposed to this, as he generally opposes her education, and her mother must intervene: " 'And why should I tell her such things?' my mother asked. 'The girl must do something for herself, to fail for herself. Do you think I have not told her her efforts will come to nothing? You know your daughter. She is wilful and headstrong. She won't listen to me. I am tired of telling her things to which she pays no attention,' she whined" (24).

The performance continues; she flatters and fawns over Jeremiah—"You know your daughter." She intimates hidden threats: "She will never forget it, never forgive you" (25). Mostly she feigns agreement—"Do you think I have not told her her efforts will come to nothing?"—to win over Jeremiah's opinion; and knowing his impressionability and laziness, she succeeds in the end. The mix of whining, agreement, disagreement, and menace succeed within the context of the mother pleading for her daughter—that is, manipulating Jeremiah within the circumscription of patriarchy by playing at the role of suppliant—"she whined." It is very difficult to argue for a clear-cut evaluation of her performance as a masquerade or a mime. She "paints herself" with the features of the suppliant, and there is no note of triumph in Tambu's narrative to suggest the nod and wink that would imply recognition of a mime. Instead, Tambu's concluding remark is matter of fact: "That is how on the Tuesday I kept an appointment with Mr. Matimba" (25).

Mr. Matimba is Tambu's teacher. He has enough authority to stand up to Jeremiah's demand for Tambu's money, just as he earlier exercised his professional and social authority in stopping the children from fighting. He is always "Mr. Matimba," never addressed by his given name like Tambu's father, Jeremiah. When Tambu obtains permission to sell her maize, he drives her into the city in his own car, and en route explains how things work in the world—the highways, the traffic lights, and so on—all of which lend status to his authority. Thus it is all the more shocking to see him, too, feigning and fawning over the whites in helping Tambu sell her mealies: " 'Excuse me, Madam,' Mr. Matimba said in English, in the softest, slipperiest voice I had ever heard him use, speaking to an old white woman who walked arm in arm with her husband. 'Excuse me, Madam, we are selling green mealies, very soft, very fresh, very sweet.' " And Tambu picks up the "mask," in imitation of Mr. Matimba: "Smiling brightly I held two cobs out while my stomach rolled itself into tight, nervous knots." Tambu finds these old white people distressingly ugly—("malignant-looking brown spots on their hands")—but overcomes her repugnancy and smiles all the more: "Making sure not to wrinkle my nose, because these were the people who had the money I needed to go back to school, I smiled more broadly, showing all my teeth, and said, 'Nice maize, good maize.' 'Nice, good,' I repeated" (27).

It is not coincidental that Ma'Shingayi (Tambu's mother), Tambu, and Mr. Matimba all resort to these acts of feigning, as the principal purpose of the masquerade can be seen as the commodification of the women. And as the quote from Aidoo's "For Whom Things Did Not Change" shows, the black man who has had to "cook and chore" for the whites has had to learn the meaning of "maquillage," of bowing and scraping and "putting on a face," not just for others to see, but for the others' desire to be satisfied. Tambu's early initiation into these acts—miming, masquerading—signals her introduction both to patriarchy and to colonialism where racial difference supersedes gender difference.

The feigning does not stop there. When Babamukuru—the head of the family clan (whose name means "father's eldest brother"[11])—returns from England, Jeremiah is now obliged to don the mask. According to Tambu, "My father had always been ingratiating in Babamukuru's presence. Even so, the performance he staged on the occasion of my uncle's return was magnificent by anyone's standards" (31). There follows a description of her father's begging ("something that my father had developed an aptitude for, having had to do it often") that is presented with the humor of the spectator who is able to laugh at the other's abjection: " 'Vakomana, vakomana,' he must have said, holding his head in his hands and shaking it, possibly even striking his forehead with the flat of his palm" (31).

The implication of Mr. Matimba's and Jeremiah's sycophancy seems clear. The conditions requiring people—all people—to wear masks for others, unnaturally assuming a false, painted face, are generalized. It is "unnatural," in terms of the novel's own binary structuration, because it is, like culture, artificially assumed and indicative of the devious means to which subservient people must resort. But as it is the strategy of the weak vis-à-vis the strong, it may be put to good uses, even if it is degrading. If it is a feminine strategy, then "feminine" would seem to denote a position of relative weakness more than it denotes gender—the position of the colonized.

But the nuances of its usage in this novel do not stop there. Tambu's mother deploys considerable ingenuity in her various acts of feigning, commensurate with her ability to read others' desires and turn them to her advantage. She doesn't always win, however, despite her careful calculations. Thus when Jeremiah and Nhamo are trying to work out the arrangements for traveling to Salisbury to meet Babamukuru on his return from England, she tries to get them to spend the night before their departure at Tambu's aunt's home. They are indeed well disposed toward the idea of doing so, but "my mother irrationally pointed out that though my aunt would feed them well while they were at her homestead, she could not be expected to provide for the journey as generously as my mother would. They should not blame her, my mother said, if they slept at my aunt's homestead only to die of hunger on the train" (32). Tambu goes on to describe the consequences of her mother's intervention. "My mother had miscalculated. She had hoped that by seeming to dissuade them from spending an extra night away from home, she would ensure that they would do so and thus be free of them for a while longer. This she had achieved, but she also landed herself with the impracticable and strenuous task of finding the provisions" (32). As usual, the men's unrealistic demands are placed on the women who are expected to fulfill them.

What is striking here is that Tambu's mother seems so clearly calculating, so clearly miming concern, and that though the men seem not to realize it, Tambu is able to decipher her mother's codes, even in their most devious turnings. Tambu's *deciphering* can be taken as the relevant point—and not the mother's *miscalculation*—because it is in Tambu's reading that her mother's discourse *becomes* effective as a tool in "recovering the place of her exploitation by *discourse*" while remaining "elsewhere." The "recovery" is for the *daughter whose* passion for reading translates into her capacity to see through discourse the intricacy of motivation and desire.

Tambu and Nyasha are the two daughters endowed with a passion to read, so it is only natural that they would "read through" the masquerades of others, and perform acts of subservience as a mime, and not as a "false" masquerade. The first time Tambu meets Nyasha on her return from England, Tambu is obliged to carry the water-dish for the family members to wash their hands. The task required precise knowledge of everyone's status since the water-dish was offered in order of descending importance for the members of the family hierarchy. By the time Tambu gets to one uncle who is a bit long about modestly protesting his status over another, she has become impatient and feigns an accident: "I grew tired and let some water slop out of the dish on to his feet (apologizing profusely) to encourage him to wash without further discussion" (41). Nyasha appears to be the only one who reads the signs correctly—seeing the feint, and communicating her perception to Tambu: "Nyasha indicated her solidarity with the ghost of a smile and a twitch of her eye" (41).

The complicity between narrator and character—Tambu as subject of enunciation and herself as subject of the énoncé—implicitly extends to the reader, and it is in the invitation to the reader to wink and grin along with Nyasha that the masquerade is to be "unmasked"—demythologized, its "nature" revealed to be "culture." But at times it is virtually impossible for the reader to be sure the wink is there. The best case involves the head of the patriarchy, Babamukuru himself, the "god" in the youthful Tambu's eyes. "He inspired confidence and obedience. He carried with him an aura from which emanated wisdom and foresight." The narrator's position seems clear—not ironic. Babamukuru's "sensibility" is such that "while you listened you couldn't help being overwhelmed by the good sense of his words and resolving to do exactly as he suggested" (44). Of course, this was the reaction of Babamukuru's audience, the ones to whom his rhetoric was directed. "While you listened" leaves open the possibility for calmer, more mature, or more clever readings on later reflection. "Overwhelmed" suggests a struggle in which "reason" functions to naturalize the patriarch's discourse—the "good sense of his words"—so that the auditor would be conquered, made to submit to his will as if to an abstract and universal reason—patriarchy's ultimate technique. But even in her reportage of being overwhelmed, Tambu-as-narrator leaves open the possibility of a counter, ironic reading by the way in which she subsequently describes, and with a wink mocks, the paterfamilias: " 'Er— what I mean,' said Babamukuru, clearing his throat and removing pieces of meat that had stuck between his teeth with the slim blade of his multiple-blade penknife, 'is that what needs to be done is this' " (44). The pretense of superior culture conferring superior intelligence is exposed, as are the commanding notes of his rhetoric that are shown to begin with the throat clearing, peremptory sound. The rapid assent of Jeremiah to everything Babamukuru subsequently says again undermines the claims for sensibility, and returns the performance to its level of a staging, with only Tambu, Nyasha, and the readers joining in the demasking.

The narrator follows this scene with a quiet, understated unmasking of Jeremiah when Babamukuru expresses his pleasure at his brother's having sent Tambu and Nhamo to school, whereas the reader and the whole of Tambu's family are already aware of Jeremiah's opposition to her schooling, his pocketing of Babamukuru's money intended for school fees (now revealed to all, including the reader), and his attempts to obtain the ten pounds from the school principal. For much of *Nervous Conditions*, the artifice of the mask—its servility and deviousness—is set off disadvantageously against reason, and by extension, nature. For nature is presented as uncultivated, as uncontrived and sufficiently empowering to permit a young girl to stand up to her unjust father. But if gender roles under patriarchy are unnaturally differentiated, it becomes less clear where the line between nature and culture is drawn, thus, as in the blurring of the distinction between masquerade and mime, making it difficult to assign responsibility and blame.

We can see this in Tambu's relation with Nhamo. At one point she makes plain the difference between her point of view as Tambu-as-narrator and Tambu-as-character. Tambu-as-narrator looks back at herself as a child responding to Nhamo's baiting, angry over his jeering, sexist remarks. Nhamo had claimed that his good fortune in being chosen by Babamukuru to go to the mission school "was unquestionably deserved, a natural consequence of the fact that he was Nhamo" (48). A little further on, just to make sure it was clear what nature this consequence obeyed, he asked, "Why are you jealous anyway? Did you ever hear of a girl being taken away to school?" (49).

At the time, Tambu-as-narrator tells us, she was sure Nhamo knew that what he was saying was unreasonable, but since then, "I have met so many men who consider themselves responsible adults and therefore ought to know better, who still subscribe to the fundamental principles of my brother's budding elitism, that to be fair to him I must conclude that he was sincere in his bigotry" (49). Nhamo's sincerity, then, in the eyes of the elder Tambu, looking back, attests not to the artifice of a masquerade, but to an underlying, natural disposition: "But in those days I took a rosy view of *male nature*" (49; my emphasis). Dangarembga comes as close, here, to a direct, mimetic, realist assertion about the nature of difference: Nhamo lies exposed, and through him "male nature." But the subsequent lines, and the episode immediately following, complicate the picture, exactly in the same way that Bhabha sees the figure of the double as exceeding the "analogical sign of resemblance." The reason can be seen in the space of writing employed by Dangarembga where, to borrow Bhabha's words, "there can be no such immediacy of a visualist perspective, no such face-to-face epiphanies in the mirror of nature" (50). Bhabha confronts the reader, the "metropolitan intellectual" "caught in the ambivalence of [his or her] desire for the Other"—just as Dangarembga catches the reader in that same doubled desire to read Nhamo as just like all the others, even while articulating the liberal humanist doctrines expected by the reader of a Dangarembga novel. Dangarembga catches herself in embodying that doubled desire, and casts it back to the reader, breaking the illusionist glaze of mimetic realism.

Her casting it back occurs in the subsequent lines in which Tambu exposes her own position with respect to her father and brother, whom she now portrays not as dominating and obnoxious, but as dominated and understandably disfigured in their natures as a result: "I wanted my father and Nhamo to stand up straight like Babamukuru, but they always looked as if they were cringing. That picture was frightening. I used to suppose that they saw it too and that it troubled them so much that they had to bully whoever they could to stay in the picture at all" (50). Tambu now reads her father's and brother's feigning as "cringing," and for her it is frightening. The empowerment, acquired by her mother's miming, is lost on her brother and father, who *look* diminished, not cleverly turning their loss to gain, but turning their loss to others' loss, bullying others.

Once this is established, Dangarembga makes a brilliant move in her narrative. Earlier Tambu's grandmother had recounted how the family had been displaced and forced to give up their land to the invading "wizards," the whites who had conquered because they were "well-versed in treachery and black magic," wizards who were "avaricious and grasping" (18). Now

Tambu-as-narrator does not stop at the patriarchy within the family, or at male nature, to explain the compensatory bullying behavior of her brother and father, but turns her eyes to the larger sociohistorical frame provided through her grandmother's *oral* account: "[F]rom my grandmother's history lessons, I knew that my father and brother suffered painfully under the evil wizards' spell" (50).

The reading of masquerade carries Tambu, and the reader, not just to the visage under the painted mask, but back to the reasons for the mask to be worn at all. When the narration continues immediately thereafter with "Babamukuru, I knew, was different," we have been prepared for the possibility of a double reading: one in which Tambu-as-narrator's voice is *miming* that of herself as Tambu-as-character, the child, the more naive "enfant noir" who, like Camara Laye, would have to experience the pain of considerably more ruptures and separations before being able to see through the fatuity and the frightening features of her uncle Babamukuru. The irony lies between the lines, as Bhabha would read the doubly inscribed colonialized discourse: "He didn't need to bully anybody *any more. Especially not Maiguru, who was so fragile and small she looked as though a breath of wind would carry her away. Nor could I see him* bullying Nyasha" (50; my emphasis). The "I" here is clearly that of the subject of the énoncé, Tambu-as-character.

Immediately after the episode in which Tambu has discovered her brother stealing and giving away the mealies she is growing to pay for her school fees, Tambu finds she has lost her voice with her brother. Her reaction might be described as hysteria, as she literally cannot speak to him, whereas she can speak with anyone else. "Not that I consciously tried to ignore him. It just happened. Try as I would, I simply could not open my mouth to talk to him" (50). Despite Tambu's understanding of the bullying, despite her grandmother's lesson about the wizards, she cannot leap over the next step up on the patriarchy, Babamukuru, who stands clearly as the Name of the Father for Tambu and her entire family. No matter how she might rationalize, understand, or fight back against her brother, or outwit her father, the Baba figure stands upright, casting his shadow, if not his spell, on the rebellious Tambu. If she sees, but cannot speak, it is because of the conflict caused in rebelling against the very figure whom she must internalize and assimilate—the évolué-cum-Father— the introjection of whom is precisely what enables the signifying process to occur. This conflict comes out in her split vision of her brother and father as lying under the wizards' spell, causing her to be frightened, while admiring her uncle, whose position as headmaster is that of a stand-in for the whites. Babamukuru had "plenty of power. Plenty of money. A lot of education. Plenty of everything" (50). Tambu cannot "bring [her]self to speak" because in fighting Nhamo's promotion over her, she is fighting Babamukuru's singling out of Nhamo "for special promotion, as he had been singled out by the good wizards at his mission" (50). Furthermore, as with Nyasha's later bouts of bulimia, her inability to speak can also be read as a mixed form of hysteria through which she expresses her resistance to patriarchy.[12]

This is the first "nervous condition" caused by the patriarchy in the novel. The limits of the masquerade and the mime seem to have been reached in her physical hysteria; but simultaneously they are supplanted by "nature," as the limits of masquerade and mime are those of artifice, whereas her physical inability to address her brother reads as a natural, not an acculturated reaction. It is at once a sign of the limits to which her revolt can go, and at the same time a sign of the adamancy of her refusal where her blockage spreads out in her resistance to her brother.

It is now up to Ma'Shingayi to take the logic of that refusal to its conclusion, following along the limits of Tambu's grandmother's account: " 'Now what evil spirits have arisen between you two?' she scolded. 'If you have been bewitched, then tell us so that something can be done. But if it is your own madness, stop it straight away!' " (51). If wizards had caused Tambu's Baba and brother to cringe and feign, and thus to bully her, her refusal and her understanding now place her against the figure of authority responsible for the masquerade, and she cannot, or will not, turn to mime so as to oppose him. By the end, what appeared to be madness, hysteria, bewitchment, seems to turn into straightforward willfulness: "Seeing how badly my mother was taking our quarrel, I nearly called a truce with Nhamo, but when he told me I would be better off with less thinking and more respect, I was glad I had stood my ground" (51). No longer a hysteric, Tambu turns her silencing into a weapon against her silencer ("better off with less thinking"), and problematizes the stratagem of the mask with its clever words.

The limits of the mask are reached when Nhamo dies, again as if nature supplants artifice/culture. Ma'Shingayi, Tambu's mother, attributes his death to his having been anglicized/acculturated. When he goes to live at the mission, his identity as a Shona speaker, as one whose "site of enunciation" sprang out of the soil of the village and homestead, is broken. He now refuses to speak Shona, and speaks English with his father as much as possible. The ironies over language are clear: "identity," the subject's position, is expressed *immediately* in discourse because overlying all other forms of difference, the difference signaling colonial identities is expressed in speech. The break in Nhamo's speech is an example: his mother is distanced as he assumes the role dictated by the new speech acquired through an English education. The break thus announced is read by his mother as the cause of his death: she pushes away Maiguru, who tries to comfort her, and cries out: "Now, when it is too late, that is when you are concerned. You pretend. You are a pretender, you. First you took his tongue so that he could not speak to me and now you have taken everything, taken everything for good. Why are you keeping quiet! Why are you not speaking! Because it is true. *You bewitched him* and now he is dead" (54; my emphasis).

We have come full circle. Ma'Shingayi, the artful manipulator of the mask, now makes Maiguru's presumed feigning the target of her accusation. It is all the more amazing an accusation when we consider the doubled turnabout in her accusation of witchcraft in that Nhamo's passage to the mission was not in opposition to the "wizards," but one that followed in their path, one that led Babamukuru, the family patriarch, to his greatest success, and which thus made possible, in turn, his largesse extended to the entire family. But that success was itself a consequence of the effects of the wizards, so that her reading of colonization as having killed her son had figuratively already occurred by the time it had distanced him from her.

If we now recall the origins of the word mask, "maschera," and its associations with witchcraft, as well as "bad woman," "false face," and theatrical disguise, we can read the full despair of Ma'Shingayi: her accusation and anguish would seem to be directed against the very strategy women were forced to resort to under patriarchy. That strategy is not "witchcraft," but the act of feigning the role demanded by male desire, a role that would bewitch, when it worked, because it would turn that desire back, satisfying her own desire while seeming to yield to the other. Ma'Shingayi assimilates this into the masquerade, and in her pain articulates it fully, charging Maiguru with pretending, and with bewitching Nhamo. Unlike Tambu's silence, her "reading" leaves her with no place to go, no strategies left with which to resist the wizards of patriarchy, and she collapses: "This time when she fell to the ground she did not pick herself up, but rolled there, tearing her hair and her clothes and grinding sand between her teeth" (54). A powerful figure of powerlessness, of the failures of the mask.

There is an abrupt shift in the novel at this point. Tambu is chosen to replace Nhamo at the mission, and despite her mother's opposition (one strikingly similar to that of Camara Laye's mother, or even to Kateb Yacine's[13]), she goes off. Here begins her life with Nyasha, and the introduction of a new element, the effects of the doubling created by her relationship with her cousin. The key issue for us to consider in our examination of this period of Tambu's life is her relation with Nyasha, and the question of *why* they are split into two. It would seem that only the radical splitting of self into doubled other could make possible a strategy of miming, the starting point for Tambu's "emancipation."

Double or Nothing

From mask to mime to double, one is led to ask, where is the threshold for the feminine, and especially for the colonized feminine self, leading us directly to Bhabha's formulaic "less than one and double," which applies specifically to the colonial situation where the colonizer views the colonized under two optics: as subhuman (less than one), and as naturally good or to be civilized (double). The hybridity of the colonized, his "sly civility," his subaltern role, is also "not one," if not "two" as Irigaray figures the feminine. What emerges from Bhabha's analysis is the impossibility of reading the oppressive relationship of colonizer to colonized as a simple binary in which two unitary entities are set in opposition. For some, this weakens or destroys the potential for real oppositionality by undermining the agency of the colonized. But agency does not exist in some abstract space apart from its articulation and implementation. Above all, agency is expressed in the act of enunciation, and it is there that Bhabha's analysis focuses our attention on the split nature of the subject.

In Judith Butler's examination of gender, she refuses to accept all forms of transcendental, unitary, fixed identities. And it is possible, in reading her analysis of doubles, to see the logic extended from gender to colonialism just as the reverse was possible with Bhabha.

Butler's discussion of the nature/culture binary enables us to work this logic through. We have already noted how the masquerade in *Nervous Conditions* functions as "culture," as artificially constructed behavior and language, and that it is assumed not only by women vis-à-vis men, but by the colonized across the entire spectrum of power. Finally, we saw how Ma'Shingayi rejected it on the occasion of her son's death, ultimately blaming the pretense and witchcraft of acculturation for his death. Butler sums up well the "strategies of domination" that are built into Lévi-Strauss's binary culture/nature: "The binary relation between culture and nature promotes a relationship of hierarchy in which culture freely imposes meaning on nature, and, hence, renders it into an 'Other' to be appropriated to its own limitless uses" (Butler 37). Butler goes on to cite the work of two anthropologists, Marilyn Strathern and Carol MacCormack, who have shown that the binary typically figures "nature as female, in need of subordination by a culture that is invariably figured as male, active, and abstract" (37).

The key point is that the sexual politics of this figuration goes unstated—it is assumed and "concealed by the discursive production of a nature and, indeed, a natural sex that postures as the unquestioned foundation of culture" (37). This view of nature, as sexed and incorporated into a dominant masculinist economy, arises from the awareness of its production as a discursive formation—exactly the same approach taken by Bhabha (and Derrida as well). What Butler's analysis leads to is the "unmasking" of the concealed assumptions about nature, assumptions that have important implications for "gender hierarchies" and for the "relations of subordination [that] they reify" (37).

While Butler's focus is on gender hierarchies, it is obvious from *Nervous Conditions* that more than gender is at stake in the "cultural" construction of hierarchies or relations of subordination. As the Aidoo quote so efficiently sums up, the relations of subordination entail a mixing of male/female, black/white, colonial/postcolonial, in which any one character enjoying a dominant position in one binary may be reduced to the inferior position in another binary under different circumstances. We are dealing with multiple and overlapping structures of difference, in which the Name of the Father appears increasingly abstracted and distanced when taken as an isolated principle.

Thus, we can appreciate the Butlerian analysis of the nature/culture binary all the more when we consider "nature" in *Nervous Conditions* as being figured not only as female, as Strathern and MacCormack argued, but also African as opposed to European, or black as opposed to white. But even that doesn't last for long when we consider Babamukuru and his anglicized family as being examples of "culture" vis-à-vis Tambu's family, still sunk in a state of "nature." This can be seen, especially for Tambu's parents, in the opposition of English to Shona, English education to Shona work, English status, power, and wealth—"everything" that Babamukuru has acquired, cultivated, to Shona dirt, "squalor," poverty, indifference and indolence that so naturally comes to Babamukuru's inverted double, his brother Jeremiah. If a black man who "cooks and chores" for a white man is a woman, as Aidoo says, then the answer to her question "what is a black man who cooks and chores for a black man" is "nature," that is, the state that is *prior* to culture, and, it goes without saying, subordinated to culture.

Thus we can understand better Ma'Shingayi's anguished accusation against poor Maiguru that she is a pretender who bewitched her son. Both pretense and magic are part and parcel of the artifice of culture, its masquerades of power that conceal its power. What greater concealment, then, of the cannon than the alphabet, the book that smashes "real men's" testicles, to borrow Okot p'Bitek's striking figure, drawn from Lawino's natural lament over the loss of her acculturated husband. And this is the real issue that emerges after all the conflict between Tambu and Nhamo over the prior rights of the males over the females to education and power—the nature of domination itself as "natural," the inevitable final word that sustains all rationalizations built on the binaries of difference: male/female, civilized/uncivilized, white/black.

But appearance and pretense can be read across another perspective, that is, Lacan's construction of gender in which the male "has" the phallus and the female "is" the phallus, both "being" and "having" entailing "culture" and not nature. Both maleness and femaleness, as ontological entities, arise out of the effects of signification—they are "effects" of being, not being-in-itself. "This ontological characterization presupposes that the *appearance or effect of being* is always produced through the structures of signification" (Butler 44; my emphasis). As such, the grounding of this effect of being lies in the symbolic, and is only misread as having an originary structure in the real, a misreading that lies at the heart of Freud's (and Kristeva's) quest for that originary moment either in the primal family or the primal cultural/historical moment. But the symbolic is grounded not in any originary being or prior historical or cultural moment; it is grounded in lack, in rupture, in the effects of a castration whose primary effect is the creation of an absence that the subject continually attempts to fill. Thus it is that gender constructions located around "being" and "having," no less than the racial constructions of black and white that also rely upon "being" and "having" the attributes of civilization and of superiority, are constructions, aptly termed by Butler "phantasmic." "Every effort to establish identity within the terms of this binary disjunction of 'being' and 'having' returns to the inevitable 'lack' and 'loss' that ground their phantasmatic construction and mark the incommensurability of the Symbolic and the real" (44).

This explains the positionality of the masculine subject. The "speaking 'I' " of the masculine subject arises from castration—from the "effect of repression," that effect being felt in the sense of the subject as an autonomous being. The "sense" is a posture, an appearance, as this "I" "postures as an autonomous and self-grounding subject" (44), but can do so only by denying, and remaining blind to its denial of the incestuous desires that have been repressed—the condition of "primary repression." As a result, the masculine subject only "*appears* to originate meanings and thereby to signify" (45), this appearance belying not only the originary act of repression that leads to his sense of himself as autonomous, but also his further dependence on the female reflection of his possession of the phallus: "the demand that women reflect the autonomous power of masculine subject/ signifier becomes essential to the construction of that autonomy and, thus, becomes the basis of a radical dependency that effectively undercuts the function it serves" (45). This dependency is all the clearer in that it is women's acquiescence in the role of embodying the desire of the other, that is, in "being" the phallus, that the masculine subject requires in order that his "having" the phallus might enable him to play his role in this dance of desire.

> Women are said to "be" the Phallus in the sense that they maintain the power to reflect or represent the "reality" of the self-grounding *postures* of the masculine subject, a power which, if withdrawn, would break up the fundamental illusions of the masculine subject position. In order to "be" the Phallus, the reflector and guarantor of an apparent masculine subject position, women must become, must "be" (in the sense of "posture as if they were") precisely what men are not and, in their very lack, establish the essential function of men. (45; my emphasis)

This can help us understand Nhamo's obnoxious behavior toward Tambu, and her refusal to accept that behavior, as she expresses it in the striking opening line of the novel, "I was not sorry when my brother died" (1). Nhamo needs Tambu in order to *be* a masculine subject. This we can see when he follows Tambu to the field to brag about his uncle's decision to take him to the mission school: "Unable to wait until I came home to begin bragging, he came to the vegetable garden, where he sat on a log and congratulated himself while I diverted one of Nyamarira's smaller tributaries into the beds of onions and rape" (47). Jeremiah's weakness, his sycophancy and pusillanimous behavior, especially when confronted by his elder brother, undermines Nhamo's efforts to *be* a *Shona* man—and Nhamo's roles in the homestead and at the local school confine him to that role. If his success in school attests to his "having" the phallus, then the even greater successes of his sister challenge that position. He has no other figure who can function as what he is not, as lacking what he possesses, but his sisters, and when his first junior sister refuses to carry his bags for him when he returns to the homestead by bus, he must turn to her younger sister to play that role. But Tambu keeps frustrating Nhamo in this endeavor: she obstructs Netsai when she is willing to carry Nhamo's bags, and when that doesn't work, Tambu sets out to insure that she herself will be able to attend school just like Nhamo. Again he endeavors to foil her resistance, her attempts to refuse her "lack," and steals her mealies. Again she frustrates his endeavors to keep her in her "place," and not only uncovers his theft, but publicly attacks him.

Tambu's fury at his behavior, then, is actually fury at the role that everyone in her family conspires to impose on her, the role needed by her brother, and indirectly her father, to be men, to be masculine subjects who can speak from that position. The effectiveness of these "phantasmatic constructions" in appearing autonomous and self-grounded can be seen in the "wiser" comment of the older Tambu-as-narrator that as she has seen more of masculine nature reproduce these prejudices against women, she has come to question her earlier "rosier view of male nature" (49), a view summed up in her decision to pursue schooling and not accept her father's admirably pithy advice to be a woman: "Can you cook books and feed them to your husband? Stay at home with your mother. Learn to cook and clean. Grow vegetables" (15).

Butler discusses the classical Lacanian notion of femininity as an act of masking a lack, so that their "being" the phallus translates into an *appearance* of being: "an 'appearing' . . . gets substituted for the 'having' . . . so as to . . . mask its lack" (46; quoted from Lacan). All being thus becomes appearing, as Butler notes, so that "gender ontology is reduced to the play of appearances" (47). Conversely, if conventional gender difference is nothing but conventional, the question then arises, what if there were a desire, let us say a feminine desire, that existed *prior* to the currently dominant patriarchally structured pattern of sexual differences—a feminine desire that is "masked and capable of disclosure, that, indeed, might promise an eventual disruption and displacement of the phallogocentric signifying economy" (47)? We seem quite close here to Kristeva's semiotic, not to mention Irigaray's morphology of the feminine.

If the latter suppositions were to be considered with respect to *Nervous Conditions*, then the question of why we find the doublings that occur, especially that of Nyasha and Tambu, might be answered by seeking the disruptions they cause. Masquerading and doubling, two of the key strategies employed in the novel, would then serve a similar economy, but in different ways. The former would enable the suppression of feminine desire, unless it turns to mime; the latter would serve as a mechanism of disruption, exactly as Bhabha saw it disrupting the colonial economy through its ruptures caused at the site of enunciation and subject positioning.

Tambu's disruptions of Nhamo's attempts to elaborate a masculine subject position are obvious—they are surface disruptions, almost the opposite of systemic disruptions as they result in reaffirmations of prevailing patriarchal values. There are other disruptions that go in the same direction: Nyasha's rebelliousness and challenges to Babamukuru's authority; Lucia's defiance of the family patriarchy; Maiguru's act of standing up to Babamukuru and leaving home, and so on. Nyasha's bulimia belongs to this set, though it expresses her revolt in atypical fashion for an African narrative, and represents an extreme example of resistance on the surface of the system. Like all the abovementioned acts of female revolt, it does not challenge the prevailing heterosexual economy of difference, but rather takes us to the borders of subversion that this novel strains so forcefully to evoke. It takes us to the edge of daring, where nervous conditions and hysteria mark refusal of lack, and where a mother pulls back at the prospect of having to deal with witchcraft.

The ultimate function of the mask comes in response to refusal. Butler cites Lacan: "the function of the mask . . . dominates the identifications through which refusals of love are resolved" (quoted in Butler 48). These somewhat enigmatic words are taken by Butler to mean that in melancholy a mask is assumed so as to permit the *incorporation* of "the attributes of the object/Other that is lost, where loss is the consequence of a refusal of love" (48). Thus are the refusals "refused"—turning loss into identity, especially female homosexual identity. Butler goes on to tax Lacan for his assumption that it is the refusal of heterosexual desire that instigates this defensive move that results in lesbian desire. She reverses the assumptions, asking whether heterosexuality itself might not result from disappointed homosexual desire.

What matters for us here is the notion that as a result of refusal, the mask that assumes the form of a gender identity is constructed, a mask that is formed by the incorporation/appropriation of the one who refuses the masquerader. Following this, we can note that Nhamo refuses Tambu, that her initial "shocking" rejection of emotion over Nhamo's death[14] reads as an act of defiance, as a mask of indifference, but that she readily appropriates his position at the mission, accepting her substitution for him, upon his death.

The reason for constructing the mask, following this reading, is clear, and emerges unscathed from Butler's dissection of Lacan's account. She puts it beautifully: "every refusal is, finally, a loyalty to some other bond in the present or the past, refusal is simultaneously preservation as well" (49). If Tambu *refuses* Nhamo's rejection of her, if she ultimately assumes his place at the mission and in the hopes of the family, it is clearly in loyalty to her bond to Nhamo and to her family, a bond made all the more fragile by the refusal of her brother, her father, and even her mother to support her efforts to follow the path of Nhamo, Babamukuru, Maiguru. And if her refusal took one direction *in the past*, in which she appeared primarily to wear the mask of the rebellious daughter, it is all the more striking that her present refusal, primarily of her mother's concerns over losing Tambu to acculturation at the mission, takes the form of her wearing the mask of the *obedient* daughter during her residence at the mission! The obedient daughter who forms the model for the father, Babamukuru, to hold up as a corrective example to his own daughter[15] (a pattern copied closely by Beyala in *Assèze l'Africaine*).

The mask functions to conceal loss, "but preserves (and negates) this loss through its concealment" (49–50). The tie between the mask and doubling is made clear: the loss is acknowledged, but only as a reality to be concealed; the Other who refuses is not the subject, but is appropriated in the mask, and made to *stand in* place of the one/subject who is refused. The desire of the subject who is refused is covered over by the mask that conceals the loss of refusal, the mask through which the construction of the Other's desire is now spoken. As with Bakhtin's notion of double-voicedness, the mask reveals in the open as it conceals beneath—it is double, and as we are speaking of a psychological condition that is centered on the body, on a body that produces an identity, the mask can be said to be inscribed on the body.

Butler begins from Joan Riviere's analysis of melancholy as the state through which this posture of the mask is formed:

> The mask has a double function which is the double function of melancholy. The mask is taken on through the process of incorporation which is a way of inscribing and then wearing a melancholic identification in and on the body; in effect, it is the signification of the body in the mold of the Other who has been refused. Dominated through appropriation, every refusal fails, and the refuser becomes part of the very identity of the refused, indeed becomes the psychic refuse of the refused. The loss of the object is never absolute because it is redistributed within a psychic/corporeal boundary that expands to incorporate that loss. This locates the process of gender incorporation into the wider orbit of melancholy. (Butler 50).

This takes us to the heart of Tambu's strategy, and Dangarembga's doublings. Tambu's loss of Nhamo is followed by her immediate appropriation of his position at the mission. His refusal, her reaction, the subsequent events that make up the substance of the first three chapters, are all bound up in the definitions of appropriate gender behavior according to Shona society, and that includes the rule of difference that prescribes education as the means for advancement for males, and growing and cooking vegetables for females. Tambu's rapid substitution for Nhamo is taken entirely along these lines by all the members of the family, as though the only issue of importance were the distribution of authority and power along the hierarchy. Nowhere is libidinal desire evoked as a feature of this struggle. Indeed, its absence is all the more remarkable in this, a novel of "a girl's coming of age," and in the intercalated references Tambu makes to the zones of her body on which gender identity is conventionally written: "when I was feeling brave, which was before my breasts grew too large, I would listen from the top of the ravine and, when I was sure I had felt no one coming, run down to the river, slip off my frock, which was usually all I was wearing, and swim blissfully for as long as I dared in the old deep places" (4); "the river flowed sparsely in a dry season, but deeply enough in places when the rains were heavy to cover a child's head and to engulf me to my nipples" (31).

Like Nhamo, then, Tambu learns "book," and to speak English, to speak even better than her father, with whom Nhamo would converse when he came home. And at the end of this first period of her life, when Nhamo dies and she replaces him, she leaves her mother brokenhearted—exactly as did Camara Laye when he departed for school at Conakry. She sums up her situation, assuming the very position of her brother who had trumpeted his triumph over her in the past: "I was vindicated!" (57). We can state that her victory was complete, even exaggerated—as victory always appears to be when written on the body as a mask.

Whereas we may, with Butler, dismiss those accounts of homosexuality that are attributed to the reaction over refusal, we can accept the notion that masks of various forms are assumed in reaction to refusals, and that it is in their fixed grins, their exaggerated forms, that we can read the features of a reaction to and appropriation of loss. Lacan reads the "mask" of "women who wish for masculinity" as "an effort to renounce the 'having' of the Phallus in order to avert retribution by those from whom it must have been procured through castration" (quoted in Butler 51). In other words, homosexuality would arise in a woman out of fear of retribution for taking the place of a man. Now, this is exactly what Tambu does in taking Nhamo's place. Further, if we can extrapolate from her successful revolt against her father—her success in obtaining schooling despite his wishes, in keeping the ten pounds away from him, and eventually in acceding to an educated position that far exceeded his own, thus placing her over him in the standard hierarchy of authority within the colonial economy—we can take it that her true struggle is with her father, and not Nhamo; her true refusal to come from her father, and not her brother; and her incorporation to be of Jeremiah, and not of Nhamo. In other words, the refusal, struggle, and incorporation involve patriarchy in its fullest sense, the African patriarchy from which the girls, and generally the women, are excluded.

Tambu's revolt and subsequent formation of the mask cannot go far enough, because in moving on to the mission she is now placed in a position where she is not only refusing her father's refusal, but also her mother's. More significantly, if her success at the mission will accomplish her goals in revolt against her father, they still leave her under the authority of the patriarchy, as Babamukuru remains in charge of her life, her education, her progress, and her "emancipation," as she repeatedly puts it. Most of all, the success of the revolt against her father puts her in the position of having "castrated" her father, and to avoid the retribution for this she needs more than the mask of femininity. Her doubling with Nyasha is the "solution" to this crisis: it represents the radical split in her subject position which she could not bring herself to face: the split occasioned in her gender identity as well as her identity as a Shona woman versus that of an English/white colonizer. In short, if she incorporates Nhamo in reaction to the refusal she opposed, Nyasha now supplants Nhamo as the double, and instead of his residing within Tambu's psyche, within her interior space, he is projected outward onto the person of her cousin Nyasha.

This choice of Nyasha as her double fits perfectly with Butler's account of Riviere's analysis of the daughter's struggle with the Other, her father, "*not over the desire of the mother*, as one might expect, but *over the place of the father in public discourse as speaker, lecturer, writer*—that is, as a user of signs rather than a sign-object, an item of exchange. This castrating desire might be understood as the desire to relinquish the status of woman-as-sign in order to appear as a subject within language" (51; my emphasis). This fits the case of Tambu/Nyasha and Babamukuru so perfectly, one might suspect Riviere of having plagiarized Dangarembga, had not Riviere written her account in 1929!

In fact, what this description fits so well is the colonial situation, obviously one that obtained for women in the early part of the twentieth century in Europe as well. In the case of the novel, it is clearly

Babamukuru who holds forth in the public discourses of the family councils as the one in charge of speaking, lecturing, writing. As the head principal of the mission school, he enjoys that same status conferred on him not only through his position in the extended family, but by the authorizing agency of the colonial powers, with the university degrees from South Africa and London. The split functions of Tambu's revolt can be seen in reaction to—and in appropriation of—the larger refusal that Babamukuru represents to her "emancipation." Tambu and Nyasha both pursue the path of education. But they are split along other lines: Nyasha reads "against" her father, reading daring, sexually explicit novels such as *Lady Chatterley's Lover*, whereas Tambu reads the prescribed curriculum to qualify her as fully educated. They both become bilingual, but whereas Nyasha openly speaks out against her father, Tambu guards her silence, and in her one moment of revolt, in her refusal to attend her parents' wedding, becomes totally silent and unresponsive, as she had been when refusing to speak to Nhamo.

Nyasha speaks English fluently, and Shona hesitantly; Tambu is the opposite. Nyasha dares to stay out late and smokes cigarettes, against her father's wishes; Tambu condemns this behavior. Most interestingly in terms of the sexual identity signaled by this revolt, Nyasha effects an openly sexual, eroticized identity, in contrast to Tambu. In fact, it is Nyasha who wears skirts that are too short by her father's standards; who dances with boys, staying out late with the white mission boy, Andrew, who is presumably teaching her new steps. It is she who is treated as "whore" by her father, and who reacts most bitterly to that epithet. In short, her rebellion takes the form of an open assertion of her sexuality, providing her with a degree of closeness to Lucia in this regard.

Tambu, on the other hand, does not dance with the boys, but sidles over to the girls when she finally gets to dancing. She makes no mention of any relationship with a boy, but when the nuns from the convent school come, expresses admiration for their sharp dress and attractive appearance. It is they who offer her the opportunity of freedom ("I was to take another step upwards in the direction of my freedom" [183]). "When the nuns came to the mission and we saw that instead of murmuring soft blessings and gliding seraphically over the grass in diaphanous habits, they wore smart blouses and skirts and walked, laughed and talked in low twanging voices very much like our own American missionaries did, we were very disappointed" (176). That disappointment might be read in seeing that the nuns offered a model of women not as subjugated to the patriarchy either through status or sexual deprivation, but as supplanting the mission patriarchy, headed by Babamukuru and his anglicized model of authorization, with a female and American patent. The "myth" about the nuns was exploded, but their school remained "glamorous," "a prestigious private school" where girls wore "pleated terylene skirts to school every day and on Sundays a tailor-made two-piece linen suit with gloves, yes, even with gloves! We all wanted to go. That was only natural" (177–78).

For the girls at the mission, the nonspiritualized appearance of the nuns, their "ordinariness," explodes the myth of chastity, and yet, in the same breath Tambu asserts, "[T]he question of sex was not an obsession with us" (176). In fact, far from being an obsession, as it clearly was within Babamukuru and Nyasha's relationship, it was the opposite—invisible, or at least *never* mentioned, as though it were not there at all. In this regard we can say that if the myth about the nuns arose out of their public personae, so, too, does Tambu's persona evoke the myth of asexuality, or even repressed female desire as expressed in her neutralized admiration of the nuns and her evocation of friendships exclusively with other girls, including especially Nyasha.

This is not to suggest that *Nervous Conditions* is built around a hidden homosexuality, but rather that the divisions of the doubled subject positions of Nyasha/Tambu, formed in conjunction with the masks assumed in their relationships with their fathers, suggest such a pattern. And as this is a pattern of appropriation and concealment in response to loss, refusal, and fear of retribution, it is all the more suggested by the tenor of this, a novel about the subversive nature of female revolt in Shona society under colonialism.

Given this reading of Nyasha as assuming the projected form of Tambu's double, and of Nyasha as occupying the position formerly assumed by Nhamo, it is interesting to see the parallels between Nyasha and Nhamo. Both are older than Tambu, and attend higher grades in school. Tambu succeeds in supplanting both of them. Both try to keep Tambu from leaving the school in which she is currently enrolled and passing on to a more prestigious school. Both stand in some degree of rivalry with her—and in each instance, Tambu ultimately indicates her higher level of achievements: in the case of Nhamo, it is higher grades; in the case of Nyasha it is help in solving a math problem that Nyasha cannot solve.

Both Nyasha and Nhamo fall, as if in proportion to Tambu's rise, as if there were some mechanical relation implying that her success were at their expense. And in each case, the issue of acceding to the father's position as "user of signs rather than sign-object" is of paramount importance. Nhamo tells Tambu to "think less" and to be more respectful (51)—to stay in her place with him away at the mission, to keep separate from the family palavers. When Nhamo wishes to demonstrate his superiority at home, he does this by speaking only English, thus breaking his mother's heart: "She did want him to be educated, she confided to me, but even more, she wanted to talk to him" (53). Tambu's conflict with Nhamo over access to a speaking position is expressed directly when she states that with his departure she would be relieved, because "I would be free to talk to whomever I wished" (51).

Similarly, when Babamukuru expresses his anger at his daughter, it is her speech that particularly troubles him. As she speaks back to him, he strikes her: " 'Never,' he hissed. 'Never,' he repeated, striking her other cheek with the back of his hand, 'speak to me like that' " (114). He attempts to control her through assigning the "sign-object" of "whore" to her because of her revolt, and engages the issue at the precise point of gender identification: " 'She has dared to challenge me. Me! Her father. I am telling you,' and he began to struggle again, 'today she will not live. *We cannot have two men in this house*' " (115; my emphasis).

In Babamukuru's relationship with her, Tambu sees a parallel to Nhamo's behavior towards her. Both girls are cast into similar positions: it was "just as I had felt victimised at home in the days when Nhamo went to school and I grew my maize" (115). And as a result of this "partial" vision, she reads the scene entirely in terms of phallocracy, female victimization: "what I didn't like was the way all the conflicts came back to this question of femaleness. Femaleness as opposed and inferior to maleness" (116). "The victimisation, I saw, was universal" (115). But whereas the "victimisation" is quickly relativized in cultural terms—" 'I know,' [Nyasha] interrupted. 'It's not England any more and I ought to adjust' "; and, "I was comfortable in England but now I'm a whore with dirty habits" (117)—it is the heterosexual economy, concealed in its workings beneath the mask, that goes unnoticed, but that is rehearsed into the "treacherous mazes" (116) of Tambu's thoughts that she dare not follow:

> [I]n those days it was easy for me to leave tangled thoughts knotted, their loose ends hanging. I didn't want to explore the treacherous mazes that such thoughts led into. I didn't want to reach the end of those mazes, because there, I knew, *I would find myself and I was afraid I would not recognize myself after having taken so many confusing directions*. . . . I was beginning to suspect that I was not the person I was expected to be, and took it as evidence that somewhere I had taken a wrong turning. (116; my emphasis).

In response, then, to the question of "what is masked by the masquerade" (Butler 53), to the question of what is doubled, we can say that the tangled knots of incorporation and concealment, of donning the masks, denying and preserving the cycles of love refused and denied, allows us only access to the knowledge of there having been a "wrong turning." And if the answers cannot be found to the questions about desire lying under the mask, prior to the doubling, at least we can register the significance of the act of revolt of the daughters, on all levels, and not just those of gender and culture, to their status of sign-object; their revolt in becoming "users of signs," of acquiring the status of "subjects within language," for which the price paid, *pace* Fanon, is the natives' nervous condition.

Double Trouble

Butler asks, "[W]hy this exclusive focus on the fall into twoness," in response to the Lacanian notion of a "fundamental split that renders the subject internally divided and that establishes the duality of the sexes" (54–55). The answer for Lacan is that "division is always the *effect* of the law" (55), whereas Butler is concerned with the possibility that division, bisexuality, doubleness, might well *precede* the effects of the law, might even resist the "division" effected by the law ("a division that *resists* division" [55]), and reemerge through the crevasses of discourse, inscribed on the body of the subject. Might not that doubleness emerge within the subject's speech as "*fêlure*, discontinuity, metonymic slippage" (56)?

For our purposes, the problem of doubling appears to be posed in *Nervous Conditions* not as an instantiation of a bisexual division that precedes the law, but rather of how the law is so firmly grounded in the inscription of racial/colonial identifications as well as sexual ones. The site of the law should normally be located in the place determined by the Name of the Father. But what if the Name of the Father is supplanted—as when Babamukuru returns to the homestead, establishing the structure of the patriarchy with himself as the head? And as *Nervous Conditions* eventually shows, even the supremacy of Babamukuru is subordinated to the wizards, the white rulers who never appear, and who, in the absence of reference to the Chimurenga, are never really challenged. The Names of the Father are multiple—at times including the brother, the mother, the father, the uncle, and so on. In their multiplicity, they introduce cultural and social factors into the issue of identity formation—questions that lead Butler to suggest that the ultimate male/female binary might actually hide a more fragmented, multiple set of gender identities. That would lead us to precisely the same questions concerning race, and not just race as black/white, but especially as colonized, to a greater or lesser degree, assimilated, acculturated, métissé, etc., all of which adds up to some quantity that is more or less than one, or double in some way, but never a simple one. "In effect, the possibility of multiple identifications (which are not finally reducible to primary or founding identifications that are fixed within masculine and feminine positions) suggests that the Law is not deterministic and that 'the' law may not even be singular" (Butler 67). Butler sees this as accounting for her contestation of "the fixity of masculine and feminine placements with respect to the paternal law" (67). This is precisely my position on the "fixity" of the colonized versus colonizer's placement within the context of a colonial society—and especially within the context of a late colonial or newly independent state in which the conflicting attitudes toward the colonial identities result in multiple identity placements.

If the effects of incorporation seem less obvious for gender identities, requiring one to work through the acrobatic permutations of the oedipus, it would seem considerably more obvious that the colonialized identifications that emerge over the course of colonialism entail increasing degrees of and opportunities for incorporation.

The focus upon identity in writings about Africa and Europe has tended to create a binary that is relatively meaningless at both ends: there is no such thing as an African or a European. The comparison with gender works because the binary principle is based on exclusion: one *becomes* European, that is, assimilated, by giving up one's Africanness; and conversely, Kurtz "went native" by losing his Europeanness, his whiteness. But "male" and "female," like "black" and "white," not only encompass gradations, they also appear to be givens, originary identities, and not constructions like character and personality. This is what Butler's work allows us to challenge, as she asks, "Can gender complexity and dissonance be accounted for by the multiplication and convergence of a variety of culturally dissonant identifications? Or is all identification constructed through the exclusion of a sexuality that puts those identifications into question?" (66).

The "exclusion of a sexuality" to which she alludes is a consequence of processes of identification, a special case of which we have been considering as incorporation. Butler goes on to follow Freud's thought through in this direction, establishing that it is not only mourning that leads to this seemingly exceptional process of incorporation, but that as a result of the Law, of the effects of castration,[16] in fact *all* ego formation follows upon the effects of mourning! That doubling is not the exception, but the rule.

If we were to look for a generalized condition that might explain the prevalence of doubling in African literature—if we were to postulate the narrative of the Great African Novel—it would not be based on *Things Fall Apart*, but *L'Enfant noir*. This we can see in the case of our two models for doubling, *Nervous Conditions* and *Assèze l'Africaine*, in which the common theme is that of the severance of the child from its home. It is a colonial story: the child who succeeds at school will have to leave home as he/she grows up, and the *mourning* this engenders, the sense of loss, of nostalgia, is what marks *L'Enfant noir*. We can now expand the mourning to include the sense of loss of the immediate family, the parents and siblings, as well as all that goes into "home" in an African setting—a painful separation, augmented by the need to adopt, change, and drop old ways in the process of integrating into the new life. The multiplicity of these changes can be seen in the kinds of changes Laye had to make in taking up residence in Conakry, versus the changes Tambu had to make at the mission, and Assèze at the uncle's home in Douala.

It is also often the *woman's* story, she forced to marry into a new family and to leave home and family behind. It is the emigrant's story: in *Assèze l'Africaine* it is then twice told, Assèze leaving both home and village, and eventually country. And I suppose it was also Okonkwo's story in Part Two of *Things Fall Apart*, there the story being about his inability to change, to become a new immigrant in his mother's land, or, in Part Three, in his own homeland.

As we have seen, Freud argues that the response of the ego to the loss of the loved one is to *incorporate* that person into the structure of the ego, and thus take on that person's attributes, " 'sustaining' the other through magical acts of imitation" (Butler 59)—for us, through the masks of mimesis. The strategy entails denial of loss: "love escapes annihilation" (58). What can complicate the process is an ambivalent attitude toward the other who is lost. We saw how Tambu came to sympathize more with her brother as she spent more time at the mission, close to the pressures he had had to experience, and indeed she sympathized with her father and other African men who had had to defer to the heavy hand of the wizards. But the loss of a brother with whom one fights, or a father who is insensitive, is felt nonetheless as a powerful loss, and in the case of an ambivalent relationship, it is the ambivalence itself that is also internalized: "that ambivalence becomes internalized as a self-critical or self-debasing disposition in which the role of the other is now occupied and directed by the ego itself" (58).

We can note Tambu's self-critical disposition from the moment she enters the home of Babamukuru, where she must chastise herself in order not to succumb to her feelings of awe. More pertinently, we can now attribute the doublings to the sense of the *split* engendered by the incorporation of the other, especially the radically different other, Nhamo or Jeremiah, with the resultant split *projected* onto two characters. If we take Nyasha and Sorraya as doubles for Tambu and Assèze, then it is possible to complete the character analysis as an example of this kind of introjection and projection. Both Tambu and Assèze felt ambivalent about those whom they lost when having to move away from home to the mission or city. Both are doubled by "sisters" who are marked by self-doubts and guilt for which they punish themselves—Nyasha by her bulimia and nervous breakdown, Sorraya by her suicide.

Both doublings arise after the "mourning," and can be taken as resulting from the processes of incorporation and projection in which "self-critical attitudes of the melancholic [are] the result of the internalization of a lost object of love" (61). "Precisely because that object is lost, even though the relationship remains ambivalent and unresolved"—the very case of our two doublings—"the object is 'brought inside' the ego where the quarrel magically resumes as an interior dialogue between two parts of the psyche" (61), here between two characters.

What becomes most uncanny in this process is the continuation of the process of reproaching, now internalized or distributed between two cousins who are often reproaching the other: "the lost object is set up within the ego as a critical voice or agency, and the anger originally felt for the object is reversed so that the internalized object now berates the ego" (61). We can see this process not only in the case of the two doublings, but also in Assèze's rapid change on learning of the death of her mother. Having quit her mother with severe recriminations, she now turns those sentiments against herself and falls into deep depression—her mother's response is carried within her own ego. This is possible because in mourning, "the ego forfeits its anger and efficiency to the ego ideal which turns against the very ego by which it is sustained; in other words, the ego constructs a way to turn against itself" (62). Freud indicates that suicide can result, as we see happen in *Assèze l'Africaine*.

Suicide, bulimia, or Tambu's hysterical inability to speak, can be seen as logical extensions not of the processes of mourning, but of the uncanny reactions that bespeak the failure of the mourning process to bring resolution to the sense of loss. Butler follows along the line suggested by Nicholas Abraham and Maria Torok, who propose a distinction between mourning and melancholia. In the former, the lost one is introjected, the loss is acknowledged, and a substitute is found to replace the loss. In melancholy, the grief is "suspended" and thus sustained; there is no substitution or resolution, no turning of the loss into something else, like words. In the former, mourning, the introjected figure creates a space within the mourner, who then finds ways in which to speak the loss, to have the loss speak. The displacement of the lost one onto words entails a process of substitution, a "metaphorical activity in which words 'figure' the absence and surpass it" (Butler 68).

In contrast to this introjection and subsequent enunciation, melancholy is marked by incorporation, which is "antimetaphorical . . . because it maintains the loss as unnameable" (68). When put in terms of the oedipus, and primary repression, introjection is followed by "the possibility of individuation and of significant speech, where speech is necessarily metaphorical, in the sense that the referent, the object of desire, is a perpetual displacement" (68). It is from the space created by the loss of the maternal body "as an object of love" that words originate. On the other hand, incorporation is so radical, the loss refused so absolutely, the maternal body is "encrypted" in the body as "a dead and deadening part of the body or as one inhabited or possessed by phantasms of various kinds" (68). The borders of this kind of refusal are reached in *Tu t'appelleras Tanga*, where Anna-Claude's incorporation of Tanga results in a kind of phantasmic possession of her ego. Between these two extremes must lie the possibility of telling the story of the loss—of displacing it, of projecting the ambivalent feelings onto characters, and of transforming the loss not into dead space, but into the site of enunciation—"destroying the emptiness of silence," in D'Almeida's rendition of Beyala's words.

Following Abraham and Torok, Butler logically enough figures the space written on the body by introjection of loss as an empty mouth since it becomes "the condition of speech and signification" (68). But speech is built on the same condition as that which enables the subject to be formed, the space through which an imago must also be internalized, "introjected" if not "incorporated." To the process of mourning we can add that of perceiving, a process that also involves introjection, substitution, and projection. In Africa, as elsewhere, there can be no speech without these processes. But in Africa, unlike elsewhere, the speech that emerges from the specific kinds of loss, the specific kinds of mourning, must pass through a filter, a glass that is marked differently by each different historical and cultural context. What *others* pass through that mirror, and what *doubles* emerge, can be seen in the form of a doubled inscription, one in which the other mirror lies between.

There are multitudinous patterns this process can take: our examples are from *Nervous Conditions* (cited as *NC*) and *Assèze l'Africaine* (cited as *Assèze*).

> *The novels' doublings face each other across the mirrored space I set between them—a space in which the complexities of incorporation and introjection are refigured in the resemblances between situations and the plagiarisms. My goal here is to let the doublings speak for themselves through the juxtapositions that permit my own commentaries, like a midrash, to emerge. Dangarembga's text permits us to begin with the vexed question of the subject position, upon which all subsequent doublings will be built. The splits in the textual formatting enable me to echo and mark off the splits in the subject positions both within each text and between the two novels, with my own commentaries positioned in between.*

"When I stepped into Babamukuru's car I was a peasant in my tight, faded frock that immodestly defined my budding breasts, in my broad-toed feet that had grown thick-skinned through daily contact with the ground in all weathers. You could see it from the way the keratin had reacted by thickening, and, having thickened, had hardened and cracked so that the dirt ground its way in but could not be washed out. It was evident from the corrugated black callouses on my knees, the scales on my skin that were due

"There was no room for what I left behind" (*NC* 58).

"At Babamukuru's I expected to find another self, a clean, hard-groomed, genteel self who could not have been bred, could not have survived, on the homestead. At Babamukuru's I would have the leisure, be encouraged to consider questions that had to do with survival of the spirit, the creation of consciousness, rather than mere sustenance of the body. This new me would not be enervated by smoky kitchens that left eyes smarting and . . ."
"This new me would not be frustrated . . ." (59)

to lack of oil, the short dull tufts of malnourished hair" (*NC* 58).		
	"This was the person I was leaving behind" (*NC* 58).	
". . . chests permanently bronchitic " . . . by wood fires that either flamed so furiously that the sadja burned, or so indifferently that it became mbodza" (59)		
	"Everytime my relatives came from the mission I stayed near Nyasha and watched her. In this way I saw her observing us all" (52)	
	"mirrors that had once been reliable but had now grown so cloudy with age that they threatened to show you images of when you looked into them,	artful and ancient spirits
instead of your own face" (62)		
"the mansion standing at the top of the drive marked '14, HEADMASTER'S HOUSE' was truly his my uncle's own . . . . had I been writing these things at the time that they happened,	*incorporation/introjection*	"Je fis quelques pas et je vis un palais. Je dis bien palais car c'est ainsi que m'apparut la maison d'Awono. De style colonial, elle avait été bâtie au début du XIXe siècle par les

there would have been many references to 'palace' and 'mansion' and 'castle' in this section . . . this particular house had been built in the early days of the mission. She said that was around the turn of the nineteenth century" (62–63)

Allemands"* (*Assèze* 58)

"When I was dressed I admired myself   in the mirror. I looked

better in that uniform than I had ever looked before, even though it was blue   (which I now know does not suit my complexion)

and had angular four-inch pleats down the front.

It was a shock to see that

I was pretty, and also making it necessary for me to   difficult to believe,

scrutinize myself for a long time, from all angles and in many different positions, to verify the suspicion.   Nyasha, returning from her bath

caught me at it and did not allow me to be embarrassed" (91).

---

*I took some steps and I saw a palace. I say that I saw a palace because that's how Awono's house seemed to me. In a colonial style, it had been built at the beginning of the nineteenth century by the Germans.

"What was needed in that kitchen was a combination of Maiguru's detachment and Lucia's direction. Everybody needed to broaden out a little, to stop and consider the alternatives, but the matter was too intimate. It stung too saltily, too sharply and agonisingly the sensitive images the women had of themselves, images that were really no more than reflections. But the women had been taught to recognise these reflections as self and it was frightening now to even begin to think that, the very facts that set them apart as a group, as women, as a certain kind of person, were only myths" (138).

"'They're too Anglicised,' explained Maiguru, with a little laugh so that it was difficult to tell whether she was censoring Nyasha for the Anglicised habits or me for my lack of them" (74).

"This did not help, because I found that

	the advantages and disadvantages of transferring myself were about equally matched. To resolve the matter I decided that the issue was not really important" (86).	
"I was not like Nyasha,		
I was always aware of my surroundings. When the surroundings were new and unfamiliar, the awareness was painful and made me behave very strangely. At times like that I wanted so badly that for practical purposes I		who could forget where she was so entirely that she could do whatever she fancied and as a result usually did it well.
		to disappear
		ceased to exist" (110).
"I was clean now, not only on special occasions but every day of the week. I was meeting, outside myself, many things that I had thought about ambiguously; things that I had always known existed although the knowledge was vague; things that		in other worlds
	made my mother wonder whether or whether	I was quite myself, I was carrying some other presence in me" (93).

"[I]t was all very well to render unto Caesar what was his, but who was to say what was Caesar's?" (100)

"I had grown much quieter and more self-effacing than was usual, even for me. Beside   Nyasha
I was a paragon of feminine decorum" (155).

"As a result of all these things that I did not think or do, I was   Babamukuru thought   the sort of young woman a daughter ought to be
and lost no opportunity to impress this point of view upon Nyasha" (155).

* * *

"Coming to the mission, continuing any education and doing well at it, these had been the things that mattered. And since these things had been progressing according to plan for nearly two years, I had thought that ambiguities no longer existed. I had thought that issues would continue to be clearly delimited, with

Babamukuru, who was nearly divine as any human being could hope to be, imposing the limits. Through him, black would remain definitely sombre

imposing the limits

and white permanently clear, even in spite of Nyasha, whose strange disposition hinted at shades and textures within the same colour.

My vagueness and my reverence for my uncle. . ." (164).

"I was an intelligent girl but I also had to develop into a good woman, he said, stressing both qualities equally and

not seeing any contradiction in this" (88).

"'What about the light?' Nyasha reminded me.

What about the light? Where was the switch and how did you work it? Should I admit my ignorance to Nyasha, to whom I was feeling so superior, or should I ignore her? It was good to be feeling superior for a change, for the first time since I entered my uncle's house, so I ignored my cousin. Nyasha climbed out of bed, advising me to make an effort to stop being a peasant, which distressed me no end. I knew what the word meant because we had come across it one day in a poem in an English lesson and our teacher had explained that a peasant was a land fowl which looked something like a guinea fowl. Nyasha must have been very annoyed, I thought, to be so rude. . . .

had explained

must have been

"'This is it,' she said, pointing to a black patch in the wall beside the door. 'It's down now, which means it's on. It's off when it's up.' She switched the light off and on in order to demonstrate" (89).

"'It's down now, which means it's on. It's off when it's up.' She switched the light off and on in order to demonstrate. 'Switch it off,' I told her nastily, 'otherwise

With introjection, the mourning creates a space in which to speak the loss. . . . With incorporation, the maternal body is "encrypted" as a dead and deadening body.

"'Autre chose encore, dit-elle en me montrant un machin noir sur le mur. Ça s'appelle un interrupteur. Quand je le baisse, j'éteins la lumière. Quand je le

you won't sleep'" (89).	When Beyala incorporates foreign texts, they tend not to speak. The lines lie in a dead space, until she has reached the point of moving Assèze and Sorraya into their own world.	remonte, j'allume la lumière.' Elle éteignit et ralluma pour me montrer. 'A tout à l'heure!' dit-elle"* (Assèze 68).
"To look at us you could have thought we were sisters" (92).	have thought	
"'Will you come with me?' asked Nyasha as I walked into the bedroom. 'To smoke a cigarette.'		'Where to?' 'You smoke cigarettes!' I was aghast" (NC 84).
"He was laughing at me as usual. Dribbling a ball gracefully through maize plants that had sprung up in the football field of our old school, he paused from time to time to pick a fat, juicy cob and stuff it into his mouth. The cobs were full of	Tambu dreamt of her brother that first night she spent at the mission, and in her dream introjected her fears of change and her guilt over Nhamo. In the middle of the dream, Nyasha is substituted for her, after which she is able to let Nhamo and	Incomprehensible why it is this key point that Beyala chooses to plagiarize. Like Tambu, Assèze has left the village, to live in the more sophisticated urban center, in this case Douala. Like Tambu, she finds her new father's house overwhelming; like her

---

*"Another thing," she said in showing me a black thingamajig on the wall. "That's called a switch. When I switch it down, it turns off the light. When I switch it up, I turn on the light."

She switched it on and off to show me.

"See you later!" she said.

white gravy. From my desk in my class at the mission, which happened to be at the top of the maize field, I saw him eat and became alarmed that he would make himself ill with the strange mealies. In one graceful leap I bounded to his side to beg him to stop, but he laughed in my face and told me that no one would take me seriously because I was smoking a cigarette. The dream became a nightmare. When I realised that my fountain pen was in fact a long smoking cigarette. Nhamo howled with vicious glee, telling me that I would come to a bad end, that I deserved it for deserting my husband, my children, my garden and my chickens. He spoke with such authority that I was ashamed of deserting this family that I did not have. So when my husband appeared at the bottom of the field I was not surprised, only terrified, to see

herself speak, each in their own tongue.

On the cusp of the subject's ego, the uncertainty of an identity disturbed by what it has introjected, what it fears it is not assimilating: a dead brother, a lost homeland, and a sister as other, under the shadow of her father as Other, the space of the abject where Tambu finds the means to speak. The "I" embraces not only Nyasha, Tambu's mother, and Tambu as the Shona child, but also Tambu being transformed into a young woman, acquiring pen and book, English, and a

finds the kitchen and linoleum at first sight splendid, but in the long run run-down. Like Tambu, she is frightened by her uncle's dogs that are described in exactly the same terms as those in Nervous Conditions; and like Tambu sits down to a first meal where she finds the food foreign, tasteless, and so difficult to eat that she makes a mess with her fork and knife. Impossible to understand Beyala's meticulous copying of detail, phrase, concept, as though the readers of her novel would not have also been interested in reading another major African women's novel, one already available in translation in French. Impossible to understand why this nightmare, with its one repulsive, unreal detail concerning corn with white sauce, its features naturally preoccupying Tambu, and so unnaturally combined in any Cameroonian cuisine, should have been lifted, incorpo-

that it was Babamukuru and his two ferocious dogs tracking me down to return me to my spouse. Then I remembered that I was at school and began to explain this to Babamukuru." (90).

"Although I gallantly placed small portions of it in my mouth, it refused to go down my throat in large quantities. In fact nothing was going down my throat in large quantities" (NC 82).

new set of parents. Divided into these fragments of subject positions, she tries to explain herself in defense against the reproaches she faces from herself.

rated, and left to occupy the dead space: "des épis de maïs grillés recouverts d'une sauce blanche"* (70).

Left with a duplicated text that sticks in the throat. . .
"Ça ne passait pas. Ça restait coincé quelque part entre le gosier et l'oesophage"** (70).

There is a way, then, in which the Dangarembga text "speaks," and that is from the introjected space created by the "loss" of the maternal body. The loss speaks through this dream in which the act of incorporation—eating—conveys the tension over Tambu's ambivalent feelings toward her brother, her mother-homestead, and her Shona life: her "I" expresses this tension: "I saw

There is a way, then, in which the Beyala text doesn't speak, and that is from the incorporated space created by the plagiarism of Dangarembga's text. The plagiarized text functions differently for those familiar with Nervous Conditions *or* White Spirits, Burt, *or many others, from those unfamiliar with the originals. Beyala's borrowings appear at first as copying to the

---

*ears of grilled corn covered with a white sauce.
**It didn't go down. It remained stuck somewhere between the gullet and the esophagus.

him eat and became alarmed that he would make himself ill with the strange mealies"—*mealies made all the more inedible by their being covered by the kind of white sauce used to excess in bad English cuisine. Most of all, Tambu's "I" comes to the act of self-expression/self-creation through the projection onto her "emancipated" double, Nyasha, for whom the first sign of occupying the space of expressing herself is naturally the pen (the sign of those who "know book"), and for whom the second sign of her emancipated space of self-expression is the cigarette. Nhamo's speech within the dream expresses Tambu's own introjection of what he represented to her—the voice of patriarchal reproach:* "He spoke with such authority that I was ashamed of deserting this family that I did not have."

It is fascinating to see how in the text, the line between dream and reality is effaced through the speech of this "mouth" written across Tambu's body. She responds, speaks up, explaining *herself, first to Babamukuru, and then to Maiguru, whose presence floats in and out of the narrative space of the dream:* "Then I remembered that I was at school and began to explain this to Babamukuru, but Maiguru interrupted to say I should wash first. I was halfway to the bathroom before I realised that I had woken up" (90).

former, and often as anachronistic to the latter. Eventually, Beyala's characters assume a life of their own—the dead space comes to life proportionately to the degree to which Beyala's "incorporation" of original texts turns to "introjection"—or, in this case, digestion—so that a proper projection onto discrete characters can take place.

In Le Petit Prince de Belleville, Beyala's fidelity to the original Howard Buten novel, Burt, *often created "indigestible" scenes, as in the reference to Loukoum's visit to his grandparents, and much of the scene in the zoo and elsewhere. With* Assèze l'Africaine, *Beyala's borrowings from* White Spirit *match, en gros, the indigestible, anachronistic reference to white sauce on grilled corn. This is particularly infelicitous as Constant's* White Spirit *seems to have been largely inspired by Conrad's* Heart of Darkness *and other colonial writings of the early part of the century. The result is the portrait of a Cameroonian village that is completely out of place for the time frame of* Assèze. *Beyala has the White Father arrive in a village that has never seen whites before, and that accepts mass conversion. Yet the Douala Assèze comes to live in as a young girl is recognizably that of the Ahidjo era, past the time of the UPC [Union des Populations du Cameroon] fighting, and just before the recent* villes mortes *activism of the 1990s.*

The problem goes beyond anachronism. Beyala's genius, like that of Oyono, lies in her esprit moqueux, *her ability to create a satirical or parodic scene. When this works, the target of the satire is biting—and in the case of the representation of African peasants as illiterate, naive, or comic, the satire turns the negative judgments back against the reader's prejudices. But when Beyala fails, the mask sticks, the mirror does not reflect the comic caricaturizations of the "cambroussards" or "pequenots" back onto a European or westernized reader, and an uncomfortable, semi-digested scene sticks, like the white sauce, halfway down the esophagus.*

Such is the case of the scene describing the children in front of Mama-Mado's shop: "Devant la boutique de Mama-Mado, les mômes étaient frappés de tournis. On aurait dit qu'on les avait posés là dans leurs haillons avec leurs ventres baillonnés, leur genoux en crotte de bique, leurs grosses veines apparentes. Ils adoptaient des poses stupides et coucouinaient"* (50). *A pose is always before another's gaze. Here it makes no sense that that gaze would be Assèze's since she is also a child of*

---

*In front of Mama-Mado's shop, the kids were struck with dizziness. You could say they had been stuck there in their rags with their bulging stomachs, their knees like goat-droppings, their large veins sticking out. They assumed stupid looking postures and squealed.

Irigaray/Bhabha, Nervous Conditions/Assèze l'Africaine   231

the village, has always known nothing but that village. In moving the observer from a character to that of the implied spectator, the reader, the parody fades into representation, with no distance implied between the reality of the children's stupidity and that assumed by an outsider.

Once launched on this path, the slide between Constant's parody of the early colonial vision of Africa, and Beyala's echo, falls into the dead space of incorporation: "[N]ous dénichons une souris dodue et grise au bout de sa queue comme une mangue pourrie. Prisonnière, elle se débattait. Nous la plaquions à sol. Nous lui attachions un fil à la patte. Nous l'éventrions d'un coup de canif rouillé. Nous lui sortons les tripes. Nous cherchions des clous de charpentier. Contre un arbre, nous clouions l'animal. Nous ramassions des feuilles mortes et des branchages. Nous allumions un feu"* (*Assèze* 14–15).

"On dénicha une chauve-souris, molle au bout de sa queue comme une figue mûre. Prisonnière, elle se débattait un peu. Les enfants crièrent, elle s'échappa et vola en rase-mottes, on la ratrappa, on lui mit un fil à la patte et on la traîna comme une petite balle tout au long du chemin, elle bondissait sur chaque pierre. On chercha des pointes, on trouva un clou de charpentier, épais et tordu, recouvert d'une rouille si épaisse qu'il avait, pour ainsi dire, proliféré, et on s'arrangea avec du barbelé, pour confectionner une chose à peu près pointu. Contre la porte de l'école, on cloua l'animal. . . . Alors un grand alluma une cigarette d'herbe roulée dans de la

---

*We dislodged a plump mouse, gray to the tip of its tail like a rotten mango. Imprisoned, it struggled. We pinned it to the ground. We attached a thread to its paw. We gutted it with the slice of a rusty knife. We dug out its intestines. We looked for carpenter nails. Against a tree, we nailed the animal. We gathered dead leaves and branches. We lit a fire.

bananier séchée, tira quelques
bouffées et mit la cigarette dans la
gueule de la chauve-souris"*
(*White Spirit,* 166–67).

> "He did not know how my mind had raced
> and spun and ended up splitting into
> two
> dis   connected entities that had
> long frightening arguments   with each other, very
> vocally, there in my head,   about what ought to be done
> the one half maniacally insisting   the other half equally maniacally
> on going,   refusing to consider it." (*NC* 167)

"For these reasons she was in two minds as to whether she should pass on Chido's message or not, but of course she had to" (*NC* 175).

Beyala reads this split correctly, in the sense that beneath the uncanny surface of resemblance, beneath the surface tale of initiation, of transformation of country cousin into town cousin, lies the introjected body, a body of ambivalence because a body of reproach. Thus, within *Nervous Conditions* the latency of the split is transformed in *Assèze l'Africaine* into the manifest hostility between Assèze and Sorraya, while latent within *Assèze* is the closeness of the two cousins. Thus doubling is grounded in an innate ambivalence that continually rejects any unitary, originary economy.

"*To look at us you would have thought we were sisters*" (*NC* 92).
"*things that had made my mother wonder whether I was quite myself, or whether I was carrying some other presence in me*" (93).

---

*They dislodged a bat, soft to the tip of its tail like a ripe fig. Imprisoned, it struggled a bit. The children cried out, it escaped and flew off skimming the ground; they caught it again, tied a string to its paw and dragged it like a small ball along the road; it bounced on every stone. They looked for something pointed, found a carpenter's nail, thick and twisted, covered with rust so thick that it had, so to speak, proliferated; and they worked it out, with some barbed wire, to make something more or less pointed. Against the door of the school, they nailed the animal . . . . Then an older boy lit a cigarette of grass rolled in a dry banana leaf, dragged a few times on it and stuck the cigarette in the bat's mouth.

"I could see that my uncle was growing more and more disappointed with his daughter. In fact, it became very embarrassing to me, because I had grown much quieter and more self-effacing than was usual, even for me. Besides Nyasha I was a paragon of feminine decorum. . . . Above all, I did not question things. . . . I was not concerned that freedom fighters were referred to as terrorists, did not demand proof of God's existence nor did I think that the missionaries, along with all the other Whites in Rhodesia, ought to have stayed at home. As a result of these things I did not think or do, Babamukuru thought

I was the sort of young woman a daughter ought to be and lost no opportunity to impress this point of view upon Nyasha" (155). "'It's the Englishness,' she said. 'It will kill them all if they aren't careful,' and she snorted" (NC 202).

"D'abord, pourquoi veux-tu qu'elle aille vivre chez toi?"
"Pour servir de modèle à ma fille. Sorraya est trop blanchissée, si tu vois ce que je veux dire"* (50).
"Grandmère avait trois ennemies: le ndolé, les cafards et, pire encore, le Poulassie, cette horreur de langue française"** (15).[17]

Nyasha too anglicized.
Tambu to receive her grandmother's word, to continue the traditional way.

Sorraya too whitened.
Assèze to receive her grandmother's word, to safeguard the traditional way.

Both Tambu and Assèze serve the father in his goal of bringing his daughter around to a vision of the ideal woman, the ideal wife—Maiguru, the Comtesse—who understands the first rule of patriarchy: first serve the man, and then yourself: "But I was closer to her than anyone else and so I sensed the conflict that she was going through of self versus surrender and the content of sin" (NC 118).

Babamukuru's final word on the matter: "We cannot have two men in this house" (115), providing us with the mirrored image of Aidoo's rendition of the issue of cultural assimilation and servitude as figured along

---

*"First of all, why do you want her to go live with you?" "To be a model to my daughter. Sorraya is too white, if you see what I mean."
**Grandmother had three enemies: ndolé, cockroaches, and, worst of all, "chicken mouths," that horror of the French language.

gender lines—what is a black man who cooks and chores for a black man? . . . The answer, nature, is no less pertinent to Babamukuru, for whom it is only natural that his daughter accept her gendered role of subservience back "at home." Patriarchy as nature always depending upon gender difference, and therefore on the need to impose the structure of gender difference as natural. This is the point of Nyasha's refusal, and through her, Tambu's eventual "refus[al] to be brainwashed" (204) as well. Nyasha: "I don't want to be anyone's underdog. It's not right for anyone to be that. But once you're used to it, well, it just seems *natural* and you just carry on" (117; my emphasis). "Nervous condition" is the condition of unnaturalness. Of uncanny doubling. Of ambivalence and of Alice's refusal of the politics of the mirror. If it is not écriture féminine, it nonetheless succeeds in finding a way to write loss and refusal across the doubled bodies of Tambu/Nyasha so as to enable them to signify that loss and refusal, and thus to gain access to the councils of speech naturally reserved for the patriarchy.

Perhaps the ultimate sign that the mourning is over, that the mouth can now speak, is when the double finally disappears. Tambu's rise is proportionate to Nyasha's fall, and in the end Sorraya has to die before Assèze can take her place, in her husband's arms, in her home. The introjection has to be completed, but so does the "digestion." And the guilt over this exigency can be seen in the sense of Tambu and Assèze as survivors who made it somehow at the other's expense.

For Assèze, there is always a kind of battle with Sorraya in which the condition of the one is proportionally linked to that of the other: "Sorraya's spectacle lasted for six months. Six months during which she grew larger, and me, I shrank" (my translation; see p. 303).

From the start, Assèze expresses her fascination for Sorraya as the talented and sophisticated one, and is seduced by her superiority—"bizarre and naughty, but superior"; she feels herself subordinated to her ideas: "I fought against her ideas, but they kept coming back to me, captive and enchanting" (my translation; see p. 92). The doubling process of incorporation, often again figured through the imagery of ingestion, soon takes control of Assèze: "Bit by bit, like a man who absorbs each day a certain kind of food and winds up being absorbed into its substance, becoming thinner or fatter, and draws energy from that food, or else, to the contrary, becomes ill, so did I find internal changes taking place within me while my resistance weakened" (my translation; see p. 92). Thus Beyala details her own processes of incorporating the narrations of others into her own, and simultaneously frees herself to speak through the new mouth this process creates: "I was overwhelmed by my own enthusiasm, to the point of seeing triple" (my translation; see p. 92). The term Assèze uses to describe her incorporation of Sorraya is "enfourner"—to gulp down, to swallow up, as an oven ("four") swallows bread or pottery. "J'enfournais toutes les lubies de Sorraya" [I gulped down all of Sorraya's caprices (my translation)]—here it being the "lubies," the capriciousness, fantasies, follies of Sorraya that Assèze accepts into her "four intérieur"; and there, under the pressures of her own ambivalent feelings toward Sorraya, a mixture of admiration and at the same time resentment over Sorraya's obnoxious treatment of her, Assèze experiences the same wrenching we noted with Tambu after her transplantation to the mission. Thus, Assèze, in anxious conflict, ultimately expresses her ambivalence, in oxymorons: "To deal with my own contradictions became a torment and they pointed to one person who was responsible: Sorraya. I envied her and that envy was as strong as *a hatred or a romantic desire*" (my emphasis; my translation; see p. 92). Elsewhere Assèze uses the verb "déteindre" to describe her incorporation of Sorraya, as if Sorraya were leached into her: "[C]ela me poussa à demander si une partie de Sorraya, 'la haine engendre la chute,' n'avait pas déteint sur moi' " (190) [That pushed me to ask whether one part of Sorraya, "hatred leads to a fall," hadn't leached onto me (my translation)].

Unlike Dangarembga, Beyala tends to put her characters' feelings up front, out in the open, and thus often turns to burlesque or miming to express her misgivings or dislikes. Assèze's feelings for Sorraya are rapidly resolved into a straightforward antagonism, rather than into the complicated coupling of Tanga/Anna-Claude or Tambu/Nyasha. "Between Sorraya and myself, there was always hatred, but a silent hostility, looks that stabbed" (my translation; see p. 184). Assèze doesn't stay country cousin for very long; soon she comes to resemble the other young women protagonists of Beyala's earlier fiction, an attractive, increasingly street-smart, or simply street, woman, dependent on her sexual attractiveness to gain her way in life. The mime of the authentic African as prostitute, Beyala's preferred shtick, serves as Assèze's model: There she finds a source of income at her lowest point, when she is forced to "prostitute" herself for Ocean, and there she self-consciously assumes the doubled persona, that of the peasant countrygirl—the monkey face—echoing Oyono's "vieux nègre," not to mention Constant's use of the same figure in *White Spirit*. Simultaneously, Beyala mounts a defense for her plagiarism, transforming it from theft into miming, from illicit expropriation to playful imitation:

> I danced in front of a crowd hot for exoticism, with pleasant or disturbing masks. I exhausted the stock of Grandmother's tales,

and those of Ahmidou [sic] Koumba. I decorated with red, tropical precipices the tales of Grimm and Perrault. I played the monkey, did headstands, was the teller of good adventures. The whites just died because they thought they were tasting the sweet cakes of African mysteries. I duped them with a flood of snobbish and bumpkin references. (My translation; see p. 276)

If such "singéries" do not form part of Dangarembga's more serious narrative, still we remember Tambu's wide grins and words, "Nice, good," when she sold the mealies to the whites on the streets of Umtali. For Beyala, even revolution turns into a street performance, so that the affectation of a "cambroussard" appears to be merely echoed in other masks, other mimings of being. Thus, the "revolutionary" oratory reported as a script: "Ladies (*pause*) gentlemen (*pause*) dear comrades (*new pause*) in this country (*pause*) everything belongs to the same families (*pause*) for generations (*long pause*). However, it is time to work to change things (*very long pause*) and that is only possible if we combine our forces and . . . (*pause, pause, pause*) . . . and say no to dictatorship (*sensation*)" (my translation; see p. 194).

In the end, all these elements of miming, masking, doubling, of hybridity and the ramifications of assimilation, acculturation, incorporation, introjection, can be found in *Assèze l'Africaine*, and especially in the relationship between Assèze and Sorraya. In the scenes in which Sorraya and Assèze appear, as reported by Assèze, it is Sorraya who dominates the stage—just as Tambu melts into the background as the battles rage between Nyasha and Babamukuru. The foregrounding of Sorraya and Nyasha takes on a particular significance if we consider them under the rubric presented above, that is, as doubles incorporated or introjected by their "sisters," the protagonists/narrators. Thus, the battles between Sorraya and Nyasha and their fathers eventually become internalized by their doubled sisters, and become their own fights as well. Assèze recognizes this, and expresses her sentiments as though they lacked logic, and were out of her control: "I loved Awono and I didn't have a single trop of rancor toward him, and that pushed me to ask myself whether one side of Sorraya, 'hatred leads to a fall,' hadn't leached onto me, which would have explained why I didn't take into account Awono's feelings" (my translation; see p. 190).

Assèze's reunion with Sorraya in Paris provides for the last stage of their relationship in which it would appear that for the process of introjection to be complete, for the mourning to be concluded, along with the processes of substitution and speech, that the death of the double would have to be accomplished as well. Nyasha fades away before our eyes, but does not die, and Tambu's narrative rests unresolved, open to the future. Assèze is able to finish her account only as she realizes her relationship with and dependency on Sorraya.

As Sorraya speaks to Assèze in Eton, Assèze simultaneously touches the mourning of her mother and her own transposition into a passive role in her relationship with Sorraya: "'God keep their souls,' she said in our language.

It was the first time I heard her speak. The last time that she had spoken to me in Africa, she had blocked my ears. There, she opened up my mind. I understood right away that all my acts had been conditioned by this woman, from the day when she had received me at the landing of the staircase in her father's house, enveloped in a peignoir, down there in Douala" (my translation; see p. 294).

Doubled in their crossed existences, Assèze takes the news that her love, Alexander, happens to be Sorraya's husband, with shock. Her "recognition" passes beyond an act of understanding to encompass a challenge to the idea of separateness, their difference. Sorraya is incorporated as being both identical to Assèze and as her figure of loss—of mourning without end, the dead space of the unspeaking mouth. For the mime, such uncanny surprise provides the occasion for laughter: "Alexander! I was knocked out. Everything jumped in my head. I burst into laughter under the astonished gaze of Sorraya. . . . This woman and me. . . ! Never could I become separate from her. Our lives, two worlds that were intertwined. That our lives were linked by communicating tubes did not pose any problems for me. Not the same fortunes, unfortunately. What had to be done, Lord?" (my translation; see p. 298)

Sorraya's last performance brings together the conflicting terms of the oxymoron under the heading of the "négresse blanchie," the hybrid whose two terms of existence, African/European, woman/man, do not "add up," but cancel each other out as if in discovery that behind the mask, beyond the mirror image reflected back to her in the eyes of the other, there is nothing—another figure for incorporation, for "dead space." Assèze seeks to reassure Sorraya, but her double Sorraya brings the contradictions of her own ambivalence into violent conflict, and thus brings to an end her own life and the logic of Assèze's projection of her own otherness onto her:

Sorraya: " 'Don't worry. I know that you hate me. Like all the others in Africa, in fact. It's true that you all don't like my way of talking, of dressing and living. You don't like my behavior with boys. You think that I feel superior to you because I don't feel at all inferior to men. I would have really liked to be one of you. You don't consider me to be one of you.'

'I always belonged to a minority,' she continued. 'You don't accept me because I believe that I have certain rights, that everything wasn't good in our traditions.

Everything is papa's fault. He should have sent me to public school with the other black children, like you, Assèze. But he thought he was doing the right thing.

Assèze: "You never suffered from all that. You have everything, and the best."

In an instant, she passed from sweet madness to infinite sadness. She sat down, clasping her knees with her arms, elbows in her hands. . . .

In France I belong to a minority. I will never be considered like a white. I belong to nothing. A hybrid. Something without meaning!

When he saw what that resulted in, he took you to the house. He wanted you to be a model for me. But it was too late'" (my translation; see pp. 311–12).

And in the final words of her performace, Sorraya, like Nyasha, is able to broaden out her own personal loss to encompass that of Africa, postcolonial Africa, Africa "bradée," sold off, on the cheap—starting with the father's initial capitulations: "Poor papa! He had sold his soul to the devil, like your mama, like the Countess. Each in our own fashion, we have sold our souls to the devil. All sold off! Africa sold on the cheap. Dispossessed of ourselves. I sold myself in attending the whites' school. You, you sold yourself in imitating me, or at least in trying to take my place. Your mother in sending you to papa's so that you would succeed, in the whites' terms. The Countess in sleeping with papa without loving him. Where is Africa in this unleashing of ambition and corruption?

Where are you? Where am I?
You thought me bad in Africa. You thought me nice here.

I am none of all that. I don't even know where I am.
I have not succeeded in my life." (my translation; see p. 312)

Assèze tries to leave, to affirm her separation—to deny the incorporation. But as Sorraya dies, it is the burden of a reproach that does not end, that she intones: "Je l'ai laissée mourir," a reproach that she cannot convince others to hear: "'I let her die. I let her die.' 'Don't listen to her,' says Delphine. 'She is in shock.' 'Don't worry madame. We have seen some weird cases in our profession.' That's how come they didn't believe me." (my translation; see p. 317).

Thus Sorraya is "encrypted" into the body of Assèze. A "dead or deadening part of the body," she ceases to speak herself, her place taken by Assèze, who is now possessed by the phantasm of the dead one whose separate existence has come to an end: "I love you," says Alexander. "Me or the dead one?" "You or she, what difference does it make?" (my translation; see p. 317). This, for Beyala, is the mark of the West, the sign of Africa's having sold out to the West. But as we have seen, the phantasm encompasses more than the moribund inscription of assimilation. It speaks across the female body and refers us back to those other critical losses and moments of mourning engendered under patriarchy and its heterosexual economy, and to the possibilities of turning such loss into speech.

NOTES

1. For a clear exposition of Freud's story of his grandson's play on the words "fort, da," see Kaja Silverman, *The Subject of Semiotics* (71). The gist of

the story lies in Freud's grandson's invention of a game in which he tossed a wooden toy attached by a string, and stated "fort" (away), and pulled it back in, saying "da" (there, or back). Freud interpreted this game as a repetition of the child's experience of his mother leaving and returning, which the child then controlled through the game. This control became a sign for the control of language over our uncontrollable emotions, and, more important, the substitution of the signifiers for the referent.

2. A fascinating, nonpsychoanalytical approach to this pattern of doubling is examined by Teresa De Lauretis in her chapter "Desire in Narrative" in *Alice Doesn't* (1984). There she lays out the structural model established by Jurij Lotman, who postulates two textual mechanisms that characterize the formation of myth, and subsequently, fictional narratives in general. The two mechanisms include a primary one that serves to assimilate various phenomena into an integrated structure, whose function is to establish a sense of a world governed by systems and norms. The second mechanism is required to establish the place for anomalies, which, "organized according to a linear, temporal succession of events, generated oral tales about incidents, calamities, crimes, chance occurrences—in short, anything contravening, or in excess of, the mythically established order of things" (117). The two mechanisms generate "plot-texts" that reflect their double genesis, thus explaining "the widespread recurrence in modern comedy, drama, and novels of character-doubles (twins or functional pairs)" (117).

Lotman goes on to divide the overall character types into two categories: those who "enjoy freedom with regard to plot-space, who can change their place in the structure of the artistic world and cross the frontier . . . and those who are immobile, who represent, in fact, a function of this space" (118). Lotman goes on to characterize the space into which the characters are introduced as bounded, so that the former character is the one who encounters the obstacles involved in crossing the boundary, while the second remains statically bound within the space. De Lauretis goes on to associate the Sphinx and Oedipus with the fixity of the boundary and the hero whose function it is to overcome the obstacle and cross the boundary. We can easily see the pattern of these types of doubled characters articulated in Tambu, who must change her place, and identity, by conquering a series of obstacles, and Nyasha, who is inexplicably trapped and incapable of moving out of her bounded space, and who, in the end, could be said to constitute a final obstacle to Tambu's "liberation."

3. See "Women with Open Eyes, Women of Stone and Hammers: Western Feminism and African Feminist Filmmaking Practice," in Harrow, *African Cinema* (1999).

4. Some of the better known novels dealing with the war include Chenjerai Hove's *Bones* (1988) and Shimmer Chinodya's *Harvest of Thorns* (1989). Less known examples are Edmund Chipamaunga's *A Fighter for Freedom* (1983) and Stanley Nyamfukudza's *The Non-Believer's Journey* (1980). Flora Veit-Wild

analyzes the writings about the liberation struggle in *Teachers, Preachers, Non-Believers* (1993), 262–65.

5. Charles Sugnet has published an essay in which he undertakes to explicate Dangarembga's strategy in choosing not to make overt reference to the war. His take on the novel is that through Dangarembga's representation of the various forms of oppression the characters experience in the novel, the most obvious arising from sexism, she is able to construct or at least imply a parallelism between sexism and colonialism. He claims that although "*Nervous Conditions* barely mentions [the Chimurenga]," still it "[foregrounds] the struggle of two young women against the simultaneous double oppression of sexism and colonialism" (33). Sugnet is able to adduce a number of times in the novel in which oblique, if not direct, references to British colonialism are made. However, much of his argument strikes me as strained.

The choice of Dangarembga's title as taken from Sartre's prefatory remarks to Fanon's *Wretched of the Earth* is magnified out of proportion when one realizes that Dangarembga had not even read *Wretched*, and that the revolutionary reference would only make sense if *Nervous Conditions* itself were somehow aligned with Fanonian struggle. Sugnet is careful not to suggest that women's struggle must be allegorized as nationalist or anticolonial struggle, yet the absence of any character committed to the war for liberation actually having been waged around the characters during the time of the events in the novel speaks more loudly than any inferred connection between the women's struggle and the nationalists'.

Sugnet overdoes the effects of colonialism as a driving force in the characters' lives. Though Jeremiah is depicted as a despicable and spineless father, it is an enormous stretch to lay the blame for this on the British, as in the claim that "Jeremiah, deprived by the British of his ancestral lands, becomes the stereotype of the shiftless 'native,' spending his children's school fees on beer" (36). There is nothing to suggest that Jeremiah would have made profitable use of his ancestral lands, any more than he did of his brother's periodic infusions of cash, which he squandered, lying at one point about having used the money for Nhamo's school fees. Nyasha's references to British oppression certainly indicate the rising consciousness of a young, rebellious daughter. But the claim that her awareness of colonial pressures on her parents, and especially her father, compelled them to oppress her, deflects our attention from the main focus on Babamukuru as an oppressive paterfamilias, not as an oppressive assimilated African. This is the effect of Sugnet's claim that Nyasha comes to realize that "the whole chain of causality [beginning with the British] oppresses her" (37). The problem is not with the weak reference to British cultural domination and the imposition of its values, but with the devaluation of the powerful sexist dimension of the oppression.

This is the pattern of Sugnet's analysis. The anorexia and bulimia become referenced to Fanon's text and to Sartre's quote through the title, as if these intense moments of female self-destruction and resistance are to be understood through the optic of a colonial presence, when that presence in the novel is sporadic and discrete in contrast to the continual and heavy-handed depictions of sexism. When Nyasha forces herself to vomit, it is a stretch to describe it as an act of "puking up colonialism." Her struggle is focused entirely on her father; it touches on British identity politics only through his own absorption of their pressures to be "civilized," but her revolt does not take the form of rejecting her own anglicized qualities of dress, speech or culture—to the contrary, her rebellion against her father is expressed in reading a British author, D.H. Lawrence, in being "too liberated" in thought and behavior for Zimbabwean norms. The woman who exemplifies Zimbabwean, or Shona, resistance, is Lucia, not Nyasha.

For Sugnet, "any struggle for freedom is likely to have an inspirational atmospheric effect on other such struggles" (46). As readers of Fanon know, he felt the reimposition of the veil after Algeria's liberation was of "strategic necessity," whereas supporting women's struggles risked creating an alignment with European oppressors who strategically used that struggle for their own purposes of opposing nationalists.

Nyasha's "nervousness" is much less about colonialism than sexism, at any point in the novel, and is even less about colonialism for the other "nervous" characters. Dangarembga's reticence to reference the Chimurenga did not arise from her subtlety in suggesting a parallel between the two forms of oppression, as Sugnet claimed, but more directly from her acceptance of a measure of British values in her struggle against sexism, and even more from her refusal to support the armed struggle—a conclusion to which her acquaintances at the time attest.

It might be more fruitful to seek an understanding of Dangarembga's position by considering Chinodya's criticisms of the sexism practiced by the members of the liberation struggle, as portrayed in his *Harvest of Thorns*. For Sugnet, *Nervous Conditions* is a novel of "anti-colonial liberation," and he asks whether it is not possible for the ambiguous open ending to suggest that the conditions of independence might not have satisfactorily brought closure to the struggle against colonialism. What Sugnet cannot imagine in his analysis is the possibility that the absence of reference to the Chimurenga solves Dangarembga's problem of having to deal with a revolutionary struggle in an unpopular fashion, i.e., in distancing herself from it, and that indeed Tambudzai's "multiple"-faceted identity permits the possibility of contradictory attitudes toward both sexism and national liberation struggles. Sugnet quotes Mouffe in querying, "How can we grasp the multiplicity of relations of subordination that can affect an individual if we envisage social agents as homogeneous and unified entities? What characterizes the struggles of these new social movements is precisely the multiplicity of subject-positions which constitutes a single agent, and the possibility for this multiplicity to become the site of an antagonism and thereby politicized" (Sugnet 34).

By imposing Fanon's revolutionary analysis of colonial-induced neuroses on Dangarembga's characters, Sugnet denies the possibility of that multiplicity, denies that one liberation struggle can function, indeed, not to have an "inspirational atmospheric effect on other such struggles," but just the opposite, even going so far as to impose a veil of silence and claustration.

In fact, as Flora Viet-Wild has shown, Zimbabwean literature has not been noted for expressions of support for the nationalist liberation struggle. The majority have taken "a cynical view of the liberation struggle" (263), with a few weak exceptions. The reasons Viet-Wild gives for this rather unexpected situation are that "urbanisation, alienation through elite education, isolation and disillusionment about African nationalism account for a highly individualistic and sceptical outlook. Liberation was a long time coming; the delay produced a generation of 'non-believers' " (264–65). Perhaps it is too bitter a pill for this generation of postcolonial critics, and readers, to accept the notion that one of its canonical texts does not stand squarely on anticolonial, liberationist grounds, and that the ambivalences the author has expressed toward feminism as a western ideology may indeed be extended to the national liberation struggle.

Finally, I was able to put the question to Dangarembga herself, in the following manner (my question and her response follow):

Harrow: "In a nutshell, Charlie argues that you transpose the revolutionary push for nationhood onto the struggles of the young women against the patriarchy, thus redefining the Chimurenga into a broader struggle. His take is that you surreptitiously express your support for the Chimurenga this way. I take the position that your novel is inexplicably silent on this struggle, despite its having been waged intensely in the region of the school. I know the fight had its ugly sides, and the silence I take as a refusal to lend support to it. I don't see any surreptitious expressions of support, which I would find strange in the face of an open silence. It would have been too difficult for you to come out directly against the Chimurenga; but I've read some pretty strong criticisms in *Harvest of Thorns* and even indirectly in *Bones,* and it seems clear that the struggle engendered divisions and bitterness, as much as it mobilized people in the struggle. . . . Tsitsi, this is a ticklish question, and in a way I am embarrassed to ask it since I do not really believe in biographical criticisms. The main interest for me is the ways in which Nyasha and Tambu come out, live in their society, at the time period in which you set the novel. You are quite precise in setting the novel at the time of the struggle for independence, and at the same time, in not representing any of the events of that struggle in the novel, despite, as I said, the well-known fact that there was much active struggle in the region of Umtali, and in the locations chosen for the setting of the novel. I am intrigued by the way in which the novel is presented to the reader (the cover on the book, the blurb in the back, and the opening epigraph, as well as the implied connections established by the first-person narrative), all of which link the author to her characters. My final concern here is entirely with the way I can come at the novel using feminist theory—but in the end one cannot use theory in a vacuum, and the social/historical context sets a frame for the local reader in ways it might not for the foreigner. If I were a Zimbabwean, and read your novel knowing the history and the region, would I be asking this question of you?" (7/6/99)

Dangarembga: "Dear Ken, What an interesting question. Thank you for asking it and what a coincidence that you ask me now when I am ready and able to answer it. In a nutshell, Charlie is more correct. In fact, the chronology of the book is very carefully structured so as to end before the war intensified. Thus, although the war had begun at the time that Tambudzai is at the mission, events were isolated and had not yet begun to affect everybody. In truth, I, as an author, have not known how to go on about the struggle. I am disgusted with the faint heartedness of many present day Zimbabweans who still do what they are told by anybody and everybody. Yet the opposite pole of valorizing war is also inappropriate. Then again, it still [remains] difficult to convince the brokers of power, for obvious material reasons, that racism is a system whose oppressive practices within a nation or between nations must be addressed and redressed. So basically, what could Tambudzai have to say? That after she emancipated herself (and was allowed to be emancipated) to some extent from patriarchy, she remained a victim of racism, in which case she has a chip on her shoulder. Or should she adopt a protective psychological state which I call (racial) homophobia, and identify with white Rhodesians and their antiliberation struggle rhetoric. I'm sure there is a sensible position somewhere along the circumference of the circle that connects these two poles, but she hasn't found it yet. . . . So, yes, I think a Zimbabwean might ask this question. Hope this is helpful. Tsitsi." (7/6/99)

When I replied to this answer that Tambu would have been trapped in the (now classical) bind of a liberation struggle against the colonizers while enduring her own liberation struggle against the traditional patriarchy at home, Dangarembga made the distinction between herself and her character clear: "Dear Ken, I, as an author, made connections in the direction of Charlie's analysis. Tambudzai, as a character, finds herself in the bind you mention. . . . Best, Tsitsi" (7/7/99).

6. This is the same structure as that employed by Camara Laye in *L'Enfant noir*, the familiar first person account; it differs from Joyce's *Portrait of the*

Artist as a Young Man, in which the narrative voice is focalized through the narrator-character, replicating the voice of the narrator-character at every age; and at the other extreme, differs from the narrative voice in the Torah, in which parts of the narrative refer to events presumably occurring after the death of Moses, the supposed author.

7. Cf. Sugnet's take on this as evidence of colonialist thought having pervaded her reactions: "Dangarembga is brilliant in presenting the specifics of how the dream's [that of succeeding within the colonial system] very success undermines its assumptions. Living at her father's farm, Tambudzia is very aware of dirt and smells, including that of the outdoor latrine. So when she moves to the mission, the toilet seems the very essence of progress" (43). "The discourse of hygiene imposed by colonial conditions in the novel seems clearly arranged at first: Africanness is related to dirtiness (bad smells on the bus, maggots in the latrine) and English-inspired progress is related to cleanliness (Maiguru's kitchen, the white porcelain of the toilet).... Dangarembga is clever enough to see that what this discourse defines as 'African' is really the debased form of indigenous ways left *after* colonialism has disrupted them.... The dirt on the bus, the maggots in the latrine, and the loss of that 'healthy pink' are all related to the disturbances in eating and nutrition caused by colonialism and its attendant 'nervous conditions' " (44). Note, however, that these reactions are present even before Tambu has left the homestead and experienced the new world of Babamukuru's home.

8. That this is truly an issue of "reader's response" is attested to by the fact that when I last taught *Nervous Conditions*, many of my students had assumed that Nyasha was based on Dangarembga, and were not surprised to learn that she fit the autobiographical profile most closely.

9. Personal communication, May 13, 1998.

10. Definitions drawn from *Dictionnaire de la langue française*, ed. E. Littré. The *Oxford English Dictionary* gives substantially the same meaning and origins as the Littré, although it adds the possibility of an Old English root "grima," meaning mask or specter. It would add greatly to psychoanalytical theorizing around the notion of the mask to bring into play African conceptions of the mask and its social role. In this novel, it is not obvious how culturally specific notions of masking, in particular of the Shona, could be brought to bear on the argument that I develop.

11. I am grateful to Thompson Tsodzo for this information.

12. Following Kaja Silverman's exposition of the Freudian Oedipus, we can interpret Tambu's reaction as classical resistance, classical here referring to the conventions of literary representation of feminine resistance. Silverman gives the standard reading of this Freudian narrative: "Given the extraordinary demands which it makes upon her, it is not surprising that the female subject often fails to conform to the scenario described by Freud, that she declines in particular either to effect or to sustain the critical displacement of her erotic interest away from her mother to her father. Many heavily traversed paths

diverge from the straight and narrow one leading to Oedipal normalization, including frigidity, lesbianism, hysteria, and paranoia. Because of the intimate links between the Oedipus complex and the larger symbolic order . . . each of these psychic 'disorders' can be read as a point of female resistance to patriarchal culture" (Silverman 144).

13. Like Laye, Kateb attended school in French, a language which his mother did not speak. He writes that the experience of separation from his mother was like a second cutting of the umbilical cord, "cet exil intérieur qui ne rapprochait plus l'écolier de sa mère que pour les arracher chaque fois un peu plus au murmure du sang. . . . Ainsi avais-je perdu tout à la fois ma mère et son langage" (quoted in Déjeux 213) [this interior exile which no longer drew the schoolboy closer to his mother except to rip him, each time a bit more, away from the murmur of the blood. . . . Thus had I lost at the same time my mother and her language].

14. Juliana Makuchi Nfah-Abbenyi has written most forcefully about the effect of Tambu's initial words in the second chapter of her study *Gender in African Women's Writing* (1997). In response to Tambu's assertion that she was not sorry at the death of her brother, Nfah-Abbenyi writes: "This is an unbelievable statement proffered by an African woman. The first shock one has to get over is, how could she not be? How could she say such a thing? First of all, given our African extended family system that demands close family ties, no one in their right mind would say such a profane thing. Secondly, this is an African woman talking about the death of her own brother, Nhamo, her only brother, and an only son and heir, essential to the continuity of the patrilineage. Yet Tambudzai is not being callous. Her statement is a blanket truth about what it means to grow up as a woman in her society" (62).

15. We can see this best in the one scene in which Tambu does revolt against Babamukuru's wishes, and that is in attending her parents' wedding. His words to her express his thoughts that she should have served as an exemplum to Nyasha: "he had been holding me up for nearly two years as an example of filial virtue for his wayward daughter to follow" (168–69).

16. For Freud ego-formation depends upon mourning since the effects of the incest taboo initiate "a loss of the love-object for the ego and . . . this ego recuperates from this loss through the internalization of the tabooed object of desire" (Butler 58).

17. Subsequent references to text from *Assèze l'Africaine* will be my translations in English.

Chapter 6
▼▼▼▼▼▼▼▼▼▼

Division, Disunity, Disturbance, and Difference: Safi Faye's Mossane *and the Challenge of Postmodern Feminism*

Feminist issues do not begin and end with issues of gender identity or essentialism. As we have seen with Lacan, Kristeva, and Irigaray, considerations of gender with respect to abjection, the subject, the ego, and ultimately the position of enunciation within a narrative, lead directly to the bases of established order, to the conventional foundations of patriarchy, and to what subverts them; and it is there that we find l'écriture féminine, a cinema of subversion, and the questioning/challenging of Lacanian presuppositions, of Freudian mythoi, from within the psychoanalytic prism. It is there we can locate Stephen Heath's extensive querying of Lacanian analysis, and it is there we can examine the degree to which Aidoo, Beyala, Dangarembga, or Safi Faye succeed or fail to challenge the prevailing patriarchal norms in current African society.

Although Laura Mulvey's seminal article "Visual Pleasure and Narrative Cinema" (1975) has achieved canonical status in introducing the debate on subjectivity, sexual difference, and spectatorship in cinema, it is in Heath's longer and more convoluted chapter, "Difference," originally published in *Screen* (Autumn 1978), that the more systematic questioning of Lacanian feminism is to be found. Virtually a monograph on difference, approached through Lacanian analysis and applied to cinema, it raises key questions about Lacanian concepts while generally acceding to the value of employing a modified version of Lacanian analysis in its inquiry into central feminist questions.

Heath's point of departure definitively sets him off from Lacanian analysis. Whereas Lacan's most notorious claim is to possess an authoritative knowledge of women, Heath continually establishes his secondary status as a male speaking to feminist issues. Thus, Lacan states, in reference to the feminist revolt of the 1960s, "There is no woman but excluded by the nature of things which is the nature of words, and it has to be said if there is one thing about which women themselves are complaining at the moment, it's well and truly that—it's just that they don't know what they are saying, which is all the difference between them and me" ([1972–73] 1999: 73). This statement, coupled with Freud's "what does the woman want," signals the notion of woman as enigma to which psychoanalysis holds the eventual key. There is so little specificity to this construction of a gendered insider-outsider binary and others, such as the racial same/other, that we are not surprised to see Freud/Lacan and their disciples carry through the description of woman as the dark continent—a pattern dependent upon slates like Chris Miller's "blank darkness" on which analysis, or other comparable hegemonies, have inscribed their lines.[1]

Repeatedly, Heath demurs from the position of one who can speak with any authority on the multitude of questions arising from feminism since he is a man. Yet, he sets up the framework for the consideration of these issues in such a way as to permit us to think them outside anatomy, that is, in a social and historical context that exceeds the considerations imposed by the constraints of the individual body and its personal history. Thus, Heath brings to the fore his own personal stake and mantra about his inauthenticity in speaking for the other:

Difficult for me, for me not a woman . . . (98)

> the impossibility of the position of writing of someone not a woman in direct discussion of those problems and questions. I can know the issues to be fundamental, politically and theoretically unavoidable for men as for women, can find them constantly in my work, feel it to be neither correct nor possible to ignore or somehow get around them or ease out with vague expressions of sympathy but, at the same time, to engage them is at once this difficulty of writing, of my return in discourse as a certain possession, the representing of me for the reader and to myself as a certain position, a confidence of knowledge or—probably and—a problematic appropriation of feminist criticisms, voices, yet another strategy of oppression. (98)

Heath's verbal twists and turns do not lead him outside the debate, do not leave him dependent upon female interventions as providing an authentic means of accessing the dark continent. He does not turn, as does Chris Miller, to the outsider's only tack on authority—the anthropological approach. Instead he insists, like Bhabha, on the priority of the site of enunciation, and not gender identification, in consideration of one's position with respect to patriarchy. It is not the nature of maleness or femaleness that emerges as the defining issue in consideration of discourse and enunciation, but difference itself, the invisible component of separation and distinction upon which the patriarchal order is founded: "Thus any answer to the questions posed will be in terms of the identification of a discourse that is finally masculine, not because of some conception of theory that is male but because in the last resort any discourse which fails to take account of sexual difference in its enunciation and address will be, within a patriarchal order, precisely indifferent, a reflection of male domination" (49).

It might be added that any discourse that fails to take into account racial difference in its enunciation and address will also reflect racist thinking in an order governed by racial discriminations, just as the elision of religious difference erases consciousness of anti-Semitism in a Christian order that takes its own values to be natural if not normative. The constructed nature of race and religion, like gender, links it to what Barthes calls "mythology," and what Louis Althusser calls "ideology." Both mythology and ideology function to normalize dominant values, making them appear to be not constructed but natural. When cultures generate mythical meaning, Barthes tells us, they seek to make their own norms seem "facts of nature."[2]

In all these cases, questions of the constructedness of religious, racial, or sexual identity are put aside. Likewise, it is easier to pose these questions when challenging the heterosexual economy from the site of gay enunciation; the racist economy from the site of métis or Creole enunciation; the colonialist economy from the site of the colonized's hybrid enunciation. Always it is the children who are the products of "miscegenation" who would seem most naturally to speak from those in-between sites that make visible the unnoticed foundations of dominant orders.[3]

But what is to be said of the black man who "se blanchit," as Beyala would put it; of the white man who has known mostly African realities, African discourses; the man, or better still, the "man" whose position in the economy of patriarchy has been self-problematized for a long period of time, who knows only the back side of the mountains of oppression? This is the convoluted place into which Heath would seem to insert himself, despite himself. We see this in his comments on his appreciation of Chantal Ackerman's discourse as displaying a certain "fineness":

> Yet as I write "fineness," I cannot prevent the return from the enunciation of a representation in which it and I as subject are held as a position of domination, as in the difference from which women are placed from men, a representation that makes the word patronizing or containing or whatever (and I cannot deny this by advancing my contrary intention, discourse pays no heed to intentions which it anyway defines in its relations, and my contrary intention is anyway already suspect, itself discursively defined and produced and positioned within an order that I wish to be against). (99)

It is not too much of a leap to see Chris Miller's insistence on the relativity of the speaker's position when addressing issues of African culture, with the same expressions of reticence and uncertainty of authority and its built-in positions of domination.[4] Not too much to see Gordimer's reversals of racial position in *July's People* as expressive of the same dis-ease in speaking of the condition of domination of the other.

But it is also possible, indeed essential, to read "women" not only as constructed, not only as deconstructed through gay or hybrid sites of enunciation, but also *and especially* as potentially offering their bodies as discursive sites of resistance, sites that precisely go beyond the very physical boundaries of gender identification and that are defined with respect to resistance to patriarchy. This is how Carole Boyce Davies reads the position of the black woman in her *Black Women, Writing and Identity* (1994): indeed, resistance is frequently taken as the cornerstone of feminism marked by Lacanian analysis, as we see in the work of Irigaray and Cixous. Thus it is now almost commonplace, following Mulvey, to read women as offering the site of resistance to patriarchy, to mainstream cinema, to the works of the dominant culture: "Women return only as resistance to and from the place thus assigned, their image as sign of the difference and guarantee of its order" (Heath 85).

The central motif of Heath's disquisition begins here, with difference as interminably bound to the social order, situated within a historical frame, and structured around the familiar site of a we/they bipolarity. The nature of the dominant structure is to display the opposition between the differing terms so as to hide the effects of differential distributions of power and authority that are built into the relationships. And the nature of dominant cinema, as of literature, is to make natural, convey a sense of normalcy at the sight of such divisions, the act of seeing or reading going unnoticed: "We find ourselves in a social representing of desire determined by and redetermining a structure of division—the social and economic distinction of male/female, man/woman—the difference assigned and confirmed in representation serving to justify and resolve the contradictions of the oppression" (87).

Heath constructs an analysis of difference that depends on Lacanian analysis, while simultaneously critiquing it, because it is the charge of the psychoanalytical approach, even in its most political Marxist phase as with Althusser, to attempt to bring out and explicate what is repressed or disguised, what is transformed by displacements and transferences. The functioning of the patriarchal order, like that of the individual psyche, is grounded in unstated, mutually accepted norms in which the divisions of power and authority appear as natural as the divisions of the sexes, races, ethnic groups, or religious groups. The consequence is a vision of "reality" that is shared and unquestionably taken as a natural given, even though it is in fact repeatedly reconstructed.

One of the most visible manifestations of the constructedness of the vision of the real appears in the cinematic record of that vision across time. Nothing appears more natural and real than the immediacy of the cinematic vision of the present; nothing appears more dated or anachronistic than yesterday's vision. Thus it has been inevitable that cinematic criticism should focus not only on the constructedness of vision, as in the case of Mulvey's analysis of the constructedness of the male gaze, but also that it should employ Lacanian analysis in its undertaking of the study of cinematic vision. Heath provides us with the quintessential statement of the joining of feminist concerns to the Lacanian approach in cinematic analysis: "It might be added, moreover, as a kind of working rule, that where discourse appeals directly to an image, to an immediacy of seeing, as a point of its argument or demonstration, one can be sure that all difference is being elided, that the unity of some accepted vision is being reproduced" (49).

Mossane the Beauty

Here, then, is the essential question for us in beginning our examination of difference in Safi Faye's *Mossane* (1996): Is it that the unity of an accepted vision is being reproduced, or has the cineaste succeeded in challenging or disrupting the unity of the accepted vision? Not surprisingly, Heath approaches this question of the accepted vision with an extended discussion of the role of the phallus and castration in Freudian/Lacanian analysis. As the phallus functions in the economy of the imaginary *and* the symbolic through its *visible* traits, its erectness, and its difference with respect to males and females, it is this quality of visibility that is given first consideration: "Freud refers to the 'strikingly visible,' Lacan to the phallus as 'something the symbolic use of which is possible because it is seen, because it is erect; of what cannot be seen, of what is hidden, there is no possible symbolic use' " (Heath 49). The symbolism of the phallus depends on its visibility, just as castration depends on its absence. Both function because of the assumption of difference to which phallus and castration can refer, a difference reduced in Lacanian discourse to the father having the phallus and to the mother being the phallus.

Mossane, like all films to a greater or lesser degree, reproduces an accepted vision in the act of representation. *Mossane* depends upon the unity of vision conferred by the conventions of realism, especially of *cinéma vérité*.[5] The plot revolves around the most conventional of conflicts in African cinema, that of a forced marriage in which the reluctant bride loves someone whom her family finds unacceptable. Mossane, the village belle, loves Fara, a poor university student, but her parents had agreed to marry her to Diogoye, the son of another couple with whom they were long-standing friends; and as Diogoye is wealthy, the choice appears both obvious and ineluctable to them. In constructing this tale, Faye has recourse to legend and folktales: the setting is entirely placed in the village, and the image of the ancestral spirits, the Pangools, appears at the beginning and at the end, offering a token of focalization through the villagers' eyes. Faye carries this focalization through by intermixing the whole gamut of village customs within the fabric of the story, so that we are treated to ceremonies of propitiation and supplication to the ancestors and gods at the shore and before the sacred tree, to rituals of healing and cleansing of evil spirits, ceremonial dances and singing, a wedding celebration, the griot's performance, and so on. All this by way of cinéma vérité—that is, the "unmediated" representation of the unified vision of Serer village life and values, the subordination of plot to an ethnographic exigency to show all the essential features in the life of the community as seen by that community. This is the unity of a shared vision bound entirely to a concept of truth, namely, that the presence of the real can be reproduced before the camera without distortion or falsification, and furthermore, in the case of African reality, that that truth can be presented authentically if the insider to that reality is given control over the voice and the vision. Safe Faye's *Mossane*, like most of her more directly ethnographic films, *Lettre paysanne*,

Fad Jol, and *Selbe*, is a home movie in the sense of the filmmaker *coming home*. Faye teaches ethnography in Paris, where she has lived for decades, but her films are usually set in the Petit Côte of Senegal, home, the site from which home truths are captured, filmed, enunciated, and authenticated.

Jean-Pierre Bekolo presents a quite different Africa. His films, *Quartier Mozart* (1992) and *Aristotle's Plot* (1995), are not set in the village but in the city, in the urban quartier. There is no compulsory return to the village, no song, dance, or sacrifice of cow, goat, or chicken. Instead, there is much magic in his films, much sorcery, but tongue-in-cheek—self-consciously mocking, and thus self-consciously modern, that is, "modern" in contrast to Faye's "authentic" presentation of "tradition." Bekolo undermines Faye's traditionalism not by presenting the other Africa, the urban, modern Africa, but by undermining the modern/traditional dualism with the sly, mocking laughter of the postmodern. It is not that Bekolo doesn't take the problems of Africa seriously, but that the only appropriate response to the *pagaille* of the present is the carnivalesque, which translates into a camera that must acknowledge simultaneously both its own presence and the inauthenticity, the constructedness, of what it presents. Yet the story Bekolo develops in *Quartier Mozart*, stripped of its ironic frame, is once again about the travails of love, about the difficulties a couple has in overcoming the obstacles to their union. And in the process of presenting the story of the couple, Bekolo, like Faye, will exploit the setting, in this case a popular quartier of Yaounde, Quartier Mozart, and thus indirectly paint the picture of life in this particular community.

Mossane ends with the kind of tragedy that supposedly brings wisdom with pain, as the Greeks would have it: the regime of truth that requires sacrifices that it might come to be known. *Quartier Mozart* ends with the chuckle and scoffing of the skeptic for whom there is no truth in love; and if there were, there would be no way to tell it. If *Mossane* belongs to the Socratic tradition, *Quartier Mozart* belongs to that of the Sophists, for whom universal truth yields to rhetoric, or, in this case, to legerdemain, the magic not of realism but of cinema. Which takes us to the portrayal of difference, to the unified vision whose constructedness is concealed by the very devices of classical cinema, realism, or even of cinéma vérité. If Heath finds psychoanalysis trapped into a debilitating appeal to the visual in its presentation of the notion of the phallus and castration, so too can cinema be taxed as being false to the image it has created of itself by its dissembling over the constructedness of the vision it creates.[6] "The vision, any vision, is constructed, not given; appealing to its certainty, psychoanalysis can only repeat the ideological impasse of the natural, the mythical representation of things" (Heath 50).

It is this sense of the "natural" on which Faye depends in her construction of difference, especially in the scenes in which the women appear naturally before the lens, that is, "au nature"—in the nude. Thus Mossane and her best friend, another young woman recently married, disrobe and bathe each other, as does Mossane's mother, who has Mossane scrub her back. These scenes celebrate the beauty of the black woman, celebrate her color and the qualities of her flesh that give Negritude poets their source of inspiration. However, there is no male presence in these scenes through which the camera's gaze is focalized, although, as Mulvey would have us observe, the action is not advanced in these scenes as much as frozen by the camera's gaze. Mossane, whose name means beauty, has the function of embodying female beauty in the story: all the men remark on her beauty; her brother becomes enamored of her and must be sent away to his uncle's; the educated university students praise her beauty, and Fara becomes her lover; her mother counts on her beauty to secure her a good catch; her future parents-in-law are delighted with the prospect of their son marrying her, despite her family's poverty; the griot sings her beauty's praises; her father takes her out of school so that she will assume the role of an appropriate woman and wife in the community, not an educated woman. Everything conspires to set up a chain of events that circle around the one inevitable feature of the typical African warning tale, that is, disaster that comes with female beauty because Beauty values her own judgment and feelings above those of her parents.[7]

Mossane's mother Mingué tells Moss that when she was young, she too was beautiful like Moss. But Moss doesn't need to be told that her mother's marriage to the village blacksmith was not an act of revolt against traditional parental authority, or that love counted more for her mother than did money. Money is seen as part of the modern world that has fallen away from the ancestors' ways. And love, like money, breaks the unity of the village. The warnings against the parents' greed, like those against the willfulness of beautiful girls, all address the power implicit in an economy of difference that will not yield to the village ideal of sameness, and the inevitable shock brought about through their encounter. That difference is sexual, the sameness phallocentric. They speak through practically every scene in the movie, so that while the village may be divided and feel itself to be broken over the wisdom/foolishness of parents who refuse to consider their daughter's emotional feelings in marriage, the underlying protocols of gendered roles continue unabated.

It is here that the conventions of a western feminist tradition strike most violently against the unity of an accepted African vision. Heath carefully lays out the foundations of the unities of that western vision. Drawing upon Freud/Lacan, he states, "Sexuality is not given in nature but produced; the individual subject is not constructed from sexuality, sexuality is constructed in the history of the subject, with difference a function of that construction, not its cause, a function which is not necessarily single (on the contrary) and which, *a fortiori*, is not necessarily the holding of that difference to anatomical difference (phallic singularity)" (59). Heath goes on, unlike Freud or Lacan, to stress that the history of the subject is also constructed by sexuality's engagement with the social relations of production, classes, and sexes.

Some of those relations do not appear visibly on the surface of the village, especially when caught in a particular historical moment and limited to a tale about love and disobedience. But the closer the African viewer to the Serer village, to those years in which the university students went on strike, the more visible will appear the social relations of production or classes. Of course this terminology is grounded in a foreign environment. The villages work together to produce crops or fish, though not all families succeed equally in becoming wealthy. Most, in fact, are visibly poor, and depend on the successes of their children in economies outside the village, as in the case of Diogoye. But even the university students do not present a future certain to bring wealth: Fara loses Moss because he is a poor student, even though he has only three years left to complete his studies; and the griot laughs at his major, agronomy, a word he pretends not to be able to pronounce, but whose sense he mocks as entailing no more than what the peasant farmers themselves already know.

Less visible are the caste differences—occasions for similar love stories, as caste becomes the reason why a young university educated couple can't marry in Fadika Kramo-Lanciné's *Djeli* (1981). The griot is clearly presented as lacking the stature or dignity of the other men in the village, especially Moss's father, who is a blacksmith, and her uncle, the healer. Unlike the other men, the griot is Mingué's confidant and ardent supporter. Faye does nothing to relativize these differences, or the effect of Islam, or preexisting caste status (as Sembène does frequently, as we can see in *Ceddo* [1977], where these factors are central). The new economic exigencies suffice by themselves to subordinate other markers of status. The irony to which this leads is highlighted by Sembène in *Guelwaar* (1991). "Guelwaar" means noble, and the eponymous hero makes much of the dignity that he ascribes to his rank. Still, he must live off the earnings of his daughter who works as a prostitute in Dakar. "Traditional" markers of difference serve increasingly to obscure or disguise new realities of difference imposed on the village by forces that lie outside of it, especially the economies of the city and the state.

Faye strives to create an atmosphere that enables her to avoid the conventions of male-driven narratives concerning the village beauty's rebellion, with its focus on the seductive powers of the male suitor, on the sense of a collective wisdom centered on the elders, and particularly on the men who are leaders of the village, the clan, or the family. Conventionally, the beauty's attractiveness is matched by her poor judgment, which we are invited to condemn in the telling, in the warning that gives us the tale's moral. The flip version, which this film gives, and which we can trace back to multitudinous versions in contemporary African film or literature, such as Jean-Pierre Dikongue-Pipa's *Muno Moto* (1976) and *Le Prix de la liberté* (1978), Cheikh Oumar Sissoko's *Finzan* (1989), Kramo-Lanciné's *Djeli* (1980), Sembène's *Xala* (1974), and Bâ's *Une si longue lettre* (1979), represents the parents as shortsighted or worse, and generally presents "modern love," romantic love, and individual feelings as the true basis for marriage.

Faye doesn't take this approach either, as the model for lovemaking, if not sentimental love, is supplied by Moss's girlfriend, whose judgment is marked by French romance magazines (*Nous deux*), with their images of dream couples kissing, and an openness toward sexuality that contrasts with Mossane's more demure attitudes. Mossane's relationship with her girlfriend, and more important, her mother, shifts the emphasis from the male account of the legend, the male sacrifice, and the ultimate male authority, to the female bonds and the strains on those bonds. Isseu Niang's character Mingué, Moss's mother, completely dominates the family drama. The father is absentminded and relatively distanced from the drama, whereas Mingué's tears, her brother Baak's attempts to heal Moss, her griot's machinations and rhetoric, all center the action around Moss's response to Mingué and her dreams, and not to Moss's father's orders. Indeed, the latter asserts his authority once, at the wedding celebration in which Mossane announces her opposition to the wedding. This provides the father with practically the only opportunity left to him to exercise his control and assert his position. He stands up to proclaim that just as every family must have only one who rules, in his family it is he who will decide whom Mossane will marry. In the subsequent scene, Mossane flees at night, and her father's declamations seem as depleted as the soil that refuses to nourish the village.

Faye's *Mossane* can be best contrasted with the films of Sembène, Idrissa Ouédraogo, and Cissé, who often portray women as victims of male oppression, or who ground the essential conflict between the youthful daughter in rebellion and the patriarchy frozen in an outmoded traditionalism. Faye will not do that because as an ethnologist she wants to validate the image of tradition, and because as a feminist she wants to give pride of place to the roles of the women in the community. Patriarchy is thus not as much the target as a condition within which the dynamics of poverty, love, and authority have to be worked out.

Most important, difference is presented as being as natural, essential, and eternal as the soil, the sea by the coast, the great sacred trees, the spirits that inhabit that world, and all the day-to-day gestures whose rhythm is caught in the camera's gaze. The world of tradition is fixed in every aspect, even in the possibilities of revolt presented by those who leave the village, and it is as unselfconscious about its constructedness, about the very notion of traditionalism itself as a recent construct in modernity's great project of world-figuration, as it is about the nature of sexuality itself as a construct. Thus "tradition" functions exactly like the ethnographer's camera, which is rendered invisible in its role of producing an image. That is why, despite Faye's reshaping of the legend and refocusing of the emphasis on the women, she still stays entirely within the conventions of the heterosexual economy laid out by the structures of patriarchy. More specifically, she stays within a logic of difference that is continually reinforced by the emphasis on Mossane's beauty as exemplary of femininity, on female sexuality across generations and within all the meaningful relationships with others, and finally on the imposition of the Name of the Father, of patriarchal Law, in the role of final arbiter in the dispute over the wedding.

Mossane's beauty is mirrored back to her, and indirectly to the audience, through the eyes of all who perceive her. She is "si belle que même les enfants succombent et laissent tomber leur ballon: 'Dès qu'ils la voient, ces deux-là [her two particular youthful admirers], ils la suivent et le match est foutu!' " (Barlet 1996: 117) [so beautiful that even children succumbed and dropped their ball. "As soon as they see her, those two follow her, and the game is all screwed up!"]. By the end of the film, when her beauty has led her only to an unwanted marriage, Mossane attempts to flee by herself from the world of mirrors, of gazes, within which she and her story have been held—the world of the village. After determining that her lover, Fara, has already left for the university without even having informed her, she goes to the well where the image of the moon is reflected back at her gaze.

But she cannot escape by giving a final embrace to the reflection, and perhaps is not as trapped by the misrecognition of the mirrored image as is the audience that would see the specular reflection as the natural site of the feminine. For Montrelay, and for feminist film critics following Mulvey, this is the natural consequence of women's emplacement outside the symbolic—or in this case, Mossane's emplacement outside the patriarchal council of elders, the real, and the Law of the Father. "Failing the symbolic, outside of representation, it is difficult then not to reproduce the woman as site of the specular, the enclosed reversibility of specularity, a cinema for the man and for herself. . . . The woman stands once more in sight, in her fascinating and fascinated duality—'I saw myself seeing myself' " (Heath 69).[8]

Mossane does not leap into the well. Instead she goes down to the shore and takes a pirogue out into the water—her destination uncertain: "Elle n'a plus qu'à s'enfuir, mais doit passer par Mamangueth, le bras de mer qui, s'il pouvait parler, dirait tout ce qu'il a déjà vu" (Barlet 1996: 117) [She only had to flee, but had to go past Mamangueth, the inlet of the sea which, if it could talk, would say everything it had already seen]. The specular, and especially spectral, underside of the feminine, all that haunts the security of the symbolic in its rationalization of the real, emerges at the end, and as in Elechi Amadi's *The Concubine*, it is that specularity that comes to the fore as the gods reclaim their wife. Safi Faye: "Si je mets en scène les Pangool (dénomination sérère pour les esprits des ancêtres), c'est parce que je crois moins aux religions monothéistes et donc je défends la religion africaine fondée sur les esprits. . . . Mossane est trop belle pour appartenir à ce monde, et ne peut appartenir qu'au monde des esprits, des ancêtres" (Interview with Olivier Barlet 1997: 9–10) [If I put the Pangools (Serer name for ancestral spirits) in the film, it is because I believe less in monotheistic religions, and thus defend African religion based on spirits. . . . Mossane is too beautiful to belong to this world, and can only belong to the world of the spirits, the ancestors.]. Thus the "bras de mer" through which Mossane attempts to flee, and which took the other youths before her who became the Pangools, is "un gouffre bien amer" (Barlet 1997: 9) [a bitter abyss] from which emerge only the groans of the spirits, as if originating in the depths of what Kristeva would term the chora.

For Heath, it is overly simplistic to reduce the mirroring, the reflections and imagings of the specular to the imaginary. Although Safi Faye, like Souleymane Cissé in *Finye*, gives imaginary form to the spirits—"Impossible de les filmer comme des humains. Je les ai donc imaginés" (Barlet 1997: 10) [Impossible to film them like humans. So I imagined them.]—

the imaginary is informed with an imagery drawn directly from the real and integrated into the symbolic. As Heath points out, even in the mirror stage, "symbolic, real are always there; the subject is a representation of the signifier held in a structuration which is the shifting imbrication—the knotting—of real, symbolic and imaginary, the latter modeling desire in the subject's image of itself from the structure, not some separate area prior to the subject that is given in some way to possess" (69). The danger Heath sees in equating the imaginary with the specular lies precisely in seeing the imaginary as given, and by extension, in seeing the specular, and thus the feminine, as equally prior, equally given, equally outside history: "the need is much rather to avoid limiting the imaginary to a biological evolution of the individual, to grasp that it is a necessary and permanent function of the history of the subject, and, simultaneously, of the subject in history" (69).

Mossane's beauty, and the tale of her demise, follow the imbrication of the real, symbolic, and imaginary in the ways in which desire, at this historical moment in Senegal's struggle with poverty, education, and production, figures the *subject's* image of herself and himself as ineluctably responsive to the biological drives of male and female natures. Difference is portrayed here as given, and the tripled threnody of Moss's name ("Moss, Moss, Moss," meaning Beauty, Beauty, Beauty) by Fara, when the two first articulate their love for each other, further echoes this sense of the inevitability of difference. It is here that Heath's analysis of this order seems to be most appropriate:

> [I]f there is a way of thinking that works in the specular—imaginary, it is well and truly that of difference—the establishment of the difference of one and the other sides from the fact of the biological division of the sexes, with its consequent motion of reversal of images, from side to side, the same images. *Difference in these terms is always treacherous, reactionary*; a tourniquet operates in which the real necessity to claim difference binds back, and precisely from the difference claimed, into the renewal of the same, a reflection of the place assigned, assigned in difference. (Heath 69–70; my emphasis)

We understand from this that no matter what choice Mossane makes, no matter what her revolt or its success, the same will still be renewed, and the iron law of difference perpetuated. This is the project of patriarchy and its eternal mantra: "Patriarchy, men in its order, has never said anything but that woman are—the woman is—different: they are *not men*, the difference maintained supports the status quo, the difference derived,

derived ideologically, from nature, the appeal to the biological, 'undeniable' " (70).

If Mossane must be claimed by the Pangools, spirits of the ancestors whose own difference can be seen in their spectral markings and upside-down positioning, it is but one step from the imaging in legend, in tale, that preserves the sense of the normal by inverting all representations of the unreal, the spiritual. Safi Faye: "Comment visualiser ces derniers [the world of spirits, the ancestors]? Impossible de les filmer commes des humains. Je les ai donc imaginés—ayant la tête en bas—la tête à l'invers" (Barlet 1997: 10) [How can one visualize the latter? Impossible to film them as humans. I thus imagined them—upside-down].

The problem, states Heath, is "to pose specificity away from the specularity of difference" (70). That is precisely the challenge contemporary feminist western film has set for itself. Faye sees herself lending validity, authenticity, and dignity to an African world, and an African womanhood, denigrated by the West. That her strategy might constitute a "tourniquet" that turns back against itself, binding back into a "renewal of the same," would not occur to her because of her unselfconscious representation of difference as ineluctable and given. The question is whether it is enough to mount a self-conscious parody of that representation in order to avoid the tourniquet, to "pose specificity away from the specularity of difference." That is the problem of Bekolo's *Quartier Mozart*; that is the problem of second wave feminism, and the parodists like Sony Labou Tansi, Bekolo, or Okri, whose work has constituted a refusal of the essentialisms produced by the tourniquet.

Stephen Heath and Quartier Difference

> The constant limit of the theory is the phallus, the phallic function, and the theorizing of that limit is constantly eluded, held off, and, for example, by collapsing castration into a scenario of vision; to say that it is through sexual reality that the signifier comes into the world is not far from deriving the phallus as privileged signifier from an essence in nature and not from an order of the symbolic—but then the problem, the debate, is precisely there. (Heath 60)

The theorizing of the phallic function always comes back to being—and the processes of identification—and having: the woman being the object of desire, the phallus that she cannot have; the man having the phallus, and being subject to castration, to the substitutions that enable the symbolic order. For Lacan, all attempts to evade this logic are doomed to failure: the failure of hysteria—the woman who rejects the conditions of identification; the failures of psychosis—the man who refuses the conditions of castration. If we were to change the terms of identity here from man/woman to black/white or Christian/Jew, it would be possible to situate the subject in the locus of hybridity, in-between, as both and neither, so as to operate outside the logic of the symbolic. But if it is given that having or being the phallus is as much bound to an either/or logic as having or not having a penis, then we will have predetermined the nature of the symbolic, and with it the conditions for hysteria, psychosis, and especially difference.

When Mon Type, in *Quartier Mozart*, looks into his underwear to see what is there, we are no longer sure what he/she will find—no longer sure what logic is governing difference. Similarly, when Panka extends his/her hand to shake other men's hands, and they find their penises have shrunk, or disappeared, we are no longer sure of the old ideas of circumcision, excision, or castration—no longer sure of the regime under which the subject is to be established.

The logic of the phallus is built upon substitution: it is not the penis that is indicated by the phallus, but that which the erect penis comes to suggest, symbolize, evoke. Through the sleight of hand of African magic, Bekolo undoes the substitution, and imposes the literal on the figurative. Thus, where Eugénie Lemoine-Luccioni, following Freud/Lacan, attributes female castration anxiety to her perception of the absence of a penis, that is, to her identification with a male whose difference from herself she notes, Bekolo transforms identification into the literal acquisition of a penis. When Chef de Quartier becomes Mon Type, she becomes a stud, the embodiment of maleness, most of all through what she *has*—that is, as Atango (Bonbon des jeunes filles)[Candy for the girls] ascertains when they both take a piss against the wall, a huge *bangala* [penis]. Lemoine-Luccioni's account of the nature of loss experienced by the woman in the course of her childhood and early womanhood has particular resonance for most of Africa where the wife is expected to leave her parents' home and live with her husband and his family: "rather than castration anxiety the woman knows the anxiety of partition; she lives under the sign of abandonment: mother, father, child, husband, penis, everybody leaves her" (quoted in Heath 62). From this, Lemoine-Luccioni is led to conclude: "Through identification with the man, the woman imagines herself lacking a penis (whereas strictly speaking it is not lacking in the man) and symbolizes in this way the lack of which all the phenomena of partition deprive her" (62). Lemoine-Luccioni goes on to describe the development of a female symbolization in which "the woman takes herself as lost object," rather than the imaginary loss of a penis, and as a result, to have lost herself "in unity": "To lose the half of oneself is indeed to lose oneself in one's unity and thus in one's being. The symbol of the lost unity would be the body as whole, without fissure" (62).

That unity Lemoine-Luccioni locates in the man "by the grace of the signifier of his lack, the phallus" (63). If in his *jouissance* he finds the Other in the woman, "this knowledge does not divide him. The man is and remains, as man, and assuming that he exists as a man who is not also a woman, one" (63). But that is exactly what the quintessential stud in *Quartier Mozart* happens to be, a man who is also a woman, and therefore not one. It might well be seen that the defining moment in postmodern African cinema comes when Mon Type encounters Chef de Quartier as she is emerging from a neighborhood car-wreck, and they stare at each other as though lost, in a work whose own symbolic has lost its moorings.

What then is the place of the woman in *Quartier Mozart* if man, as one, is found to be divided, fractured? For Lemoine-Luccioni, "the *jouissance* of the woman is the revelation of this one in the Other, which makes her one for the duration of love. But being one makes her Other and separates her from her 'mother bark,' like bark from a tree" (63). Alienated, except in the moment of lovemaking, and even then alienated "from her specificity" (62), she can find oneness only in the Other, in man as "the very ideal of unity" (63). But Chef de Quartier doesn't only find this oneness, she commands it, incorporates, embodies, impersonates it. And she does this not in defiance of her alienated position as a girl, "badly castrated" (63), but as a disciple of the sorcière whose own knowledge appears as the only one to be complete.

Quartier Mozart is not staged, like *Mossane*, as a village fable. It is resolutely and entirely set in the city, and, to be specific, in the popular quartier of the African city. For the purposes of quartier humor, it might as easily have been set in Lagos, Abidjan, Dakar, or Nairobi—because virtually everywhere on the continent, Africa's large cities have become emblems for a new Africa, one marked by poverty, corruption, and authoritarian governments, but also by vibrancy and dynamism. These vast urban conglomerates that have generated their own languages, cultures, and mores. The terms "modern" or "postmodern" do not seem to apply so well in describing their new cultures. Rather, they might be seen as sites in which the exercise of social control is extremely fragile, if not illusory—where terms like quartier, quartier général, location, or 'hood become evocatory. We can see this in Chien Méchant's feeble, fruitless attempts to control the disapproval of his first wife when he takes a second. Failing to control her through the elders, through the priest's holy water, or even through his own deputy, he is forced to appeal to his gardien-de-nuit, Panka, the sorceress/woman in disguise, to have her thrown out. And the film leaves the viewer with the impression that it is the wife's subsequent complaints to the commissaire that get Chien Méchant demoted from his own position.

Quartier Mozart is not about sexual revolution: that is the business of the older generation of filmmakers, as we see in *Xala*, or those that have not passed beyond that logic, as in *Finzan*. *Quartier Mozart* is not programmatic; it is unprogrammatic in the sense that Cameroonian humor is broad and omnidimensional. It lends itself not to the shift in existing sexual roles, but to the effects on social institutions generated by the humor through the use of parody and mime, and thus addresses the more fundamental bases of patriarchal authority, those bound in social institutions.

In response to Lemoine-Luccioni's claims that "no sexual revolution will shift these lines of division [between male and female]" (quoted in Heath 63), Heath frames the problem of change as one of effecting not a sexual revolution, but a social revolution: "Privileging the sexual has nothing necessarily liberating about it; on the contrary, the sexual functions only too readily as an instance by development of and reference to which the social guarantees its order outside of any real process of transformation, produces exactly a containing ideology of 'liberation' " (63).

Quartier Mozart is as liberatory as the distracting laughter of neighborhood wits that inevitably is turned back on them—as in farce. As in farce that is grounded in a critique, and that encompasses, and transcends, the usual features of quartier sexism and African patriarchy. The key question posed for us by the film is whether Bekolo has succeeded in approaching any of the goals of the feminist agenda set by those concerned with écriture féminine or feminist film practice, that is, whether Bekolo has succeeded in transforming conventional African film practice into a transgressive or subversive act that undermines patriarchy, or whether he has merely reproduced a "containing ideology of 'liberation.' "

What might be the measure of such subversion? For Kristeva, it is the ruptures effected by the modernists that attest to the eruption of the semiotic, appearing through the crevasses of the symbolic. But the project of modernism, from the late nineteenth century, beginning with Baudelaire, and continuing with Pablo Picasso, Gertrude Stein, and T.S. Eliot, et al., has depended upon its writing of traditionalism as the foil for the modern/experimental schools of the twentieth century. It seems not at all incidental that woman, unrepresentable and "partially castrated," should be the dark continent, the mystery, the site of excessive, inexplicable *jouissance* for Freud/Lacan. Post-Lacanian feminism has assumed this burden with defiance and laughter, often mockingly, at times bitterly. For Gallop, Lacan is a "prick," though she dedicates years of study and several books to his work. For Cixous and Irigaray, writing out of female jouissance enables women to go beyond the phallocentric logic of the symbolic order as grounded in the phallus as the key to signification. For both, as for Butler, writing the female body has the advantage of drawing upon female specificity while operating outside the order of the symbolic. "[A] woman's writing thus 'jams the machinery of theory' " (Irigaray, quoted in Heath 71); goes beyond the limited logic or subject/object, is fluid, closer to spoken language than meta-language, and finally, expresses difference without having recourse to a politics of sexual identity, of a binary, heterosexual economy (Heath 70–71). Vivian Forrester carries this latter point to its logical conclusion: it is not a question of male or female authorship that determines écriture féminine, it is rather one of going beyond the strictures of a discourse that is unified in its subordination to a patriarchal symbolic order: "It remains to them [male or female authors] to practice the forgetting of the hierarchical orders, the categories. . . . Forgetting, it is exactly in that that any writer, man or woman, must become woman in order to operate" (Forrester, quoted in Heath 71). Heath sums it up beautifully: either woman accepts silence, "she silenced in the discursive reality, the reality of discourse," or she turns silence into something other, and not only thinks other (or otherwise), "pense autre," as Khatibi would have it,[9] but writes "autre," transforming silence in the process of disrupting discourse: "or writing as silence, her silencing—Forrester's 'forgetting'—of the orders of language, her practice of a language that is wild, on the body, unauthorized" (73). A subversion, or a breakup of unity: "I name myself in two languages in unnaming myself; I unname myself in telling my story. Speaking in this no-name sense, the body experiences pleasure in outbursts of rage, in breakup" (Khatibi 79).

Where is the resistance to be located, how figured in writing (in one language) without returning to a new symbolic order, how imaged in film without returning to images that represent, that give unity, albeit through what is new or transgressive? And obviously, how maintain transgression or subversion without those categories becoming new prisons, new prisons of light that reflects the self back onto a conventional practice? Newness by itself is not only meaningless, it is inevitable, and in fact is no less patriarchal in its movement than convention. For the moment, then, it must be necessary to fix, at least provisionally, the notion of patriarchy in terms of a resistance to it, recognizing that both terms—patriarchy and resistance—are relative, and meaningless outside of their specific historical and cultural context.

That said, we can attribute resistance in film—that is, in the contemporary film produced in the West and in Africa—in relation to a dominant Hollywood model, or even to a Hindu or Kung-fu model, that is inevitably a narrative film that relies upon a heterosexual economy, and that ties or sutures spectator, specular image, look, and character (i.e., the subject constructed through the identities represented), into a closed world, a symbolic in which the *sense* of the film is created with respect to a plot whose ending implies completeness.[10] "The narrative film has tried always to *complete* an interpretation of the subject (the image, the identity, it proposes, the reading of the spectator it maintains), resisting resistance as best it can, its best being the constant image, and *of the woman*" (Heath 90; my emphasis).

For Mulvey, the image of woman in film as fetishistic object held in a male gaze can be broken by destroying the illusion that the camera is invisible/not present and that there is no audience watching the screen:

> The first blow against the monolithic accumulation of traditional film conventions (already taken by radical filmmakers) is to free the look of the camera into its materiality in time and space and the look of the audience into dialectics, passionate detachment. There is no doubt that this destroys the satisfaction, pleasure and privilege of the "invisible guest," and highlights how film has depended on voyeuristic active/passive mechanisms. Women, whose image has continually been stolen and used for this end, cannot view the decline of traditional film with anything more than sentimental regret. (18)

However, highlighting the presence of the camera and the audience's act of looking may itself become conventional—François Truffaut's *Tirez sur le pianiste* (1960), which jolted audiences with its funky, direct addressing of the audience, is now quite dated in terms of this innovation, and the eroticization of the female image seems not to have been diminished by the self-conscious references employed by mainstream cinema that easily bridges the gaps that engage the audience's act of viewing with the erotic image of the woman. We seem to be caught up in an inevitable bind in which the look upon which cinema depends requires the female image.

This can be seen in Heath's powerful dictum that "woman is not the ruin of representation but its veritable support in the patriarchal order" (74). If representation, like the mirror image, misconveys to the viewer the nothing of identity as wholeness or unity, then woman-as-lack, woman-as-castrated, is the ruin of representation. But the symbolic order itself is constructed against division and lack, is itself the effect of castration, and is subject to the same division as the subject itself. Language is the stitching back together of the subject into an effect of wholeness that is continually to be reconstituted, respoken with each discursive act. These acts are originally made possible by an economy of desire that accounts for the repression of the phallus and its transformation into signifier. As the signifying system is constructed, the effects of castration are surmounted and the illusion of wholeness is returned. Woman-as-lack, then, must return with the newly constructed symbolic system, as whole—and it is that sense of wholeness that the representation of woman supplies. Each culture may figure her representation differently, may construct different features of a symbolic order into which her image is integrated, but in the end a patriarchal order cannot sustain the notion of the unrepresentable and the divided identity of woman, but rather must return her to the signifying chain as a coherent and desirable figure: represented, named, and figured, she joins imaginary and symbolic so strongly as to be [mis]-taken for a fact of nature—eternal, unchanging, ever-desirable. "What is designated unrepresentable is what is finally the most strongly represented, an absence or lack named and figured as such, a real which comes back to the subject in its system, its suture of symbolic and imaginary" (Heath 73–74). It is on the basis of this claim that Heath argues that woman is the support of the patriarchal order, and at the same time the basis for representation itself functioning (as in cinema) so as to provide the effect of unity and wholeness:

> In this sense the woman is not the ruin of representation but its veritable support in the patriarchal order, the assigned point at—on—which representation holds and makes up lack, the vanishing point on which the subject that representation represents *fixes* to close the division of which it is the effect; setting in place then, in the alienation-separation return, of a modeling of desire in which the woman takes the (imaginary) place of the Other, is procured as the truth of the man. What is always in question is a *closure of the subject*, of subjects, in a specific join—the suture—of symbolic and imaginary as field of the representation of the subject that ceaselessly holds in desire, puts it into a perspective, and the per-

spective above all of *man* and *woman*. (Heath 74; my emphasis, except for last two)

Heath sees this effect of the suturing of imaginary and symbolic around the circuit of difference as accounting for the eroticization of castration where the division of man and woman is assumed as "difference around the penis-phallus as 'normal' fetish . . . which is the relation of men, women and desire in a particular economy of representation" (74), that is, that of "recognition and refusal of lack."

Given this eroticization that depends on the image of women, and the dependency of the patriarchal order on the reconstructed image of woman as that which makes up for or refuses lack, it is no surprise that the logic of resistance has gone beyond Mulvey's notion of a self-conscious cinematography to one that refuses to collaborate in the very construction of the image of woman as desirable object. It is not just a question of narrative cinema imposing a structure of closure, not just mainstream cinema dependent on the male gaze and the fetishization of the image of the woman, but the very voyeurism inherent in the look upon which cinema itself depends *and* the representation of woman whose image, cast within the specific, recognizable forms given in any specific culture that will bring with it an economy of difference, serves to sustain the dominant patriarchy. This is the edge of resistance, its limits, where the challenge falls upon the very act of representing women in cinema—its limits also being "those of the cinema within which [resistance] operates and is defined, the voyeurism it repeats as the grounds of its struggle" (85). This leads to the crucial point: "one implication of such a questioning then [is] that *any image* of a woman in a film, by the fact of its engagement in a process of representation that brings with it, as preconstruction, the significance of the showing of the woman as difference, her representing (a significance, a representing, to which cinema in its institution is historically committed) *inevitably re-encloses women in a structure of cultural oppression* that functions precisely by the currency of 'images of women' " (Heath 85; my emphasis). The controlling question of whether resistance is ever possible is shifted back onto subjectivity and its relation in the production of enunciation, "the movement against the single unity of the subject, the confirmation of the difference" (85).

Heath points out Chantal Akerman's and Mulvey's attempts to get past this point of blockage, as indeed has been seen in the strategies of écriture féminine intended to do the same for writing. But once this issue has been reduced to representation itself, and especially to the representation of difference in terms of sexuality, the possibilities of alternatives, of resistance, seem to vanish. Where is the line, for instance, between mimicking sexual difference—Irigaray's strategy—and representing it, when the voyeur's relationship to the mimicked image is the same to the eroticized image? "[I]t is no surprise that [the representation of sexuality—'masculine,' 'feminine'—] should be the great problem, the great affair, of dominant cinema today (with its 'new sexuality'). An urgent question for any alternate practice is thus how *not* to contribute to this representation, how not to valorize its terms of identity and identification" (91).

The eroticization of castration works in cinema because of the voyeurism inherent in the specularization of the image in cinema. The image that is represented, perceived, and apprehended is bound up with character, and character with narration, in such a manner as to confer unity, wholeness, the oneness of identity on the image—another suture, and precisely the process carried out in the mirror stage. The effect of this is to ward off the threat of castration—its essentially divisive function: "the perceived image of the body gives the principle of unity, the one, identity—an identity that can never be other than that imaginary, in which, through the look, castration can be eluded, held off" (Heath 78). This look—the scopic drive, voyeurism—depends initially upon the safety of the audience's anonymity insured by the darkness of the theatre, the unselfconscious representations of the actors/actresses, the frozen status of the fetish. This has provided the occasion for the image of woman, in cinema, to assume her role as support for this voyeurism: " *'The'* woman is support of this eroticization, the whole scene of the phallus, *is* representation" (79).

But what happens when the woman looks back? As image, she has no "look," is image, not subject. When that pose is refused, when the image turns back on the voyeur with her own gaze, her own look, the eluding of castration is confounded, the anxiety returns, and with it the division of the subject: "The scopic drive may elude the term of castration but the look returns the other, castration, the other—the evil—eye" (78).

In *Quartier Mozart*, Chef de Quartier wants to know what is going on under the roofs of people's houses. Maman Thécla, the sorceress, gives her the "dog's eye" so she can see. In *Mossane*, it is we who have access to the scene of "chevauchée" where Dibor mounts her husband Daouda during the afternoon "siesta." Safi Faye, aware of the delicacy of challenging the conventions of modesty in African women's films, asks: "Quel mal y a-t-il à montrer une bonne sieste? Peut-être ai-je osé montrer ce qui se fait la nuit dont on ne parle pas le jour. Chevaucher n'est pas un problème" (Barlet 1997: 10–11). The problem of voyeurism, and its implications for the voyeur who seeks to accomplish it, is lost on Faye, for as Heath points out, closely following Lacan, the voyeur seeks "not the phallus on the body of the other but its absence as the definition of the mastering presence, the security of his position, his seeing, his phallus . . . ; the desire is for the Other to be spectacle not subject" (Heath 79). When Dibor mounts Daouda in the "chevauchée," she is projecting her image for our eyes—the classical posture, according to Mulvey, for the woman as fetish, focalized through the gaze of Daouda, who lies beneath her, and whose gaze directs our eyes at her. The suture that fashions the spectator as subject through identification with the character that gazes is grounded in classical sexual difference: Daouda serves as "mount" not only for Dibor, but also for our own gaze to be situated in a subject position—a male position.

When Mon Type (Chef de Quartier) looks inside his (her) briefs, checking for himself (herself) what the audience cannot see, the flip side of scopophilia is displayed: Freud's identification of its autoerotic dimension: "for the beginning of its activity the scopophilic instinct is auto-erotic; it has indeed an object, but that object is the subject's own body" (Freud, quoted in Heath 77). By denying the audience a share in the sight, Bekolo toys with the scopic drive inherent in representation, refusing to return unity to the division posited in Mon Type/Chef de Quartier. Similarly, when Chef de Quartier is given the "dog's eye" by the sorceress, and sees Atango in bed with his current girlfriend, it is not the fetishized image of the nude woman that is displayed, but once again the mockery of "ce qui se fait la nuit": Atango's premature ejaculation provides the opposite of the eroticization of castration and through Chef de Quartier's eyes denies the audience the mastering presence of the voyeur.

Still, Bekolo cannot escape the inevitability of sexual representation. Cinema, as Heath reminds us, "is an institution of representing" (95). The importance of representation for us lies in its relationship to the construction of the subject. Lacanian analysis, for all its flaws, enables us to see this process as one involving the mis-recognized unity of self involved in the act of looking, in cinema, in a spectator seeing unity in character, images, and closure—finally attaining suture, the telos of the cinematic process—guaranteed by the effect of representation. But representation does not occur in a vacuum, and Heath is correct in reminding us that "the bind of representation" involves the subject *in history*, within a specific social formation that encompasses political and economic conditions as well as individual specificities, that is, "the production of the individual in structures of difference and desire" (95). As the film functions as a message, representing an image, constructing a narrative for an audience, its effect in the process of construction of the subject is effected both in the process of creating character, image, and narration, and in its reception by the spectator. The exchange, the "bind of representation," is given its completion in the process by which film assumes a status of universality, a standard for the subject through which unity, oneness, is achieved.

It is, in the final analysis, in the disruption of the processes that lead to this completion, this closure, that resistance, "alternative" cinema, and its equivalence in a "cinéma féminine," is to be located. "Alternative practices are then alternative insofar as they transform the relations of the symbolic in representation *against* representing, against the universalizing conditions of exchange; representation held to use (a definition of Brechtian distanciation); to another difference again, division, disunity, disturbance of the (social) contract (of cinema, film, the spectator)" (96).

And in "division, disunity, and disturbance," we are led back again to difference, because it is there not only that the question of the subject arises, but that the mechanism of cinema, as with patriarchy itself, is grounded. As long as cinema holds to representation as its fundamental principle, the issue of sexual difference will define the standards by which patriarchy governs cinema and its effects. Nowhere more than in the struggles involving representation are the implications of difference to be felt: "Nowhere perhaps is that struggle more important today than in the 'reality' of sexual difference and the stabilization of sexuality there, in the representation of difference and the representing of men and women as that, the hold of the difference. Men and women may be differentiated on the basis of biological sex but that differentiation is always a position in representation, a specification of the individual as subject in meaning" (96).

It is no coincidence that *écriture féminine* seeks to disrupt the conventions of the dominant modes of representation and to destabilize the borders of sexual difference. New wave African women's literature, carrying on some of the work begun by Aidoo in *Sister Killroy* or Ken Bugul in *Le Baobab fou*, has moved those efforts onto a new plane where it has begun to make sense to approach them through the same critical apparatus that as has been applied to women's écriture féminine in the West.

Notes

1. Heath cites two well-known Lacanian analysts who carry through with this same approach to woman as having imperfectly experienced the Oedipal castration fear, and therefore having imperfectly entered into the symbolic. For Michèle Montrelay, "the woman pulls towards the unrepresentable, toward the ruin of representation. Feminine sexuality is 'unexplorable,' a dark continent 'outside the circuit of the symbolic economy' which the woman's *jouissance* contains and exceeds as an end of language" (quoted in Heath 65). Similarly, Eugénie Lemoine-Luccioni shares this notion of women's partial entry into the symbolic, as does Kristeva, who thereby attributes the capacity to subvert that order, to break with the symbolic, only to men.

2. For Althusser, it is interpellation that accounts for the way in which ideology intervenes in our lives and installs its presence. He claims that it is only in ideology that we can locate our subjectivity and our social reality: "ideology 'acts' or 'functions' in such a way that it 'recruits' subjects among the individuals (it recruits them all) or 'transforms' the individuals into subjects (it transforms them all) by that very precise operation I have called *interpellation* or hailing, and which can be imagined along the lines of the most commonplace police (or other) hailing: 'Hey, you there!' " (174). The standard treatment of interpellation and ideology is to be found in Althusser's treatment of ideology and state apparatuses in *Lenin and Philosophy* (1971), where he claims that individuals are "always-already interpellated by ideology as subjects" (176).

3. Although it is Bhabha who has given us the well-established usage of hybridity for postcolonial studies, it is useful to see Appiah's older treatment in his *In My Father's House* (1992), which is largely cast in personal tones, and Robert Young's *Colonial Desire* (1995), in which he traces the history of hybridity in western (mostly English) culture, especially from the eighteenth century to the early twentieth century, i.e., under imperialism.

4. In *Theories of Africans* (1990), Miller shifts the problem of authoritative knowledge from literature to anthropology, so that it is in "dialogue" with an anthropological knowledge that an adequate response to the literary text can be generated, especially for those "outside" the culture: "Thinking programmatically about Western approaches to African literature leads me to one major hypothesis, around which the rest of this book will turn: that a fair Western reading of African literatures demands engagement with, and even dependence on, anthropology. The demonstration of this point begins with the premise that good reading does not result from ignorance and that Westerners simply do not know enough about Africa. Much of what I will be arguing here grows out of my basic belief that no responsible Western reading

of African literature can take place in the vacuum of a 'direct' and unmediated relationship with the text. What the literary text says is necesssary but not sufficient; other texts must be brought into the dialogical exercise of a good reading" (4).

The problem of the adequateness of anthropological knowledge is glossed over. By shifting onto anthropology, one might well fill in the blanks of one's ignorance, but at the same time fill them in with a constructed vision of wholeness that is as inadequate to the multifaceted and divided nature of culture as is the literary text. Despite his disclaimer—"The task here is to seek a better understanding of francophone African literature by placing it within its historical, political, but especially anthropological context. This is not intended to place anthropology in a position of dominance or to let it block out other concerns" (5)—the dominance of anthropological knowledge is ultimately asserted in his analyses.

This is a problem that will arise in any theorizing of a primary text, as I realize is the case with my attempt to employ western feminist thought in this study, without giving that thought any more dominance than Miller wished to give to anthropology.

5. Safi Faye began her career in filmmaking as an assistant to Jean Rouch, the "father" of cinéma vérité—an anthropologist who originally trained under Marcel Griaule and did much to create the field of French ethnographic filmmaking.

6. Silverman supplies the basic definition of "suture" as "the name given to the procedures by means of which cinematic texts confer subjectivity upon their viewers" (195). The key to the notion lies in the fact that the camera must hide its existence from the spectators for the spectators to be able to identify with either the camera's gaze or the gaze focalized through one of the characters. Silverman returns to this point repeatedly: the 180 degree rule, i.e., the generally accepted range of the camera's viewing field, is "derive[d] from the imperative that the camera deny its own existence as much as possible, fostering the illusion that what is shown has an autonomous existence, independent of any technological interference, or any coercive gaze" (201–12). This is the classical view of shot/reverse shot where "the subject of the speech seems to be the speaking subject, or to state it differently, the gaze which directs our look seems to belong to a fictional character rather than to the camera" (202). Finally, "the shot/reverse shot formation derives its real importance and interest for many of the theoreticians of suture because it demonstrates so lucidly the way in which cinema operates to reduplicate the history of the subject" (203). "Oudart insists that the classic film text must at all costs conceal from the viewing subject the passivity of that subject's position, and this necessitates denying the fact that there is any reality outside of the fiction" (204).

The subject solves its own need to compensate for its own "lack" due to the wound of castration by seeking meaning and narrative, and this is provided by classical cinema's proffering of the fictional character, and the narrative itself, as stand-ins for the viewing subject. Thus Heath's notion that "the classic cinematic organization depends upon the subject's willingness to become absent to itself by permitting a fictional character to 'stand in' for it, or by allowing a particular point of view to define what it sees. The operation of suture is successful at the moment that the viewing subject says, 'Yes, that's me,' or 'That's what I see' " (205).

7. There are innumerable versions of this tale, the best known of which might be found in Amos Tutuola's *The Palm-Wine Drinkard* (1952). There it is the story of the handsome stranger "the complete gentleman," who seduces the vainglorious, strongheaded belle in the village market and leads her home, in opposition to her parents' wishes. As the couple make the journey through the forest, the groom gradually returns the various body parts he had borrowed en route to the market, until nothing is left but a talking skull. By that point, the young woman has realized that she has run away with an evil spirit; but by then it is too late. As the various versions continue, the young woman often escapes with the aid of a brother or some other helper, and she returns home having learnt the lesson.

See Carmela Garritano's "Restaging the Past: The Rewriting of *The Tale of the Beautiful Daughter* by Abrahams, Tutuola, Ogali and Aidoo," in Eke et al., *African Images: Recent Studies in Cinema and Text* (2000).

8. Silverman takes up the issue of specularity in her *The Subject of Semiotics*, and in the process points to its centrality for both psychoanalytical and cinematic theorizing. The relationship between the visual and the erection of the ego appears in her discussion of Lacan's approach to the imaginary. She cites Lacan's crucial statement concerning the mirror stage as marking the formation of the subject. When the child perceives itself as reflected in a mirrored image (be it literally a mirror image or some comparable reflection of itself from the other), it experiences jubilation: "This jubilant assumption of the specular image by the child at the *infans* stage, still sunk in his motor incapacity and nursling dependence, would seem to exhibit in an exemplary situation the symbolic matrix in which the *I* is precipitated in a primordial fashion, before it is objectified in the dialectic of identification with the other, and before language restores to it, in the universal, its function as subject" (Lacan, quoted in Silverman 157–58). She goes on to extend this aspect of the imaginary order with the functioning of the cinematic image. "The important role played by visual images in the identifications of the imaginary order has made this part of Lacan's model particularly rich in implications for the study of film. Indeed . . . Christian Metz in *Le Significant imaginaire* has defined the cinematic signifier as an imaginary one—as one which induces by means of visual images the same sort of identifications which occur early in the subject's life, and within which absence plays the same structuring role" (159).

Finally, lest the "mirror" be taken too literally or abstractly, Silverman extends her analysis of the formation of the "I" and the subject to the broader effects of cultural mediation: "Careful scrutiny of the account given to us of the mirror stage reveals undeniable traces of cultural intervention, most notably in the term 'ideal' by means of which Lacan qualifies the pronoun 'I.' 'Ideal' is a term which has meaning only within a system of values. It indicates that social norms play an important role in the mirror stage, and that the child's identity is from the very beginning culturally mediated.... As most readers of the 'mirror stage' are quick to point out, we cannot interpret the reflection within which the child finds its identity too literally; it must be understood at least to some degree as a cultural construct" (160).

In Susan Handelman's approach to the visual, she links it to the Greek philosophical tradition for which the *eidos* or visual image is associated with the universal concept or idea. This provides Derrida with the basis for his critique of western logocentrism whereby the "natural" assumptions of western metaphysics can be seen to rely upon a visual metaphor:

> Behind the aspiration to the invisible, nonsensible world was the Greek desire to *see*, a concept of thought in terms of the image (*idea*, from the Greek *eidos, image*). Words were merely conventional signs, as Aristotle said, but thoughts were *likenesses* of things.... Derrida will try to unmask the whole metaphysical basis upon which thought about metaphor takes place, and will label all of Western metaphysics a "white mythology"—a mythology which has "whitened," that is, blanked out the recognition of itself as mythology and taken itself for literal truth.
>
> Writes Derrida: "But if we turn the most critical and most properly Cartesian part of the critical process to the point of hyperbolic doubt . . . to the point at which doubt attacks not only ideas of sensible origin, but 'clear and distinct' ideas, and the self-evident truths of mathematics . . . the natural light and all the axioms which it enables us to see are never subjected to the most radical doubt." (17)

This link between Greek philosophical speculation and the preeminence of the visual is nicely summed up in Thorlief Boman's account. "Boman argues that the Greeks . . . considered reality to be an 'objective, given quantity with which our own senses, particularly our sight, bring us into contact.' The Greeks recount and describe what they see, but show no inclination for verbose narration. Greek perception, he claims, has been of decisive significance for philosophy, for all our concepts are given through sight, even time. If sight is the predominant mode, then in the search for identity in knowledge, resemblance is bound to be defined in terms of copy, re-presentation, mirroring—and thought, therefore, is *spec*ulative.

One seeks the reflection of true being in one's own consciousness" (Handelman 33).

9. "Je suis persuadé que ce temps de l'impuissance de penser et de méditer, n'était pas dû uniquement à un manque d'amour, selon les usages courants, mais à l'absence d'une pensée—autre" (Khatibi 1983: 88) [I am convinced that this time when I was powerless to think or meditate was not due uniquely to a lack of love, as current usage would have it, but rather for want of a thought—other (trans. in Khatibi 1990: 78)]; "Oui, mais ce que j'essaie de reconstituer n'appartient plus à ces lois tellement universelles qu'elles sont absurdes. Ces généralités: désolation nulle de l'esprit, et parler d'une épreuve singuliére exige une pensée-autre" (104) [Yes, but what I'm trying to put back together no longer obeys those laws which are so universal they're absurd. These generalities: empty desolation of the spirit; speaking of a singular ordeal demands an other-thought. (trans. in Khatibi 1990: 93)].

10. Edward Said's notion of finality, developed in *Beginnings*, provides one definition of completeness. Handleman summarizes it thusly: "*Finality* is the maintenance of the unity of the text through genealogical connections, such as the author-text, beginning-middle-end, text-meaning, and reader-interpretation" (Handleman 78). We might equally turn to Catherine Belsey's analysis of the classical realist text as providing closure, stabilizing the subject, following Emile Benveniste's propositions concerning the declarative text (Belsey 90–91). Finally, we could also evoke Barthes's notion of the readerly text in which the reader is not expected to contribute to the solution of the issues raised by the text, but passively to accept the author's position as definitive.

Chapter 7

City of Mud and Diamonds, City of Dis: Tanella Boni, Véronique Tadjo—A Feminism of the Cities

Coquery-Vidrovitch: City Life Chez les Femmes

The women writers of the 1980s and especially the 1990s with whom I am associating a second wave African feminism have turned to the city for their setting. In *African Women: A Modern History* (1997), Catherine Coquery-Vidrovitch has made a compelling case to explain the migration of African women to urban centers. During the nineteenth century, before the impress of colonialism, women generally lived under the strict control of a patriarchal system. Despite the great variations to be expected from culture to culture, region to region, it was usually the case that men disposed of the wealth of the family or community, ruled the clan or family, and enjoyed far greater prestige than the women. Aidoo's syllogism about a man who adopts the woman's role of cooking and choring for her husband expresses the two qualities that marked most women's lot: they performed the lowest level of manual labor, almost invariably farming, and represented the lowest status among the workers in society. Coquery-Vidrovitch sums it up succinctly: "A slave man was an individual made to perform a task that a woman would normally do [such as carrying water]. There is no clearer way to describe the condition of women, slave or free, at the dawn of colonization" (26–27).[1]

Colonization did not bring an improvement of the women's condition, but the contrary. Not only were jobs and education within the colonial economy reserved for men, laws intended to keep women in the village and subordinated to male rule extended the dominion of traditional patriarchy beyond its original scope. Coquery-Vidrovitch provides the economic basis for the ideology that emerged under colonialism:

> Whatever their prior status, peasant women's fate worsened under colonial rule, which upset the fragile balance between dependence and autonomy in relations between the sexes in work as at all levels of social organization. The imbalance increased for two reasons: the intensification of cash-crop cultivation (peanuts, coffee, cocoa) and the production of surplus foodstuffs (corn, yams, rice) for sale, which took up part of the cycle of subsistence cultivation, and the collection of these latter for sale by foreign companies, which often destroyed preexisting female networks. (59)

Coquery-Vidrovitch goes on to describe the multitudinous reasons that compelled women to migrate to the cities, reasons that figure as familiar tropes in first wave feminist literature and Agenda criticism: unwanted or unhappy marriages, including forced marriages, marriages to older polygamous husbands, harsh living and working conditions aggravated by colonial authorities, oppressive conditions of widowhood or divorce[2] (Coquery-Vidrovitch 75), all of which were no longer terminal conditions for women who could appeal to a colonial court that superseded traditional authority, and who recognized opportunities for autonomous lives in cities—"a chance at a new life, free from the pressures of rural customs" (75).[3]

However, despite the attractive call for freedom represented by the cities, only a very small minority could actually follow the path of "modernization" laid out by Flora Nwapa in Nigeria, or Mariama Bâ and Nafissatou Diallo in describing their inscription in the French schools under colonialism in Senegal. Most African women migrated to cities *despite*, not because of, colonial rule, as colonial administrators did their best to block the process so as to keep the women back "on the farm." Not surprisingly, when women did manage to make it to the cities, they usually occupied the bottom ranks of the work force, coming *after* the men in the competition even for domestic occupations like house servants or cooks (in Francophone Africa such domestics have been termed "boys" regardless of age or gender).

What is striking is to see the statistics that quantify the movement to the cities. Until World War II, only middle class African girls and women were seen to profit from increased benefits of schooling or health available in the cities. After World War II, a gradual shift in favor of female migration began. Outside of Madagascar, there was a heavy imbalance of male migrants over females as late as the 1960s and 1970s. Now, according to Coquery-Vidrovitch, the urban migration is gender-balanced, and indeed "there are more women than men in many black African cities" (81). Where Africans have had to leave their countries to seek work abroad, it has been men who have usually left, leaving the women behind, so that those few countries where men remain in the urban majority are the exception. Further, men's migration to the cities has been only partial in the sense that the men have often retained close connections with the village, often retiring to their "homes" in the village. Women have more often moved to the city permanently. A touching picture of such a migration is painted in Beyala's *Les Honneurs perdus* (1996). There it is a grandmother who reluctantly leaves the village after everyone else has abandoned it, and who ends her days without being able to return and reestablish her life in her village. Even more telling, in three of Beyala's recent novels (*Assèze l'Africaine*, *Les Honneurs perdus*, and *La Petite Fille du réverbère* [1998]), one finds the trajectory described by the young female protagonists as orienting their lives not back to the villages, the locus of a past that is depicted as lost, but "forward" to Europe, to the great metropole.

These last factors seem quite pertinent to the development of second wave feminism. While African men were dreaming of success in the cities enabling them to build substantial houses in the village, women were migrating, at least in part, with the intention of distancing themselves permanently from village ways, beliefs, economies, and laboring. The village was a yoke—*their* yoke. Thus, according to Coquery-Vidrovitch, interviews conducted in Nairobi

> revealed that the number of men who wanted to return in their native village was much higher than the number of women. . . . Women preferred to settle permanently in the city, where they had developed neighborhood networks and new affinities based on religion. . . . Men remained more attached to their ethnic group.
> All this contributes to freeing women from their rural yoke. (82–83)

Strikingly, it is not the case that independence has brought new legislation and social conditions that have led to the improvement of conditions for women. They are still disfavored when it comes to land ownership and economic opportunities. But the demographic shift of the past twenty years has had two major consequences: women are now as well established in cities as men, and retain more permanent attachments there than the men. Further, the vital forces driving urban expansion have meant that a large percentage of the urban population consists of young adults and children, many of whom cannot find jobs. The old men dream of returning "home" to the village, whereas the old women,

> the poorest and least adaptable of all . . . remain in the city. The migration of couples to the cities is increasing more rapidly than the migration of single men, but independent women have become real and increasingly visible actors, often numerically a majority. Some are poor village girls seeking work, and some are young unmarried women who come to the city for the diploma they need for their social and professional advancement. Only among the marginal European-style urban bourgeoisie does one encounter the Western model of the supposedly dependent women at home. (85)

We will return to the urban landscape as we look more closely at Boni's *Une vie de crabe* (1990), but for now what this pattern of migration suggests is a connection between the changes in African feminism and those in the city. First wave feminism looks to the burden of the African woman as marked by the village. First wave African women writers often depicted their protagonists as occupying a space that is marked by both the village and the city. It might be the story of women migrating to the city, as in Aidoo's "In the Cutting of a Drink" or Emecheta's *Joys of Motherhood*, or women whose lives in the village are marked by changes in the city, such as Safi Faye's *Selbe* (1982). Even as recent a novel as Aidoo's *Changes* (1991) posits that village mores still have an impact on the lives of the couples in the city—even though those couples are members of a wealthy and westernized bourgeoisie. Novels that seek to evoke the violence and disruption that mark the lives of women moving away from the village, like Ken Bugel's *Le Baobab fou* or Dangarembga's *Nervous Conditions*, seem anxious to embrace a spirit of subversion that cannot be separated from the reactions toward—and against—the village, and that inevitably construct those reactions in terms of an urbanized discourse in which the urban environment represents the locus of change and autonomy, even if the "price of liberty" comes too high.

With Beyala's recent novels, and especially with the fiction of Véronique Tadjo, Tanella Boni—and, on a parallel track, the fiction of Ben Okri and the films of Jean-Pierre Bekolo—we are moving into an urban landscape in which second wave feminism is set, with the city no longer cast in the shadow of the village. The features of this city are becoming similar across much of the continent. The contradictions that account for its landscape include great poverty and unemployment (with "la crise," "la conjunction," or the International Monetary Fund listed variously as descriptions of the situation and its cause), set over against signs of great wealth (Benzes spawning various Wabenzi), matched by sprawling "bidonvilles," newly formed slums often lacking water and electricity, and wealthy quartiers with expensive villas, night watchmen, and so on. In *Une vie de crabe*, the symbolism for these radical oppositions in the city may be seen in Boni's use of the tropes of mud and diamonds. There is much more mud than diamonds, but it is the glitter and excitement associated with urban life, and the possibility of gaining wealth rather than eking out a poor existence in the village, that continues to account for urban migration.

In fact, in *Les Honneurs perdus* and *La Petite Fille du réverbère*, Beyala depicts New Bell, a popular quartier in Douala, as animated by a poor but lively community—somewhat reminiscent of the typical scenes in Naguib Mafouz's novels set in Midaq alley. Beyala's grandmother sells cassava sticks and traditional medicines, maintaining herself and her granddaughter in poverty. The small-scale commerce, and the need for many to make do on tiny margins of profit, account for the inevitable pressure placed on the poorest women to trade on sexual favors for anything from school grades or employment to outright cash. More than prostitution, it is the market of buyem-sellem[4] that drives most of the transactions in the quartier, providing the prevailing morality. Thus Léti goes to the wealthy Dramane-le-Bègue, in *Une vie de crabe*, when she needs his help to enroll Niyous in a private school. She dresses "comme une femme du monde" [like a worldly woman], and he receives her with the conventional wisdom, "Ma fille . . . ça . . . ça s'arrangera. Tout peut s'arranger" (83) [My daughter . . . it . . . it will work out. Everything can be worked out.].

Coquery-Vidrovitch's summary of the lot of the great majority of the women living in cities, poor and lacking in resources, marks the irony that despite the fact that today "more than ever, city life is in women's hands," women must go begging in order to survive. Given the insufficiency of men's salaries, and the rampant unemployment of young people, poor women live on the margins:

> Socially marginal in the extreme, in the cities in disproportionate numbers in relation to their work, increasing numbers of women—

widows, unmarried mothers, orphaned girls—are excluded from any regular work. Gradually, all that is left to them is prostitution, actually a disguised form of begging. The schoolgirl sells herself for a few treats, the college student sleeps with her teachers for a few more points, the employee becomes the boss's mistress to keep her job, the market woman compensates for mediocre sales by going out with some of her clients, the partner or wife of a polygamous man takes other lovers to make up for his insufficient income, and especially young rural women, driven from their villages by poverty, fall prey to the prostitution that is commonplace in many large African cities—Addis Ababa, Abidjan, Kisangani, and Accra. (137)

Mud, Diamonds and Palu: Tanella Boni's *Une vie de crabe*

The urban setting for Boni's novel, ostensibly Abidjan, is not identified, although the quartiers are all named. As the site for subversion, the city is marked by the polar opposites of beauty and disease: viewed through the bus window, it presents "une vue superbe sur la ville belle et impaludée" (42). The beauty comes from the women. If the city is attractive, exciting, enticing, it is so because the women make it so, and in most cases through their embellishment not of the urban environment—not of their lawns, their flowers, their interior designs, for which all but the bourgeoisie lack the resources—but of themselves. They become the signs of the night life, and it is they, much more than the men, who represent the radical transformation from villagers to city dwellers. They have become strangers—transformed by their commercialization of sexuality into foreigners, different from what they had been at home. Like Duayaw's new friend in Accra: "She is as beautiful as sunrise, but she does not come from our parts" ("In the Cutting of a Drink," Aidoo 1970: 33). For the villager who has come to the city to find his sister, everything is new and different: the dancing, the drink, the languages, and most of all the women:

> I kept looking at her so much I think I was all the time stepping on her feet. I say, she was as black as you and I, but her hair was very long and fell on her shoulders like that of a white woman. I did not touch it but I saw it was very soft. Her lips with that red paint looked like a fresh wound. There was no space between her skin and her dress. Yes, I danced with her. When the music ended, I went back to where I was sitting. I do not know what she told her companions about me, but I heard them laugh.

> It was this time that something made me realize that they were all bad women of the city. (35–36)

The villagers weep when they hear that it was Mansa, their daughter, who was now lost to them, but her brother's bitter truth comes closest to the mark from the city's point of view: "What is there to weep about? I was sent to find a lost child. I found a woman" (37). The city's harsh truth is dictated, like the village's, by the economic law of survival: "Any kind of work is work" (36, 37).

If Mansa's brother finds her truths as harsh as her new appearance ("Any kind of work is work. . . . This is what Mansa told me with a mouth that looked like clotted blood" [37]), Beyala's prostitutes often represent excitement and beauty, without any accompanying guilt over having betrayed village values. The two settings Beyala employs to evoke the "belles de nuit" are New Bell and Belleville, the popular quartiers of Douala and Paris. In her recent autobiographical novel, *La Petite Fille du réverbère*, Beyala evokes this image of excitement for the young girl that she was, an excitement always accentuated by the prostitutes' assertiveness and eroticism:

> [V]oir Douala *by night*, c'était pénétrer dans un sanctuaire aveuglé par des lingots de bonheur; c'était côtoyer des Anges noirs aux seins imposants et les voir déguisés en charbon des Blancs à l'énergie féroce. C'était lire un livre magnifique mais compliqué où s'inversaient les rôles: les maîtres devenaient esclaves et les soumis les divinités. (66–67) [(S)eeing Douala by night meant to enter into a sanctuary blinded by ingots of happiness; it meant rubbing elbows with black angels with remarkable breasts, and to see them disguised with the whites' bleaching agents, those with ferocious energy. It meant reading a magnificent but complicated book where the roles were inverted: masters became slaves who submitted to divinities.]

The mixture of the forbidden and the pleasurable recurs in Beyala's writings, especially from *Le Petit Prince de Belleville* on to her more recent work. The house of prostitution of Madame Kimoto in *La Petite Fille du réverbère* exercised that kind of fascination for the young Beyala: "Dans la nuit qui s'annonçait on entendait glapir les filles de Madame Kimoto et leurs yeux à éclats et à éclipses clignotaient déjà, indiquant par les mouvements humains des paupières: 'C'est moi. Je suis le désir, je suis le sens, je suis le bonheur!'" (186) [In the night that was coming on, you could hear the yapping of Madame Kimoto's girls, and with their eyes, already opening wide and narrowing, the blinking indicated by the human movements of eyelids, "It's me. I am desire, I am feeling, I am happiness!"].

The attractiveness is linked to licentiousness for Beyala's grandmother, for whom the growing sexuality of Beyala's friend, Marie-Magdalena, represents evil, while for Beyala she is an object of desire in the process of its formation:

> "Cette fille est le démon," dit-elle. . . .
> Je regardai autour de moi et vis Maria-Magdalena-les-Saints-Amours. Elle portait une jupe en strass si courte et lumineuse que chacun de ses pas faisait suinter les pulsations sanguines de coeur, goutte à goutte. Je vis la naissance de ses fesses, mais aucun diable. (89)
>
> ["This girl is a demon," she said . . . .
> I looked around me and saw Maria-Magdalena-The-Holy-Loves. She wore a skirt with sequins so short and shiny that each one of her steps made bloody heartbeats drip out, drop by drop. I saw the emergence of her buttocks, but no devil.]

Later, when Beyala and her class are down at the port, they see the prostitutes approach the sailors, calling out to them in English. Libertinage and depravity are combined with gaiety: Beyala's portrayal of urban sexuality does not differ substantially from that of Aidoo in this regard:

> Ici, la vie continuait avec sa libertine insolence. Les doudous se répandaient en tendresses: "Very beautiful girl!" criaient-elles. "Cinq cents francs la tasse de tendresse." Des marins occidentaux ou africains s'approchaient, vêtus de pantalons bleus, leurs casquettes enfoncées sur leurs crânes: "Come here, darling!" Les filles se retournaient pour qu'ils vérifient la nature non évanescente de la marchandise: "What do you think, brother?" Ils riraient, se tapaient dans les paumes: "Ouah!", scellant ainsi un pacte avec la veulerie, avec la bonne dépravation qui leur permettait de libérer en toute impunité leurs plus bas instincts. (127) [Here life carried on with its insolent promiscuity. The hookers spread their tenderness everywhere: "Very beautiful girl!" they called out. "Five hundred francs a cup of tenderness." Some western or African sailors approached, dressed in blue pants, their caps pushed down on their heads: "Come here, darling!" The girls turned around to allow their permanent merchandise

> to be looked over. "What do you think, brother?" They laughed, clapped their hands: "Yeah!," sealing a pact with apathy, with that good old-time depravity that let them unleash their lowest instincts with total impunity.]

With her eroticized and spirited portraits of prostitutes in Douala and in Paris, Beyala has come to a comforting, reassuring depiction of sexual difference, one that conforms to established norms that go back in French literature and art to the late nineteenth century with Zola's Nana and the Impressionist can-can dancers, Moulin Rouge and all. Further, the Madame Kimotos and Mademoiselle Etoundis, warm-hearted and vulnerable women, offer easy alternatives to the hard mother figures who rejected or exploited their daughters—as with Tanga or with Beyala herself in *La Petite Fille du réverbère*.

This conventional view of sexuality is a far cry from that generally evoked in Beyala's early fiction, where male violence toward women was met by a discourse of outrage and anguish. We have passed from a universe in radical disarray to the Beverly Hillbillies where the *quartier général*, the popular quartier, may be seen to suffer from its poverty, but where the men are now "characters" who no longer represent any threat to anyone:

> où des hommes assis sous les vérandas se saoulaient au vin de palme, où nos démocrates parlaient des prochaines élections en jurant sur la tête de leur mère que le Président-à-vie avait des pouvoirs surnaturels qui lui permettaient de se déplacer sous l'eau et d'y parcourir milles kilomètres. Je les écoutais sans les écouter et haussais les épaules. (94) [where men seated on verandas got drunk on palm wine, where our democrats spoke of the next elections, swearing on their mothers' heads that the President-for-life had supernatural powers which permitted him to move about under sea and to go for thousands of miles. I listened to them without hearing them and shrugged my shoulders.]

The pinnacle of the Beverly Hillbillies depiction of quartier life comes in *Les Honneurs perdus* with characters like the pharmacist, the "journaliste-news," the chef de quartier, or the carpenter who always wants to make someone a coffin.[5] What Beyala has become is the complete modernist, one whose feminism is now comfortably arranged, like the depiction of Africa, so as not to disturb.

How ironic that her initial entry onto the literary scene should have been so controversial. In referring to the moment in which Ateba reaches out to touch Irène's knee in *C'est le soleil qui m'a brûlée*, a moment in which Ateba trembles with emotion and with a sense of sin, Juliana Nfah-Abbenyi writes, "This is what I see as the erotic and (un)spoken moment of/for lesbianism in *Soleil*, an issue, among others, that has been highly controversial with some readers and critics" (93). Nfah-Abbenyi goes on to detail the accusations of pornography, of commercialization of sex, and of scandalous lesbianism for the African reader and critic. Indeed, throughout Beyala's writings, the eroticization of women as seen through the eyes of other women has been a common feature, though hardly a subversive one. We have seen how the young Beyala-character in *La Petite Fille du réverbère* found the emergent sexuality of Marie-Magdalene attractive, but not, as her grandmother said, evil—"but no devil." The "lesbian" desire with which Ateba trembles, the description of which evoked such strong reactions, has devolved into much more hesitant, attenuated forms, as we see in Aminata's advances to Assèze:

> "Poor little Assèze who doesn't see how she is loved. . . . Who knows nothing about love and waits for marriage to discover it."
> "Aminata spoke as if in a dream, her voice purring, her cheek against mine, her hand covered with flour sliding under my dress. I remained in a stupor, incapable of making sense of what her hands were obviously doing, when the bell rang." (Beyala 1994: 93; my translation)

If Assèze is saved by the bell from transgression, she differs enormously from Ateba or Tanga, who lived the violence of their lives *through* the extremity of their sexual experiences, through an eroticism that was inevitably an outlaw experience, an eroticism that gradually changed in the course of Beyala's writings to the conventionalized experimentation of adolescence and the clichés about warm-hearted prostitutes. The discourse of subversion turned into a parody of itself—Cameroon's *villes mortes* no longer serious as political engagements; Aminata's advances no longer skirting along the precipice; Tanga's death replaced by the girl-character embodying Beyala's success, in *La Petite Fille du réverbère*, in which the line is effaced between the author's celebrity and her eponymous hero's inevitable transplantation to Paris.

The city in such a context becomes the setting for a first wave feminism because the features of its landscape and inhabitants are drawn according to the charts of modernism—the locus for contemporary humanist thought in which western values prevail, and the locus in the African novel for the struggle over women constructed in terms of tradition versus modernity. It is hardly surprising, then, that *Les Honneurs perdus*, the novel that most reduces African agency to a satiric joke, and that establishes Paris as the ultimate setting for a successful heterosexual love relationship, should have been the one to win the approval of the Académie Française with its Grand Prix du Roman.

In *Une vie de crabe*, the city does not resolve itself into the kinds of patterns with which one could associate the norms of a traditional/modern binary. To be sure, there are rich and poor quartiers, but each invades the space of the other; each experiences time in similar fashion; each is marked by the key indices that signify not only wealth and poverty, but life and death. The mud contains the diamond in the rough, the gold nugget: "Dans les bas-fonds de la ville, la propreté enseignée dans les écoles et autres lieux aseptisés reste invisible. Mais quelque pépite d'or brille dans la boue" (11) [In the slummy parts of town, the cleanliness taught in the schools and other sterilized locations remains invisible. But some nugget of gold shines in the mud.]. Niyous forges his way through the city. When we first meet him, he is a true child of the streets, on the lookout for car parts to steal. His way leads him through the garbage and mud in the lower courtyards of the urban landscape for which the borrowed rural vocabulary, "les bas fonds de la ville," only signals the transformation and not the connection to the village. Life is contained within the mud, within the city's lower depths, not as a figure for purity, but rather as one of activity, motion, and noise—life gleaned from the discarded waste that forms the urban landscape: "Mais la vie, elle, continue son chemin, infatigable, près des poubelles de la ville. Elle devient mouches et asticots. Elle rampe, elle vole, elle bourdonne. Dans vos oreilles, vos narines, vos entrailles. Oui, ici, la vie colle à la peau" (12) [But life itself carries on, indefatigable, near the city garbage dumps. It creeps, it soars, it buzzes. In your ears, your nostrils, your innards. Yes, here life sticks to the skin.]. Perhaps because life in the lower courtyards, the chicken coop of the city, is so uncertain, "short, nasty, brutish," it cannot be separated from death—so that the signs of life, flies and maggots, are also signs of death. Butler sees the regulatory function that creates the boundaries of sexual identity as also creating that which lies outside those boundaries, that which is defined by opposition. The mud of life and death, of movement and stillness, of dirt and shining gold, holds in its embrace the same contradictory forces.

These are the lines that inscribe themselves on the city. They etch in the trajectory that takes Niyous along his path at night, through the streets of Terre-Sèche, where the wealthy go to see movies, and back to Djomo-La-Lutte, the quartier where mud and life meet: "Ici, à Djomo-La-Lutte, la vie semble avoir été branché sur du courant alternatif, celui de la guerre, celui de la mort, celui de la survie" (12) [Here, at Djomo-the-Struggle, life seems to have been plugged in to alternating current, the current of war, of death, of survival.]. The words that follow the direction of Niyous's steps seem to fade into each other, the signifying chain sliding, as his steps turn from "marche" to "marché" to "poches" and "hanches" (walk, market, pockets, hips). They are led, with Niyous, as he descends the street, to the center of life and activity in the city, the market, the domain of the women:

> Niyous joue, rit aux éclats, fait un clin d'oeil aux enfants qui se bousculent et rient et pleurent. Puis il sautille par-dessus un caniveau. Il descend dans la rue, en direction du marché.
> Il marche et marche. Mains dans les poches ou sur les hanches.
> . . . Niyous va vers sa mère, la Mère, le marché. (12–13)
>
> [Niyous plays, breaks into laughter, winks at children who rush about and laugh and cry. Then he hops over a canal. He goes down into the street, towards the market.
> He walks and walks. Hands in his pockets or on his hips. . . .
> Niyous goes towards his mother, the Mother, the market.]

"La Mère, le marché"—market of food, of clothes, of those comings and goings that draw people together for needs that begin with the sediment of life, but go on to its adornment: the essentials of city life in Djomo-La-Lutte:

> Au marché de Djomo-La-Lutte, la surprise n'a pas cours et le reproche ne se vend guère. Des denrées alimentaires de première nécessité. Des feuilles, des écorces d'arbres, des pagnes par rangées, par brassées, des chaussures de forêt ou de savane. De quoi nourrir, habiller, chausser, parer, soigner l'âme et le corps de la tête jusqu'aux pieds. (13) [At the market of Djomo-the-Struggle, surprises don't usually happen and reproaches are hardly to be found. Foodstuffs of the most basic kind. Leaves, bark of trees, cloth by the yard in neat rows, armfuls, shoes for the forest or the savannah. What you need to eat, to dress yourself,

to wear on your feet, to adorn yourself, to care for the soul and the body from head to toe.]

With its own food, its local spices and herbs, its own pagnes, its bazins, its sandals, its stalls and stalls, at times extending in all directions like a world unto itself, the market gives to the city or the town an atmosphere, if not an identity, a space that cannot be assimilated to the European urbanscape. It forms "un autre univers" [another universe], one in which the beauty of the women is noticed, formed, and sold. In the midst of the mud, a diamond: "Toi aussi dans le marché?" [You too here in the market?] Niyous asks his friend, Bakari-Service. " 'Je ne sors pas de là, *jo*!' répond l'ami avec assurrance. Et comme pour lui en mettre plein la vue: '. . . c'est que, j'ai un de ces diamants ici . . . dans le marché-aux-tresses. Viens, viens voir' (17)[6] ["I don't leave it, jo!" the friend answers with assurrance. And as if to put on a show for him, " . . . it's that, I've got one of these diamonds here . . . in the market for braiding women's hair. Come, come and see."]. Niyous and Bakari-Service then make their way to that "other" universe of the women where the new space is being forced, one that is neither this nor that, but the meeting place, the rendez-vous of all the women's cultures:

> Bakari-Service et Niyous se dirigent vers *un autre univers* où l'on rencontre les mêmes transactions, la même soif de consommation. Mais où les traditions et les cultures se côtoient ou se mélangent. Ils aperçoivent les hangars du marché-aux-tresses qui ne sont pas encore les salons de coiffeur super équipés de Bellevue. Qui ne sont plus la natte ancestrale de grand-mère. (17; my emphasis) [Bakari-Service and Niyous make their way toward *another universe* where one finds the same transactions, the same thirst for consumption. But where traditions and cultures find themselves side by side or mixed together. They perceive the sheds of the market for braiding women's hair which weren't yet the superequipped hairdressing salons of Bellevue. And which are not grandmother's ancestral braiding either.]

There, at the heart of the women's corner of the market, Bakari-Service sees his "joyau adoré" [adored jewel], and Niyous encounters Mam'Djan, his mother's co-wife, from whom he had begged some coins the night before. Mam'Djan establishes the standard for beauty, having captured the wealthiest man in town, Dramane-le-Bègue, with her looks. She is the prize, the winner of all the best adornments offered by the market, from its braids, to its kohl for the eyes, to its finest clothes. "Elle était femme" (51) [She was a woman] for a city that measured female beauty by its own standards:

> Elle se parait de bijoux hors de prix. Elle possédait une garde-robe inouïee. Robes brodées, pagnes tissés, brillants ou de bazin riche se côtoyaient pêle-mêle. Elle avait appris à se faire belle. Elle excellait dans l'art de la coquetterie. Ses yeux en noir de palme rendaient ses rivales folles de jalousie. (50) [She adorned herself with priceless jewels. She possessed an unheard of wardrobe. Embroidered dresses, woven yards of cloth, glossy or of rich damask, spread haphazardly side by side. She excelled in the art of flirtation. Her eyes darkened with palm nut mascara made her rivals crazy with jealousy.]

Following Beauvoir, one can say that Mam'Djan, or Léti, didn't merely learn to make herself beautiful, but to make herself a woman. The regulatory agency that set out the standards for her wardrobe, her makeup, her coquettishness, was there to be found at the end of the road leading to the marché-aux-tresses. She is a woman, but *for* her husband:

> Elle avait appris que son époux devenait, pour ainsi dire, le maître de son corps et de sa maison. Elle était femme, elle agirait en épouse, puis en mère. Elle acceptait avec joie de s'allier à Monsieur Dramane Youni dit le Bègue alias Roi-du-commerce. (51) [She had learned that her spouse had become, so to speak, the master of her body and her house. She was a woman, she would act like a spouse, then a mother. She accepted with joy the alliance with Monsieur Drama Youni called the Stutterer alias King-of-Trade.]

It is against this backdrop of conventional female beauty, of conventional male prerogatives (next to the marché-aux-tresses Niyous and Bakari-Service install themselves at a bar, "L'endroit d'où ils peuvent observer les femmes à loisir" (18) [The place where they could observe the women with leisure]), that the drama of rupture is played out. We can approach this rupture from two directions—that of the disjunctive chords struck by Léti and Niyous's affair, and that struck by the very negativity ensconced within the city, the city of mud and disease. We can begin with the latter, as it surrounds and sets off the very beauty of the women delineated above.

If the city, "la ville," is "belle," it is also "impaludée," and the "palu," the malaria, seems to rise from the mud itself, just as the death arose from the polluted waters of the canals of Venice in Thomas Mann's allegory of love and death. "Terre humide" [Humid earth]. The city cannot contain the water that bursts the drainpipes:

> Il y avait beaucoup de monde dans la rue. Les enfants jouaient sous la pluie, dans des mares boueuses. Des canalisations rouillées par le temps avaient sauté sous la pression de l'eau et de la masse de déchets. Les gens vivaient dans les odeurs fortes, celles des égouts, celles de la vie souterraine. Ils attendaient, les pieds dans la boue où ils vivaient depuis des temps immémoriaux. (68) [There were lots of people in the street. The children played in the rain, in the muddy puddles. Pipes rusted over time had burst under the pressure of water and the mass of sewerage. The people lived with the powerful odors, those of sewers, of underground life. They waited, feet in the mud where they lived since time immemorial.]

The mud and the "palu," the malaria that has become everyday, like the mud, the streets whose paving could not be maintained, define the lives of the people in the city. And as if in defiance of the optimism of the modernist paradigm, the streets are not getting better, the mud is not being reduced, the malaria not being cured. To the contrary:

> Les pères et les mères avaient connu moins de boue que les enfants qui y jouaient à présent, les grands-parents moins de boue que les parents.... Mais depuis trois générations le palu hantait tous les sangs, échauffait tous les sangs. Tout le monde attendait, riait, jouant depuis le jour de sa naissance, malgré la pluie, malgré le palu. (68) [The fathers and mothers had known less mud than the children who were presently playing there, the grandparents less than the parents.... But for three generations malaria had haunted all of their blood, heated up all of their blood. Everyone waited, laughed, playing since the day of their birth, in spite of the rain, in spite of the malaria.]

Gradually Boni constructs the portrait of "la ville impaludée"—the city of mud and disease. From the first small indications, it grows like a virus into epidemic proportions, invading the atmosphere and the lives of all, rich and poor alike. It plays ironically and incessantly like a theme that repeats itself, a performance of death, constantly reiterated, constantly fought off by medicines and practices that fall short, as if the rupture to which they are linked were an inevitable feature in the performance.

When Niyous first goes to see his mother, it is her preventative medicine that he first notices:

> La [main] droite fermée sur un morceau de branche de nim, l'arbre remède miracle contre le palu, contre l'hépatite virale. Elle se blanchit les dents avec, tous les matins. Traitement préventif, par la même occasion, de la malaria latente qui sévit alentour, dans le marché, dans les cours, près des ruelles moites du quartier. (14) [Her right hand closed over a bit of a stick of nim, a tree that provides a miraculous remedy against malaria, against viral hepatitis. She whitens her teeth with it every morning. At the same time it's a preventative treatment against the latent malaria that is spread around, in the market, in the courtyards, near the wet narrow streets of the neighborhood.]

At the beginning of the novel, the mud, the disease seem distant and manageable, the threats of love and jealousy represented metaphorically. When Niyous raises the topic of Mam'Djan with his mother, she reacts with pain, experiencing the memory of her displacement by her rival as a crack, a "lézarde" opened in the mind, an "abcès" [abscess], a "brèche" [crack], a "ver de Cayor" [Guinea worm] which emerges through her skin (14). Similarly, Niyous, struck by the sight of Mam'Djan, experiences the attraction as though bitten, stung—"piqué par une femme. Ou une guêpe. Piqué à mort. A vif. Engourdi par un venin jusque-là inconnu" (18) [stung by a woman. Or a wasp. Stung to death. Alive. Dulled by the venom up till then unknown]. These metaphorical descriptors shade into the real with Niyous's observations of "les paralytiques," the handicapped beggars reduced to the status of subhumans due to the effects of disease. Malaria, endemic and not hitherto regarded as a major risk, now returns, like the memory of Mam'Djan for Niyous's mother, in virulent form:

> C'était des bouts d'êtres humains, diminués, aplatis, ratatinés. Ils marchaient sur les mains et les genoux, à quatre pattes, sous le soleil ardent. Ils avaient été parmi les nombreuses victimes de la poliomyélite ou autres maladies endémiques, bien avant que le paludisme ne prenne la relève avec ses accès pernicieux qui sèment la terreur dans toutes les familles. (45) [They were bits of human beings, diminished, flattened, shrunk. They

walked on their hands and knees, on all fours, under the burning sun. They had been some of the numerous victims of polio or other endemic diseases, long before malaria had taken their place with its pernicious onslaught, planting terror in all the cities' families.

Niyous, reduced figuratively to their state, is also "démuni." But the material difference remains: "Il avait des pieds et des mains. Il marchait debout, souvent les mains dans les poches, tête haute. Toute la différence était là" (45) [He had feet and hands. He walked upright, often hands in his pockets, head up. That was the whole difference.].

Here Boni permits a slippage between the figurative language of Niyous's condition—emotional, economic—and the more realistic description of the city's most disadvantaged population. The gap, the difference, is emphasized, but a few pages later Léti (Mam'Djan), married to the city's most favored son, the "richissisme" Dramane-le-Bègue, herself falls victim to the dangers in the air. Her new husband had expelled all his other lovers and wives at Léti's insistence; but eventually she succumbs to the same fate when she discovers that her husband has a favorite mistress: "Une adversaire de taille. Une ombre. Qui passe sans avoir l'air de passer" (54) [A worthy adversary. A shadow. Which passes by without seeming to pass by.]. From this semi-figurative language, the narrative proceeds to the literal language in speaking of the infection, ending once more with "palu": "Elle attrapa froid. La grippe? Puis un certain palu flotta dans l'air englué qui circulait loin de la demeure royale. Elle devint la cible préférée des cauchemars, ceux-ci lui labouraient le corps et le crâne tout entier à longueur de journée" (54) [She caught a cold. The grippe? Then a certain malarial strain floated through the thick air that circulated far from the royal household. She became the preferred target of nightmares, those that worked over the body and the skull throughout the length of the day.].

When Léti returns to the present in her thoughts, it is to the image of Niyous who "traînait dans les rues de la ville impaludée" (57) [dragged through the streets of the malarial city]. Here the imagery of palu grows and takes on even greater proportions, just as the struggle against it seems increasingly delusory. The medieval dance of death becomes, in modern usage, musicotherapy, whereby the music produced by humans would combat the discordant tones of the mosquitoes:

> La musique produite par les humains, disait-on, brisait les envolées lyriques des moustiques. Puissant antidote contre le paludisme, le

mal des maux dont souffrait Watouville. On essayait de conjurer le mauvais sort, par homéopathie. Guérir le semblable par le semblable. On chantait et dansait de concert. Question de santé physique et morale. Et éloigner les moustiques des portes officielles de la ville. (57) [The music produced by humans, they say, broke the lyrical clouds of mosquitoes. A powerful antidote against malaria, the worst of the ills from which Watouville suffered. People sang and danced in concert. It was a question of physical and psychological health. And of pushing the mosquitoes away from the official doors of the city.]

As Léti and Niyous approach each other, the warning tones of the disease multiply, the attempted cures failing to slow its progress: "Mais rien n'y faisait. Musique contre musique, les bourdonnements désagréables et les fêtes foraines des moustiques se magnifiaient, devenaient plus beaux, plus malins" (57). [But nothing helped. Music against music, the disagreeable buzzing and the country fair atmosphere of the mosquitoes became magnified, became more beautiful, more clever.].

Niyous is stabbed at the dance, and recuperates at Léti's apartment. The rains increase. The mud puddles proliferate, and with them the mosquitoes. Before the inevitable course is run, the city's means to contain the threat cannot hold. The forces of order, those surrounding the market, occasionally invading it; patrolling the streets, seeking bribes for their efforts to control the traffic; intervening at the dance after the stabbing of Niyous had taken place—they are the forces of a regulatory mechanism as extravagant in its threatening appearance as it is helpless to maintain order, on the retreat before the onset of the rain, the disease, the mud—and Niyous and Léti's affair.

> Octobre. Il pleuvait sur Watouville. Une de ces pluies fines que la ville connaissait depuis des siècles.
> Léti se dirigeait, sous un parapluie bleu, vers la demeure de Niyous à Djomo-La-Lutte. . . .
> Il y avait beaucoup de monde dans les rues. Les enfants jouaient sous la pluie, dans les mares boueuses. Des canalisations rouillées par le temps avaient sauté la pression de l'eau et de la masse des déchets. Les gens vivaient dans les odeurs fortes, celles des égouts, celle de la vie souterraine. Ils attendaient, les pieds dans la boue où ils vivaient depuis des temps immémoriaux. (68)

> [October. It rained on Watouville. One of those fine rains which the city has experienced for centuries.

Under a blue umbrella, Leti went towards Niyous's house in Djomo-the Struggle. . . . There were lots of people in the streets. Children played in the rain, in muddy puddles. Pipes rusted over time had burst under the pressure of water and the mass of sewerage. The people lived with the powerful odors, those of sewers, of underground life. They waited, feet in the mud where they lived since time immemorial.]

It is at such a moment, with the poor vulnerable to the worst of the forces of nature and the noxious discharges of the city, that the wealthy Massahacre, "le roi du sucre" [the king of sugar], succumbs to the rampaging palu—the everyday disease that has now become, like AIDS, the inevitable punishment for those living in the city. The comments of the awole players capture the fatalistic tone of the people:

Premier joueur: "tu as entendu ça? Massahacre est mort. Le palu a fini par l'emporter."
Deuxième joueur: "moi qui pensais qu'il prenait sa Nivaquine, tous les matins, depuis cinquante ans qu'il était là!"
Troisième joueur: "tu parles! La forme pernicieuse, propre à Watouville, est rebelle à tout comprimé, à tout injection, à toute pillule. . . . On invente de nouveaux remèdes, authentiques, très efficaces semble-t-il."
Premier joueur: "en attendant, vieux Massahacre est déjà mort, paix à son âme!" (68)

[*First player:* "Have you heard? Massahacre died. Malaria finally carried him off."
Second player: "Me who thought he was taking his Nivaquine, every morning, for the fifty years he was around."
Third player: "You think! This pernicious form we've got in Watouville is resistant to every kind of pill, injection, tablet. . . . They are inventing new cures, authentic and really efficacious, so it seems."
First player: "While we're waiting, old Massahacre is already dead, may he rest in peace!"]

As in *Death in Venice*, the pestilential atmosphere gains more and more ground, especially as the poor now recognize that even the wealthy are vulnerable. Faith in traditional cures fades away—"Les sacrifices n'ont jamais soigné personne. On en fait . . . on n'en fait pas, on meurt quand même!" (69) [Sacrifices have never cured anyone. We make them . . . or don't make them, and we die anyway!]. The ordinariness of the corrupt order, the ordinariness of the roads becoming unusable, the insalubriousness of the infrastructure matching the inadequacies of the schooling system, all lend themselves to the general condition of life in the city. For the inhabitants of the popular quartier, trapped in the nets of their existence, it is the life of the crab—trapped and waiting to be saved: "Ils guettaient toujours l'arrivée de la main salvatrice. Qui les purifierait. Qui les sortirait enfin de leur trou de crabes!" (68) [They always looked for the arrival of the hand of redemption. That would purify them. That would finally lead them out of their crab-holes!]. In the meanwhile, with the death of the king of sugar, the people now anticipate that it will be their turn next, and that they should quickly find what honey they can while there still is time: "Moi, plus que j'écoutais ce discours sur le palu, plus je me disais: maintenant que le roi du sucre est mort on va consommer du miel, du miel à gogo" (69) [As for me, the more I listen to this talk about malaria, the more I say to myself: now that the king of sugar is dead, we're going to eat honey, honey by the ton].

Léti seeks a place for Niyous in some school, hoping to rescue him from his life in the street. As she is looking, missing her own classes in the school where she teaches, her absences begin to weigh against her. The spread of the disease through the city is compounded by the journalists who fail to report on the problems within the school system, by the general lassitude of the population, and, by metonymic extension, by Léti's efforts on Niyous's behalf that cannot be explained within the strictures of the governing order. Léti's license, half unacknowledged by herself, gains ground along with the diseased economy of life in Watouville. Thus, the newspaper reports: "Il n'y a pas de problèmes, la rentrée se fait *sous la signe de l'ombre*" (69; my emphasis) [There are no problems, school opening is taking place under the sign of the shadow]. And the readers' apathy constitutes their response:

> Curieusement, tous ceux qui lisaient cette page ne disaient mot. Silence. C'était comme s'ils ne voyaient rien, n'entendaient rien à ce qui était écrit. Les gens avaient le visage dur, la mine sombre, l'air fatigué ce midi-là. A peine répondit-on au bonjour du voisin.
>
> Puis les jours passèrent, les uns semblables aux autres. Et ce malaise, indescriptible, gagna aussi Djomo-La-Lutte, ses enfants, ses joueurs. La nouvelle maladie n'avait pas encore de nom qui se répandait, comme une tache d'huile, sur tous les visages, sur tous les corps, dans tous les esprits. . . .

Léti fut atteinte, elle aussi, de ce nouveau virus. (70)

[Strangely, all those who read this page didn't say a word. Silence. It was as if they hadn't seen anything, hadn't heard a word about what had been written. The people had hard faces, a somber look to their faces, a tired appearance this noon. They hardly responded to their neighbors' greetings.

Then days passed, each one like the other. And this illness, indescribable, also took over Djomo-the-Struggle, its children, its players. The new illness didn't yet have a name to be spread, like a spot of oil, on all the faces, the bodies, the minds. . . .

Léti too came down with this new virus.]

The dream and the real become mixed, confused. Léti dreams she loses her job, and the next day is fired for having missed so many classes. Later she will learn she was fired to make room for a young man who had been searching desperately for a position, and that it was Dramane-le-Bègue who had been responsible for her losing her post. Her feelings for Dramane were not yet gone, and those for Niyous uncertain, incompletely acknowledged—"Sans l'ombre d'un doute, elle avait aimé Dramane. Mais l'accident l'avait rapprochée, terriblement rapprochée de Niyous" (67) [Without the shadow of a doubt, she had loved Dramane. But the accident had brought her closer, terribly closer to Niyous.]. Léti moves into the uncertain, ill-defined, disordered time and space of subversion.

Without the clearly defined signposts of traditional order, without the dictates of the new, modern forces of order, Léti and Niyous sketch out the lineaments of an incestuous love that is manifest entirely in terms of "la ville belle et impaludée." It is both desirable and destructive, because the regime that dictates the path of love within the established, patriarchal order also defines the externalized spaces that go beyond their limits. In the city, limits are easily recognized. Dramane lives in the wealthy quartier, in a luxurious house, with expensive cars and many servants. Djomo-La-Lutte has its mud puddles, its market, its palu. The two worlds see themselves as miles apart, but cross over continually. Cast-off wives fall from the luxury of Bellevue to the poverty of Djomo-La-Lutte in the space of a divorce, and their children lose favored status to become street children. If the example is extreme, the chain of signifiers linking the ruling elite to the ruled masses is continually imbricated with relatives and friends whose ties extend into networks throughout the city. Léti lives alone, her life caught up in the space that lies between the father and the son, casting her into a temporal zone that lies outside the margins defined by the forces that construct its order:

> Elle pensa à Niyous. Niyous. Niyous. Niyous, mille fois Niyous! Si tu savais ce que tu me coûtes dans la vie, rêvasses-t-elle le temps d'un éclair. Elle rentra chez elle, la mort dans l'âme. Et la semaine fut, à ses yeux, interminable. Elle n'avait aucune envie de jouer avec le temps, ce temps qui s'imposait à elle et qui, de tout son poids, lui pesait si lourd sur les épaules. (72) [She thought of Niyous. Niyous. Niyous. Niyous, a thousand times, Niyous! If you knew what you cost me in my life, she dreamed in the flash of an instant. She returned home, death in her soul. The week seemed interminable, in her eyes. She had no desire to play with time, this time that imposed itself on her and which, with all its weight, weighed down so heavily on her shoulders.]

Trapped, the space of her apartment closes in on her—"Cet espace restreint qui lui collait presqu'à la peau" (72) [This narrow space which practically stuck to her skin]—until her inner world and the disease-ridden atmosphere become one: "Elle finit par attraper *la* maladie. . . . Au creux de ce profond paludisme elle entrovoyait deux têtes d'hommes: l'une colossale, l'autre en miniature. La tête du père et celle du fils. Elle dêlirait" (72) [She wound up catching *the* disease. . . . At the full depths of this malaria she caught a glimpse of two human heads: one colossal, the other in miniature. The head of the father and that of the son. She raved in delirium.].

In her delirium the borders dissolve—the time-space of her incest dissolves the distinction between father and son; and her role—that particular role of favored "rivale" in the polygamous marriage, that particular role of young, beautiful co-wife in the menage of the wealthy and powerful "Roi-du-commerce," that particular role of second mother to her co-wives' children, all that fades before the elements that comprise "la ville impaludée," its mud and disease. "Les choses devenaient liquides autour d'elle. Il y avait des mares boueuses partout. Sa chambre était une énorme flaque d'eau couleur de terre sur laquelle elle flottait, elle, inerte, sans vie" (73) [Things became liquified around her. There were muddy pools everywhere. Her chamber was an enormous puddle of water the color of earth on which she floated, she, inert, without life.].

Once cured, she goes out into the city, and there, everywhere before her eyes, the signs of the forbidden *and* of its inexpungeable presence present themselves to her eyes: "Elle voyait des flaques d'eau boueuse en pleine chaussée, des routes barrées pour travaux. Elle aperçut des déviations, de nouveaux sens interdits. Une circulation fortement réglementée" (73) [She saw the puddles of muddy water in the middle of the sidewalk, roads blocked off for repairs. She saw the detours, the new no entrance signs. Traffic heavily regulated]. At the same time, she sees holes, crevices, mounds of dirt—signs of a disorder fatally resistant to the efforts of the construction company, Michel Ruzé et Cie: "un ravin sans fond restait sourd et rebelle aux efforts d'Hercule de Michel Ruzé et Cie qui accueillait avec grâce tous les véhicules roulant à tombeau ouvert dans cette rue" (73) [a ditch without bottom remained unresponsive and rebellious to the efforts of Hercule de Michel Ruzé and Company, which welcomed with grace every vehicle driving full speed down the street.].

As Butler puts it, the order that generates the law also generates the very exclusions that work against it, so that subversion arises "from within the terms of the law, through the possibilities that emerge when the law turns against itself and spawns unexpected permutations of itself" (93). Léti's love is one such unexpected permutation of the law of patriarchal order. Turning against the law, against the social construction intended to define the direction through which the traffic would pass, like that through which the time too would pass, she catches the new disease that proves resistant to all the old remedies. A victim of the city, she defines a new form of beauty, that grounded in the possibilities posed openly by the future. Her poem to Niyous exposes us to that spirit—one in search of an indefinite face that lies before her, unknown, undelineated, free:

> Je cherche un nuage
> Je cherche un passage
> Je cherche un paysage
> Je cherche un visage
> Sur une feuille de canne à sucre
> Une nervure sur fond vert
> Un nuage une nébuleuse
> *Je te* cherche
> Toi l'inconnu
> Dans les charmes secret
> De la liberté! (73)
>
> [I am looking for a cloud
> I am looking for a passage
> I am looking for a countryside
> I am looking for a face

> On a leaf of sugar cane
> A vein on a green background
> A cloud a nebulousness
> I am looking for you
> You the unknown
> In secret charms!]

Léti does not turn to her traditional past, nor does she rely upon the Other, not even Niyous, to define her future. What marks her thoroughly subversive stance is not a spirit of revolt, defined by the lineaments of a patriarchy, postulated in negativity, but her insistence on constructing her future for herself. Her subversion *is* her openness, which does not fade into a vague indefiniteness, but which enables her to find and perform that identity that conforms to her conception. She thus would seem to match perfectly Butler's notion of the liberated body: "The culturally constructed body will then be liberated neither to its 'natural' past nor to its original pleasures, but to an open future of cultural possibilities" (93).

We can hear an echo of Freud's question "what does the woman want?" in the exclamation of a conventional taxi driver who cannot easily accept the new visage of the African woman wearing panther T-shirt, jeans, and leather boots: "*Walahahi*! S'exclama le taximan en freinant brusquement. Qu'est-ce que femme veut? Un homme comme moi peut-il avoir une femme militaire de ce gabarit-là?" (30) [God! Exclaimed the taxi driver, braking brusquely. What does woman want. A man like me, can he have a military woman in that get-up?]. The "gabarit-là" that shocked the Muslim taxidriver might not represent an "open future of cultural possibilities" as much as a performance of liberation in borrowed clothes. But as all gender performances are rehearsals without opening nights, are reiterations of previous performances, with "original" borrowings, with improvisations on "original" themes, and at the same time are completely contemporary, completely figurations of their time and place, the scene played out before the taxi man at the popular eating establishment "Forfait conjuncture" is, like its name, a playful exhibition—performance as play. Somewhere in that play lie the possibilities for a grin without a cat, just as the repression is there in the very effect of subversion it has produced. We can read the leather boots as signs of new possibilities opened up, and we can read them as pseudo-liberation decked out in foreign clothes. *Une vie de crabe* does not involve itself so much with the taxi man's immediate concern, but more with the larger question "what does the woman want?" played out against the backdrop of order. We can see this in the scenes leading up to the consummation of Léti and Niyous's love affair.

For the father, Dramane-le-Bègue, the "maître-de-maison," order is implied in his status, established by his wealth. He has lost Léti and no longer enjoys a satisfactory sex life, so he undertakes a voyage to the village where he can seek the aid of a powerful "guérisseur," Kabako. His "phantasm" of gender, that of the powerful male, is reiterated in virtually every encounter he has. When his pickup is stopped by a customs official on the road for the usual hassles and bribes, Dramane threatens to have the official's career and life ruined, and the customs man is reduced to a pathetic figure. The visit to the healer, the prescription for winning the woman's love, the exchange of large sums of money, all play into a familiar scene of power and mystery long established in the narratives of heterosexual economies: sex and conquest married to wealth and status; the mastery and the role of master defined against a backdrop of phallic power. Phallocracy never so literal as in this staging; never so convinced of the substantiality of its embodiment.

On his return from the healer, Dramane throws a party, inviting Léti to attend. There he grants her request to help Niyous enroll in his school, and at the same time reestablishes his relationship with her. She is reintegrated into his scene—reincorporated into a setting in which he, like the sun king, sheds his "rayons de soleil," dispersing the shadows that hitherto had haunted Léti's imaginary. Léti senses the presence of "[l]es boues multicolores de la ville" (84) [the city's multicolor muds], but given the ease and security provided by Dramane, succumbs: "Elle trébucha. Tomba à la renverse dans une mare. Douce. Chaude. Moelleuse. Cette mare sentait le miel" (84) [She stumbled. Fell backwards into a pool of water. Soft. Warm. Luxuriant. This puddle smelled of honey.]. The honey, the "mare," represent transvaluations of the disease-ridden puddles of Djomo-La-Lutte. Struggle is replaced by Lethean ease; the honey, Dramane's sweet wealth, has replaced the sugar trade run by Dramane's dead rival, Massahacre. The sexual dances of the phantasms are played out in all seriousness, with their magic potions and well-rehearsed discourses of love: " 'Tu es belle, tu sais!' murmura-t-il" (85) ["You are beautiful, you know!" he murmured.], and the healer's triumph of masculinist sexuality is made apparent:

> Il avait avalé à l'insu de la femme, quelques gorgées de cette eau sacrificielle à laquelle il tenait tant. Potion magique, infaillible, qui lui permettait de recouvrer tout son honneur, toute sa dignité d'homme.

> Il la caressait du regard. Un désir infini. . . .
> Toute une nuit durant, la guerre s'était estompée entre l'homme et la femme qui reformèrent un couple tendre, amoureux, paisible. Ils glissèrent ensemble dans les eaux profondes et tumultueuses, ces eaux mille fois millénaires des fantasmes qui passent. Sans pouvoir passer entièrement. (85)

> [He had swallowed, without the woman knowing it, a few mouthfuls of that sacrificial water that he counted on so much. Magical potion, infallible. Which permitted him to recover all his honor, all his dignity as a man.
> He caressed her with his look. An infinite desire . . .
> During a whole night, the war was erased between the man and the woman who reformulated themselves as a tender, loving, peaceful couple. They slid together into deep and tumultuous waters, those thousand-fold millennium waters of phantasms which passed by, without passing by entirely.]

Who are these phantasms that pass? And why does an excess, a supplement remain? For Butler the repetitive act of heterosexual gender practice, constructed within the regulatory structures of the patriarchal order, is phantasmic, not given—as much constructed performances as any other, including the gay performances playfully parodying them:

> The "real" and the "sexually factic" are phantasmic constructions—illusions of substance—that bodies are compelled to approximate, but never can. What, then, enables the exposure of the rift between the phantasmatic and the real whereby the real admits itself as phantasmatic? Does this offer the possibility for a repetition that is not fully constrained by the injunction to consolidate naturalized identities? Just as bodily surfaces are enacted *as* the natural, so these surfaces can become the site of a dissonant and denaturalized performance that reveals the performative status of the natural itself. (146)

If Léti's return to Dramane signifies a return of things to their natural place, Boni's discourse of that return slyly suggests its inherent instability. If the waters in which the couple is formed are deep, they are also tumultuous, a force requiring containment. They are haunted by constructions whose play is excluded, as incest is always present as the excluded act or thought in every act of phallic substitution. And the phantasmic nature of the act, so natural in appearance, is seen in the very quality of substitution itself. Dramane-le-Bègue will be followed by Dramane junior, no matter how infinite the gap between the streetwise child and his father the Roi-du-commerce.

Dramane's intervention into Niyous's life, his placement of Niyous in school, like his intervention into Léti's school that resulted in her dismissal, represents his natural efforts to bring them both into the orbit of his ordered universe—actually his ordered city-state. But Léti and Niyous, separately and together, like the city itself, remain features of a law that continues to construct and produce the very objects that deny it. From within the scholarly community into which Niyous entered emerges the rebellion against its authority:

> "Ainsi vous tomberez vous aussi dans l'illégalité, la rébellion. . . ."
> "On a toujours été des hors-la-loi. Qu'est-ce que tu veux? La société est si peu fait pour nous . . . nous les mains vides." (89)
>
> ["Thus you will fall into a life of illegality, of rebelliousness. . . ."
> "We were always operating outside the law. What do you want? Society is so little made . . . for us . . . we the empty-handed."]

As Niyous continues to talk to Léti, the narrative describes the declining force of the "faibles rayons de soleil" [weak sunrays], the decline of the sun, as Dramane's influence over them fades. The motif of the excluded urban waste returns, marking the "natural" environment with its polluting effects: "De[s] petites boules d'une pâte noire collante durcie par le soleil se mélangeaient çà et là aux feuilles mortes qui recouvraient à peu près le tiers de la plage. Des restes de goudron sans doute. Ou les déchets industriels déversés dans les eaux de la ville. La lagune, la mer aussi" (89) [Small black, sticky balls, hardened by the sun, mixed here and there with dead leaves which covered over, more or less, a third of the beach. The leftover tar no doubt. Or industrial waste thrown into the waters of the city. The lagoon, the sea too.].

As Léti returns to her apartment, her feelings for Niyous rekindled, she notes in her notebook, "C'est maintenant que le voyage interdit commence" (90) [It's now that the forbidden voyage begins.]. Her reestablishment of her relationship with Dramane was needed for her feelings for Niyous—"Dramane-le-Jeune"—to be experienced as forbidden. For both herself and Niyous, their roles required names that would mark their separation from the Roi-du-Commerce: Niyous and Léti, not Dramane-le-Jeune and Mam'Djan (i.e., mother of Djan).

The student strike in which Niyous takes a leading role is strongly reminiscent of Souleymane Cissé's *Finye*, in which the direct confrontation between the younger generation (the daughter of the commandant and her boyfriend) and the older generation (the father-commandant) results in the expulsion of the students and their incarceration in harsh military camps. Obviously this is a struggle that is "real," even if psychologically or figuratively symbolic. In *Une vie de crabe*, the two orders of meaning are maintained and overlap. As the students strike, disorder and disease spread:

> Au cours de cette même période les accès palustres et l'hépatite virale continuaient leurs ravages. En moins d'un semaine ils avaient terrassé deux enseignants du Lycée.
> Les autorités politiques s'inquietèrent de cette forme de désordre si peu habituelle à Watouville. Des forces de l'ordre envahirent les rues de la ville comme un nuage de criquets. (92)

[During this same period the incidents of malaria and viral hepatitis continued their ravages. In less than a week they had done in two highschool teachers.
The political authorities were worried about this unaccustomed form of disorder in Watouville. The forces of order invaded the streets of the city like a cloud of crickets.]

Niyous and the other student protesters are arrested and sent to "un camp sans nom" [a nameless camp] where they are treated to the rigors of initiation (exactly as had been the case in *Finye*). The city authorities unleash insecticide bombs on the infested sites throughout the city. But the infection has already spread too far: Léti marks in her notebook, "C'est l'heure du voyage interdit" (95) [it was the hour of the forbidden voyage], as if the two of them have already entered, as accomplices, into a new play. The time and space containing Niyous—"le temps et l'espace carcéraux" (94) [the prison time and space]—the time of an order governing their lives in the city, marking their days, hours, and seconds according to a regulatory calendar inscribed by the forces of order, yields to their reinscriptions of disorder and of incest. Niyous returns, they meet, and as she comes close to him, taking his hand, "[l]e temps devenait une fusée qui brisait tous les espaces rêvés, inconnus, interdits. Leurs paroles venaient de loin" (97) [time became a rocket which broke up all the dreamed, unknown, forbidden places. Their words came from far away.].

In contradiction to and in rebellion against the order of the sun—against Dramane's "rays"—they bed down together as the rain continues to fall. Desire, love, death, and life slide along a chain of signifiers disordering their names, their roles: "l'homme et la femme attendaient la fin de la pluie. Mais la pluie n'avait pas de fin. . . . Comme le désir. La fin du désir c'est la mort de l'amour. La fin de la pluie c'est la mort de la vie" (97) [the man and the woman await the end of the rain. But the rain didn't end. . . . Like desire. The end of desire is the death of love. The end of the rain is the death of life.].

Not since Sembène's powerful *Véhi Ciosane* (1965) have incest and the sense of transgression been treated with such force. And nothing better exemplifies the distance beween the kind of reformist first wave feminism embraced by Sembène, and the possibilities for more radical subversion opened up by Boni, than this scene between Niyous and Léti. Léti, always the more articulate and reflective of the two, expresses perfectly the sense of entering into unknown waters: "Je ne vois pas la tête que j'aurai en sortant d'ici" (97) [I can't imagine what face I'll wear leaving here.].

As they make love, and then as Niyous falls asleep, Léti remains awake, drawing the reader into her full awareness of the situation through the use of free indirect discourse. The delicate slide from narrative description to the interiority of the thoughts enables us to approach her character more closely, to share in the awareness of the transgression she has now accepted: "Léti avait les yeux grands ouverts. Elle cherchait à comprendre. Dramane venait à mourir, symboliquement mais sûrement, assassiné par son propre fils. Désormais, il y aurait Dramane Junior dit Niyous. Un homme à mi-chemin entre l'enfance et l'âge adulte" (97) [Léti's eyes were wide open. She tried to understand. Dramane had just died, symbolically but surely, killed by his own son. From now on, there was Dramane Jr. called Niyous. A man half-way between childhood and adulthood.].

That evening she enters into her notebook: "Toi sans nom, accepte que je t'appelle amour" (98) [You who have no name, accept that I call you love]. Aware of her inscription within the inevitable masculinist discourse, Léti shrugs off the constraints of names, of nouns whose meanings are lit up, made clear, through the order of sense and purpose. She embraces, if only temporarily, their entrance into "les ombres de la nuit" (98) [shadows of the night], and in her jouissance outside the order of time, sketches the ephemeral contours of a grin—without the body, and without the overseeing, of the cat.

The novel ends with Léti losing her notebooks. They had been kept in a drawer where they rested on the solid surface of a wooden board—"Oui de bois, question de toucher du dur, du solide" (35) [Yes of wood, a matter of touching something solid, hard]. But with the rain, the mud, and the new disease, all that had been solid began to dissolve. Even the powerful Dramane-le-Bègue succumbed to the viral hepatitis, dying with the word "ombre. L'o-o-o-o-m-bre!!!" (100) [shadow. The sha-a-a-a-dow] on his lips, as though losing his senses. Léti's notebooks represented her efforts to record, to give substance within the confining of her narratives, to all the events that animated her life: "Ils sont jaunes, vieillis, pétris d'idées, de sourires, de clins d'oeil, de coups de dards, de regards, de soleil, de mer, de fleurs, de pleurs, d'odeurs, de vie, de lutte, de tumulte, de silence farouche" (35) [They are yellow, old, molded with ideas, smiles, winks, struck by spears, glances, the sun, the sea, flowers, tears, odors, life, struggling, tumultuous, a savage silence.]. The one word that is missing from this enumeration is "amour," the fullness of which she hopes to find at the end, without the need to record and reinscribe it; but to be able to experience in the present moment. "Léti pense à ses cahiers morts noyés. Mais, pour une fois, elle rêva d'amour sans écrire. Un amour fort, dense, immense, inachevé" (107) [Léti thinks of her dead, drowned notebooks. But, for once, she dreamed of love without writing. A strong love, deep, immense, unfinished.]. The dream of love without writing, a presymbolic écriture, strong, dense, and immense, evokes the inscriptions of the body, when viewed in light of Kristeva's powerful image of the semiotic, or the laugh of Medusa, Cixous's equally vivid image of the force of feminine desire unconstrained by patriarchy.

The drowned notebooks provide a kind of culmination of the final, hallucinatory scenes of the novel in which the forces of order come for Léti and are met by a resistance led by women and children, resulting in a riotous, carnivalesque riposte. The "deluge" breaks forth. Kitchen implements rain down on the police, whose reinforcements fall on the city like swarms of bees, butterflies. A veritable war of cheeses breaks out,[7] as the norms of language and order disintegrate:

> Dehors, des sirènes ameutèrent le quartier, la ville entière, le pays profond, le pays tout court. Des uniformes kaki ou gris ou vert-de-gris arrivèrent sur les lieux de la scène fantastique, en musique, comme un essaim d'abeilles. Cependant, ils étaient attendus de pied ferme par une fête gigantesque qui ne manqua point de leur couper le souffle. Il y avait partout, des barrages de femmes et d'enfants auxquels se joignaient des hommes, puis des hommes. (106) [Outside, sirens woke up the neighborhood, the whole city, the heart of the country, the country altogether. Khaki, gray, or gray-green uniforms appeared on the sites of

the fantastic scene, with music, like a swarm of bees. However, they were greeted with resolution by a gigantic festival which didn't fail to take away their breath. Everywhere there were roadblocks made up of women and children who were joined by men, and then more men.]

Helicopters bring millions of parachutists—"[i]ls atterrirent comme des papillons échappés d'un grand filet" [they landed like butterflies that escaped from a large net]. And the rains fall and fall, bringing more pools of water, "des mares de plusieurs mètres de profondeur [qui] roulèrent jusqu'aux égouts, jusqu'aux caniveaux" (106–7) [pools of several meters depth that spread out as far as the sewers, as far as the sewerage ditches]. It is then that the prehistoric creatures lying beneath the surface, constantly brought under control by the network of regulatory agencies, make their appearance: "Et l'on vit même des crocodiles, des crabes de terre et de mer et de lagune dans la rue. Trempés dans les mares boueuses" (107) [You could even see crocodiles, land and sea and lagoon crabs in the streets. Soaked in the muddy pools.]. In this setting the final battle is waged:

> Les victimes du déluge se battaient, conscientes du lien, le sang ou l'alliance, qui les unissait. Léti se trouvait parmi la foule. . . . Puis arrivèrent, sans tambour ni cora, des gorilles-barracudas. Ils avaient été téléguidés de l'extérieur et ils oublièrent, arrivés à destination, leur mission périlleuse de sauveurs de crocodiles ou autres animaux préhistoriques. Car ceux-ci se faisaient pincer très fort ou assommer en pleine gueule par des femmes. (107) [The victims of the deluge fought against each other, aware of the tie, by blood or marriage, that brought them together. Léti found herself among the crowd. . . . Then the gorilla-barracudas, without drumbeat or cora, arrived. They had been teleguided from the outside and they forgot, once they had arrived at their destination, their perilous mission to save the crocodiles or other prehistoric animals. Because they were being pinched very strongly or smacked right in the puss by the women.]

The law has "spawned unexpectedly permutations of itself"—the force of Léti's desire, denied and liberated, does not return either as a natural being or as an imaginary flight from being, but as a subversive performance. The return is played out as a text without writing, a new discourse "liberated, not to its 'natural' past, nor to its original pleasures, but to an open future of cultural possibilities" (Butler 93). The women turn their pincers on the gorrilla-barracudas, stinging them into forgetting their missions of control, of "saving" the submarine forces from themselves, channeling their dangerous parts, taming them, transforming their pincers, their hides, their teeth into commodities for the wealthy and the tourists to consume. The reign of the metaphysics of substance, teleguided by the ancient kings—of commerce, of sugar, of the city—comes to an end in this figuration, and a new temporal order emerges, alive and open: "Le passé mourait et il n'y avait pas d'avenir. Car on était, dans le déluge, sur le qui-vive. Sur le qui-vive à l'infini" (107) [The past died and there wasn't any future. Because one was, in the deluge, on the lookout. On the lookout forever.].

City of Dis: Véronique Tadjo's Urban Landscapes

The sense of incongruity between western feminism and African culture and society derives in part from the fact that conditions in Africa are substantially different from those in the West, so that strategies developed to advance feminist issues in the West should not be viewed as universally applicable elsewhere. Further, the tendency to apply western thinking in other domains—an extension of colonialist beliefs that all civilization resided in the West, and that Europe bore the duty of bringing civilization to the rest of the world—has an exact parallel in feminist thought: hence Butler's warning against the globalizing of Irigaray's notions of the woman or of l'écriture féminine. Thus, patriarchy may be seen to be widespread, but not to take the same form everywhere, nor to elicit the same combat everywhere.

Indeed it would be foolish to look for solutions in the West, and to "apply" them to "underdeveloped" countries. It would be foolish to ignore the fact that issues such as polygamy, forced marriages, clitorectomy and infibulation, and a multitude of practices and beliefs of primary concern in some parts of Africa play a small role in the West; it would be foolish to ignore the discrepancies between the African state or city and the western state or city. Each has its own virtues, each its own problems. The formulation of political struggle, and by extension, feminist political struggle, is local, even if it can be informed by other struggles elsewhere. This is Mohanty's point when she argues in her seminal essay "Under Western Eyes" (1991) against western feminist practices that totalize Third World women.

When Butler writes that "new possibilities for gender . . . contest the rigid codes of hierarchical binarisms" (145), one's first reaction is to ask whether the heavy load borne by women in Africa derives from hierarchical binarisms as much as from corrupt and oppressive governments, and from the weight of sexist thinking, in the countryside and in the cities, that reduce the status of women in the economy and society. And even if that sexist thinking is grounded in a fundamental heterosexual binary, one has to wonder about the possibilities of challenging it along the more radical lesbian lines of a Monique Wittig, through the Irigarayan opposition to masculinist discourse, or with the development of l'écriture féminine, as opposed to the more straightforward humanist lines of first wave feminism.

But still one cannot avoid the question of the subject and its constitution; what is the basis for the discourse that frames her liberation; how do we avoid reinscribing patriarchy back into the struggle against it? We cannot avoid these questions, as if theorizing about discourse or the subject were more properly concerns of the West than of people elsewhere. And if the context and particularities of the political debate are best understood in local terms, still the border between the local and the larger sphere is not an absolute or impermeable one.

Indeed, in the case of Africa, borders have long, in fact probably always, been porous: between different African peoples, between African and Arab, between African and European. And nowhere is the porosity of the line between insider and outsider more evident, more of an issue, than in the world of letters. African writers, reading and writing in European languages, being read and taught in the West, living and often studying or teaching in the West, have created a literature that has not only "written back" against the Empire, but, more important, has been written through the Empire, often being written "by" the same discourse against which it has seen itself to be rebelling. As Mudimbe has put it, "l'odeur du père" has penetrated the very revolt of the sons and daughters.

If Butler's political frame seems slightly out of kilter with African priorities at times, still her analysis permits us to approach the important issues for African feminism, and for African women's writing, in ways that seem vital and productive. As with Lacan, and with Kristeva, Irigaray, and other psychoanalytical feminists, powerful tools of theoretical analysis can be turned to "other" writings across and through the mirror, often turning back against the theorist when seen in the "other" light, but also permitting the insights gleaned within the frame of western institutions to illuminate African texts.

Still, much of the theoretical apparatus that has been employed in this study has been used in the consideration of more recent, second wave feminist texts, those for whom the immediacy and clarity of a struggle for independence have yielded to the uncertainty and inconsistency of a post-independent Africa, and whose geographical and psychological locus has often wandered, as if an Assèze or Nyasha, from one continent to another. With the writings of Véronique Tadjo as well, we enter into a world that is both nowhere and everywhere, as we see in *Le Royaume des aveugles*—an allegory that touches much of the blindness of contemporary societies, even if it is African in spirit—within a diffuse space that has multiple centers, with its Europeanized city of stone, its American black urban centers, its African home. Above all, the struggle to free the homeland and to create a new age has now given way for Tadjo, as for Okri, Boni, Rawiri, and many others, to the problems involving love and survival in the City of Dis—the city of dystopia, of dysfunctionality; of hell's bottom circles where the infernal rounds of beauty and death take their turns. For Tadjo, in *A vol d'oiseau*, and Ben Okri, in "When the Lights Return" ([1988] 1989), it is the city where Eurydice's drama is played out.

Tadjo associates the city with love. It is a site of departures and arrivals—of departures after disappointed love, of flights in anticipation of reunification with a lover; of painful separations from loved ones at home; of entering into a new world where love compensates for coldness and strangeness. Like Persephone, Eurydice comes to the realm of Hades reluctantly, and is almost brought back to the land of the living by her lover. Persephone's mother, Ceres, proved more capable than Orpheus, winning for Persephone a return to earth for six months each year. Persephone's triumph is always a temporary one: she has to leave the earth each year, cycling back and forth, from airport to airport, driven by love and death in continual anticipation, till reaching maturity, and achieving completion; death and reappearance.

For Persephone, the trajectory is cyclic, seasonal, a pattern of leaving and returning driven by nature: she is nature's servant, the embodiment of the natural principles of the seasons. Hers is the mythos for a metaphysics of substance. Eurydice's tale is more tragic. Bitten by a serpent, she is separated from a lover whom all the other women of Greece desired, the handsome, supreme player of the lyre, Orpheus. His music was such that wild beasts would come and listen tamely to his playing, and even the streams would mute their flow in response to his music. But if his playing enabled him to win a reprieve over Eurydice's death, the conditions of the reprieve were too hard for him to meet: he could not refrain from turning back as they were leaving the underworld, and Eurydice was lost to him forever.

The Greeks go on with the tale of Orpheus after his failure to rescue Eurydice, as if her return were all that mattered for her—as if her separation from Orpheus were the end of her tale. But we know well, as Aidoo has so effectively shown in "Certain Winds from the South," that there is more to the story of a husband's emigration than the account of his adventure. Not only does life go on for those who stay behind, so too does the story, and the narration, of their life.

Eurydice not only returns to Hades, the lord of the underworld, she comes back to his embrace, as does Persephone. The young, handsome musician must be left for the older, mature god-man whose power extends over life itself, especially over the lives of young women whose fertility is what brings fruit to the earth each year. The Great African Novel of departure and change also has its reverse side, that of the been-to's return, the turn away from assimilation and loss, the reclamation of the past (even Camara Laye has his *Dramouss*).

Tadjo plays on all the notes of this journey, of these departures and returns. And indeed, one finds notes of rejuvenation, hope for the future, and calmness. Most of all, the flight is not governed by the calm certainties of nature's cycles, of fertility and rebirth, but rather by the necessity to survive in the city of Dis, or rather the cities of Dis, as his realm reaches across the continents into the troubled geographies of Tadjo's several worlds.

At first *she* encounters Dis in Washington, D.C., or some such American city. It is a world apart—"un monde à part"—distant, different, the site where a meeting, and love, will take place. "Ils se rencontrèrent dans un aeroport. Arrivait de loin, il est venu la chercher comme prévu" (Tadjo 3) [They met in an airport. Come from afar, he came to fetch her as agreed.]. But the expectation of love and its more sordid realization prove to be ironically different. The calmness and middle-class affluence of her life there belie an emotional nightmare; the city becomes the setting for imprisonment and failure: "La ville était devenue une prison, son séjour un échec. Elle se sentait traquée, diminuée, blessée" (5) [The city had become a prison, her trip a failure. She felt tracked down, diminished, wounded.]. Love in Dis becomes "une sale affaire" (6)—a dirty, sorry affair for a tired city, with its "grand bâtiments blancs et ses jardins bien tracés" (6) [large white buildings with their well-marked gardens].

Dis then first makes its appearance not at home, but in the distant lands of wealth and power. It doesn't present itself in the form of racial prejudice or arrogant imperialism, but as love turned sour. The quiet anonymous narrative voice speaks of it in brief, disjointed paragraphs, not in the manner of some postmodernist, but with the intimacy of a first person diarist. She speaks to those who already know the names of the people and cities, to remind herself of what had already passed, to repeat it in a new performance of words, so that the one who had known the love and the city will emerge through her words as a subject-author: the creator of those texts, often allusive, paradigmatic stories; tale-like rather than tales, when they are not in the form of testimonial diary-like entries. Entries often about cities as prisons, which *she* must leave: "C'est un ghetto. Dans une grande ville des Etats-Unis. Washington, D.C. Il est Noir. S'en sortir . . . A tout prix" (9) [It is a ghetto. In a large city in the U.S. Washington, D.C. He is black. To get out . . . at any price.].

City of Dis. City where men practice their trade of cruelty and laughter: "J'ai lu dans le journal qu'un homme a tué toute sa famille. Découpé chacun en petits morceaux: le père, la mère, la petite soeur. *This is a bad neighborhood*. Mauvais quartier" (9) [I read in the newspaper that a man killed his whole family. Cut up each one in little pieces: the father, the mother, the little sister. This is a bad neighborhood. Bad neighborhood.] . Site and symbol of power, the city might as well be nameless: its streets will reverberate with sirens, sooner or later: the helicopters overhead pursue a man, its prisons hold dozens of drug dealers. The White House stands silent, apart, white—the empty color of Dis's house: "La ville paraît belle. La Maison Blanche est blanche" (9) [The city seems beautiful. The White House is beautiful.]. For the traveler—and not for the migrant or the ones denied visas—the city as prison extends its reach everywhere: "Il n'y a pas de frontière" (10) [There's no border].

Another look, and the city is now a war-zone, or the site for battles: "Les canons ont cessé de tonner. Le feu des mitraillettes s'est arrêté et les hommes ramassent les cadavres. On soigne les blessés. Seul le bruit sourd d'un râle vient troubler le silence du champ de la bataille" (52) [The cannons stopped booming. The machine-gun fire stopped and the men gathered up the corpses. They treated the wounded. Only the dull noise of a deathrattle troubled the silence of the battlefield.]. The moment of peace is installed, and hope makes its appearance. But the peace, like love, is an interlude; it is broken, always, by the devices of destruction. Thus she creates the story of the child of love who is sent by his parents throughout the continents to be their messenger, to recreate the cities "détruites par la violence et l'oppression" (69) [destroyed by the violence and the oppression]. He comes to "la ville," the only site for Tadjo's dramas to be played out, as it now seems to stretch out indefinitely—"la ville qui s'étalait le long de l'horizon" (70) [the city which spread out along the horizon]. There he finds the beauty and the ugliness of all cities, but especially in this case the African city that feels the breath of the harmattan: "Bien sûr, la ville était brillante de lumières et d'envies mais il suffisait de faire un pas pour rencontrer la boue et la saleté" (70) [Of course the city was shining with light and desires, but in just one step there was mud and dirtiness.]. There the wealthy, adorned in gold, live along with the poor in their rags, the children of the street. Worst of all, hope and freedom are empty words, "paroles inutiles," the people beaten down by forces that seem as distant and powerful as the forces of nature: "L'harmattan pouvait souffler pendant des semaines et blanchir la peau des hommes mais la chaleur s'abattait ensuite plus forte et plus puante" (70) [The harmattan could blow for weeks and whiten the skin of men, but the heat beat down afterwards even more powerfully, increasing the stink.].

The young emissary meets a beautiful woman who awakens his desire. She gives the city its beauty, it illuminates her gaze: "La ville était dans son regard" (71) [The city was in her gaze.]. He seeks to possess her, takes her by stealth, against her will, betraying their love. Eurydice's return is destroyed, and a love betrayed enters the city, the perfect location for destruction to complete its work:

> Soudain, il y est un éclair gigantesque, bousculant les nuages. Le ciel se mit à fuir et les arbres hurlèrent. En même temps, une chaleur infernale plongea. Une fumée lourde et poussiéreuse encercla la nature qui s'enflamma. Un souffle d'air violent brûla les êtres et renversa les buildings. La peau se détacha en plaques. Les yeux s'asséchèrent. Les cheveux tombèrent par touffes. Tous moururent violemment. Le fer se mit à fondre et coula le long du sol. Un énorme nuage-champignon sculpta l'horizon incendié. (72) [Suddenly there is a giant lightning bolt, shaking up the clouds. The sky began to flee and the trees shrieked. At the same time, an infernal heat broke out. Skin came off in patches. Eyes dried up. Hair fell out in tufts. Everyone died violently. Iron began to melt and flow along the earth. An enormous mushroom-cloud sculpted the burnt-up horizon.]

City of loss. Labyrinth of the lost, ruled by those mad with power. Site of the absence of love, whose power must be turned back against itself if there is to be any renewal of the land and the people: "L'éclatement du vent. Le fer du ciel gronde. La pluie sera sèche et dure. Il n'y aura abri nulle part. Il faudra offrir son visage et découvrir sa tête. La rite aura lieu au milieu de la ville et à travers le pays. Les détritus dégrindoleront des allées du pouvoir" (67) [The smacking of the wind. The iron of the sky groaned. The rain will be dry and hard. There won't be a tree to be found anywhere. You'll have to offer up your face and uncover your head. The rite will take place in the midst of the city and across the country. The rubbish will tumble down the alleys of power.].

Site for the murder of a child, the city is beaten down by the sun, its inhabitants reduced to silence: "La ville était agenouillée sous le ciel" (25) [The city was on its knees under the sky]; for the deaf-mute child it becomes a sepulcher: "L'enfant était seul, la ville tel un spectacle sans musique, une piste de danse sans orchestre" (27) [The child was alone, the city like a show without music, a dancefloor without band.]. When the child is found beaten to death in the morning, the rotten odors that fill the atmosphere mark the city: "C'était la saison des mangues et les fruits pourrissaient sous les arbres gorgés de sève. Une odeur forte envahissait l'atmosphère. Un nuage de poussière passait dans le ciel. La ville s'éveillait. Il devait être six heures passées" (28) [It was the season of mangos and the fruit rotted under the trees engorged with sap. A strong odor invaded the air. A cloud of dust passed in the sky. The city woke up. It was probably after six o'clock.].

Finally, African city, African quartier. Like Boni's Djomo-La-Lutte, Tadjo's Marcory is where the poor live alongside streets filled with street vendors and mud—poto-poto—the base of the mud blocks that form the modest houses of the poor. "Marcory poto-poto. Je vois un enfant morveux qui dévale la rue suintante de boue noirâtre. Je vois les pantalons retroussés. Les chaussures à la main. Je vois les pagnes relevés jusqu'aux genous. Les pieds nus et salis par la terre malmenée. Les taxis s'immobilisent au milieu des flaques" (11) [Marcory mud. I see a snotty child who runs down the street oozing with blackish mud. I see the pantlegs rolled up. Shoes in hand. I see the wrappers rolled up to the knees. Feet bare and dirtied by the worked-over earth. Taxis were stuck in the middle of puddles of water.]. The same children and women in the street, the same mud, the same insecurity—the city of Dis in its commonest form—poverty, and the visible signs written on those most marginal to the villas of power:

> Marcory poto-poto. Je vois la ville qui agonise de ses maux. Je vois les concessions, les maquis, les bars, les taos, les mauvais types.
>
> Je vois une femme qui fait de l'aloco. L'huile chaude. Les bananes rougissent. Ses pieds sont sales. La fumée brûle ses yeux. Un gosse attend sa part. Il a cinq francs. Ça fait trois alocos. (11)

> [Marcory mud. I see the city in agony from its troubles. I see compounds, the bush, bars, nightclubs, bad dudes.

I see a woman who makes aloco. Hot oil. Reddening bananas. Her feet dirty. Smoke burns her eyes. A kid waits for his share. He has five francs. That makes three alocos.]

Marcory poto-poto. Je vois les bandes de quartiers. Ces garçons qui sont déjà des hommes. (13) [Marcory mud. I see the neighborhood gangs. These boys are already men.]

At the other end of the voyage, away from home, she comes to another city, the great city of stone. Not Washington, D.C., or anything resembling an American agglomeration; this large, cold city, city of early darkness not unlike London, is the place of exile to which love has led her. It is the other space to which she must go if she is to be reunited with her lover—even if that union turns out to be temporary.

With love, the city shows its other side. Abidjan is painted in rainbows, and life becomes unrecognizable: "Tu as changé ma ville. Tu l'as peinte en arc-en-ciel. Je ne reconnais plus les noms des rues" (37) [You changed my city. You painted it in rainbow hues. I don't recognize the names of the streets any more.]. But love is marked by departure, and the city of stone marks the destination: "Tu t'envole vers un autre espace. Chez toi. Dans la grande ville de pierre" (37) [You soared toward another space. Your home. In the great city of stone.]. *She* must ultimately go toward him, after their love has been discovered. The patrilineal narrative is almost always the same: she leaves her home and family to go to his. *She* repeats the performance, with the play on pronouns evoking the full drama: "Tu pars comme il se doit. On part toujours. Mais tu ne sais pas si tu reviendras. Et c'est encore la même question répétée à l'infini: 'je pars, je pars, est-ce que je reviendrai' " (37) [You leave as you have to. One always leaves. But you don't know if you will return. And it is always the same question repeated over and over: "I am leaving, I am leaving, will I return"]. And for those of hers left behind, now the plural "vous": "Je vous quitte aujourd'hui. Hier je vous avais quittés déjà" (37) [I am leaving you today. Yesterday I had already left you.].

This is not going to be the cautionary tale of the foolish, headstrong daughter who ignores her parents, chooses the handsome stranger by herself, and finds herself captive of the bodiless spirit. *That* version springs out of a village paradigm intended to authenticate the regulatory agency of the lineage and family patriarchy, a warning intended to check the powerful anarchic force of female desire and to bring it under the control of the heads of the households.

What is so striking in Tadjo's account of *her* stress and conflict over the voyage to her lover's land is the absence of the reigning patriarchy's codes. The straightforward revolution of first wave feminism cannot be sustained in Tadjo's narrative because the tradition/modernity binary on which it depended has been supplanted. The *city* is all that is there. The village is a memory—an authenticating construction for Achebe, who had to consult with the elders of his father's and grandfather's generations to reconstruct the world of Umuofia before the coming of the whites; an artificial, imaginary construct for Beyala, who had to plagiarize Paule Constant's version in *White Spirit*, that version itself being a kind of parodic rendition of Conrad's equally imaginary invention in *Heart of Darkness*, all of which makes the Beyala version doubly removed from the village. Beyala's recent *La Petite Fille du réverbère* puts us in New Bell—"Couscousville." Boni and Tadjo give us various versions of Abidjan and its quartiers. From Rawiri's Libreville to Bâ's Dakar, the struggle in these urban environments that marks people's lives is based on the need to earn money, not to grow and sell crops; and the results of that struggle are written on the urban landscape, and on the goods people purchase. Bellevue (or Cocody), Djomo-La-Lutte or Marcory. *There* Mammywatta will make her appearance—in the bars and nightclubs where the music is electric and the rhythms decidedly mixed.

When *she* makes up her mind to leave them for "la grande ville de pierre," for her lover's home, there is no one to oppose her departure, to advise her against it, to arrange a better match, to poison her adventure. Whatever serpent strikes Eurydice's heel, she will have to make the decision about the journey alone, decide alone whether to stay or go. *She* is, in fact, alone in her narrative of this voyage whose nature may change from adventure to nightmare. There will be no Orpheus to rescue the helpless maiden—she *knows* what earth she is leaving, what ties she is breaking, what price she must pay. The brideprice is her own life: "Il faut partir avant de mourir, avant que ne s'éteigne le feu qui anime ton espoir. Partir avant l'indifférence, avant d'en avoir trop dit et scellé le silence" (48) [You have to leave before dying, before the fire that lights your hope dies out. Leave before indifference, before having said too much and sealed the silence.].

The warnings against the handsome stranger in the "original" cautionary tale could be read as subtextual warnings against female desire going unchecked.[8] Now her desire is her force, the force of her account, her words that have the strength to forge Eurydice's path where *she* wants to go—to *another world*, to be sure, beyond the sea, beyond the confining prison of home: "Partir quand il est encore temps avec ton désir qui fend la mer. Fort. La mer, rien que la mer. Souveraine et belle. Placenta immense, prison liquide" (48) [To leave while there is still time, with your desire that splits the sea. Strong. The sea, nothing but the sea. Sovereign and beautiful. An immense placenta, a liquid prison.]. The language of rupture succeeds that of individual desire. Or rather, the locus of desire, which drives the journey, shifts from a subject located in the position of the first person pronoun, the one with the name, to a space in which the impulsion or *jouissance* exceeds the boundaries. There time loses its diachronous regularity, and agency its personalized nature: "Il n'y aura plus de demain mais l'eau et le ciel se frayant un chemin à travers l'horizon" (48) [There will no longer be a tomorrow, but the water and the sky forging a path across the horizon.].

In "The Tale of the Complete Gentleman," the dangers and warnings are clear: the stranger returns his borrowed bodily parts and assumes his *true* form, his natural substance, as evil spirit. It is so that she can learn to recognize and distinguish good from evil that the disobedient, headstrong, beautiful daughter undergoes this trial. In the account of Tadjo's Eurydice, there is no clear distinction between a good that is here and an evil of others over there. If the seaside home is a "[p]lacenta immense," a "prison liquide," and if desire lends her the power to forge a new path ("frayer un chemin"), the love she discovers reveals itself to be no less confining: there is no departure without simultaneous attachment:

> L'étau se referme, le cercle se rétrécit. Je sens que je ne peux plus bouger.
> Serait-ce ton amour qui brise tant d'énergies? Cet amour qui *me possède* et me fait rompre les liens. (37)

> [The vice closed up again, the circle shrank. I feel that I can't budge any more.
> Would it be your love that breaks up so much energy? This love which possesses me and causes me to break all ties.]

Motifs of separation and adherence assume ambiguous proportions, as if the difference between them has become obscured. Her journey away, to the loved one, is the journey to Hades, to Dis, to the city of stone. Through death, love and desire are worked out, as it is the mourning over the death of the loved one, before the separation from the mother, that finally enables the mouth to speak. "Aller te rejoindre . . . Partir avec toi . . . n'est-ce pas mourir un peu? Mourir de cette mort qui trompe. Pas la vraie. Mais celle qui sépare de tout et descend sur la terre une voile de solitude" (37) [To go join you . . . Leave with you . . . isn't that to die a bit? To die of that death that betrays. Not the real one. But that which separates one from everything and covers the earth with a veil of solitude.].

So the mourning is joined to love, and the power to speak love: it is written across the body, it speaks the body, it is the body's desire and pain, and especially its need to move that pain through words. For Tadjo, it is expressed through the feelings of absence:

> C'est l'absence qui me tue. C'est l'absence qui aura ma peau. Je te le dis, elle aura ma peau. Je devrais y être habituée, mais chaque jour, elle me surprend, m'agrippe au collet, me met le couteau à la gorge et me tranche les forces.
>
> Ce sont toujours les autres qui meurent. Ils te laissent là, au milieu de la vie et tu ne sais plus si tu as rêvé ou si le temps existe encore. C'est cette absence qui me guette. (38)

> [It's absence that kills me. It's absence that will have my skin. I tell you, it will have my skin. I ought to be used to it, but every day, it surprises me, grabs me by the collar, puts the knife to my throat and cuts up my force.
>
> It's always other people who die. They leave you, in the midst of life, and you don't know any more whether you dreamed it or if time still exists. It's this absence that lies in waiting for me.]

This, too, is Dis—where time and the real escape the control of the subject, where "I" speaks through "tu," and where the struggle in the streets moves onto the fields of the body—to the head and knees that make the effort not to bow, but to speak:

> Le combattant salue l'adversaire. Le combat se fera contre lui-même. C'est la peur qu'il faut vaincre. Il ne baisse jamais la tête. Il refuse qu'on s'agenouille devant lui.
>
> . . . Le combattant a le coeur fier. Ce n'est pas moi qui le dis. Je l'ai lu quelque part. (38)

> [The combatant salutes the adversary. The combat will be against himself. It's fear he has to conquer. He never lowers his head. He refuses to have anyone kneel before him.
>
> The combatant has a proud heart. It's not I who says it. I read it somewhere.]

How will Eurydice take charge of her story, a story that was already given to her before her departure? No sooner has *she* made the journey than she discovers the placenta, the prison, the vice closing in on her all over again. She writes her way through the city of stone—through its cold beauty, its grandeur, its coldness, to the discovery that her desire was always her own. "En fin de compte, je ne t'ai jamais quitté" (55) [In the final analysis, I never left you.]. Eurydice's Orpheus remains silent, invisible—but always present. An absence and a presence—the substitutions of Dis, like those of the mother, of the other, a doubling of substance made possible through the act of enunciation: "Au creux de cette grande ville de pierre, le soleil a une autre lumière et toujours quelque fraîcheur. On dirait que les mots ont un double sens et que les gens marchent sur des coussins d'air" (55) [At the hollow point of this great city of stone, the sun takes on another light and there is always a coolness. It's as if words have a double meaning and the people walk on air cushions.].

Eurydice whispers to the absent-presence who is as close as her skin. Now she waits at his place for him: "Hier, j'étais chez moi. Aujourd'hui, je suis là. Je t'attends mais tu es tout près" [Yesterday, I was at home. Today I am here. I await you but you are nearby.]. She invites him, chez *lui*, the home of the handsome stranger: "Je t'attends et nous descendrons dans la rue" (56) [I await you and we will go into the street.]. At the beginning, the beauty of his fingers, his skin like hers, attracted her. But now, after the time of mourning, of absence, she discovers "l'autre espace," and it is cold. "Sous l'édredon, je grelotte de froid" (56) [Under the down comforter, I shake with cold.]. It is gray; there are stones, but no mud, no dust. And love, the city, the stranger, close in on her: "La vie est une piège. Je deviens folle dans cette ville qui tourne autour de toi, où ma vie a pris l'allure d'une promesse. Je m'essouffle. C'est l'amour qui m'a conduite ici et qui me laisse comateuse jusqu'au lever du ciel" (57) [Life is a trap. I am going crazy in this city of which you are the center, where my life has taken on the rhythm of a promise. I run out of breath. It's love that led me here and that leaves me comatose until the morning sky's clearing].

Perhaps for Eurydice the whole adventure turned on the city. Orpheus, of course, took it to be fate that she was bitten, that she went unwillingly to that other space, to that other realm whose king must have been death itself. He must have thought she needed to be rescued, and that when she turned back at the end it was because of his mistake. How could he have known what she felt—*he never asked!*

But *she* discovers the cold and the darkness without anybody's help, and learns of the treachery and pain through her body. In effect, her body is forged through the experience of Dis, and the permutations she will make of the journey will conduct her—construct her—to the borders of the city where light turns gray, where energy flows away, and the rehearsal of the actions of her daily life seem like a death. The cold city so like a London in the wintertime:

> Nous voilà revenus dans la grande ville de pierre qui maintenant a froid. Le soir descend plus vite. A quatre heures de l'après-midi, il fait déjà noir. Les lumières s'allument étrangement. C'est terrible cette obscurité qui s'étire à n'en plus finir. . . . C'est comme une trahison. . . .
> Nous sommes devenus de petits êtres gris. Les épaules voûtées, le ventre rebondi. Je traine mon air maussade, ne sachant pas ce qui brise ma voix et inonde mon âme. (63)
>
> [Here we are back in the great city of stone which now is cold. Night comes on more quickly. At four in the afternoon, it is already dark. The lights come on strangely. It's terrible this darkness that spreads out without stopping. . . . It's like a betrayal. . . .
> We have become little gray beings. Hunched-over shoulders, potbellied. I drag around with my grumpy look, not knowing what is cracking my voice and inundating my soul.]

The city holds her in its grip, and she struggles: "Depuis des jours, je tourne en cage, le malaise épais dans ma gorge" (63) [For days I go round and round as if in a cage, uneasiness weighing heavily on my throat].

If gender is a reiterated performance, and if it is mourning and introjection that enable that new mouth to speak, then her speech, her text, must arise from the repeated discovery of this experience in Dis—a repetition born of the daily encounter with both love and death, desire and mourning, all necessary for incorporation and speech. This is experienced and expressed through her body. Here it is through the experience of a city that is lacking warmth, lacking body: "Que m'arrive-t-il dans cette ville qui n'a pas d'odeur?" (63) [What is happening to me in this city that doesn't have any odor?].

In the end, *she* no longer recognizes *herself*. The city is no longer the other space; love no longer holds her, and she is not torn away from her own loved ones. She is now used to the city of stones—indeed, "Cette ville est belle après tout, avec ses bâtiments en pierres immenses et ses maisons serrées les unes contre les autres. Il suffira de marcher dans les parcs, de nourrir les canards et d'acheter des marrons chauds" (89) [This city is beautiful, after all, with its immense buildings made of stone and its houses squeezed against each other. It will be enough just to walk in the parks, to feed the ducks and buy hot chestnuts.]. Ironically, her body now gives off the sweat whose absence she had earlier noted in the city: "Dehors, elle transpirait sous son manteau. Son odeur emprisonnée ne lui plaisait pas. Sans cesse le vent frappait son visage. Sa peau se desséchait. Elle passait la main dans ses cheveux et elle avait l'impression de toucher du coton" (89) [Outside, she sweated under her overcoat. Her closed-in odor displeased her. The wind struck her face without stopping. Her skin dried out. She ran her hand through her hair and had the impression she was touching cotton.].

By the end of the voyage, slowly she moves toward the Eurydice, as another might move toward the Oedipus. There is a kind of definitiveness at the end of each performance, which can be summed up in the name of another whose story was marked by a beginning, middle, and end. For her, the end will take us back into the writing through which she has written herself—written herself, at times, as Eurydice, so that that would be where we would expect to find her.

For Eurydice, Dis is a tomb. She leaves us with a city of the dead, so as to mark the end of her affair with Orpheus, and perhaps the beginning of a new one with less Hellenic tragic overtones. "La grande ville de pierre est couverte d'un voile opaque. De ma fenêtre les arbres squelettiques dansent les gestes d'une mer silencieuse. Il est parti" (90) [The great city of stone is covered with an opaque sail. From my window the skeletal trees dance with the gestures of a silent sea. He is gone.]. She begins the solitary dance of repetition like Léti after her rupture with Niyous, with her words. Not words anchored in law and affirmations of truth, but words without baggage: "Et je suis là, dépossédée de tous mes biens. Il ne me reste que l'écriture. Ces mots sur du papier blanc. Ce sont eux qui me disent à l'oreille les souvenirs. Qui chuchotent à mon âme les paroles momifiées" (90) [And I am here, dispossessed of all my belongings. Only writing remains for me. These words on the white paper. They speak in my ear of souvenirs. That whisper to my soul mummified words.]. In the legend, Eurydice remains imprisoned in Hades. *She*, however, has given herself her own account, at the end of which, despite the pain of the loss, she discovers that freedom from the constraints of all narratives based on the metaphysics of substance: "Il n'y a pas de loi. Il n'y pas de juge. Dans la jungle du coeur, on perd parfois son sang" (91) [There isn't any law. There isn't any judge. In the jungle of the heart, sometimes one loses one's blood.].

Her call for love is her own. She gives voice to Eurydice, gives body to herself through her call, her desire. It is a new, strong voice that reverberates, repeats itself, at the end:

> "Désire-moi, désire-moi: ou j'en mourrai de solitude.
> Je veux que la vérité bouscule mon corps. Qu'elle fasse éclater le carcan de ma chair personnelle. (91)]
>
> [Desire me, desire me: or I will die of solitude.
> I want the truth to shake up my body. May it cause the yoke of my personal flesh to burst open.]

Eurydice

In the legend of Eurydice, she dies and is taken to the underworld. The legend gives expression to a certain law, one not unlike "The Tale of the Complete Gentleman," in which Eurydice's role is to be a relatively passive one. For the Greeks rescue comes from Orpheus, if it is to come at all; for the Yoruba, rescue comes from the foolish girl's brother, who defeats the evil spirit and brings his sister back home. In the end, it is an affair of men. For the Greeks it will end in the transformation of Orpheus into a transcendental being—his music immortalized among the stars. For the Yoruba, it will end in her acceptance of her parents' choice, in her acceptance of a reasonable offer of a young man; in her acceptance, not her revolt.

For Butler, subversion will be possible within the law. *She* cannot exist in any space that does not return her, in the end, to the same propositions that she faced at the outset: desire, the formation of the body. The constraint of the lines of meaning that hold the words within the recognizable space of the lines requires that she repeat her words and gestures in forms always already given. But repetition does not mean sameness. Every oral performance contains the possibility for difference, even if that possibility is denied by the self-promoting words of the griot.[9] And the talented performer can take a text and turn its meaning against the "original."[10] The obvious means of verbal, performative subversion are always available in parody, satire.

Tadjo is involved in another kind of rewriting. It is one that starts with the city in Africa—the city that is both "belle et impaludée"—as the setting for an unsettling, unfamiliar performance. A performance that occurs "when the law turns against itself and spawns unexpected permutations of itself" (Butler 93). The expected permutation begins with a dying Eurydice and a desperate Orpheus: " 'J'irai avec toi jusqu'à la mort,' lui dit-il. 'Je veux t'aimer jusqu'au bout de ta souffrance' " (40) ["I will go with you until death," he said to her. "I want to love you until the end of your suffering."]. It is she who then writes them into the lines of the Greek legend, already introducing the first permutation absent from the Greek version, self-consciousness: " 'Tu ne peux arrêter la mort,' murmura-t-elle. 'Elle est forte. Souviens-toi d'Orphée et d'Euridice. Que ferons-nous dans cette ville abandonnée au désespoir et aux incroyants?' " (40) ["You can't stop death," she murmured. "It is strong. Do you remember Orpheus and Eurydice? What will we do in this city given up to despair and unbelievers?"].

Love and death are possible for them in this version only when they have gone to the end of the world, to the borders of the desert, where they have escaped the impurities of the city. She can write this version, telling Orpheus when they have arrived, where to deposit her, and when to make love, knowing that it is not the final draft. The story of the serpent's bite, of Dis, of the long voyage of separation will be repeated over and over.

It returns in the segment numbered 64, where a magician encounters another young woman making yet another "voyage finale" (76). Perhaps this time it is she who reigns over the magical kingdom, and not the young interloper trying to steal Eurydice away. In any event, in this version the young woman is not without powers of her own. She arrives one evening from parts unknown, ready to meet the handsome magician whose reputation has extended so far that people from distant lands sought him out. Whereas others were baffled by the magician's words, she sought to approach him through her own meditations, her own powers. After all, she, too, was the daughter of parents with extraordinary powers.

When the magician meets the young woman, he accepts her, and agrees to lead her on condition that she not ask him any questions. He takes her to a labyrinth with walls of glass. "Elle voyait tout ce qui se passait à l'extérieur mais elle savait qu'elle ne pourrait jamais retrouver son chemin" (75) [She saw what took place on the outside but knew that she could never find her path again.]. Finally they arrive at the last chamber. It has thick curtains, and she wonders if there are windows. It is another version of Dis, a place removed from the earth of growth, flowering, pain, suffering, and death. "Une paix régnait dans un dépouillement total. Pas d'objet inutile. Pas de fioriture" (75) [A peace reigned amidst a total asceticism. Not one useless object. No flowery decoration.].

Why Eurydice should have wanted to travel to Dis is unclear. She never gets to tell us why. Perhaps it had to do with the handsome ruler, perhaps with the excitement of a city located in "another place." Here in the heart of the labyrinth, she and the magician make love, and afterwards, when he is asleep, she opens his skull and looks within. What permutation of sight will turn against itself, to spawn new visions and new words? She sees Dis in all its horror: "un désert de tristesse et de solitude. On aurait dit un champ de bataille. Des tranchées, du fil de fer barbelé, des traces d'obus. Des cadavres jonchaient le sol"—an "endroit de désolation" (75) [a desert of sadness and solitude. One would have said it was a battlefield. Trenches, barbed wire, traces of shells. Corpses strewn over the earth—a place of desolation.]. Had she not been one whose mother was endowed with "des pouvoirs d'initiée" [powers of an initiate], she might have despaired and sought some city of light, some city of stone, far from the cannons and shells. Assèze seemed to cross all the frontiers between Douala and Paris without effort; "la petite fille" Saïda could leave, too, when she wanted. And Beyala, as she tells us in *La Petite Fille du réverbère*, was to become a famous writer who would be harassed by small-minded men.

But the daughter of the initiated mother looks beyond the desolation, and seeks a lake, a plain, where the grass is rich and luxuriant. For Birago Diop in "L'Héritage," appearances were deceiving: ultimate reality always wears clothes that hide more than they reveal. But Birago's truths wore an eternal face, grounded in Sufi mysticism—and not in the subversive garments of a new Zoroaster.

The young woman undertakes the voyage of love and discovery with the magician several times. For the final trip, she takes all the precautions she can: she breaks an egg, washes her face three times, and again enters the magician's realm while he sleeps. And while Orpheus dreams, Eurydice passes through all the portals of Hell, past the genocide and terrible amphitheatres of destruction:

> Elle marcha avec précaution mais déchira sa robe en passant sous des barbelés. Elle se blessa à une jambe en tombant dans une piège. Néaumoins tout cela n'était rien car elle réussit à éviter les mines enfouies dans le sol et à retenir sa respiration devant la puanteur des cadavres en putréfaction. (76) [She walked carefully but tore her robe while going under the barbed wire. She received a wound in a leg while falling in a trap. Nonetheless, all of that was nothing since she succeeded in avoiding mines buried in the

soil and in holding her breath when encountering the stink of putrefying corpses.]

"What does the woman want?" For Freud the enigma rested at the door of feminine desire. The young woman does not fall asleep with the magician after they make love. Eurydice did not stay at home with Orpheus: his music was enough for him, but what was she to do? Eurydice plunges into the lake, on the far side of the fields of devastation, of the cities of night, and swims for the other side.

We could leave her there—seeking new shores—if that weren't an old story for Orpheus, who would surely be waiting for her in "another place." But this version has the magician wake up, and, in his despair over the absence of the young girl, fail to perceive her swimming through the reaches of his dream. In a twist on the original, it is his waking and foolish crying out that cause her to drown: "La fille se sentait tirée vers le fond du lac par une force supérieure. Elle s'enfonçait de plus en plus. L'eau rentrait dans sa bouche, dans ses oreilles, dans son nez. Elle voyait les algues exécuter leur danse. Elle ne pouvait pas crier. Elle ne pouvait penser qu'à la rive" (77) [The girl felt herself drawn toward the bottom of the lake by a superior force. She sank in deeper and deeper. Water entered her mouth, her ears, her nose. She saw the algae executing dance steps. She couldn't cry out. She couldn't think about anything except the riverbank.].

Tadjo leaves Eurydice en route. Her permutations on the theme of love return us to one question: is it possible for the woman's body to speak her desire, is there a language that will take us beyond the frontiers of the regulatory agencies of the natural, the normal, the ordered society of the city whose borders are manned by the soldiers of Dis: "Est-il possible de laisser parler les corps?" (81) [Is it possible to let the body speak?]. We ask this question of Eurydice, whose answer is inscribed in Tadjo's question, "Est-il possible de laisser parler les corps, de les laisser dire leur langage qui dépasse les frontières du silence?" (81) [Is it possible to let the bodies speak, to let them speak their language which goes beyond the borders of silence?].

Notes

1. For views challenging Coquery-Vidrovitch's general conclusion, see Newell's chapter "Anatomy of Masculine Power," in *Writing African Women* (1997), in which she critiques the text *Motherism: The Afrocentric Alternative to Feminism* (1995) by Catherine Acholonu and then critiques Chinweizu's response to the text in his book, *Anatomy of Female Power*. Acholonu makes a

case for prehistorical female ruled societies as preceding the historical patriarchal patterns. Ifi Amadiume carries a similar theme forward in her *Male Daughters, Female Husbands: Gender and Sex in an African Society* (1995 [1987]). Amadiume rejects anthropological and feminist studies of Africa generally as racist, and as imposing their own agendas on their African subjects. This can be seen, she argues, in claims for African lesbianism and in conclusions like Coquery-Vidrovitch's that African women have been oppressed victims of African patriarchy. Western feminists have had "the persistent intention . . . to seek a false solidarity on the basis of what they see as 'common roots of oppression' " (8).

It is not my intention to assess Amadiume's claims over against Coquery-Vidrovitch's or others. But it is worthwhile to point out that as an "outsider," I am excluded on Amadiume's own terms from being capable of forming a valid judgment, an inference to be drawn from her statement that "Western women have proved, by their inability to consolidate their own women's movement, that they are in no position to tell Third World women what is good for them" (9), and from her self-authorizing claim that "[i]t was, of course, from my knowledge of my own people that I recognized that a great deal of what anthropologists and Western feminists were saying about African women's power was incorrect" (9).

It is perhaps also worthwhile to point out that inasmuch as Amadiume has published her study, she thereby presents it to an informed audience for their judgment. My reading of her claims is that they appear forced, especially in her notions of what defines gender.

2. It is interesting to note that virtually all these themes are to be found in Buchi Emecheta's *Joys of Motherhood* (1979).

3. Again a common theme in the literature, from such stories as Aidoo's "In the Cutting of a Drink" (in *No Sweetness Here*), to such films as Dikongue-Pipa's *Le Prix de la liberté*. It is implicit in the depictions of independent urban women, such as Esi in Aidoo's *Changes* or Nwapa's *Women Are Different*.

4. Beyala uses a quaint spelling for this term, "bayam-sellam" (1998: 21).

5. Some of the flavor of the hillbilly style can be discerned in the following scene in which the pharmacist is addressing a crowd. He spoke, and you could hear the beating of a fly's wings as he adjusted his pince-nez:

—Chères compatriotesses (silence). Très chers compatriotes, très chères amies et fidèles (très longue silence). Depuis trentes ans que j'exerce parmi vous, répandant dans vos foyers la semence de mes recherches, les plus hautaines et enveloppées des plus complexes théories . . .
—A l'essentiel! Cria quelqu'un. . . . .
—On s'en tape, nous, des théories, dit un autre. On veut des faits. . . .
—J'y arrive, dit le pharmacien. Les événements les plus savoureux sont ceux qui se font attendre, n'est-ce pas?

—Ouais, dit le chef. Mais à ce rythme, on va se fatiguer avant que t'aies commencé.

—Je disais donc qu'étant donné les résultats de mes recherches en physique, en chimie et en biologie, après études comparatives de mes travaux et lesdites conclusions, appliqués à la personne ici présente dénommée, habitant . . .

—Tout le monde connaît Saïda, dit quelqu'un.

—C'est de la perte de temps sensible et manifeste, dit le journaliste-news.

—Bande de tarés! Hurla le pharmacien. Vous ne comprendrez jamais rien aux théories nouvelles, à la tellurie universelle, à la connaissance sidérale. Je perds un temps précieux avec vous et sur ce, je vous salue bien, messieurs, mesdames.

As he left, the disappointed crowd got excited:

"Faites quelque chose, chef!" et: "Retenez-le, chef!" Mais avant que le chef réagisse, le journaliste-news courut après le pharmacien: "Faut pas se mettre dans cet état pour si peu! Un peu de *flair play*, très cher!" Il s'agitait, suppliait: "Qu'allons-nous devenir sans vous?"

Il en perdait son froc, et se prenait les pieds dans les fils tarabiscotés de son magnétophone. Le chef se joignit au journaliste et des Couscoussiers, très chiens affamés sentant l'os leur échapper , se mirent aussi à supplier le pharmacien-docteur, à le dorloter. (Beyala 1996: 114–15)

[—Dear lady compatriots (silence). Dearest compatriots, dearest lady-friends and faithful friends (very long silence). For the thirty years that I've been exercising my trade among you, bringing to your foyers the harvest of my research. The highest and most convoluted of the most complex theories . . .

—Get to the point, someone cried out.

—We're fed up with theories, someone else said. We want the facts.

—I'm getting there, said the pharmacist. What is most pleasurable requires most waiting for it, right?

—Yeah, said the chief. But at this rate, we'll be worn out before you've started.

—I said that given the results of my research in physics, chemistry, biology, after the comparative study of my labors and the selfsame conclusions, applied to the person here present and named, living . . .

—Everyone knows Saïda, someone said.

—It is the loss of perceptible and manifest time, said the news journalist.

—Bunch of degenerates! Screamed the pharmacist. You'll never understand anything about new theories, universal tellurism, about sidereal knowledge. I am wasting precious time on you, and with that, my greetings, ladies and gentlemen.

... "Do something chief!" and "Stop him, chief!" But before the chief could react, the news journalist ran after the pharmacist: "Don't put yourself in such a state over so little. A bit of *flair play*, dear fellow!" He got excited, begged, "What would we become without you?"

He lost his frock, and his feet got all tangled in the complicated wires of his loudspeaker. The chief rejoined the journalist and the Couscousiers, famished dogs sensing the loss of their bone, also began to beg the pharmacist-doctor, to coddle him.]

It is little wonder that it was this totally nonsubversive version of a picturesque, "rocambolesque" Africa that the Académie Française chose to honor with their Grand Prix, rather than Beyala's more disconcerting early novels of abjection.

6. There is an interesting parallel with a similar moment in *Death and the King's Horseman* when Elesin catches a glimpse of a beauty in the market while surrounded by the women:

> Tell me who was that goddess through whose lips
> I saw the ivory pebbles of Oya's riverbed.
> Iyaloja, who is she? I saw her enter
> Your stall; all your daughters I know well.
> No, not even Ogun-of-the-farm toiling
> Dawn till dusk on his tuber patch
> Not even Ogun with the finest hoe he ever
> Forged at the anvil could have shaped
> That rise of buttocks, not though he had
> The richest earth between his fingers. (Soyinka 1975: 19)

In approaching Iyaloja's prospective daughter-in-law, Elesin trespasses on relatively forbidden ground, not unlike Niyous in his attraction for Léti.

7. Cf. *Aucassin et Nicolete*, a medieval romance with a similar war of apples and cheeses. The hero, Aucassin, comes upon the strange battle, as is here recounted:

> Anon rode Aucassin and the King even till they came to that place where the Queen was, and lo! Men were warring with baked apples and with eggs and with fresh cheeses, and Aucassin began to look on them, and made great marvel.
>
> > Here one singeth:
> > Aucassin his horse doth stay,
> > From the saddle watched the fray,
> > All the fight and fierce array;

>   Right fresh cheeses carried they,
>   Apples baked, and mushrooms gray,
>   Whoso splasheth most the ford
>   He is master called and lord.
>   Aucassin doth gaze awhile,
>   Then began to laugh and smile
>   And made game. (Loomis and Loomis 275)

8. See Denise Paulme's *La Mère dévorante* (1976), which explores this theme.

9. Of the many examples one could cite from Niane's *Sundiata* (1965) the following example: "I, Djeli Mamoudou Kouyaté, am the result of a long tradition. For generations we have passed on the history of kings from father to son. The narrative was passed on to me without alteration and I deliver it without alteration, for I received it free from all untruth" (41).

10. In his *Allegorical Speculation in an Oral Society: The Tabwa Narrative Tradition* (1988), Robert Cancel records an excellent example of this performance-based take on a conventional story in his analysis of the Tabwa narrative tradition. There he shows how each performance varied according to circumstance, including the political point the storyteller wished to make.

Conclusion:
Rebuilding Dis: Words of a Second Wave

It is there, in the strangest corners of Dis, that the echoes of Eurydice and Orpheus can be glimpsed again, since it is there that Ben Okri sets his story of Maria and Ede, "When the Lights Return" ([1988] 1989). It, too, is a story of Dis—the city of nightmares, destruction, chaos—and excitement. Ede is the magician who is to lose his girlfriend, Maria. As in most of Okri's writing, the vision of Africa—or Nigeria, in any event—is one in which the law has gone mad, and the orderly process of legend that underwrites the regulatory agencies of power as normalizing and natural is turned on its head. If the permutations of this law are turned into monstrous caricatures of themselves, so, too, is the legendary force of the Orpheus-Eurydice mythos rendered in this new, self-consciously parodic, dystopic version. Ede's song is the plaint of the African Dis, and of the helplessness of the western legend before its African other:

> He had never sung for anyone in the streets before. He sang of the bicycle-repairer who had crazy dreams of riding on the sea. He sang of friends who died in the Civil War, of mad soldiers and hungry policemen, of children who grow leaner, of buildings in the city that were sinking into the earth. He sang of love, his love for Maria, her love for the world. He got carried away with his improvisations and sang loudly, outdoing the record shops and the bellowing hawkers. She touched him on his arm and said:
> "It's alright."
> He sang on. Then she added:
> "Or do you think you are Orpheus?"
> He stopped singing. (173)

With the city of Dis, we come full circle and return to our initial excursus through Zobeide, "this ugly city, this trap," in whose mazes the voyager wanders, seeking that image of the woman to lead him through. But she is not to be found there, the city existing only in the voyager's imagination or dream. She has been writing, while he was searching, while he was tracing the echoes of the old question, what does the woman want, forgetting to look in the pages she had penned about the streets of mud and diamonds. Streets of Douala, New Bell, Belleville, Bellevue, Couscousville, Umtali, Abidjan, Dakar, London, Washington, Djomo-La-Lutte—Dis. And tracing the dream of the magician, the voyage leads inexorably within—past the corridors of the real, the names of streets, markets, cities, states, dissolving in an interior landscape whose markings reveal only the lineaments of a symbolic heritage.

The critical approach taken in this volume does not pretend to answer all the questions frequently posed to African literature or to works written by women—that is, how did you live and what steps can be taken to improve your lot? That is, this is not cultural, historical, or sociological critique. Not that those approaches are unworthy or secondary. That work will always be done. Furthermore, this study has not been undertaken with the notion of divorcing my critical approach from the concrete context within which the works were produced: the symbolic order is nothing if not a cultural and social order, shaped by an evolving set of historical forces. To that extent one can say that Dis is a real place. But it is real, also, in the way that Lacan defines the real as beyond the scope of mediation, inaccessible to symbolization, whose limits are those of language. Which returns us to the subject of this study: texts produced in English and French; texts susceptible to psychoanalytical readings that seek, finally, not to explicate their meanings, but to suggest possible avenues of approach of common concern to those for whom feminist thought is indispensable.

Starting with Freud's Dora, feminists have struggled mightily to turn psychoanalytical approaches into positive means for action. The earliest female analysts, like Melanie Klein and Karen Horney, worked through models largely framed by Freudian thought. Post-Lacanian feminists have carried on those labors. It seems to me that Lacan, "prick" though he may be in Gallop's words, provided the real break from the possible reading of the oedipus as a question of "anatomy," of physical beings, their instincts, and relationships embodied in the immediacy of the biological sphere, to one turned in the direction of desire and its displacement into language. That provided the opening for the French feminists to break the stranglehold of the notion of the symbolic as inexorably shaped by a phallocentric order.

Kristeva's conception of the break was not subversive—her privileging of the borderline cases, of modernist poets, focused our attention on the abject and the disruptive, not so as to overturn the order but to highlight its constraints. The semiotic remains subordinated, no matter what its poetic eruptions. Irigaray, Cixous, Wittig, and a generation later, Gallop and Butler have set the agenda for more thoroughgoing challenges to patriarchy. En route, we have seen their strategies of masquerading, performing, and writing inspire a new generation, a new wave of authors who have claimed droit de cité. African masks, displaying new dance steps, wearing the old clothes of English or French texts, now shape this body of works. We have begun the study of those masks by exploring just one facet of them—the interior, psychoanalytical side, especially as conveyed though their language. Colleagues will continue the exploration with a fuller understanding than I have of the richness of Africa's masking and dancing traditions, and, I hope, will continue to trace the steps of a dancer whose full text will be read for its outer appearance, its inner shapes, and its unstated spaces and silences, which sometimes can be sensed in the interstices of language.

The main concern of this study has been to engage those feminist writers whose work in psychoanalytical criticism has enabled us to challenge the phallocentric order that remains dominant in Africa. It is my conviction that second wave African feminism, African women's literature, and African women's cinema are reconstituting the walls and structures of Zobeide, of Dis, with their own words—that Maria has heard Ede's song, his mythologizing gesture, even his crazy dreams, and now has spoken up: "Or do you think you are Orpheus?" She is there. He thinks, "What does woman want?" He waits, and she begins . . .

Bibliography

Achebe, Chinua. (1958) 1972. *Things Fall Apart*. London: Heinemann.
———. 1988. *Anthills of the Savannah*. Ibadan and London: Heinemann.
Ahmed, Leila . 1992. *Women and Gender in Islam*. New Haven: Yale University Press.
Aidoo, Ama Ata. 1970. *No Sweetness Here*. Burnt Mill, Harlow: Longman.
———. 1991. *Changes*. London: The Women's Press.
Althusser, Louis. 1971. *Lenin and Philosophy*. Trans. Ben Brewster. London: Monthly Review Press.
Amadiume, Ifi. (1987). 1995. *Male Daughters, Female Husbands: Gender and Sex in an African Society*. Highland Park, NJ: Zed Books.
Appiah, Kwame Anthony. 1992. *In My Father's House*. London: Methuen.
Ashcroft, Bill, Gareth Griffiths, and Helen Tiffin. 1989. *The Empire Writes Back*. New York: Routledge.
Assouline, Pierre. "L'Affaire Beyala rebondit." 1997. *Lire* 252 (February): 8–11.
Bâ, Mariama. 1979. *Une si longue lettre*. Dakar: Nouvelles Editions Africaines.
———. 1981. *Le Chant écarlate*. Dakar: Nouvelles Editions Africaines.
Barlet, Olivier. 1996. *Les Cinémas d'Afrique noire*. Paris: L'Harmattan.
———. 1997. "Entretien avec Safi Faye." *Africultures* 2 (November): 8–11.
Beauvoir, Simone de. 1973. *The Second Sex*. Trans. E. M. Parshley. New York: Vintage.
Bekolo, Jean-Pierre, dir. 1992. *Quartier Mozart*.
———, dir. 1995. *Aristotle's Plot*.
Belsey, Catherine. 1980. *Critical Practice*. London: Methuen.

Beyala, Calixthe. 1987. *C'est le soleil qui m'a brulée.* Paris: Stock. (Trans. by Marjolijn de Jager as *The Sun Hath Looked Upon Me.* Portsmouth, NH: Heinemann, 1996.)
———. 1988. *Tu t'appelleras Tanga.* Paris: Stock. (Trans. by Marolijn de Jager as *Your Name Shall Be Tanga.* Portsmouth, NH: Heinemann, 1996.)
———. 1990. *Seul le diable le savait.* Paris: L'Harmattan.
———. 1992. *Le Petit Prince de Belleville.* Paris: Albin Michel. (Trans. by Marjolijn de Jager as *Loukoum.* Portsmouth, NH: Heinemann, 1995.)
———. 1994. *Assèze l'Africaine.* Paris: Albin Michel.
———. 1995. *Lettre d'une africaine à ses soeurs occidentales.* Paris: Spengler.
———. 1996. *Les Honneurs perdus.* Paris: Albin Michel.
———. 1997. "Moi, Calixthe Beyala, la plagiaire!" *Figaro,* January 25–26: 23.
———. 1998. *La Petite Fille du réverbère.* Paris: Albin Michel.
Bhabha, Homi. 1994. *The Location of Culture.* New York: Routledge.
Boni, Tanella. 1990. *Une vie de crabe.* Dakar: Nouvelles Editions Africaines.
Borch-Jacobsen, Mikkel. 1991. *Lacan: The Absolute Master.* Trans. Douglas Brick. Stanford: Stanford University Press.
Borgomano, Madeleine. 1997. " 'L'Affaire' Calixthe Beyala ou les frontières des champs littéraires." Paper presented at the APELA (Association pour l'Etude du Littératures Africaines) conference Brussels, September 1997.
Bottéro, Jean. 1986. *Naissance de Dieu: La Bible et l'historien.* Paris: Gallimard.
Boyce-Davies, Carole. 1994. *Black Women, Writing and Identity: Migrations of the Subject.* New York: Routledge.
Braxton, Joanne and Andree Nicola-McLaughlin, eds. 1990. *Wild Women in the Whirlwind: Afra-American Culture and the Contemporary Literary Renaissance.* New Brunswick: Rutgers University Press.
Bugul, Ken. 1983. *Le Baobab fou.* Dakar: Nouvelles Editions Africaines.
Burke, Carolyn, Naomi Schor, and Margaret Whitford, eds. 1994. *Engaging with Irigaray.* New York: Columbia University Press.
Buten, Howard. 1981. *Burt.* New York: Holt, Rinehart and Winston. (Trans. by Jean-Pierre Carasso as *Quand j'avais cinq ans, je m'ai tué.* Paris: De Seuil, 1981.)
Butler, Judith. 1990. *Gender Trouble.* New York: Routledge.
———. 1993. *Bodies that Matter* New York: Routledge.
Calvino, Italo. 1974. *Invisible Cities.* Trans. William Weaver. New York: Harcourt Brace Jovanovich. (Originally published as *Le citta invisibili.* Turin: Einaudi, 1972).
Cancel, Robert. 1988. *Allegorical Speculation in an Oral Society: The Tabwa Narrative Tradition.* Berkeley: University California Press.

Cazenave, Odile. 1996. *Femmes rebelles*. Paris: L'Harmattan.
Chinodya, Shimmer. 1989. *Harvest of Thorns*. Harare: Baobab Books.
Chinweizu, Onwuchekwa Jemie, and Ihechukwu Madubuike. 1980. *Towards the Decolonization of African Literature*. Enugu, Nigeria: Fourth Dimension.
Chipamaunga, Edmund. 1983. *A Fighter for Freedom*. Gweru, Zimbabwe: Mambo Press.
Christian, Barbara. 1986. *Black Feminist Criticism: Perspectives on Black Women Writers*. New York: Pergamon.
Cissé, Souleymane, dir. 1982. *Finye*.
Constant, Paule. 1992. *White Spirit*. Paris: Folio.
Coquery-Vidrovitch, Catherine. 1997. *African Women: A Modern History*. Trans. Beth Gillian Raps. Boulder, CO: Westview Press.
D'Almeida, Irène. 1994. *Francophone African Women Writers*. Gainesville: University Press of Florida.
Dangarembga, Tsitsi. (1988) 1989. *Nervous Conditions*. Seattle: Seal Press.
Davies, Carole Boyce, and Anne Adams Graves. (1986) 1990. *Ngambika*. Trenton: Africa World Press.
de Gaudemar, A. "Livres." 1997. *Libération*, May 29: 7.
Déjeux, Jean. 1973. *Littérature maghrébine de langue française*. Ottawa: Naaman.
De Lauretis, Teresa. 1984. *Alice Doesn't*. Bloomington: Indiana University Press.
Derrida, Jacques. "The Purveyor of Truth." 1975. *Yale French Studies* 52: 31–113.
———. 1976. *Of Grammatology*. Trans. Gayatri Spivak. Baltimore: Johns Hopkins University Press.
———. 1979. *Spurs/Eperons*. Chicago: University of Chicago Press.
Dikongue-Pipa, Jean-Pierre, dir. 1976. *Muno Moto*.
———. dir. 1978. *Le Prix de la liberté*.
Douglas, Mary. 1966. *Purity and Danger*. London: Routledge and Kegan Paul.
Eke, Maureen, Kenneth Harrow, and Emmanuel Yewah, eds. 2000. *African Images: Recent Studies in Cinema and Text*. Trenton: Africa World Press.
Emecheta, Buchi. 1979. *The Joys of Motherhood*. London: Allison and Busby.
Fanon, Frantz. 1961. *Les Damnés de la terre*. Paris: Maspero. (Trans. by Constance Farrington as *The Wretched of the Earth*. New York: Grove Press, 1968.)
Faye, Safi, dir. 1982. *Selbe*.
———, dir. 1996. *Mossane*.
Felman, Shoshana. 1987. *Jacques Lacan and the Adventure of Insight: Psychoanalysis in Contemporary Culture*. Cambridge, MA: Harvard University Press.

Foucault, Michel, ed. (1978) 1980. *Herculine Barbin, Being the Recently Discovered Memoirs of a Nineteenth-Century Hermaphrodite*. Trans. Richard McDougall. New York: Colophon.

Folly, Anne-Laure, dir. 1993. *Femmes aux yeux ouverts*.

Fox, Everett. (1983) 1995. *The Five Books of Moses*. New York: Schocken Books.

Freud, Sigmund. (1913) 1960. *Totem and Taboo*. Trans. James Strachey. London: Routledge and Kegan Paul.

———. 1930. *Civilization and Its Discontents*. Trans. Joan Rivière. London: Hogarth Press.

———. 1939. *Moses and Monotheism*. Trans. Katherine Jones. New York: Random House.

———. 1958. *Standard Edition of the Complete Psychological Works of Sigmund Freud*. Vol. 17. Trans. and ed. James Strachey. London: Hogarth Press.

Gallimore, Rangira Béatrice. 1997. *L'Oeuvre romanesque de Calixthe Beyala*. Paris: L'Harmattan.

Garritano, Carmela. 2000. "Restaging the Past: The Rewriting of *The Tale of the Beautiful Daughter* by Abrahams, Tutuola, Ogali and Aidoo." In Maureen Eke, Kenneth Harrow, and Emmanuel Yewah, eds., *African Images: Recent Studies in Cinema and Text*. Trenton, NJ: Africa World Press.

Gary, Romain. 1975. *La Vie devant soi*. Paris: Mercure de France.

Grosz, Elizabeth. (1990) 1991. *Jacques Lacan: A Feminist Introduction*. New York: Routledge.

Handelman, Susan. 1982. *The Slayers of Moses*. Albany: SUNY Press.

Harrow, Kenneth. 1998. " 'I'm Not a (Western) Feminist but . . .'—A Review of Recent Critical Writings on African Women's Literature." *Research in African Literature* 29, no. 3 (Fall): 171–90.

———. 1999. *African Cinema*. Trenton: Africa World Press.

Head, Bessie. 1977. *The Collector of Treasures*. London: Heinemann.

Heath, Stephen. "Difference." 1978. *Screen* 19, no. 3 (Autumn): 51–112. Reprinted in *The Sexual Subject: A Screen Reader in Sexuality*. New York: Routledge, 1992.

Hove, Chenjerai. 1988. *Bones*. Harare: Baobab Books.

Ilboudi, Monique. 1992. *Le Mal de peau*. Ouagadougou: Imprimerie Nationale.

Irigaray, Luce. (1977) 1985. *This Sex Which Is Not One*. Trans. Catherine Porter. Ithaca: Cornell University Press.

———. (1985) 1992. *Speculum of the Other Woman*. Trans. Gillian Gill. Ithaca: Cornell University Press.

Jameson, Frederic. 1986. "Third World Literature in the Era of Multinational Capitalism." *Social Text* (Fall).

Kane, Cheikh Hamidou. 1961. *L'Aventure ambiguë*. Paris: Juillard.

Khatibi, Abdelkebir. 1983. *L'Amour bilingue*. Montpellier: Fata Morgana. (Trans. by Richard Howard as *Love in Two Languages*. Minneapolis: University of Minnesota Press, 1990.)

Kom, Ambroise. 1996. "L'Univers zombifié de Calixthe Beyala." *Notre Librairie* 125 (January-March).

Kramo-Lanciné, Fadika, dir. 1980. *Djeli*.

Kristeva, Julia. (1980) 1982. *Powers of Horror: An Essay on Abjection*. Trans. Leon Roudiez. New York: Columbia University Press.

―――. 1984. *The Revolution in Poetic Language*. Trans. Margaret Waller. New York: Columbia University Press.

Lacan, Jacques. 1953. "Some Reflections on the Ego." *International Journal of Psychoanalysis* 34: 11–17.

―――. (1968) 1975. *The Language of the Self*. Trans. Anthony Wilden. New York: Delta.

―――. (1972–73) 1999. *On Feminine Sexuality: The Limits of Love and Knowledge, 1972–1973*. (Seminar XX). Ed. Jacques-Alain Miller. Trans. Bruce Fink. New York: Norton.

―――. 1977. *Ecrits: A Selection*. Trans. Anthony Wilden. New York: Norton.

―――. [1938] 1984. *Les Complexes familiaux dans la formation de l'individu*. Paris: Navarin Editeur.

Laye, Camara. (1953) 1972. *L'Enfant noir*. Paris: Plon (Livre de Poche).

Lee, Spike, dir. 1988. *Do the Right Thing*.

―――, dir. 1994. *Crooklyn*.

Littré, E., ed. 1863. *Dictionnaire de la langue française*. Paris: Librairie Hachette.

Loomis, Roger Sherman, and Luari Hibbard Loomis. 1957. *Medieval Romances*. New York: Modern Library.

Mataillet, Dominique. 1996. "Le Cas Beyala." *Jeune Afrique* 1876–77 (18–31 December): 70–77.

McClintock, Anne. 1995. *Imperial Leather*. New York: Routledge.

Miller, Christopher. 1985. *Blank Darkness: Africanist Discourse in French*. Chicago: University of Chicago Press.

―――. 1990. *Theories of Africans: Francophone Literature and Anthropology in Africa*. Chicago: Chicago University Press.

Mitchell, Juliet and Jacqueline Rose, eds. 1983. *Feminine Sexuality: Jacques Lacan and the Ecole Freudienne*. Trans. Jacqueline Rose. New York: Norton.

Mohanty, Chandra Talpade. 1991. "Under Western Eyes." In Chandra Talpade Mohanty, Ann Russo, and Lourdes Torres, eds., *Third World Women and the Politics of Feminism*. Bloomington: Indiana University Press.

Mohanty, Chandra Talpade, Ann Russo, and Lourdes Torres, eds. 1991. *Third World Women and the Politics of Feminism*. Bloomington: Indiana University Press.

Mudimbe, V. Y. 1988. *The Invention of Africa*. Bloomington: Indiana University Press.

Mulvey, Laura. 1975. "Visual Pleasure and Narrative Cinema." *Screen* 16, no. 3 (Autumn): 6–18.

Newell, Stephanie, ed. 1997. *Writing African Women*. Atlantic Highlands, NJ: Zed Books.

Nfah-Abbenyi, Juliana Makuchi. 1997. *Gender in African Women's Writing*. Bloomington: Indiana University Press.

Ngugi wa Thiong'o. 1977. *Petals of Blood*. London: Heinemann.

Niane, D. T. 1965. *Sundiata: An Epic of Old Mali*. Trans. G.D. Pickett. Burnt Mill, Harlow, U.K.: Longman.

Nnaemeka, Obioma. 1997. *The Politics of (M)Othering*. New York: Routledge.

Nwapa, Flora. (1986) 1995. *Women Are Different*. Enugu, Nigeria: Tana Press.

Nyamfukudza, Stanley. 1980. *The Non-Believer's Journey*. London: Heinemann.

Okri, Ben. (1988) 1989. *Stars of the New Curfew*. London: Penguin.

———. 1991. *The Famished Road*. London: Vintage. (Trans. as *La Route de la faim*. Paris: Juillard, 1994.)

———. 1996. "Famished Road Feeds French Book Fever." *The Guardian*, 26 November.

Ortigues, Marie-Cécile, and Edmond Ortigues. (1964) 1966. *Oedipe africain*. Paris: Plon.

Oyono, Ferdinand. 1956. *Une vie de boy*. Paris: Juillard.

———. 1956. *Le Vieux Nègre et la médaille*. Paris: Juillard.

Paulme, Denise. 1976. *La Mère dévorante*. Paris: Gallimard.

Rouch, Jean, dir. 1954. *Les Maîtres fous*.

Sembène, Ousmane. 1965. *Véhi Ciosane ou blanche genèse suivi du Mandat*. Paris: Présence Africaine.

———, dir. 1974. *Xala*.

———, dir. 1977. *Ceddo*.

———, dir. 1991. *Guelwaar*.

Silverman, Kaja. 1983. *The Subject of Semiotics*. New York: Oxford University Press.

Sissoko, Cheikh Oumar, dir. 1989. *Finzan*.

Smith, Barbara. 1977. "Toward a Black Feminist Criticism." *Conditions: Two* 1, no. 2 (October). Reprinted in Gloria T. Hull, Patricia Bell Scott, and Barbara Smith, eds., *But Some of Us Are Brave*. New York: The Feminist Press, 1982.

Soncino Chumash (1947) 1985. Ed. A. Cohen. New York: Soncino Press.

Sow, I. 1977. *Psychiatrie dynamique africaine*. Paris: Payot.

Sow Fall, Aminata. 1993. *Le Jujubier du patriarche*. Dakar: Editions Khoudia.

Soyinka, Wole. 1964. *The Strong Breed*. London: Oxford University Press.

———.1965. *The Road*. London: Oxford University Press.

———. 1971. *Madmen and Specialists*. London: Methuen.

———. 1975. *Death and the King's Horseman*. New York: Norton.

Spillers, Hortense. 1996. "All the Things You Could Be by Now, if Sigmund Freud's Wife Was Your Mother: Psychoanalysis and Race." *Boundary 2* 23, no. 3 (Fall): 75–141.
Sugnet, Charles. 1997. "*Nervous Conditions*: Dangarembga's Feminist Reinvention of Fanon." In Obioma Nnaemeka, *The Politics of (M)Othering* (New York: Routledge).
Tadjo, Véronique. 1986. *A vol d'oiseau*. Paris: Nathan.
Trinh T. Minh-ha, dir. 1982. *Reassemblage*.
———. 1989. *Woman, Native, Other: Writing Postcoloniality and Feminism*. Bloomington: Indiana University Press.
Tutuola, Amos. 1952. *The Palm-Wine Drinkard*. London: Faber.
Veit-Wild, Flora. 1993. *Teachers, Preachers, Non-Believers*. Harare: Baobab Books.
Walker, Alice. 1982. *The Color Purple*. New York: Harvest/Harcourt Brace Jovanovich. (Trans. as *La Couleur poupre*. Paris: J'ai Lu, 1987.)
———.1984. *In Search of Our Mother's Gardens: Womenist Prose*. New York: Harcourt Brace Jovanovich.
Warner-Vieyra, Myriam. 1982. *Juletane*. Paris: Présence Africaine.
Young, Robert. 1995. *Colonial Desire: Hybridity in Theory, Culture and Race*. London: Routledge.

Index

A vol d'oiseau (Véronique Tadjo), 310–22
  and Beyala, 316, 324
  and Butler (*see also* Butler, Judith), 308, 309, 322–23
  City of Dis: 310, 311; of Africa, 322, 323; of exile, 315, 318, 319; Marcory, 314–15; and Okri, 331; of stone, 316, 319, 320, 321; Washington, D.C., 312, 313
  Eurydice, 310–11, 316, 317, 319, 321; and legend, 322–25; and Okri, 331
  mourning (absence), 318–20
  mud (and poverty), 314–15
  Orpheus, 310–11, 319; and legend, 322–25; and Okri, 331
  Persephone, 310
  "Tale of Complete Gentleman" (Tutuola), 316, 317, 322
Abiku, 88, 89, 90, 91, 92, 166
Abjection, 51, 63, 70, 76; Biblical and Kristeva, 43; Black/African, 60, 62, 73, 76, 77, 86, 90; Black/primitive, 49; and borderline individual, 46, 76, 83; Jewish, 45, 49, 52, 53–54, 55–56, 59, 60, 61, 62; Jewish-black, 45; and Kadjaba, 73, 74, 78–79; and Kristeva, 48, 49, 51, 79–81, 82, 84; of self, 49; and sniveling, 61; and Tanga, 70, 77, 80, 85; and Tanga, femme-abject, 88, 89, 90, 91; and *Tu t'appelleras Tanga*, 59, 63, 69, 76, 77, 78, 81, 82, 84, 85
Achebe, Chinua, 26, 33, 35, 162; *Anthills of the Savannah*, 2
Acholonu, Catherine, *Motherism: The Afrocentric Alternative to Feminism*, 325–26 n.1
Agency, 162–63, 201
Ahmed, Leila, *Women and Gender in Islam,* 19–20 n.1
Aidoo, Ama Ata, 25–26; *Changes*, 160*;* "For Whom Things Did Not Change," 177, 193; "In the Cutting of a Drink," 282–83; *No Sweetness Here*, 25
Althusser, Louis, *Lenin and Philosophy*, 271 n.2
Amadiume, Ifi, *Male Daughters, Female Husbands: Gender and Sex in an African Society*, 326 n.1

Appiah, Anthony, *In My Father's House*, 271 n.3
Assouline, Pierre, *Lire*, 103, 115, 117, 118, 119, 150 n.9
Aucassin et Nicolete, 328–29 n.7

Bâ, Mariama, 3; *Une si longue lettre*, 2, 157, 159–60
Beauvoir, Simone de, 10–11
Bekolo, Jean-Pierre, 170
  compared with *Mossane*, 253
  and mimicry, 168, 253
    Quartier Mozart, 261–63, 269; Chef de Quartier, 261, 262, 269; Chien Méchant, 262, 263; Mon Type, 261, 262, 269; phallus, 261
  and urban setting, 253
Beti, Mongo, 84
Beyala, Calixthe, xxv, 16, 59–96, 97–155
  l'affaire Beyala, 103, 110–21
  Assèze l'Africaine, xxv, 19; Assèze and Tambu, 234, 239; and Sorraya, 236–39; Sorraya, 234–39; split text, 218–33; 237–39
  C'est le soleil qui m'a brulée, 75, 96 n.16, 104, 285–86
  Les Honneurs perdus, 119, 281, 285, 326–28 n. 5
  Lettre d'une africaine à ses soeurs occidentales, 102
  "Moi, Calixthe Beyala, la plagaire," 114–15
  La Petite fille du réverbère, 281, 283; and Mme. Kimoto, 285
  Plagiarism (*see also* Plagiarism), 103–4, 109–21
Bhabha, Homi (*see also* Double; Mimicry), 161–62, 164, 171, 173–84; and doubling, 183–84, 197, 198; hybridity, 76, 176; identity, 177–78, 179, 180, 181, 183; *The Location of Culture*, 162; mimicry, 161, 162, 163, 171, 182, 183, 184; Third Space, 174–75, 182; unhomely, 173
Bolekaja critics (Chinweizu, Onwuchekwa Jemie, and Ihechukwu Madubuike), 14, 26
Borch-Jacobsen, Mikkel, 99, 100, 101, 102, 123, 124, 126, 128, 129; and ego, 148 n.1, 151–52 n.13, 153–54 n.18
Borgomano, Madeleine, 150 n.11
Buten, Howard, *Quand j'avais cinq ans, je m'ai tué*, (*Burt*), 104–9, 113, 118, 133, 140, 143, 144, 146. *See also* Beyala, Calixthe, Plagiarism
Butler, Judith (*see also* Identity; Incorporation/introjection; Mask; Riviere), xxv, 1, 15, 16, 18, 19
  Bodies that Matter, 21 n.4
  doubling, 213
  Gender Trouble, 5–8, 10, 12–13, 15–19
  and Lacan, 206, 208
  mask, 206–7, 213
  melancholia: Abraham and Torok, 216–17; and mask, 206; and Riviere, 207
  metaphysics of substance, 8, 14
  mourning: Abraham and Torok, 216–17, 246 n.16; and African literature, 214–15; and incorporation, 215
  and *Nervous Conditions*: and gendering, 203, 204, 208
  subversion, and Eurycide, 322–33
  and *Une vie de Crabe*, 299–300; phantasmic, 302

Calvino, Italo, *Invisible Cities*, xvi
Cancel, Robert, *Allegorical Speculation in an Oral Society: The Tabwa Narrative*, 329 n.10
Cartesian Ego, 78

Cartesian self, 48
Cartesian Subject, 8
Castration, xxiv–xxv, 36–38, 47, 50, 54, 84, 86, 104, 120–31, 151 n.12, 152–53 n.16; and Butler, 203; Freud, 121–23, 124, 126, 127, 128, 130, 152–53 n.16; and Heath, 268; Irigaray, 131; Kristeva, 122, 128, 131; Lacan, 121–31, 134, 153 n.16; in *Le Petit Prince de Belleville*, 104, 147; and representation, 266
Cazenave, Odile, 36, 42
Céline, Louis Ferdinand, 43–44, 46, 48, 51–52
"Certain Winds from the South," 25–41
    act of enunciating, 28, 36, 40
    circumcision, 38
    cola nuts, 30, 31–32, 33
    and Fanon, 32, 33
    Felman-Lacanian approach, 29, 35–36; and castration, 37
    Fuseni, 37–38
    Hawa, 27
    Issa, 27, 30, 34, 37–38
    kernel story, 28, 32, 36
    Memunat, 27, 39; story of, 40–41 and migration, 171
    M'ma Asana, 27, 30, 31, 34; and husband, 39; and Issa, 37–38; and Memunat, 40–41
    M'ma Asana's husband, 27–28, 32, 34–38, 40–41
    narrator's position, 31, 35
    Rules for Reading, 26, 29
Chevrier, Jacques, 104, 112–13, 118
Chinweizu, *Towards the Decolonization of African Literature*, 26. See also Bolekaja critics
Conrad, Joseph, "The Secret Sharer," 66
Constant, Paule, *White Spirit*, 111, 150 n.8; split text, 229–32

Coquery-Vidrovitch, Catherine, *African Women: A Modern History*, urbanization of women, 277–82, 325 n.1

D'Almeida, Irène, 42; *Francophone African Women Writers*, 36, 98, 121
Dangarembga, Tsitsi, 184, 185, 186, 188, 189, 243–44 n.5, 245 n.7
    Babamukuru, 192–93, 196, 198; and Dangarembga's biography, 188–89; and Lucia, 189–90; meaning of name, 193; Name of the Father (and patriarchy), 184, 199, 210, 233–34; and Nyasha, 212; standing upright, 197–98; and Tambu, 195, 197, 198, 233–34
    Jeremiah (Tambu's father), 191, 192, 193, 194, 196, 204, 241 n.5
    Lucia, 189–90
    Ma'Shingayi (Tambu's mother), 192, 193, 194, 195, 199, 200
    Maiguru, 198, 200, 233
    Nervous Conditions (*see also* Double; Masque; Masquerade; Mime; Patriarchy; Sugnet), 174, 184, 213, 215–16, 218–29; and Fanon, 241–43 n.5; split text, 232–36
    Nhamo, 187, 191, 192, 194, 196, 197, 199, 204, 206, 207, 208
    Nyasha, 185, 210, 225, 233–34; and Babamukuru, 212; and Dangarembga's biography, 188, 189; and "nervous condition," 190, 199, 241–42 n.5; and Nhamo, 211–12; and Tambu, 195, 200–2, 211
    Tambu, 185; and cleanliness, 187–88; and Damgarembga biography, 188; and feigning, 191–93; and grandmother, 197–98; and

Jeremiah, 191–93; and mask (*see also* Mask), 205, 206, 207, 209; and masquerade, 185, 186, 187, 189, 198; and Mr. Matimba, 193; and mother, 194, 195; narrator/character, 187, 195, 198; and Nhamo, 196–99, 204–9

Davies, Carole Boyce, 20 n.3. See also *Ngambika*

De Lauretis, Teresa, xvi, xviii; *Alice Doesn't* (City of Zobeide) xvi–xviii; doubling (*see also* Lotman, Jurij)

Derrida, Jacques, 66, 152 n.14, 159; visual image, 274 n.8

Diop, Birago, 177

Double, 159, 160–64; and African literature (incorporation of other), 215–16; Assèze/Sorraya, 234, 236, 238; and Bhabha, 175, 177, 179, 180, 182; and Butler, mourning, 213, 214; and Freud, 66–68, 85, 99; and Lacan, 101, 102, 125, 137; and de Lauretis, 240 n.2; and mask, 207; and mimicry, 183, 184; and *Nervous Conditions*, 197, 201, 209; *Petit Prince de Belleville* (Abdou/l'ami), 141, 142, 144, 146; phallic, 128; split text, *Nervous Conditions* and *Assèze*, 218–39; Tanga/Toundi, 98, 99, 100; and *Tu t'appelleras Tanga*, 62

Douglas, Mary, 51–52, 93 n.3, 94 n.5

Ecriture féminine, 75; and African *écriture féminine*, 85, 101, 133, 184; and resistance in cinema, 270

Empire Writes Back, The (Ashcroft), 3

Exodus (the book of), 53, 55–56, 93 n.4

Fanon, Frantz, *Black Skin, White Masks*, 171; *Damnés de la terre* ("Wretched of the Earth"), 32–34; and *Nervous Conditions*, 241–43, n.5

Felman, Shoshana, 25, 35; Felman-Lacan, 29, 36–37, 40–41, 53

Feminism
 African, 1, 148 n.2
 First wave, 2–4, 7–8, 11–14, 16–17, 75, 280, 286, 287, 305
 Second wave, 2, 5, 7, 11–14, 76, 279–81, 305, 309–10
 Western, xi, 41 n.1; problem of relating to African literature, 309

Figaro, 114–17

Foucault, Michel, 8, 10, 14; Herculine, 13

Fox, Everett, 93 n.3, 94 n.4, 94 n.5

French Feminism, xi, xv, xviii, xxiv

Freud, Sigmund, xviii, xix, xxi–xxii, 49–50, 99, 121, 125; "Dark continent," xvii; Fort, da, 159, 239–40 n.1; *Moses and Monotheism*, 52, 94 n.8; Oedipal Complex (see Oedipal Complex), 57, 125, 126; *Totem and Taboo*, xxi, xxv, 49–50, 57; Uncanny, 66, 67, 95 n.10, 110

Gallimore, Rangira Béatrice, *L'Oeuvre romanesque de Calixthe Beyala*, 96 n.15, 149–50 n.8

Great Mother. See Mother Goddess

Grosz, Elizabeth, 121, 130, 131, 132, 133–34, 139

Handelman, Susan, 92–93 n.2; speculation, 274–75 n.8

Head, Bessie, "The Collector of Treasures," 4; Dikeledi, 120

Heath, Stephen, 153 n.17; and castration, 268; "Difference," xxv, 247, 248, 249, 250; and Lacanian analysis, 251; and Mossane, 254, 255, 259; and phallus, 260; and

Quartier Mozart, 263; representation and patriarchy, 266, 269, 270, 271 n.1; and resistance to patriarchy, 264–65, 267, 268; the visible, 252, 264

Holy/Unholy. See Kadosh (holy)

Identity (*see also* Bhabha, Homi, identity), 199; and Butler, 203, 206; and sexuality, 213–14

Ilboudi, Monique, *Le Mal de peau*, 3

Incest (incest taboo), xix, xxi, xxiii, 203–4; and Freud, 246 n.16; and Kristeva, 49, 50, 51, 55, 56, 58, 83; and Tanga, 79

Incorporation/Introjection: *Nervous Conditions/Assèze*, 225–29; *Assèze*, 234–36, 239

Irigaray, Luce, xix, xx, 6–7, 11–13, 18, 90, 131–34, 164–70, 171; and doubling, 161, 169, 170; and Lacan, 169; mask, 161; masquerade (*see also* Masquerade), 161, 168; mimicry 163, 168, 169; mime, 191; mirror, 169–70; and *Nervous Conditions*, 189–90; not one, 164, 165, 166; *This Sex Which Is Not One*, 164

Jewish: Abject (*see* Abjection), Bible (*see* Exodus [the book of]; Leviticus [Book of]); Impurity (see Pure/impure)

Jouissance (*see also* Lacan); Kristeva, 44, 45, 100

Jussawalla, Adil: and evil eye, 176, 181, 182, 183

Kadosh (holy), 53, 59, 92 n.1

Khatibi, Abdelkebir, xxiv, 264; penser autre, 275 n.9

Kojève, Alexandre, 129

Kom, Ambroise, "L'univers zombifié de Calixthe Beyala," 114

Kristeva, Julia (*see also* Abjection; Castration), 43–61, 64, 67, 79–85, 94 n.5 & n.8, 131–34, 140, 144; Abject, 46–47, 59, 60, 80, 81, 82–92; borderline, 64–65, 71, 76, 77, 79, 83, 84, 86; castration, 122, 125; chora, 131; *Powers of Horror*, 43; Semiotic, 46–47, 131–32, 140; Symbolic, 43, 131–34

Lacan, xviii–xix, xxii–xxiv, 8, 25, 29, 36–37, 47, 49, 58, 66, 90, 93 n.2, 94 n.8, 95 n.11, 98–99, 100, 101, 121–31, 139, 152 n.14; Imaginary, xx; Imago, 35, 71, 100, 101, 125, 141; Law of the father, 58, 122, 131; Mirror stage, xxiii, 35, 46–47, 62, 63, 69, 70, 90, 125–26, 159, 273 n.8; Name of the Father, xix, xxi–xxiii, 15, 46, 58, 84, 109, 122, 123, 127; Phallus, 49, 123–31, 134; Real, xx; Subject Presumed to Know, 57, 59, 60, 63, 64, 114, 123, 131; Symbolic, xix, xx, xxiii, 47, 51–55, 60, 62, 132; and *Tu t'appelleras Tanga*, 69

Lee, Spike, 104, 148 n.3

Lemoine-Luccioni, Eugénie, 261–63, 271 n.1

Levi-Strauss, Claude, 49, 50, 52

Leviticus, Book of, 52–53, 59, 92 n.1, 93 n.3, 94 n.5

Levy-Bruhl, Lucien, 95 n.1

Lotman, Jurij, 240 n.2

Makhélé, Caya, 113–14

Mask (*see also* Masquerade), 190–91, 200, 201; and Butler, 206; and *Nervous Conditions*, 201, 206, 209

Masque, 190

Masquerade (*see also* Bhabha, Homi; Irigaray, Luce), 161; *Nervous Conditions*, 184, 185, 186, 187,

189, 191, 193, 194, 195, 196, 197, 199, 200, 213
McClintock, Anne, critique of Bhabha and Irigaray, 161, 162, 163, 167, 183
Miller, Christopher, 149 n.5, 248, 250; *Theories of Africans*, 271–72 n.4
Mime (*see also* Irigaray, Luce), 161, 182; and *Nervous Conditions*, 191, 192, 193, 194, 195, 196, 198, 199, 201
Mimicry, 18, 161–63, 164, 166, 168, 169; Assèze, 235; and Bekolo, Genet, Oyono, Rouch, 168; *Nervous Conditions*, 184, 189, 190, 191,195
Minh-ha, Trinh T. *See* Trinh T. Minh-ha
Mirror Stage. *See* Lacan, mirror stage
Mitchell, Juliet, *Feminine Sexuality: Jacques Lacan and the Ecole Freudienne*, 151 n.12, 152 n.16
Mohanty, Chandra Talpade, *Third World Women and the Politics of Feminism*, 41, 308
Montrelay, Michèle, 271 n.1
Mossane (Safi Faye), xii, xxv, 251–260; compared with *Quartier Mozart*, 253; and difference, 254, 257, 259; Fara, 253, 254, 255, 257; Mingué (Mossane's mother), 254, 256; Mossane, 252, 254, 256, 257–59, 260; Mossane's father, 256; Pangools, 252, 258, 260; and vision, 252, 260
Mother Goddess (Great Mother), 54, 56–59, 94 n.5
Mudimbe, V.Y., 15; *The Invention of Africa*, 76, 95–96 n.15
Mulvey, Laura, 265

Nfah-Abbenyi, Juliana Makuchi, *C'est le soleil qui m'a brulée*, 286; *Gender in African Women's Writing*; and *Nervous Conditions*, 246 n.14
Ngambika (Adams Graves & Davies), 3, 5, 8–12, 14, 20–21 n.3
Ngugi wa Thiong'o, 2, 14; *Petals of Blood*, 2
Nnaemekas, Obioma, *The Politics of (M)Othering*, 95 n.11
Nwapa, Flora, xviii; *Women Are Different*, 2, 20 n.2, 157

oedipus, the, xix–xxii, xxv, 46, 58, 83, 97, 98, 123–31, 137, 140, 153–54 n.18, 332
Oedipus Complex, xii, xx, xxi, 47, 50, 57, 121, 122, 125, 127, 128, 129, 130, 151 n.13, 152 n.16, 153–54 n.18. *See also* Freud, Sigmund; oedipus, the
Okri, Ben, 111, 118, 150 n.11; *The Famished Road*, 112, 119; "Feeds French Book Fever," 118; "When the Light Returns," Orpheus and Eurydice, 331
Ortigues, Marie-Cécile and Edmond, *Oedipe africain*, xx
Ouologuem, Yambo, 113, 115, 149 n.5; *Lettre à la France nègre*, 149 n.5
Ousmane, Sembène. *See* Sembène Ousmane
Oyono, Ferdinand, 168, 170; Toundi, 61, 62, 67, 68, 84, 97–99, 100, 101, 102, 138, 169; *Une vie de boy*, 61

Patriarchy (*see also* Lacan, Name of the Father), 233, 234; African, 146; and castration, 266; "Certain Winds from the South," 26; and difference, 249; first wave feminism, 14–15; institutional, in "Collector of Treasures," 4; and Irigaray, 133, 134, 165; and

Kristeva, 54, 134; and *Mossane*, 257, 259; and *Nervous Conditions*, 178, 182, 193, 195, 196, 198, 199, 209, 210, 213; and *Petit Prince de Belleville*, 139; and *Quartier Mozart*, 263; and resistance, 250, 264–65; second wave feminism, 5; and Tadjo, 315–16;

Péju, Marcel, 111–12, 113, 115

Petit Prince de Belleville, Le, 104–10, 134–55
   Abdou (Father), 140, 143, 154 n.20; and l'ami, 109, 141–42; interior monologue, 135–36, 154–55 n.21; and Loukoum, 137, 138, 139; and Madame Saddock, 145
   l'ami, 141–42, 143
   Lolita, 140, 147
   Loukoum, 143, 154 n.20; and Abdou 135–7, 139, 140, 147; and Burt, 104–5, 109, 140; and M'am, 109, 135, 142, 144, 154 n.20
   Mme. Garnier, 143, 144
   Mme. Saddock, 145, 146; and Gil, 140, 147
   Soumane, 109, 135, 142, 144, 145, 146, 147

Phallocracy, 3; Irigaray, 165, 167; *Une Vie de Crabe*, 301

Phallus (*see also* Lacan), xii, xix, xx, xxv, 123–31, 138, 139, 153 n.17; and Heath, 260–61; and Lemoine-Lucioni, 261–63

Plagiarism, 103, 104, 109, 121, 149 n.4, 150 n.11. *See also* Beyala, Calixthe; *Petit Prince de Belleville, Le*

Pure/impure (tahor/tamei), 43, 45, 52–55, 58, 67, 92 n.1. *See* Kristeva, Julia

Riviere, Joan, 207. *See also* Butler

Rules of Reading, 26, 29

Saro-Wiwa, Ken, 28
Sartre, Jean-Paul, 129
Sembène Ousmane, 2, 3, 14, 15, 26, 172; *Guelwaar*, 172, 255–56; *Vehi Ciosane*, 84
Silverman, Kaja, 245–46 n.12; *The Subject of Semiotics*, specularity and mirror stage 273–74 n.8; suture, 272–73 n.6
Sniveling, 61, 62
Sophocles, xxii
Sow, Ibrahim, xxi–xxiv
Sow Fall, Aminata, 113
Soyinka, Wole, 51; *Death and the King's Horseman*, 328 n.6
Spillers, Hortense, xx
Sugnet, Charles, 186, 187; on *Nervous Conditions*, 241–43 n.5, 245 n.7

Tadjo, Véronique (*see also A vol d'oiseau*); *Le Royaume des aveugles*, 310
Tahor/Tamei (Clean, Unclean). *See* Pure/impure
Thiong'o, Ngugi wa. *See* Ngugi wa Thiong'o
Todorov, Tzvetan, 158
Trinh T. Minh-ha, 24; *Reassemblage*, 176–77
Tsodzo, Thompson, 188
Tu t'appelleras Tanga
   Anna-Claude, 64, 69, 101; and abjection, 62, 64, 65, 81; and borderline, 83; less than one and double, 70; and Ousmane, 65–66; and sniveling, 61; and Tanga, 62, 63, 64, 66, 68, 86, 87, 91, 92; and Tanga's story, 86, 87, 91; and la vieille la mère, 68
   Camilla, 75, 87, 88

Cul-de-jatte, 85, 86, 89, 90, 91
Hassan, 70, 71, 72, 75, 85, 86, 88
Kadjaba Dongo (grandmother), 73, 74, 78
Ousmane, 62, 65
Pieds-gâtés (Mala), 72, 75, 85, 86, 90, 104
Tanga, 61, 62, 68, 69, 72, 73, 75, 85, 86, 89, 90; abiku-analyst, 88–89; and abject, 70, 73, 77, 78, 80, 81, 88, 99, 101; and borderline, 71; and Camille, 87–88; and ego, 78, 81, 88, 99, 101; and Hassan, 70, 71; and her story, 63, 66, 70, 86, 91; and Toundi, 67, 68, 98, 99, 100, 102; and la vieille la mère, 68, 69, 73, 85
Tanga's mother (la vieille la mère; see Tanga), 68, 69, 73, 74, 75, 77; and abject, 74, 75, 77
Tanga's father (le vieux le père), 65–66, 77–78, 83–84, 86
Tutuola, Amos, "The Complete Gentleman," 73, 273 n.7, 316–17

Uncanny, 62, 63, 66, 67, 68, 69, 79, 141. See also Freud, Sigmund
Urban environment, 277–82; and Beyala, 282–87; and Boni, 287–89, 291–93, 298–99; and Dis, 331–32; and Tadjo, 310–16

Vie de crabe, Une (Tonella Boni), 281, 282, 287–308
  and Butler, 299–300; phantasmic, 302
  Djomo-La-Lutte, 288, 294–97, 301
  Dramane-le-Bègue, 289, 290, 293, 297, 301, 302; and order, 303, 306
  incest, 297, 298; phantasmic, 302, 304, 305
  Mam' Djan (Léti), 289–90, 292, 293, 294, 296, 297, 298; love for Niyous, 299; and Dramane-le-Bègue, 301–03; notebooks, 305–6
  market, 288–89
  mud (and malaria), 291, 292, 293, 294, 295, 296, 297, 298, 299, 301, 304, 306
  Niyous, 287–88, 292–93, 294, 296, 298, 303
  oxymorons, 287, 291, 297, 304
  subversion, 300–301; student strikes, disease, 304, 306–7
Vieyra, Myriam Warner, *Juletane*, 3

Walker, Alice, *The Color Purple*, 109, 110, 145, 146, 147
Wittig Monique, 12–13

Yewah, Emmanuel, 95 n.13
Young, Robert, *Colonial Desire*, 20 n.1, 271 n.3

About the Author

KENNETH W. HARROW is a professor in the English Department of Michigan State University. His previous Heinemann books include *Faces of Islam in African Literature*, *Thresholds of Change in African Literature*, and *The Marabout and the Muse*.